ARMS
AND
THE MEN

IAN HAY

LONDON
HER MAJESTY'S STATIONERY OFFICE

© Crown copyright 1977

First published 1950

Paperback edition 1977

ISBN 0 11 772195 6

Produced in England for Her Majesty's Stationery Office
by Unwin Brothers Limited, The Gresham Press, Old Woking, Surrey
Dd. 497697   K28   4/77

Prefatory Note

TOWARDS the end of the Second World War the Committee for the Control of Official Histories recommended to the War Cabinet that the Government should commission and publish a series of popular military histories. These were to present a broad view of the military events of 1939-45, and each volume was to deal with a particular campaign. They were to be forerunners of, and not in any sense substitutes for, the more detailed Official Histories of the Second World War then planned and since published.

Soon after the war, distinguished authors were commissioned to write the texts for six books, and they were given full access to official documents and sources of information. The authors were, however, to be individually responsible for the presentation of their material, the statements they made and the opinions they expressed.

The first book was *Arms and the Men*. Written by Ian Hay, it was the story of the evolution of the British Army and how it acquitted itself throughout the war. The second was Eric Linklater's *The Campaign in Italy*, an account of the Eighth and Fifth Armies' fighting between May 1943 and May 1945. Christopher Buckley, the well-known war correspondent who was tragically killed in Korea in 1950, wrote the next three: *Greece and Crete, 1941*; a tale of heroic failure; *Norway, the Commandos, Dieppe* and *Five Ventures: Iraq, Syria, Persia, Madagascar, the Dodecanese*, which deal with smaller expeditions and campaigns, chiefly in countryside that presented problems of unusual character. The last book, *North West Europe, 1944-5*, by John North, was the story of the achievement of the British 21st Army Group in the Allied invasion of North West Europe.

When these books were first published they were well received, and second impressions were produced of two of them. In recent years, the rapid expansion of interest in military history of all kinds – and in the Second World War in particular – has stimulated a demand from a wide spectrum of the public for copies of these volumes from libraries, museums and other sources. The demand appears to be growing and the reprinting of all six books in this new format is in response to it.

These new impressions are straight reprints. Except for minor changes to one or two of the preliminary pages, there are no alterations. The volumes are essentially just as they were a quarter of a century ago.

1977

FOREWORD

THE TITLE of this book should explain itself. My purpose and hope in compiling it has been to tell the story, in terms acceptable to the general reader, of the part played by the British Army during the Second World War.

It would be impossible within the limits of a single volume to give a detailed technical or tactical description of all the tremendous operations involved therein: that is a task for the professional military historian. I have devoted most of my attention to what may be called the internal history of those events—the growth and development, from the most meagre beginnings, of our vast citizen Army, and of the changes brought about in its composition, training, leadership, and administration by the introduction of total mechanised warfare. The reader will also find that there has been a good deal to say regarding the revolution effected during these years in certain army traditions. Some of these have been altered almost out of recognition, especially on what may be called the social side—but the best remain intact, as we shall see.

By way of emphasising the contrast between past and present, I have devoted my earlier chapters—which I hope the reader will study with patience—to an account of the inception and growth of our Army from the time of the New Model, including the sweeping reforms, almost forgotten today, of those two great administrators Cardwell and Haldane. It is always instructive to study the foundations—originally rather insecure foundations—upon which a great and stable edifice has finally been reared. It is no bad thing either, in reviewing recent triumphs, to remind ourselves of the valour and achievement of those who went before us, without whose service and sacrifice we should not be here today. *Vixere fortes ante Agamemnona.*

A list of the authorities upon whom I have relied for most of my information will be found at the end of this volume. I take this opportunity of offering my grateful thanks for the aid and counsel which I have received, through a long and laborious task, from various commanders in the field and highly placed officials in the War Office.

IAN HAY

vii

CONTENTS

MAPS AND ILLUSTRATIONS

MAPS

ILLUSTRATIONS

A Coastal Defence Post: England 1941
An Anti-Aircraft Battery: England 1941
A Rocket Battery (Anti-Aircraft) in Action
Home Guard Instruction
A Daimler Armoured Car
A.T.S. on Anti-Aircraft Gun Site

The 5·5-inch Gun Howitzer
The Valentine Bridge-Layer
The 'Flail' Tank in Action
The 'DUKW'
An Early Type of Landing Craft (M)
The Crusader Tank

North Africa 1941
North Africa 1942
North Africa 1943: The Mareth Line
Italy
Italy

North-West Europe 1944
North-West Europe 1944
North-West Europe 1944: Into Arnhem
North Burma 1944
Burma: The Road to Kalewa
Burma 1945

(The photographs are Crown copyright and were supplied by the Imperial War Museum)

CHAPTER I

ARMA VIROSQUE

~*(1)*~

WE are so accustomed today, and have been throughout the centuries, alas, to the idea of every country maintaining an army of some kind as a matter of course, that it does not always occur to us to consider what exactly an army is for.

Primarily an army should be a defence and shield against aggression from without, just as it is the function of a police force to maintain security and good order within. Some countries are so well protected from potential enemies by nature—the United States, for instance— that they stand (or stood) in no particular need of an elaborate defence scheme; others, lying embedded in a continent inhabited by peoples of different races and conflicting ambitions, must for ever be prepared against sudden and overwhelming onslaught; which means that every able-bodied citizen of a country so placed must receive some measure of training in the noble art of self-defence.

But armies have been raised for many other purposes than home defence; indeed, it is not too much to say that throughout history, and all over the globe, no two countries—or at any rate governments—have ever required an army for precisely the same purpose.

In ancient times, and not merely among primitive communities, war was the natural pursuit of man—or at any rate the inherited Sport of Kings. The Pharaohs of highly civilised Ancient Egypt, during the period of the great dynasties, were accustomed to launch an almost annual campaign against their Asiatic neighbours, return-ing at the end of the season in triumphal procession up the Nile, with captured kings hanging head downwards from the prows of their ships.

In later centuries the Medes and Persians favoured similar excursions, but upon more methodical lines. Cyrus, Xerxes and Darius, less concerned with promiscuous plunder than permanent territorial aggrandisement, set out to convert western Asia into a single consolidated empire, controlled by the royal armies and ruled by royally appointed satraps. They failed only when they came into contact with the better-armed and more intelligently controlled Greeks at Marathon and Plataea.

Then came the turn of the Greeks themselves, who discovered yet another opening for the employment of arms. They were a small and homogeneous nation, but not too small nor sufficiently homogeneous to avoid the fatal error of internal dissension and warring faction. In this tendency they were assisted by the nature of the country in which they lived, which cut them off from one another by mountain ranges and arms of the sea, stunting the growth of a national spirit and encouraging a narrow provincialism. The result was a century and more of internecine warfare between such great and notable city-states as Athens, Sparta and Thebes. Each achieved a certain hegemony in turn, until the intrusion upon the scene, in the middle of the fourth century B.C., of King Philip of Macedon, a man of outstanding personality and single aim. He had improved upon current tactical methods by the invention of the phalanx, and, assisted by the skilful employment of those propaganda methods which have become such an essential feature of international diplomacy today, created an atmosphere of suspicion and mistrust among his opponents which effectually prevented them from combining against him. (He was the author of the saying that no city is invulnerable whose gates are wide enough to admit a single mule-load of silver.) He defeated the Athenians at the battle of Chaeronea, and in due course all Greece lay prostrate before him.

Assassination in the prime of life precluded him from further enterprise, but his son Alexander the Great, comparable only to Napoleon as a single-handed organiser of victory and architect of empire, promptly took his place and set out to conquer the world. What is more, he succeeded. He occupied Egypt and overran what had once been the Persian Empire, leaving behind him in one captured country after another a military garrison, a settled constitution, and a new capital called Alexandria.

He actually reached India, and so lasting is his fame that today the Khassadars who keep watch over the frontier at Michni Kandao will still point out to you the winding track by which he led his invading Macedonians up from the Afghan passes to the head of the Khyber. But he died in Babylon at the age of thirty-six, and the great instrument of conquest which he forged—that was its sole purpose—and the vast empire which he had founded, withered and perished.

Then came Rome, and the Legions, and the Legions really conquered the world. But not until they had served a hard and humble apprenticeship in the capacity of Home Guard, one might say; for the young republic was compelled to fight long and desperately for its very existence. It had to subdue its own warlike neighbours and repel the invasions of such external aggressors as Pyrrhus; only to become locked, for more than a century, in a death grapple with Carthage. At one time that great lone wolf Hannibal, with his marooned but invincible army, ranged up and down the length and breadth of Italy, practically unmolested, for more than fifteen years. But Carthage was 'deleted' at last, and the Roman soldier had achieved the first of his destinies: he had established beyond all doubt that in the centuries to come Europe was to be ruled by Europeans and not by Asiatics. But it had been a long struggle. In Rome the Temple of Janus, kept closed in peacetime, had stood open night and day for close on two hundred years.

Then the Roman turned, all unconsciously, to his second destiny— as a civilising influence, once the rapine and bloodshed of actual military occupations were overpast, throughout the whole of the then known world. Wherever the Legions penetrated they built roads, founded cities, set up public works and schools of learning, inculcated the principles of Roman law, and taught the people they had conquered to govern themselves under the protecting shadow of the Eagles. So, perhaps, like the British colonisers and merchant venturers of a later day, these men builded better than they knew.

Such, in brief review, are some of the purposes for which an army can be employed, and were employed in the early days of the world's history—mass invasion in frank pursuit of captives and plunder; deliberately planned campaigns of territorial expansion; civil war between peoples of the same race and speech; ambitious individual attempts at world conquest; finally an ordered scheme of world settlement and standardised government, imposed upon that world by a genuine master-race of soldiers, engineers and lawgivers.

So far we have found no trace of any successful attempt—except perhaps in the early struggles of Rome herself—to employ an army in its primary and legitimate function, that of home defence. This, perhaps, is not altogether surprising, for the attacker, being in possession of the initiative, enjoys an immense advantage over the defender. He knows exactly what he is going to do and when he is going to do it, while his opponent exists in an atmosphere of conjecture and suspense.

⤙(2)⤚

With the break-up of the Roman Empire the Dark Ages descended upon Europe and History. From these we emerge into the Medieval Age, the age of so-called Chivalry.

The world we find is still at war, but we are now in the Christian era, and a new source of international discord has been discovered in differences of religious belief. Cross and Crescent are at grips, and pious European monarchs, with their attendant knights, embark periodically upon a species of devout emotional spree known as a Crusade, with the liberation of Jerusalem from the Saracen as its objective, and a reasonable expectation of loot and silken dalliance on the side.

The armies here employed, we note, were composed of the personal followers of the various leaders engaged, for the feudal system had now superseded the general levy or fyrd. In these fantastic enterprises the Captains and the Kings, well protected by shield and armour, performed prodigies of valour, and if they had the misfortune to be taken prisoner could be ransomed or exchanged. On what happened to the Other Ranks no information is forthcoming, nor is any needed.

Mention of the feudal system brings us at last to our own island, and its long and variegated military history.

Since the departure of the Romans, Britain, as we know, had been cut up into various small kingdoms. She possessed no particular national consciousness and nothing whatever in the shape of a national army or defence scheme. Factious and disunited, she lay almost wholly at the mercy of any roving invader. The Norsemen came at will, and until the time of Alfred the Great were usually bought off: *Danegelt* seems to have been the crude forerunner of modern appeasement.

Alfred passed, and disunity reigned again. So complete had it grown in 1066 that when William the Conqueror descended upon our shores a single battle was able to give him possession of the whole country, and Britain, though a sea-girt island fortress, became annexed to the continent of Europe.

Later on, somewhat surprisingly, the positions were reversed, and Europe, or a considerable slice of it, became annexed to Britain. Even so, these oversea dominions were not conquered or occupied by a regularly constituted British Army: Crécy and Agincourt were won, and the Hundred Years War subsequently lost, by the same English lords and their feudal followers as in the Crusades. The common people were little interested in or affected by these martial enterprises (except in so far as they were taxed to pay for them), nor for that matter in the subsequent Wars of the Roses, nor in the two dynastic factions who took part in them. The true spirit of England had yet to be awakened.

~(3)~

And it awoke at last, under the never-failing spur of common peril. But that awakening was neither sudden nor simultaneous: it had been in progress for some time. In other words, it had become apparent to a slow-thinking people that their true heritage and bond of union was to be found not ashore but afloat.

For the world's horizon was widening. Man had at last mastered the elements sufficiently to have lost his dread of the open sea. He no longer hugged the coast, landing at night; he struck boldly across the ocean, and the great era of exploration and discovery set in. People talked now not of the Mediterranean and Scandinavia, but of the Barbary Coast, and the Indies, and Cipango. It was by this time agreed that the earth was a globe, and the great ones of that globe began to look toward the other side of it for their next conquests. Thither they set out, mingling as usual pious aspiration with a sound instinct for material profit. Vasco da Gama rounded the Cape and reached India, whose inhabitants he informed that he had come 'in search of Christians and spices'. Spain, already the greatest power in Europe, staked out a vast claim in Central and South America, from which her generals extracted gold and silver for the Imperial Treasury, while the army of ecclesiastics who accompanied them converted the original owners thereof, by their accustomed methods, to the True Faith.

But this time Spain was not to have an unrestricted field, for the English were awakening to their destiny and Elizabeth was on the throne. Tension between the two countries increased steadily: Drake plundered the Imperial gold-ships in mid-Atlantic, and singed the King of Spain's beard in Cadiz harbour.

All this could have but one end, and presently the news came that the Invincible Armada was on its way to chastise presumption. But of late the English people, fired by the exploits of their seamen, had been growing steadily towards one another, and now the menace of invasion closed all ranks. The Queen herself ceased to temporise and issued a trumpet-call to her subjects. The beacons blazed from Dartmoor to Skiddaw; the trained bands and other forerunners of the Home Guard stood to arms, and for the first time the hearts of Englishmen beat as one in the defence of their country.

As it happened, there was little for them to do, for God blew with His wind and the enemy were scattered. The Navy did the rest. But as a direct consequence England emerged from her experience with enormously enhanced prestige—not yet as a military power but as an influence to be reckoned with in a new era of sea-rovers and merchant venturers.

Another century was to elapse before the British Army as we know it today was to play its part upon the stage of History, and a leading part at that.

~(4)~

The begetter and director of that army was Oliver Cromwell, whom we may class with Robert Clive as one of the great self-made Captains of History. Up to the age of forty-three he was a peaceful gentleman-farmer in East Anglia: after that he took up arms and became the foremost soldier of his time. He was the founder of the British Army in the sense that he introduced method, good order and obedience among the raw levies which comprised the forces of the Parliament (and indeed of both sides) in the Civil War. Such troops, besides being sketchily trained and too lacking in discipline to fit into any co-ordinated plan, were prone to sudden and self-granted periods of leave, especially about harvest time.

After Edgehill, that untidy scramble, Cromwell warned his friends that the Parliament must have soldiers of a better stamp, and that to the spirit of chivalrous gentry must be added that of a 'God-fearing Yeomanry'. Upon this principle he formed his incomparable Ironsides. In this famous corps he combined strict discipline, sober enthusiasm, and a rigid code of morals. Men could even be punished for swearing.

It was upon such a foundation that the New Model Army was built up. It consisted of horse, foot, and artillery, regularly paid and systematically trained. For the first time in English history, too, troops were uniformly attired—in scarlet, with different coloured facings according to regiment. These unusual methods more than justified themselves, and in due course the Royalists were swept from the field, at Naseby, Dunbar and Worcester. The New Model had come to stay.

With the end of the Civil War and the execution of Charles I, Cromwell, as Lord Protector, rose to a height of authority unprecedented in an English commoner either before or since. But his path was both difficult and perilous. It was his constant desire to revert to constitutional government, but circumstances were too strong for him. The two Houses of Parliament were in constant collision, and once he had to dissolve them, employing military compulsion as his instrument. His life, too, was perpetually in danger from the plottings of Royalists who regarded him, quite simply, as a rebel and a regicide. Consequently he had to rely both for the enforcement of his decrees and the protection of his own life upon his troops. Thus almost the earliest appearance of the British Army was in the role of personal appanage and bodyguard to the head of the State—yet another method of employing an army, of which the people of England took due note.

But he employed that army for other purposes too. Under him the English Commonwealth became the head and protector of Protestant Europe, and a new and wholesome respect grew up for the country which had produced these terrible russet-coated warriors, who rode storming into battle with a psalm upon their lips and wielded so lustily the sword of the Lord and of Gideon.

That respect was enhanced by the exploits at sea of Cromwell's great contemporary and brother-in-arms, Admiral Blake, the earliest and, after Nelson, the greatest sea captain that this country (until perhaps quite recently) has produced.

In the interests of religious liberty Cromwell even allied himself with that singularly undemocratic monarch, Louis XIV, against Catholic Spain. The alliance proved highly successful, for, while Blake commanded the sea approaches, Cromwell and the French fought and defeated the Spaniards at the battle of the Dunes, hard by Dunkirk. Dunkirk itself became the prize of victory, and remained a British possession until Charles II sold it back to the French five years later. In a sense, Dunkirk has since come back to us.

Thus, while he lived, the name of Oliver Cromwell resounded throughout Europe. He had sworn that he would make the name of Englishman respected throughout that continent as once the name of Roman had been. And, thanks very largely to the New Model, it was so.

CHAPTER II

THE BIRTH OF AN ARMY

~*(1)*~

CROMWELL died at fifty-eight, and the English military system was back in the melting-pot. So, for that matter was the British constitution. But not for long. George Monck, Admiral-General, soldier of fortune, and shrewd opportunist, who had fought on both sides during the Civil War and subsequently distinguished himself under Cromwell and Blake in the continental operations which followed it, was at the time of Cromwell's death in command of the Parliamentary troops in Scotland. All about him was confusion and uncertainty; the Commonwealth was on its last legs and constitutional government almost at a standstill. Here was a heaven-sent opportunity for a man who knew his own mind.

Monck did not hesitate. He assembled 6,000 men at Coldstream on the border and marched on London, where he was welcomed on all sides. Here, people felt, was a man who could create order out of chaos, and whose lead in consequence all were prepared to follow, if only from the instinct of self-preservation. In a short time Charles II had been recalled from exile and the Restoration was an established fact.

With the King on the throne again, it became obvious that the New Model Army could not be retained upon its republican basis. Something must be done to regularise the situation, and at the same time save as many faces as possible.

This was effected by a simple change of label. General Monck's own regiment—that same infantry force which had followed him from Coldstream to London—were mustered upon Tower Hill. Upon the word of command the men laid down their arms as soldiers of the Commonwealth and took them up again as His Majesty's Regiment of Foot Guards—or, as they came to be known, and are known to this day, the Coldstream Guards.

Thus, the British Regular Army came to birth. It was as simple as that. Presently it was supplemented by certain other units, mostly composed of Royalist gentlemen who had been fighting for the King abroad. These were the 1st Foot Guards (afterwards the Grenadiers) and the 1st and 2nd Life Guards. Another cavalry regiment, the Horse Guards, was added, recruited mainly from disbanded soldiers of the New Model. And therefore today we number among our Household Troops three regiments which trace their ancestry back to the Royalists of King Charles's day, and two representing the sturdy stock of the New Model Parliamentary Army.

⁓(2)⤝

The New Army (Royal Army now) was soon augmented by units returning from service abroad.

A word must be said here about the origin and composition of some of the first few at least of these early Regiments of the Line. From the Restoration onward they came progressively into being, and were numbered accordingly. Thus the senior regiment of the Infantry of the Line today is The Royal Scots, or 1st Foot. At the time of the Restoration the regiment was in the service of a foreign country—a by no means uncommon circumstance in those days—having been lent to Louis XIII by Charles I. It had been raised in 1633 under the command of Sir John Hepburn, and was called by the name of its leader—a common practice of the time[1] and a sore trial to subsequent regimental historians, especially since upon the continent of Europe British names and titles are apt to undergo strange transmogrifications. (The nearest that the French could ever get to Hepburn's regiment was *Le Regiment d'Hebron*.) But although this famous regiment was nominally embodied in the seventeenth century, its history, authentic if unofficial, goes back some two centuries farther; for it had its roots in the days when Scotland was perpetually allied with France against the traditional enemy, England, and the person of the French monarch was protected by a Scottish bodyguard—as we may read in the pages of *Quentin Durward*.

The Second Regiment of the Line, the Queen's Royal Regiment (West Surrey), was of more recent origin, having been raised to protect Tangier, which Charles II had acquired as part of the dowry

[1] The practice survives today—in the case, e.g., of The Green Howards.

of his Portuguese Queen, Catherine of Braganza. Another cavalry regiment, the Royal Dragoons, was created for the same end about the same time, and shares with the Queen's the distinction of the first battle honours in our history—*Tangier* 1662–80.

The Third Regiment came from abroad, like The Royal Scots, and consisted of a body of English mercenaries who had been in Dutch service. Early in Charles II's reign war broke out between England and Holland, and these expatriates, having very properly declined to fight against their own countrymen, were sent home and received into the Royal Army. They are now known as the Royal East Kent Regiment, the Buffs. A Fourth Regiment, the King's Own Royal Regiment (Lancasters) was also raised, to assist the garrison of Tangier.

The death of Charles II and the accession of his brother James II, followed almost immediately by Monmouth's rebellion, was the occasion for quite a spate of fresh units. More troops were withdrawn from Holland, and from these additional regiments were formed, two of which survive today as the Royal Northumberland Fusiliers and the Royal Warwickshire. This period also witnessed the creation of six regiments of Dragoon Guards, two of Hussars, and a fresh batch of infantry regiments sufficiently numerous to bring their serial notation into double figures.

There is no need to extend the list further: enough has been said to indicate that the New Army was now a lusty and growing infant.

❦(3)❧

The days of James II were few and evil. In three years he was driven into exile, and William of Orange, his son-in-law and cousin, reigned in his stead.

Still pursuing our researches into the various uses to which an army can be put, we have to observe that from its foundation at the time of the Restoration the Royal Army, apart from a few units engaged in garrison duty abroad, had been enlisted and employed almost entirely in the defence of the Stuart dynasty.

Now the Stuarts were gone, but their very banishment involved us in a renewed series of wars of a type already familiar since the time of Elizabeth—the bitter, unending struggle between Protestant and Catholic.

Into the details of these campaigns there is no need to enter here. They were mostly fought in Belgium, the 'Cockpit of Europe'.

Belgium's high favour in the seventeenth and eighteenth centuries as a convenient arena for the settlement of other people's differences was due principally to the fact that it was flat, and therefore suited to the formal, parade-ground battles of that period; that it was well furnished with waterways, which assisted transport; and that it was fertile and could so support a considerable army of invasion. Such considerations carry little weight today.

The campaigns of Marlborough, which followed close on those of William, necessitated a further increase in the strength of the British Army. Its establishment was brought up to eighteen regiments of cavalry, including the Household Troops, the regiments of Foot Guards, and forty-six regiments of Infantry of the Line. Artillery, as a composite body, had not yet come to its own. With this force during the next ten years the great John Churchill, like Cromwell before him, made the name of British soldier ring round the world.

But the main point to observe is that the Army was still the Royal Army, the personal appanage of the throne, and as such was subject to considerable suspicion by Parliament and people. The day of its transference to popular control was still far distant.

~*(4)*~

As this is a narrative less of army operations than of army development and growth, we need not concern ourselves overmuch with the campaigns launched and the battles fought and won by our soldiers during the seventeenth and eighteenth centuries—the wars of the Spanish and Austrian Successions, and the Seven Years War in particular—beyond giving a brief summary of successive increases in personnel and equipment. Special mention, however, must be made of the Seven Years War, in which the British Army achieved triumphs hitherto undreamed of.

It was a tense moment in our history, for the great powers of Europe, headed by the French King, had combined to crush the vigorous young kingdom of Prussia—an enterprise which, if successful, would have meant the supremacy of France in the world and the wreck of British hopes and commitments in India and America, and not improbably the end of Britain herself.

But again we produced a man capable of dealing with the situation: William Pitt, later Earl of Chatham. Besides introducing a Militia Act, which provided that the whole manhood of the country should undergo a three years' period of military training, he raised no less than twenty-one new regiments. Many of these, we note, were named the Second this and the Second that—indicating that the supply of fresh recruiting areas throughout the country was becoming exhausted.

The Seven Years War raged all over the world. Those were the days of which Macaulay wrote:

On the head of Frederick (the Great) is all the blood which was shed in a war which raged during so many years and in every quarter of the globe . . . in lands where the very name of Prussia was unknown; and in order that he might rob a neighbour whom he had sworn to defend, black men fought on the coast of Coromandel and red men scalped one another by the Great Lakes of North America.

They were the days, too, in which Walpole remarked that one could never afford to miss a single copy of the newspaper for fear of missing a victory somewhere. Nearly two hundred years later History was to repeat both of these commentaries almost to the letter.

In 1775 the American War of Independence broke out, and the tide of conquest ebbed swiftly. In 1777 Burgoyne and his army were surrounded and captured at Saratoga. This disaster was hardly the fault of Burgoyne: the blame lay at the door of the British military authorities in London, who insisted, instead of trusting the men on the spot, upon directing the war from a base more than 3,000 miles away. But the first British Empire had been dealt a mortal blow.

The results were immediate and startling. France promptly hurried to the assistance of what she now plainly regarded as the winning side: Spain followed her example shortly after, and presently Britain found herself engaged in a world war which was to continue, practically without intermission, until Napoleon was securely immured in St. Helena thirty-five years later.

Further new regiments were raised, but these proved a mere instalment, for a few years later the French Revolution burst forth in all its fury, and the struggle deepened in horror and intensity. So more infantry regiments were embodied, some dozen in all, composed mainly of Scottish (especially Highland) troops. Apparently Scotland had reconciled herself by this time to the Hanoverian regime.

About this time, too, the Royal Artillery came to its own as a regular formation—two Horse Artillery battalions, with their own drivers instead of the casual and undisciplined civilian teamsters who had discharged that office hitherto.

And here also we have glimpses of the first beginnings of the Army Service Corps, in the shape of a 'Corps of Waggoners'. Unfortunately the authorities saw fit to recruit this force from the dregs of the population—they were known and esteemed as the Newgate Blues—and the experiment was abandoned.

The same years saw the gradual abandonment of the old smooth-bore musket, Brown Bess, in favour of a weapon with a rifled barrel, the tremendous possibilities of which had yet to be realised. For a start a Corps of Riflemen was formed, famous today as the Rifle Brigade.

~*(5)*~

Now for a word regarding the internal administration of the Army of those days.

In Waterloo Place, London, at the foot of Lower Regent Street, stands an imposing monument known as The Duke of York's Column, second only in prominence to that of Nelson himself, from the summit of which a plump gentleman in a martial cloak, sword in hand, looks down upon the Horse Guards' Parade. Thousands of people pass it by every day, on bus-top or on foot, but few have any idea who this particular Duke of York was, or how he came to achieve such an exalted memorial. The information that he was one of the numerous progeny of George III is not likely to increase either the interest or enthusiasm of the inquirer.

Yet Frederick, Duke of York, must have been a remarkable man, and no record of British Army administration or reform would be complete without his name. The second son of his father, and thus born out of direct succession to the throne, he followed the practice of the time and embarked upon a military career.

He took over as Commander-in-Chief at the Horse Guards in 1795, after a series of disastrous ventures in leadership in the field against the French Revolutionary Armies. His failure there had been largely due to insufficient support from home and chaotic conditions within the Army itself; so, armed with that most infallible of weapons, first-hand experience, he devoted himself to a vigorous and far-sighted campaign of reform.

He began, very properly, at the top, by establishing a Headquarters Staff to collect intelligence and plan operations. He disciplined the officers of the Army, too many of whom were neglecting their men by absenting themselves from duty upon the slightest pretext. He established the system, bitterly resented at the time, of confidential reports upon individual officers, with most stimulating results, and abolished some of the worst features of the Purchase system—of which there will be more to say hereafter.

Realising that soldiering was a serious profession and a whole-time job, and not merely an agreeable occupation for young men of family, he founded the Staff College, to enable capable officers without influence to qualify for promotion by merit. He also established what is now the Royal Military Academy at Sandhurst, for the training of cadets.

Turning to the rank and file, he made vigorous efforts to alleviate some of the hardships and privations of the common soldier upon active service, by improvements in transport and supply. He mitigated the sufferings of the wounded by the provision of a Regimental Doctor, with commissioned rank, to each unit. He established a veterinary service for the much enduring cavalry and transport horses. He tried, with a fair measure of success, to start a service of Regimental Chaplains. In short, he endeavoured to humanise the conditions under which the British soldier had long been compelled to exist. He did not succeed in all his schemes, but every one of them has long since been recognised as of fundamental importance and carried to fruition.

As a final proof of his humanity he established The Duke of York's Military School for soldiers' children in Chelsea.[1]

In short, Frederick, Duke of York, was not only a reformer of advanced ideas, but he was the first member of the reigning House to evince that practical interest in the welfare of the soldier, however humble, which has since become almost a commonplace in the benevolent activities of our Royal Family today. Hard things have been said about other aspects of his character, but students of military history will tell you that by his new treatment of the soldier he planted the seed which Sir John Moore and Wellington afterwards watered, the ultimate result being the victorious Peninsular campaign and the crowning achievement of Waterloo.

The rank and file at least should remember him, for he gave them what no British soldier has ever had before—hope for the future and the treatment of a human being.

---

[1] It has since been removed to Dover.

CHAPTER III

THE CRIMEA AND
CARDWELL

⁓(1)⁓

THE answer to our inquiry as to the ultimate purpose and function of the British Army, beyond its obvious and primary duty of defending our Island and Empire, has now emerged and taken definite shape.

In time of war our general strategic plan, rendered possible by British seapower, has been to dispatch an expeditionary force, under naval protection, to carry the war into the enemy's country. Such was the policy of Marlborough and of the two Pitts. It was further exemplified in the nineteenth century by our conduct of the Crimean and South African Wars.

Upon each of these two latter occasions, unfortunately, the organisation, direction and administration of the force employed lagged far behind the valour of its soldiers. The result was a lamentable waste of military energy and the sacrifice of thousands of gallant lives.

The Crimean War we fought for no particular reason, except a vague fear of Russia and an amiable compliance with the grandiose ambitions of a French Emperor who was destined, had he but known it, to lose his throne and end his life in exile in England.

The combined Franco-Turco-British expeditionary force, to which our country contributed 27,000 men under the command of Lord Raglan (a Wellingtonian veteran so imbued with the spirit of the Peninsular War that he constantly referred to the enemy as 'the French') was landed in 1854 upon the south-west corner of the Crimean Peninsula (not far from Yalta of more recent and historic

memory), and proceeded to the investment of the fortress of Sevasto-
pol, an operation which occupied and practically constituted the
whole war, except for a naval blockade of the Baltic.

Our men spent the first winter upon the exposed Upland, so called,
which lay eight miles from their base of supplies and possessed no
roads of any kind—a contingency for which no provision seems to
have been made. The troops were raw and their officers inexperienced,
for our country had been at peace since the Congress of Vienna—for
forty-four years, the longest period of tranquillity in our history.

But, ill-prepared though we were on the operational side, upon the
administrative side matters seem to have been even worse. There was
no organised system of supply and transport, and the commissariat
was in the hands of civilian contractors who were both incompetent
and corrupt. (Upon one occasion a shipload of sorely needed army
boots arrived, but it was found that the boots were for the left foot
only.) In the end we lost over twenty thousand dead, of whom only
twelve per cent fell in battle. No wonder the sick and wounded in the
Scutari hospital regarded Florence Nightingale, when she came, as
an angel from Heaven.

~∗(2)∗~

In 1868, with the Crimean War and Indian Mutiny now relegated to
an uncomfortable memory, a General Election was held, and a
Liberal Government, with Mr. Gladstone at its head for the first time,
swept Mr. Disraeli and the Conservatives from power.

One of the most vital and immediate questions facing the new
Prime Minister was that of Army reform. The public conscience had
been deeply stirred by the blunders and scandals of the Crimea, and
the world at large was perturbed by the general state of political and
military unrest everywhere prevalent. The American Civil War was
only recently over, and in Europe itself Prussia, a *parvenu* among the
older nations, had developed a new and terribly efficient warlike
technique of her own. She had smitten Austria-Hungary to the
ground in a campaign of only seven weeks, and now Bismarck was
quite openly engineering a head-on collision with the pinchbeck
Second Empire of France. If the British Army in its present state were
to become involved in these operations, no one could foretell the
consequences—though many could make a melancholy guess.

Mr. Gladstone's choice of a Secretary of State for War fell, somewhat unexpectedly, upon Mr. Edward Cardwell, who had abandoned

a prosperous practice at the Bar in favour of a political career, and had already held various Government offices. He had no experience or knowledge of military matters. Still, it is doubtful whether there was any military expert living at this time who understood, or could have explained in full, the system under which our unfortunate Army was governed and directed.

At the outbreak of the Crimean War, army affairs had been in the hands of seven distinct and separate authorities, of a disunity quite unique—the Secretary of State for War, who was also Secretary for the Colonies; the Commander-in-Chief, at that time Queen Victoria's cousin the Duke of Cambridge, who held what amounted to a life-tenure of the office; the Secretary of State *at* War; the Master-General of Ordnance; the Home Secretary; a Board of General Officers for the Inspection of Clothing; and, needless to say, the Treasury.

It is not necessary here to describe at full length the respective and conflicting duties of these individuals, but briefly their functions were as follows:

The Secretary of State for War was responsible for maintaining the Army at its allotted strength in time of peace. He had also (in theory) entire control of operations bearing on war.

The Commander-in-Chief was responsible for the discipline and efficiency of the cavalry and infantry (but not of the artillery, engineers, or other arms), and as the Sovereign's deputy also held a post equivalent to that of Commander-in-Chief of the home forces. But he exercised no control over their arms and equipment, nor power to move a single man without the sanction of the Secretary for War. Finally he dwelt apart in the Horse Guards, some distance removed from the War Office—then situated in Pall Mall, where the Royal Automobile Club now stands. The Commander-in-Chief was genuinely devoted to the Army and showed himself a good friend to the soldier; but he treated the War Office, we are told, with polite disdain, and frequently submitted questions to the Queen direct.

The Secretary at War was a Minister of the Crown, usually with a seat in the Cabinet, and his control of army affairs was chiefly financial. He had no jurisdiction where the artillery or engineers were concerned, nor in the matter of army *matériel*.

The Treasury, besides being in general control of army finance, had the management of the Commissariat, providing food, fuel, and light for troops serving overseas. (There was no Army Service Corps in those days. That magnificent machine was not fully assembled until 1888.)

The Master-General of Ordnance had charge of the discipline, pay, and allowances of the Royal Artillery and the Royal Engineers, and exercised supreme control over the whole business of the issue of ordnance supplies, not only to the Army but the Navy.

The Home Secretary was responsible to the Secretary of State for 'general military questions relating to Great Britain'. He also controlled the militia and yeomanry, but only so long as they remained disembodied.

The Board of General Officers dated from the time of George I, when it seems to have discharged a number of diverse duties connected with 'matters of general importance to the Army'. After the institution of the office of Commander-in-Chief in 1793 its powers dwindled, and by 1854 these were practically limited to the control of army clothing.

These seven departments were independent of one another, and communicated with one another by letter only! At one time they had been under the supreme co-ordinating control of the Sovereign, but with the establishment of a constitutional monarchy the Crown had ceased to exercise this function. So, for lack of an equivalent substitute, chaos reigned supreme.

⇥(3)⇤

Such was the state of affairs which confronted Mr. Cardwell in 1868. True, certain reforms had been effected during the Crimean War itself, but a Herculean task still awaited him.

This fell into two parts. In the first place the diverse administrative elements just described had to be combined into a homogeneous whole under single control—the control of Parliament and, behind Parliament, of the electorate. It was particularly important to bridge the gap between the War Office and the Horse Guards, which at this time practically divided the Army under two separate and opposite factions.

Secondly, Mr. Cardwell had to remodel the British Army itself, and bring it up to the highly modernised standard imposed by the events of the Austro-Prussian and Franco-Prussian Wars.

It is a signal proof of the man's greatness that he was equally successful in both parts of his task. For the first of these he was fully qualified by his legal training and experience; but the second, an intricate, exclusively military problem, he was compelled to approach as a civilian and amateur.

By way of comparison, it may be interesting for a moment to consider the status and function of the War Office today, and so discover to what extent Mr. Cardwell laid the foundations of the present edifice.

The Army of today (except the Army of India, which is[1] the affair of the Indian Government) has for long been under the supreme control of the Secretary of State for War, a civilian Cabinet Minister, who is himself the servant of Parliament and People. The most important of the heterogeneous collection of divided authorities just described, that of Commander-in-Chief, lapsed shortly after the South African War, and its functions have been assumed by the Chief of the Imperial General Staff, a military officer of the highest standing, presiding over a General Staff which now formulates the strategic policy of the whole Empire.

Today all these departments are housed normally under one roof—though in 1941 they overflowed into twenty-three buildings in the London area alone—and each contributes a member or members to the Army Council, in regular session under the presidency of the Secretary of State for War.

Mr. Cardwell could hardly have been expected, within his term of office, to achieve in the way of War Office reform what it has taken years of agitation and two world wars to evolve today; but he undoubtedly accomplished wonders, and performed an enormous public service with the opportunities at his disposal. He abolished various obsolete institutions, contrived to eliminate the overlapping of the duties of one department with those of another, healed the breach between the War Office and the Horse Guards, and finally brought the Army and all its operations under the direct control of Parliament. He was also able to strengthen War Office representation therein by the appointment of a Financial Secretary, who could relieve his chief of the heavy burden of satisfying inquisitive members upon questions of pounds, shillings and pence.

~*(4)*~

Having reduced the War Office and administrative services to something like order and cohesion, Mr. Cardwell was now confronted with his second and even more difficult task, the complete reorganisation of the British Army.

[1] Or was, until 1947.

He was hampered at the outset by finding himself called upon, like every British War Minister before or since, to bring about two equal and opposite consummations—render the Army more efficient and at the same time reduce its cost.

The first requisite of an efficient army, he realised, is that it must be of a size adequate to its duties; the second, that it must be perfectly trained and equipped with the most modern weapons. Mr. Cardwell solved the problem of size quite simply, and with the full concurrence of Mr. Gladstone, by recalling various battalions which had been stagnating, sometimes for years, in distant Colonial stations, and restoring them to the home establishment.

These stations fell into two categories—Imperial stations, such as Malta and Bermuda, which served as essential bases and coaling-stations for the Fleet; and contributing colonies, such as Canada and Australia—they were still called colonies in those days—which it was felt and agreed should now be prepared to assume some responsibility for their own defence. The Imperial stations then were left very much as they were, but troops were withdrawn from the colonies to the extent of more than 15,000—a considerable addition to a home force which at this time numbered less than 100,000. Moreover, since their upkeep at home cost the taxpayer considerably less than abroad, Mr. Cardwell had been able to combine two seemingly incompatible undertakings—increase the size of the home force and reduce the Army Estimates by a million pounds.

But the real value of this move lay less in its economy of manpower and money than in the boon which it conferred upon the soldier himself. A man might, and frequently did, spend the whole of his service as an exile from his native land; and since in the seventeenth and a great part of the eighteenth centuries that service was for life, this meant that he might never come home at all. The 38th Foot, now the 1st Battalion the South Staffordshire Regiment, were sent to the West Indies in 1706 and remained there for sixty years, utterly forgotten; while such units as did return from such trying service were mere relics of their former selves. The Cameron Highlanders were once so reduced in numbers by privation and disease during a tour of duty in the West Indies that the survivors of the rank and file were actually transferred *en masse* to the 42nd, the Black Watch. However, officers and non-commissioned officers contrived to return to Scotland, where they speedily found recruits and saved a famous regiment from extinction.

These were not by any means extreme instances, and it was little wonder that defaulters in home units, confronted with the alternative sentences of a thousand lashes or 'Colonial service', almost invariably chose the thousand lashes.

By 1868 these conditions had been considerably ameliorated. A soldier was no longer enlisted for life: the system had finally been abolished in 1848. But a fundamental weakness persisted, and Mr. Cardwell immediately laid his finger upon it. What he wanted, what the times demanded, was a small, efficient army which could rapidly be expanded in time of emergency into a really formidable force. And this could only be accomplished by the creation of an ample army reserve.

His available reserves at this time consisted of the Militia, which could be embodied only in time of war; the Volunteers, who from their first inception had grown to a considerable body but could only be called up in case of invasion; and two classes of Regular Army Reserves, of which only the first class could be sent abroad, the second being retained for home service. It will thus be seen that his only available reserve in time of peace was the First Army Reserve, roughly one thousand men. Plainly, if he desired a really adequate Army Reserve he must go to the Regular Army for it.

In 1870, therefore, he introduced a new Army Enlistment Act, under the provisions of which a Regular soldier's first term of engagement was fixed at twelve years, part to be served with the Colours and part in the Reserve. Obviously, the shorter a man's period of service with the Colours, the larger the number of men available for the Reserve at the end of each year. These periods have varied from time to time, but in Cardwell's Act they were fixed at six years for each, and it was calculated that thereby and in due course a reserve of 60,000 men would be permanently available. To that system, with slight variations, we have adhered ever since.[1]

By a further and most sensible provision, the bounty formerly paid to a recruit upon enlistment was abolished, and his good conduct allowance increased. This put an end to a practice all too common, under which a recruit, having received his bounty, promptly deserted, to enlist again elsewhere and so have his patriotism rewarded a second time.

The immediate result of the introduction of the short-service system was to make soldiering much more popular than ever before. This popularity was increased about the same time by the exclusion of bad characters from the Army and the abolition of flogging. The last year under the old system was 1869, when 11,742 recruits were enlisted. In 1871, the first year which saw the new scheme in working

---

[1] That is, until 1947, when the linked battalion system was suspended.

order, the number jumped to 23,165, or more than double. In 1885 the number had risen to close on 40,000.

But the Act of 1870 still made no provision against the possibility of a soldier having to spend the whole of his Colour service abroad. True, six years are better than sixty, but the principle was utterly wrong. So Mr. Cardwell embarked upon his second great innovation. He divided the Army[1] into a series of double or 'linked' battalions, some seventy pairs in all, with interchangeable personnel both in officers and men, one battalion serving a term overseas while the other remained at home and acted as feeder—a much more satisfactory and far less expensive system than that hitherto prevailing of filling vacancies in the overseas battalion from a depot maintained abroad.

But, as usual, there were difficulties to be overcome. The first was that of linking the battalions in an appropriate and tactful fashion. In the case of those regiments which already possessed two battalions the problem solved itself, but to unite two single-battalion regiments, each with its own traditions and *amour propre*, in a harmonious partnership, was not so easy. Secondly, the scheme made no provision for the systematic employment of the militia in the new reserve system. This body had always stood somewhat aloof from the Regular Army. It was not fully controlled by the War Office, being merely under the executive direction of an Inspector-General of Reserve Forces, while the officers received their commissions, not from the Queen, but from the Lord-Lieutenant of the county.

Obviously, this was no time for half-measures, so Mr. Cardwell took a third and even bolder step.

Hitherto each regiment in the Army had been known by a number, which incidentally indicated its age and seniority. Mr. Cardwell now decided to localise enlistment upon a territorial basis, and to call each regiment not by its number but by the name of the county or town in which it was raised. To this end he divided the country into seventy districts—a large county would naturally contain more than one of these—and allotted two line battalions to each, affiliating to them the militia and volunteer corps belonging to that district. Each district was furnished with its appropriate quota of artillery, cavalry and other arms, and the whole force served under the direction of the Major-General commanding the district.

As already noted, if a regiment already possessed two battalions, these were now linked as a matter of course; a regiment possessing but one battalion was wedded to a second regiment in a similar state

[1] The Guards and certain Rifle units were excluded from the scheme.

of single blessedness, each losing its original number and receiving the same territorial designation. (For example, the old 30th Foot became the 1st Battalion the East Lancashire Regiment, and the 59th Foot became the 2nd Battalion.) A good deal of conjugal incompatibility sometimes resulted.

The affiliation of the militia battalions incidentally disposed of a question to which the linked battalion scheme had supplied no answer: 'Supposing the country were to be involved in a serious war and it became necessary to send *both* Regular battalions of a regiment overseas, from where would they draw their reinforcements?' The reply was: 'From their affiliated militia battalions'. Moreover, recruits to the militia were now to be trained as far as possible with those of the Regular Army. In this way a county regiment formed a really homogeneous whole. The Royal Loamshire Regiment, we will say, was now comprised as follows: 1st and 2nd Loamshires, Regular; 3rd and 4th Loamshires, Militia; 5th (or more) Loamshires, Volunteers. Thus all enjoyed the same regimental name, tradition, uniform and pride of county.

Of course, the new system did not spring up in a night. It encountered fierce opposition from the sentimentalists, and was itself of a character which precluded speedy growth. But by 1881, when Mr. Childers was Secretary of State for War, the changeover was completed and the new machinery running smoothly.

Still, to this day you will encounter veterans of all ranks who still prefer to refer to their old regiment by its number rather than its name.

~⊰(5)⊱~

Mr. Cardwell now embarked upon his final and most hotly contested reform, the abolition of the peculiar system, unknown in any other country or age, under which officers of the British Army were permitted, instead of qualifying for the King's Commission by merit or experience, to purchase them for cash.

Indefensible as the practice may appear today, it was at least hallowed by an understandable tradition, dating back to the time when our Army was less an army than a collection of independent regimental units, and the colonel practically owned his regiment. His officers purchased their commissions from him, which made each of them the proprietor of his own company or troop, and to that extent a shareholder in a business venture—not always a profitable venture, for he had to keep his company up to strength. Recruits, as always in the history of our country, were hard to come by, and to obtain a sufficiency of these the officer had frequently to pay a bounty, or bonus, out of his own pocket over and above that granted by the nation for each man enlisted; so when the time came for him to retire he recouped himself for all this expense by selling his company to the highest bidder, much as a man today may dispose of the lease of his house or sell a medical practice.

The system persisted after the establishment of the new Regular Army. Charles II himself recognised it by purchasing the command of a regiment of Guards from one Colonel Russel and bestowing it upon his own natural son, the Duke of Grafton, a young man who had seen no military service whatever. Charles extended his recognition still further, and more profitably, by exacting a 'rake-off' of five per cent on all Purchase transactions as a contribution to the new Chelsea Hospital, then in course of erection.

The first monarch to exhibit any active aversion to the practice was George I, not so much by reason of its inherent rottenness as because the prices asked for commissions were growing beyond the bounds of reason. He issued a Royal Warrant on the subject, imposing certain limitations, but no one appears to have taken any particular notice of it, and it soon became a dead letter.

In 1766, however, a more serious effort was made to control the traffic, and a regular tariff of prices was set up with the approval of George III. The authorised charges varied from £6,700 for a colonelcy in the Foot Guards to £400 for an ensignship in a marching regiment of foot. It was strictly forbidden to pay any price in excess of that laid down, but there is no doubt that the regulation was regularly evaded. Thus an iniquitous system was stabilised. It imposed a grievous handicap upon officers compelled through lack of means to work their way up by merit alone, while the frequent admission to all commissioned appointments (up to the rank of Colonel) of wealthy, incompetent amateurs constituted a direct menace to the morale and efficiency of the Army itself.

A single instance will serve to illustrate either aspect of this evil. Lord Clyde (Sir Colin Campbell), who had himself fought his way up to the rank of Field-Marshal in campaigns extending from the Peninsula to the Indian Mutiny, giving evidence before a Royal Commission (which was investigating the incidents of the Crimean War) in 1856, told the following story of an officer of the 55th Regiment.

'This officer', he said, 'had been promoted for service in the field, having led the assault at Ching Kiang-foo, and so attained his brevet-majority. He next became a brevet-colonel. Then, when he was actually in command of his regiment in the field, in the presence of the enemy, that command was purchased over his head by a very young and totally inexperienced captain who had just come out, and he himself was compelled to descend to the command of a company! He was afterwards killed leading that company in the assault on the Redan.'

The time had come, Mr. Cardwell decided, not only for the sake of the good name of the Army but for the protection of the brave men who fought in its ranks, to bring Purchase to an end once and for all. So in 1871 he embodied a proposal to that effect in his Army Regulation Bill, undertaking at the same time to pay reasonable compensation to the officers for the loss of their vested interests.

The abolition of Purchase was more strenuously resisted than any of the other reforms. It was objected in the first place that the country could not afford to pay the sum required for compensation—some seven or eight million pounds. Secondly, it was argued, the Army had always done well under its present type of officer, the dashing, high-spirited soldier of the traditional Cavalier type; and to entrust its fortunes and fate to leaders of a lower social category—this was begging the question with a vengeance—would have a demoralising effect upon both efficiency and discipline. Thirdly, it was claimed that the system actually favoured the officer who had won his commission by merit alone, for upon leaving the service he could sell it for cash. Finally, to appoint officers by selection, as now proposed, would be no improvement, since it would lead to favouritism and backstairs influence.

To these mixed and inconclusive arguments Mr. Cardwell returned a single, unequivocal answer.

'The Army', he said, 'must be rendered efficient. To render it efficient the officers must belong to the Army, and not the Army to the officers. So Purchase must go, and judicious selection take its place.'

And to that contention he steadfastly adhered, backed by his Prime Minister, all through a long and tempestuous Session.

Finally the Army Regulation Bill, of which the abolition of Purchase formed the core, was forced through the House of Commons and passed to the Lords.

Here the Opposition changed their tactics. With the permanent majority at their disposal, they could have rejected the Bill outright. This they refrained from doing, probably because the country was by this time strongly in favour of it, and fell back upon a policy of obstruction and a series of blocking amendments.

But Mr. Cardwell was determined that the Bill should become law. So he had recourse to a simple expedient. The Purchase system, he recollected, had been amended, and to that extent legalised, by a Royal Warrant of George III. But what the Sovereign could sanction the Sovereign could annul. So Mr. Gladstone asked the Queen to cancel the Royal Warrant of 1766 altogether. The Queen did so, and at a stroke the purchase of commissions stood bereft either of sanction or sanctity.

There was a fierce outcry, of course. It was said that the prerogative of the Crown had been abused, and the authority of Parliament flouted. But the Prime Minister and the Secretary of State were within their rights. They rode out the storm, and the Army Regulation Bill became law. Purchase was dead.

Such, in brief review, were the Cardwell Reforms[1]—the reorganisation of the War Office; the institution of the short service system; the provision of an adequate reserve by the device of linked battalions; the establishment of the seventy regimental districts; the affiliation of the militia to the Regular Army; the transference of the bestowal of commissions upon the officers of the Auxiliary forces from the Lord-Lieutenants to the Crown; and the abolition of Purchase.

The name of Cardwell is almost forgotten now, but the great edifice which he erected so laboriously has stood up well. Its superstructure has been altered more than once by the hand of time and the progress of military science; but the foundations endure.

---

[1] These have not all been described in their exact chronological order.

CHAPTER IV

THE SOUTH AFRICAN
WAR AND HALDANE

~(1)~

FROM the end of the Indian Mutiny to the outbreak of the Great Boer War our country enjoyed the second longest period of rest—forty years—from wars of major importance in its history.

Indeed, during the Victorian era we turned over what almost amounted to a new leaf. We allowed the Russo-Turkish War, the Austro-Prussian War, the Franco-Prussian War, and various revolutionary upheavals in Spain, Italy and the Balkans, to be conducted without us. Apart from the unnecessary folly of the Crimea, not a single British soldier fell in action upon the continent of Europe between Waterloo and Mons—a period of close on a hundred years.

Not that the Army was not seriously engaged elsewhere. It fought, not without some humiliating setbacks (as Isandhlwana and Majuba remind us) against the Zulus and Cape Dutch, in numerous operations upon the North-West Frontier of India, and in particular in Egypt and the Sudan, beginning with Tel-el-Kebir in 1882 and achieving no final settlement until sixteen years later, when a hitherto unknown general named Sir Herbert Kitchener, with a mixed force of British and Egyptian troops, routed 50,000 Dervishes at Omdurman, avenged the murder of Gordon, and established peace and civilised government from the Nile Delta to Khartoum.

But these, apart from certain preliminary clashes with the Boers, were wars fought against native troops, fearless and fanatical fighters, but unprovided with modern weapons. They gave our Army and its leaders no practical experience in the employment of more scientific methods.

Then came the Great Boer War of 1899–1902. With its operational history we are not concerned, except to take note how far the new military machinery lived up to expectations, and to summarise the lessons learned.

It was obvious from the start that the Cardwell reforms had produced an army capable of immediate and rapid expansion. A reserve of 80,000 men, ninety-six per cent efficient, was at once forthcoming, and during the next two years not less than 130,000 troops—the largest force ever commanded by a British general—were maintained continuously in the field. Also, the infantry were now equipped with the new Lee Metford magazine rifle, using smokeless powder, which replaced the hard-kicking, cloud-compelling Martini Henry. Discipline was excellent and morale high.

A good deal has been said and written, not always temperately, about muddle and inefficiency during the South African War. Those charges can hardly be laid at the door of the Army itself. It was a very different force from that which had fought in the Crimea. It was well trained, well equipped, and well fed, and it was led by officers who knew their job, and knew their men.

But the Cardwell reforms had not penetrated deeply enough into the higher regions—in other words, the War Office. War had threatened for months, yet little provision or planning seems to have been made for it. Apparently the old fatal theory still held good, that the best way to avoid war is to avoid all appearance of preparing for it. It was only after urgent representations from responsible military commanders that the meagre garrisons of Cape Colony and Natal were reinforced; and even when war was at last declared our total force in South Africa numbered only about 22,000 men.

These, thrown at once upon the defensive, soon found themselves closely beleaguered in Ladysmith, Kimberley and Mafeking. It is difficult to understand why the Boers, who were fully mobilised and highly mobile—every man of them was mounted—did not swoop upon Cape Town itself before the British Expeditionary Force could arrive.

The energies of that body upon landing were immediately applied to a series of unrelated and disastrous attempts to relieve the besieged garrisons. Within a single week in December 1899—a week never to be forgotten by those old enough to remember it, for it was perhaps the blackest week in British military history—came the news of heavy defeats at Colenso, Stormberg and Magersfontein.

The public mind at home was profoundly shocked, for no one had expected the Boers to put up such a resistance. But they might have been told, or at any rate the Army might have been told, what to expect. An efficient intelligence system could have informed them that the Boers could raise a force of some 60,000 men, whose extreme mobility practically doubled their numbers; and that every Boer was an expert sharpshooter and an adept in the art of taking cover. Under the British infantry training system of that time the accepted method of attack was by short rushes in open order, the men lying down and firing at the end of each rush. Upon arriving within 350 yards of the enemy, bayonets were fixed and a charge delivered. Such methods, directed against an invisible opponent, merely provided him with the target best suited to his methods, especially if he could cause that target to 'bunch' at a suitable range by the aid of a few strands of barbed wire.

As usual, news of disaster immediately roused Government and country to a real effort. The supreme command was placed in the hands of Britain's foremost soldier, Lord Roberts, with Kitchener, fresh from his Sudan triumphs, as Chief-of-Staff. All the remaining reserves were called up, and two fresh divisions dispatched forthwith, accompanied by considerable reinforcements, including a howitzer brigade. Eleven militia battalions went, too—another feather in the cap of the Cardwell system—followed by volunteer and yeomanry units. Here, indeed, was the promise of something entirely new to our peaceful, sheltered Island—the idea, destined to come to full fruition fifteen and forty years later, of a nation in arms.

And the idea did not stop there, for loyal offers of contingents from the Empire overseas were immediately received and gratefully accepted. But for some strange reason the acceptance was at first accompanied by the proviso, 'Unmounted men preferred'. This, against a force of some 60,000 mounted infantrymen!

Lord Roberts, upon arrival in South Africa, took the offensive from the start, marching straight up country with the enemy capitals, Bloemfontein and Pretoria, as his objective. This operation had the effect which he desired and had foreseen. The forces besieging Ladysmith and Kimberley, finding themselves in danger of being outflanked, relaxed their hold and retreated northward, with the result that both places were shortly relieved without further difficulty. Following up his advantage at top speed, Roberts gained a decisive victory at Paardeburg, where he isolated and rounded up a Boer force of 4,000 men under Cronje, and captured the whole of it.

This turned the tide. The way to Bloemfontein and Pretoria now lay open, and the war, so far as any hope of a Boer victory was concerned, was over. President Kruger certainly thought so: he decamped with all his available assets, and was no more seen.

But hopeless though the prospect might be, the enemy fought on, putting up a most gallant and resourceful defence for two years, under the leadership of such truly remarkable men as Botha, de Wet and, lastly, Jan Christian Smuts, today a Field-Marshal of the British Empire.

The final surrender came in May 1902, and the Transvaäl and Orange Free State were annexed to Britain. A few years later, by an act of magnanimity unparalleled in history, the two countries were handed back by the British people to their previous owners—with results which abide to this day as a matter for mutual confidence and respect.

~⚹(2)⚹~

Fas est et ab hoste doceri. Those two long years of guerrilla warfare against such a past-master in the art as 'Brother Boer' taught the British soldier certain lessons which were destined to be invaluable to him in the years to come, and to a certain extent revolutionised his entire attitude towards his own profession.

In the first place, as already noted, the Boer taught him the importance of mobility, intelligent scouting, and skilful use of ground and cover. From him, too, he learned that it is not always possible or desirable to attack in drill-book formation, but that troops must learn to fight if necessary in small, detached groups, where each man will have to think for himself and employ his own intelligence.

But it was a hard schooling. British 'mobile' columns, valiant but inexperienced and hampered by too much transport, tramped stolidly up and down the veldt in hopeless pursuit of a will-o'-the-wisp opponent seemingly possessed of no encumbrances of any kind, and capable at one moment of vanishing into thin air only to materialise at another, with stunning unexpectedness, to cut off a party of stragglers or catch an ox-waggon convoy crossing a river.[1]

It is only fair to add that in the end the pupil learned his lessons, to the frequent discomfiture of his preceptor. In fact, it is not too much to say that in South Africa Thomas Atkins first imbibed and developed the spirit and tradition of the commando soldier, with his unconventional methods and highly developed sense of camouflage, of more than forty years later.

---

[1] Any young soldier desiring a further and more intimate picture of the highly irregular warfare of those days is recommended to read a little book, *The Defence of Duffer's Drift*, by Major-General Sir Ernest Swinton, C.B., D.S.O. It was written some forty years ago, but the reader will find it both instructive and entertaining.

And, as also noted, warfare of this character definitely affected the soldier's attitude towards what may be called the ethics of soldiering. He learned from his opponents that in war to the death—which is what war should be if it is to effect its purpose in the shortest possible time—a certain amount of low cunning, or 'slimness', is not only necessary but justifiable. The Boer, for instance, declined to provide himself with a uniform. He went into battle attired in a frock-coat, a sombrero and a bandolier, which enabled him, at a moment's notice, to double the part of first-class fighting man with that of a peaceful civilian tiller of the soil. He was fond of ambushes and booby-traps, and when cornered himself was apt to be a little careless in his employment of the white flag. All of which taught the British soldier that you must be prepared at times, and up to a point, to fight your opponent with his own weapons.

But the most notable and heartening outcome of the South African War was the spontaneous awakening of the British Empire as a whole to its joint obligations and responsibilities.

That Empire had first become wholly conscious of itself in 1897, the year of Queen Victoria's Diamond Jubilee, when contingents from India, Canada, Australasia and the colonies, down to the remotest island settlements of the Pacific, had marched in variegated procession through the streets of London, lined by cheering citizens. But that had been in time of profound peace, and was merely a demonstration of the affection and loyalty of her subjects towards their aged Queen Empress. The South African War evoked a different spirit. This time loyalty to the old Queen and the old country had been translated into terms of action. From all over the world they came again, not to demonstrate this time, but to fight. Never had any military leader commanded so representative and comprehensive a force as Lord Roberts in the year 1900. And twice during the next half-century that same force was destined to assemble again, and fight upon a far wider battleground, for an infinitely higher cause.

~(3)~

After the South African War the usual (or rather, inevitable) Royal Commission[1] was appointed to consider its conduct. The ultimate outcome, a year or two later, was a valuable document known as the War Office (Reconstruction) Committee Report, or more briefly, the Esher Report.

[1] The Elgin Commission.

The Committee had not been required to criticise the record or performances of the Army itself, but rather its direction from above; and it put forward certain drastic recommendations, designed to remedy various undetected flaws in the Cardwell system, for the reorganisation of the War Office.

The outstanding point made by the Committee[1] was that the sole duty of a War Office is to prepare for war, and that the main weakness of the War Office in the past had been its tendency to favour routine at the expense of preparedness. 'For many years', they announced, 'this Department of State has been administered from the point of view of peace.' In other words, the War Office had been conducted more like a well-ordered department-store than as a machine which might at any moment be called upon to spring into furious and unexampled activity.

The remedies proposed, put briefly, were twofold—the constant and regular infusion of new blood to prevent routine stagnation, and a redistribution of duties which would entirely separate the Executive from the Administrative Staff; free the Commander-in-Chief and his colleagues from the perpetual drudgery of minutes and files, and enable them to devote their entire energy to preparation for active warfare.

Paradoxically enough, the Committee's very first recommendation was that the post of Commander-in-Chief should be abolished altogether; for the simple reason that (unlike the schoolmaster in Goldsmith's *Deserted Village*) one small head could not possibly carry all he was supposed to know; for he was nominally responsible for, and cognisant of, every detail of army practice and administration.

In future, his duties were to be divided among various duly qualified individuals, each with his own department and range of responsibility. Further, to relieve the intense and unnecessary concentration of army business within the War Office in London, a plan of drastic decentralisation was recommended, to enable certain duties to be distributed further afield and discharged locally.[2]

As a preliminary and most important step, the Committee put forward suggestions for the standardisation of the functions and membership of the so-called Defence Committee. The purpose of this body was to co-ordinate the activities of the Navy and Army, and at the same time consider all questions of Imperial defence from the point of view of India and the Dominions. This, of course, was not exclusively an Army problem, but the success of any scheme of Army

[1] The Committee was composed as follows: Viscount Esher, Admiral Sir John Fisher, and Sir George Sydenham Clarke.
[2] Most of these reforms had already been suggested by a Royal Commission (Lord Hartington's) in 1890; but the Report had been shelved.

or War Office reform must of necessity depend upon its effective solution. The Esher Committee therefore suggested that the Defence Committee should consist of a Permanent Secretary in place of the Prime Minister (whose views on Imperial matters might be tinged one way or the other by political bias), two naval officers, two military officers, two officers of the Indian Army nominated by the Viceroy, and one or more representatives from the Dominions.[1]

This question disposed of, the Committee turned to their appointed task, the evolution of a scheme of War Office reform.

They began by laying it down as a fundamental principle that in future the Secretary of State for War should be placed on exactly the same footing as the First Lord of the Admiralty; which meant that all submissions to the Crown in regard to military matters must be made by him alone. They followed this up by proposing that an Army Council should be created upon the general principles obtaining at the Admiralty. It was to consist of seven members, four military and three civil, deliberating under the direction of the Secretary of State for War. It may be interesting to enumerate these members, and compare their duties with those of their 'opposite numbers' on the Board of Admiralty of that time.

The First Military Member, the Chief of the Imperial General Staff, whose status corresponded to that of the First Sea Lord (or Senior Naval Lord), was responsible for military strategy, intelligence, and war organisation in general. The Second, the Adjutant-General, like the Second Sea Lord, was entrusted with all matters relating to personnel—in other words, with the recruiting and organisation of the Army, including the Medical Services and Auxiliary Forces. To the Third, the Quartermaster-General, were committed the multi-farious problems connected with the housing, feeding, clothing and transporting of the British soldier wherever the exigencies of military service might place him or the fortune of war dispatch him. (The duties of the Third Sea Lord, *mutatis mutandis*, were similar.) The Fourth Military Member, the Master-General of Ordnance, was entrusted with all questions of armaments and fortifications.

The Secretary of State for War was himself the principal Civil Member and Chairman of the Council, and was solely responsible to Parliament and the Sovereign not only for army administration but for its discipline and control. Then came the so-called Civil Member. The Third was the Finance Member, in general control of army finance. All three Civil Members were members of one or other of the Houses of Parliament.

[1] This body grew subsequently into the Committee of Imperial Defence.

The entire structure of the Council was held together by the Secretary to the War Office, a civil servant of high rank, who acted as Secretary of the War Office and Secretary to the Army Council, with general control over office business.[1] Nominally all correspondence was addressed to him.

Having thus provided for administrative needs, the Esher Committee now turned to the creation of a General Staff, or 'thinking department', dedicated solely to the preparation of the Army for war. Upon this the C.I.G.S. was to be assisted by the Adjutant-General, Quartermaster-General and Master-General of Ordnance, all of whose duties had now been clearly defined and could not overlap. In conformity with the 'new blood' principle, it was laid down that these should hold their appointments for four years only.

The Committee next put forward its proposals for decentralisation. For this purpose the United Kingdom was divided into five military commands—the Aldershot and Salisbury, Northern, Eastern, Western and Ireland—each under a General Officer Commanding-in-Chief, upon whom devolved the co-ordination of training and preparation, with the necessary administration services. For administration purposes each command (except in Ireland) was divided into two districts, under a Major-General. London was to have a separate district of its own. This arrangement set combatant officers free from routine administrative duty in order to devote their entire energy to training.

Finally, in order that the Army Council as supreme administrative body should be kept continuously informed of the training and efficiency of the troops throughout the country, an Inspector-General of the Forces should be appointed, to act, with his assistants, as the eyes and ears of the Council.

Such were the recommendations of the Esher Committee. They were at once acclaimed by the country, and were accepted *en bloc* by Parliament. Thus ended the long struggle for supremacy between the civil and military authorities of the State. 'The Generals belonged to the Army, and not the Army to the Generals.'

⤙(4)⤚

Thanks to the labours of the Esher Committee, the military machine had been brought up to date. The War Office had been overhauled and reconditioned, and its administration modernised. It now remained to reorganise the Army on the operational side—that is to

[1] He is now known as the Permanent Under Secretary to the War Office.

say, create a fully trained and equipped expeditionary force for immediate dispatch overseas in the event of war, while leaving sufficient troops at home to defend our coasts against the possibility of invasion.

And, indeed, it was high time, for once more the war clouds were gathering over Europe. Germany was not only maintaining an enormous army, but was steadily increasing her navy; it was reckoned that by 1915 the number of her capital ships would equal our own. The German press were beginning to talk with ominous unanimity about Germany's right to 'a place in the sun', the Kaiser was posturing in 'shining armour', and in German naval and military messes German officers were solemnly raising their glasses to '*der Tag*'.

The first attempt to create the military force necessary in these circumstances was made by Mr. St. John Brodrick, who succeeded Lord Lansdowne as Secretary of State for War in 1900. He proposed to establish six 'Army Corps Districts', but the scheme was too nebulous and came to nothing. His successor, Mr. Arnold-Forster, a most able administrator with a reformed and rejuvenated War Office behind him, enjoyed but a short innings, for the Government's lease of life was drawing rapidly to its close. Early in 1906 came a General Election, and the Conservative Party, after ten years of office, went down to a defeat as devastating as that suffered by Mr. Churchill's National Government forty years later. The Liberals came in with a huge majority, and Sir Henry Campbell-Bannerman was able to form a Government of quite exceptional ability and resource, containing as it did such men as Mr. Asquith, Sir Edward Grey, Mr. Lloyd George, and Mr. Churchill.

In selecting his Secretary of State for War, the Prime Minister followed the example of Mr. Gladstone in 1872, by appointing to that office a minister without any previous knowledge or experience of army affairs. The appointment was a complete surprise, and its effect was heightened by the fact that his nominee, Mr. R. B. Haldane, an eminent Scottish lawyer, who had already declined the Speakership of the House of Commons, had long been 'spotted' as the next Lord Chancellor. But Mr. Haldane went to the War Office instead, with consequences momentous in the history of the Army, and possibly in the destiny of our country. But much had to happen before these could make themselves felt.

When, in 1906, the new Secretary of State presented his first Army Estimates to the House he found himself faced, like Mr. Cardwell before him, with the old and familiar demand for 'a more efficient Army at a reduced cost'. His task was rendered no easier by the fact that a considerable section of the Party behind him favoured peace almost at any price, while he was faced by an Opposition fiercely opposed to any assault upon army establishment or tradition.

But Mr. Haldane possessed three great assets. He brought an entirely fresh and extremely powerful mind to his subject, he was utterly fearless, and he was a most persuasive speaker.

From his 'preliminary observations' to the House (which occupied something like two hours), it was obvious that he had devoted his capacious and impartial mind to a profound study of the whole science of war, and that, within the limits of human prescience, his views were sound and his plans far-sighted.

He began by repeating, in rather more elaborate form, the question asked in the opening sentence of this book: 'What is our Army for? What are the things that it must be able to do, and what are the things that it need not now be called upon to do at all? If we can eliminate these latter we shall effect an enormous economy of men and money.'

His answer can be summed up in the phrase, much in favour at that time: 'Blue Water School'. So long as Britannia ruled the waves, he declared—and we possessed at that time a Navy equal to the combined navies of any two other countries—no enemy could hope successfully to invade our coasts. Any such attempt must be limited to a force of 5,000 to 10,000 men, thrown ashore in a surprise raid. 'They might cause some annoyance, but they would all be cut off, and most of them would never get back. The Fleet would prevent any real invasion.'

With this confident and then perfectly justifiable assertion both sides of the House cheerfully agreed. This was not altogether surprising, for Mr. A. J. Balfour, the Leader of the Opposition, was himself the protagonist of the Blue Water School.

The Minister next proceeded, logically enough, to announce that, our island being admittedly immune from invasion, he proposed to dismantle most of our coastal defences, together with those of London. These consisted of some 300 guns, mostly obsolete, and employed 2,000 gunners, who could now be set free for more important duties.

Secondly, he intended to reduce the garrisons of various outlying colonies and coaling stations, such as Malta, Ceylon and St. Helena, which could perfectly well be left to the protection of our vast and mobile Navy, and bring the men home.

So far, so good. But his next announcement put an immediate end to the unanimity of his audience. 'These returning battalions', he said, 'would not be added to the strength of the home army, but would be abolished altogether, as an essential step in the reduction of army expenditure.'

After this ominous beginning, the Minister proceeded to reveal his intentions in full. 'I propose,' he said, 'in the name of my colleagues, that in future the number of British soldiers shall be 20,000 fewer Regulars than exist at the present date.'

Then he gave details. He began by laying his hand upon the Ark of the Covenant: the ten battalions of the Brigade of Guards were to be reduced by two—the 3rd Scots Guards and the 3rd Coldstream. Two battalions of the Northumberland Fusiliers were to go as well, with two from the Royal Warwickshire Regiment, two from the Lancashire Fusiliers, and two from the Manchester Regiment. These being 'linked' battalions, the liquidation of the battalion abroad would of necessity be accompanied by that of the battalion at home. Hence the double elimination.

All this was drastic enough, but there were further shocks in store, especially for the Service and country Members. Not only was the artillery to be reduced—partly in order to create a larger reserve and partly because the new quick-firing gun required an increased ammunition column and more men to serve it—but it was proposed to scrap the militia, with all its hoary tradition of general levy, ballot and control by the Lord-Lieutenants of the Counties, and reassemble it in quite unrecognisable form.

The militia, he pointed out, as at present constituted, fell between two stools. It occupied an intermediate and indeterminate position between the Regulars and the volunteers. Originally intended for home defence only, it had frequently served overseas; indeed, during the South African War no fewer than 45,000 officers and men of the militia had volunteered for that duty. It was neither one thing nor the other; it was a hybrid, evincing the weaknesses of both and the virtues of neither. 'It is plundered by the Line at one end and encroached on by the volunteers at the other,' Lord Lansdowne had said.

There was only one possible remedy; the three-line defence system of the Cardwellian scheme—Regular, militia, volunteers—must be reduced to two. To this end the militia would be taken over from the Lord-Lieutenants, put under the control of the War Office, and converted into a reserve for the Regular Army. Each Regular battalion would have its own ancillary militia battalion. The two battalions would wear the same uniform, be similarly armed, undergo the same training on manœuvres, and draw the same pay. In time of war the militia battalion could either act as a feeder to the Regular battalion from the regimental depot, or go abroad as a unit, leaving the defence of the country to the volunteers.

Finally, the ancient title, the militia, would be abolished,[1] and the name 'Special Reserve' substituted.

Having run amuck among these ancient and revered institutions, and so gratified the economists sitting behind him, Mr. Haldane became suddenly and entirely constructive—and, it should be added, irresistibly persuasive, for the scheme which he now laid before the House was in its scope, breadth of vision, and clarity of exposition, masterly. And for once in the annals of Army reform, it was destined to withstand the test of time.

∼(5)∼

Mr. Haldane began by describing the composition and purpose of his new expeditionary force. It was to consist of six infantry divisions and four cavalry brigades, with artillery, engineers, and ancillary services in proportion. It was to be kept completely equipped, and in the event of war could be dispatched overseas in a matter of days.

The Minister laid particular stress upon one point. A continental country, he remarked, which lived cheek by jowl with its neighbours, stood in constant danger, at times of international unrest, of immediate and overwhelming invasion. Upon the threat of war it must mobilise its entire military potential *instanter*, or perish. That was why such countries were compelled to maintain a system of universal conscription and an enormous standing army.

The United Kingdom was in a privileged position. Owing to our command of the sea and presumable immunity from mass invasion, we could afford to take our time, in the event of a war, in preparing those forces upon which we depended for the expansion of the Regular Army. For that expansion anything in the nature of compulsory service, he said, was unnecessary and unthinkable. Volunteers, he was confident, would instantly be forthcoming, under the spur of patriotic necessity, in more than sufficient numbers. They would be trained and equipped during the months following the outbreak of hostilities and dispatched, when ready, to join the fighting men in the field.

Having communicated his plan for the transformation of the militia, Mr. Haldane now turned to the volunteers; and of that body

[1] It came back in 1939 in a somewhat different connotation, with the institution of Universal National Service.

he had some trenchant things to say. Their present organisation, he announced, was 'probably the most confused thing in the British Empire'. It was subject to no particular order or system, and its various units were a law unto themselves. They were paid, when embodied, in twenty-two different ways. Far too great a burden was imposed upon commanding officers, who were made personally liable not only for the training and efficiency of their battalions, but if they failed to get a grant from the Commissioners must foot the bill. The actual establishment of the force was 340,000: its present strength was 240,000.

The force itself had a variegated and spasmodic history. It dated back to 1794, when the French Revolution was threatening the security and peace of the whole of Europe, and the first Volunteer Act was passed. A second followed in 1802, while Napoleon was massing his 'Army of England' on the cliffs above Boulogne. The numbers of the Volunteer force at this time swelled to 400,000. Then, with Napoleon safely lodged in St. Helena, patriotic enthusiasm languished, and nearly forty years of torpor intervened until 1849, the period of the Second French Revolution, when a fresh outburst of Anglophobia upon the part of the French people brought the Volunteer movement suddenly and violently to life again.

This time the Government took definite action. They proceeded to canalise the new flood of martial enthusiasm into an ordered system. Capitation grants were awarded in return for the performance of a certain number of drills and attendance at an annual camp. But the plan never came fully to life: discipline was slack; attendance at drill and camp was far from regular, and sometimes a unit failed to qualify for its grant. The general public became mildly derisive, and dropped into the habit of referring to the volunteers as 'Saturday Afternoon Soldiers'. In 1906 the movement remained as haphazard and unsystematic as it had been fifty years before.

Here, said Mr. Haldane truly, was some splendid material going to waste, and the waste must stop, for under his new scheme the volunteers would have a clear and definite national duty to perform— the defence, no less, of their native land during the absence abroad of the Regular Army. To that end the present inefficient system would be scrapped, and the volunteers organised, trained and equipped, like the Regulars, upon a divisional basis.

Fortunately, the new structure could be erected upon a foundation already existing. The United Kingdom had for some time been divided into twelve groups, or regimental districts, each composed of four or five counties and commanded by a Brigadier-General. Each of these districts, it was revealed, contained the material for a volunteer division. Indeed, more than one of them contained more: the Lancashire and London districts, for example, could produce two out of the material available. Scotland could do the same. There would be fourteen such divisions in all.

Moreover, they were to be real divisions, in the full sense of the word. ('Division' is the term applied to the smallest self-sufficient formation of the British Army—a mixed force, that is to say, about 15,000 strong, composed of infantry, cavalry, artillery and engineers, together with the essential transport, medical and other services; in other words, a miniature expeditionary force.) The cavalry for these 'Territorial' divisions, as they were to be called—the old volunteers had gone for ever—would be supplied, appropriately, by the Yeomanry; the artillery units were to be armed with 15-pounder guns recently relinquished by the Regulars, which when converted into quick-firers would be more than adequate for home defence.

The term of enlistment would be for four years. In the event of war the entire division would be embodied for six months' training. Each division would be commanded by a Regular Major-General, who would devote his whole time to his duties and would be supported by a Regular administrative staff. The brigade commanders, Mr. Haldane hoped—a hope destined to more than complete fulfilment—could in time be obtained from the Territorial force itself.

Finally, in order to maintain and intensify the Territorial motif, each division would be placed under the supervision of a so-called County Territorial Association. The Lord-Lieutenant, recently dispossessed of his responsibility for the local militia, would now come to his own again as President of this body, which would consist of a Committee of Commanding Officers of the Auxiliary forces concerned, together with the District Brigadier-General, who would furnish the needful link between the Territorial force and the General Staff.

─≺(6)≻─

Finally, the Minister addressed himself to the serious problem of the perennial shortage of officers. Here he looked in the main to the universities and public schools, most of which maintained their own cadet corps.

All these, he announced, would be amalgamated and standardised into a single organisation under War Office control, with the style and title of The Officers' Training Corps, Senior and Junior. The great universities could probably contribute a battalion apiece, perhaps with cavalry, artillery and engineering units thrown in. The average public school would at least muster a company of a hundred.[1] There would be regular drills, musketry instruction either on a full or miniature range, and an annual fortnight under canvas. The cadets would wear standard khaki uniforms, and their officers would receive full commissions in the Territorial force. Every unit would be subject to periodical inspection by a Regular officer.

Proficiency would be encouraged by the award of two certificates, A and B. The former would be bestowed upon any member of the Junior O.T.C. who could demonstrate that he had reached the standard of a 2nd Lieutenant of ,the volunteers: the latter was reserved for members of the University Corps, and to gain it the candidate must attain to the standard of a cadet who had undergone six months' training at Sandhurst or Woolwich. This involved real application and hard work, including a period of attachment to a Regular unit.

Here was no paper scheme of Saturday afternoon soldiering, but a serious and considered effort to convert material, splendid material, which had hitherto taken its duties somewhat lightly, into a keen and responsibly minded reserve of officers. It stood far in advance of anything hitherto proposed or even dreamed of, and was destined to succeed beyond all expectation. The present writer still cherishes vivid recollections of Windsor Great Park some five years later—July 15th, 1911—during the series of ceremonies attendant upon the Coronation of King George V. Here upon that day the King held a great review of the Officers' Training Corps—its first public appearance as a corporate body—at which 20,000 undergraduates and schoolboys, representing some 400 distinct and separate units, gathered from all over the country, marched past in perfect formation to the music of their own bands and pipers.

Most of those boys and young men, though they did not know it then, were destined some three years later to lead into action platoons and companies of Regular, Service, and Territorial battalions of the British Army in the greatest war yet fought in the history of their country. There are not many of them left today, for they were among the first to hold the fort and man the breach. But they were ready and willing at a moment when all were willing but few were ready; and for that we should never forget the O.T.C. or its creator.

Such were the historic Haldane reforms. They were fiercely assailed at the time, and from various quarters—by the soldiers and ex-soldiers

[1] At that time the eight-company system still obtained in infantry battalions.

who resented the abolition of famous infantry and artillery units, by the mourners for the departed glory of the ancient militia, and by the out-and-out advocates of universal and compulsory military service, headed by no less an authority than Lord Roberts himself. But they passed into law and ultimately proved their worth.

Mr. Haldane's prescience failed him in only two respects; first when he prophesied that our country stood in no danger of serious aggression from without—he had not foreseen the air-raids—and secondly when he declared that in Great Britain compulsory service was unthinkable. In these points he was wrong, but in everything else he was right, and more than right. Indeed, his faith and vision far outran the bare limits of his scheme, especially where the Territorial force was concerned. Here is his final word on that subject:

My belief is (and in this I am confirmed by high military authority) that not only would they be enormously more efficient than the volunteer or Yeomanry force is at the present time, but that they would be ready to say:—'We wish to go abroad and take our part in the theatre of war, to fight in the interests of the nation and for the defence of the Empire.' *It might be that they would not only go in their battalions, but in their brigades and even their divisions.*

In which bold forecast, as the event proved, he was more than justified.

CHAPTER V

THE FIRST WORLD WAR

AND AFTER

⭑(1)⭑

UPON August 4th, 1914, the seething pot of Europe boiled over, and
Bethmann Hollweg, the German Chancellor, acting under orders
long premeditated, tore up the 'Scrap of Paper' which guaranteed
the neutrality of Belgium. Britain immediately honoured her pledge
to that little country and declared war upon Germany. In one way
and another the world has been at war ever since.

The Haldane scheme came into immediate operation. Mobilisation
was effected with smoothness and celerity, and the British Expeditionary Force was dispatched to Flanders.

Simultaneously at home a nation-wide appeal was issued for men.
Here another of Mr. Haldane's prognostications was fulfilled: the
spirit of the nation soared, and recruits poured in from every side.
Men waited for hours, frequently all night, to obtain admission to
the recruiting offices. Indeed, the regular machinery devised for the
purpose proved totally inadequate, and steps had to be taken to open
extra offices all over the country—in town halls, libraries, even public
baths. So vast was the intake of recruits that upon more than one
occasion the number of enlistments in a single day (30,000) exceeded
the total for the whole of a normal year.

But the problems of 'manpower' (of which we were to hear so
much during the Second World War) are not limited to the finding of
recruits. Such men must be housed, fed, and clothed from the outset,
and in due course armed, equipped and trained as well. From this
point of view the flood had grown beyond control, and something

had to be done to abate it. So after five weeks the standard of physique was raised to a higher level, and this had the desired effect.

In due course the arrears of administration were overtaken, and the original appeal renewed. But the flood did not return: the first fine frenzy had evaporated. Men had grown tired of waiting and found another job, many of them in munition factories, and having become indispensable in their new occupations, could not be displaced. Here we note the first signs of the problem of the correct allocation of manpower between the fighting forces and the ancillary industrial services;[1] a problem destined to grow acute not only during the First World War but to an even greater degree in the longer and far more perilous conflict which was to follow it twenty-five years later, and which we shall have to examine presently.

However, there was no attempt at present to discover a scientific solution, and further recourse was had to rule of thumb and sentimental appeal. An army of speakers was mobilised, representing every class of the community, from professional 'spell-binders' to wounded officers whose very appearance was its own appeal. Some 20,000 harangues were delivered throughout the country. Rival Parliamentary candidates joined forces on the same platform. Private individuals and municipal corporations were inspired to raise whole units from a single neighbourhood, in which friends, or men of the same trade or walk of life could serve together. 'Pals' battalions of this type were recruited in such cities as Manchester (cotton operatives), Newcastle (coal-miners), and Glasgow (shipyard workers). There was a special battalion for public school boys, and another for 'Sportsmen'.

These, it should be noted, were known as Service battalions of the Regular Army. The mention of them calls for some explanation here, for their inception ran counter to the whole Haldane scheme, which was designed to build up a great voluntary reserve by automatic expansion of the Territorial force alone.

The explanation can be supplied in a single word—'Kitchener'. That famous soldier was now Secretary of State for War, having been called to the War Office by Mr. Asquith (in circumstances to be described later) upon the outbreak of hostilities.

The appointment, though universally acclaimed, was not entirely felicitous. Lord Kitchener had spent most of his professional life abroad, in Egypt, South Africa and India, and was singularly unfamiliar with conditions at home, even with the brilliantly conceived and eminently workable Haldane scheme. His inability to understand

[1] This point is dealt with more fully in Chap. XII, Sec. 3, p. 148.

and appreciate its merits was increased by the fact that upon the outbreak of war various highly placed officers of the War Office, who might have enlightened him, had abandoned their desks and gone overseas to command divisions.

So, having been accustomed through most of his life to organise and improvise upon his own initiative and responsibility, and cherishing as he did an ancient prejudice against 'Saturday Afternoon Soldiers', he decided upon a plan of his own. This was to raise a force of Service battalions, so called, to be added as Regular units to existing Line regiments. Somebody christened it 'Kitchener's Army', which of course it was not, but the sobriquet achieved instant popularity. The glamour of Kitchener's name and the idea of being classed as Regular soldiers proved an irresistible attraction. This was hard on the Territorial Army, who frequently found themselves at this time pushed somewhat into the background. Ultimately they were to prove themselves second to none in the field of action, but their training and equipment were undoubtedly retarded, as was that of Kitchener's Army itself, by this system of dual organisation and control, involving as it did a perpetual struggle between the War Office and the County Territorial Associations for the necessary priorities. Indeed, it has been maintained by men well qualified to speak, that if Kitchener had been content to use Haldane's system as it was meant to be used, and if the same assistance in the provision of Regular officers and non-commissioned officers had been given to the Territorial Army as was given to Kitchener's Army, the expansion of our military forces would have been far more expeditious than was the case. It is even affirmed that if this had been done we should, in April 1915, have had sufficient troops available to render the Dardanelles campaign a success instead of a glorious failure.

Lord Kitchener's appointment was open to criticism for two other reasons. In the first place it installed the Secretary of State for War in the House of Lords instead of in the Commons, which is the natural and proper link between the Army and the electorate, and in the second Kitchener had been accustomed all his life to handle comparatively small forces single handed, by the light of his own judgement. This had made him autocratic, aloof, uncommunicative, and disinclined to delegate authority. Moreover, he was a soldier, and constitutional usage required that the head of the War Office should be a civilian.

But his prestige was immense, and a coloured poster of him pointing a commanding finger and saying 'I want *you*!' drew hundreds and thousands to the Colours. Moreover, he was one of the few men to envisage a war lasting at least three years, and upon this more than correct calculation all recruits were enlisted for that period—or the duration.

~(2)~

By the middle of 1915 over 2,000,000 volunteers had enlisted either in Kitchener's or the Territorial Army; but the tide of patriotic enthusiasm was now definitely on the ebb, and a shortage of recruits ensued, which a foolish parrot-cry of 'Business as Usual!' did nothing to allay. Our most effective recruiting propaganda at this time came from the enemy: the sinking of the giant Cunarder *Lusitania*, with the loss of over 1,100 civilian lives, produced a temporary spurt; but it was clear that the voluntary system was being put to a severe test. So, during 1915 a series of organised efforts was made to revivify it. In the end these all failed, but their very failure, disheartening though it was at the time, was teaching us an unconscious lesson, destined to be of the utmost value when we found ourselves called upon to face an even more desperate emergency a generation later.

The following were the steps taken. In June 1915 the maximum standard of age was raised from thirty-eight to forty years and the minimum standard of height was lowered to 5 feet 2 inches. A month later a National Registration Act was passed in which at last a systematic attempt was made to 'number the people' and size up our resources in man- and womanpower. All men between the ages of fifteen and sixty-five received a registration card similar to that in use today, and the cards of the men between eighteen and forty were handed over to the recruiting authorities, for canvassing purposes. But still recruiting lagged, for vast numbers of able-bodied men were segregated in 'reserved occupations' and were 'starred' as such on their cards.

So, in October 1915, a highly popular and universally trusted public servant, in the person of Lord Derby, was called in as Director-General of Recruiting. He immediately instituted an ingenious device, ultimately celebrated as the Derby scheme, under which the men in the eighteen to forty class were divided into groups by years, twenty-three groups in all, and each group was sub-divided into two, married and single, giving forty-six groups altogether. Every man in each group was invited to 'attest' forthwith—that is, place himself at the disposal of the Government should they consider it desirable to call him up—with this proviso, that the younger men should be called up first and in rotation, according to age, and that the single men should be called up before the married men.

The scheme was well received, and produced 2,250,000 attestations in two months. But many of those who attested were already in reserved occupations, and it was further discovered that a large number—far too large a number—of single men had neither attested nor enlisted. So a comprehensive Military Service Bill was brought in, rendering all single men within the prescribed ages liable at once for military duty. This was not put into immediate effect, but its mere imminence was sufficient to bring in a large crop of previous defaulters.

But plainly the voluntary system had served its turn. In June 1916 the Act was extended to married men as well, and from that time forward all men of military age were liable to military service.

As a mitigation, local tribunals were set up composed of men to whom most of the applicants were personally known, to consider appeals for exemption or postponement upon grounds either of personal hardship or conscience. Of the claimants for exemption it is noteworthy that less than two per cent were conscientious objectors.

Finally, upon November 1st, 1917, the whole administration of recruiting was taken from the hands of the authorities previously concerned and placed under a new Ministry of National Service.

Still, voluntary enlistment had produced over 5,000,000 recruits.

⤚(3)⤙

Meanwhile, it may be asked, what had become of the creator of the British Expeditionary Force and the Territorial Army?

It is a strange story, and a sad reflection upon human gullibility and readiness to clamour for scapegoats in times of stress.

In 1912 Mr. Haldane, considering that his work at the War Office was done, consented to go to the House of Lords and take his long-deferred seat upon the Woolsack. And then the tragedy occurred. Public opinion was strained and unsettled at this time, for the Agadir crisis was newly over and suspicion of German intentions was deepening. Rumours were flying about—rumours of hidden hands and subversive influences. Spy fever was rampant. Then somebody remembered that the late Secretary of State for War was a lifelong admirer of Germany. Why had such a man been left for so long in the War Office, and what had he done while he was there? All that his critics could remember was that he had cut down the size of the Army—reduced the artillery and abolished whole battalions of infantry. He had also visited Berlin as the guest of the Kaiser.[1] He could speak German fluently, too.

This last was natural enough, for the Minister had been educated at the University of Göttingen when a youth, and had been an ardent student of German philosophy ever since. Sir Henry Campbell-Bannerman used facetiously to address him as 'Schopenhauer'. He was also much interested in the German University system, especially the manner in which it had contrived to graft modern scientific and technical education on to the classic culture of previous generations. But this was no sort of proof that he was an admirer of Kaiserdom or the Prussian jack-boot.

However, public opinion was on edge, and ripe for a witch-hunt. So the most irresponsible and mischievous section of the press fastened upon Robert Burton Haldane, statesman and patriot, and the public followed suit. Mr. Asquith, the Prime Minister, and Mr. Balfour, the Leader of the Opposition, supported their friend loyally. So did Mr. Churchill, from the Admiralty: so did the soldiers, who had cause to realise the greatness of his achievements on behalf of the Army. His King bestowed upon him the Order of Merit. But the mud stuck, and when at the outbreak of war the Prime Minister invited Lord Haldane, as he had now become, to return to the helm at the War Office, such an outcry was raised that Haldane himself, who with his usual perception had realised that what the War Office needed above all at that moment was a figure-head rather than a steersman, urged that Lord Kitchener should be appointed to the post. As we know, his advice was followed.

But that was not all. Some of his colleagues, who should have known better, became infected with the virus. In 1915, when it was proposed to form a Coalition Government, certain of these declined to serve in it if Lord Haldane were included. He at once withdrew, retiring practically into private life, and solaced himself with his philosophic studies and the society of his friends. Upon his rare appearances in public he was greeted with disapproving howls.

In due course the First World War was won, and the nation abandoned itself, deservedly, to the celebration of victory. But when Earl Haig led his troops in triumphant procession through the streets of London, no official invitation to be present on the occasion was

[1] In point of fact he had been sent to Berlin by Mr. Asquith to conduct some extremely delicate and confidential negotiations regarding a mutual reduction of naval armaments. Naturally this had to be camouflaged as a private visit on personal matters.

issued to the man who had been the earliest architect of the victory in question. He watched the procession pass up Birdcage Walk, on its way to the Palace, from a window in his own solitary bachelor establishment in Queen Anne's Gate.

That same day, however, after the march was over and the troops had been dismissed, Lord Haig walked across to Queen Anne's Gate to pay a call. He brought with him a set of his War Dispatches, bound in two volumes and inscribed: '*To Viscount Haldane of Cloan, the greatest War Minister England has ever had*'.

The wheel has turned full circle since then, and a great man now enjoys his rightful place in the memory of his countrymen. But one likes to think that it was Lord Haig's knightly gesture which set it in motion.

~✠(4)✠~

We now return to the conditions prevailing at the outbreak of the First World War, and the difficulties incident to the creation of a huge and sudden addition to the fighting forces of the country.

As already noted, it is one thing to summon spirits from the vasty deep and another to feed, clothe and house these visitants after they have materialised. Here authority had its hands full. Food, fortunately, was abundant. The lessons of the South African War had not been thrown away, and for some two years previously this situation had been anticipated and provided for; so as soon as the necessary arrangements could be made for transportation and distribution, generous rations on a uniform scale were immediately forthcoming from central depots operated by the Army Service Corps. Indeed, these proved to be too generous, for every man was issued with a pound of meat a day. This, in the course of time, had to be reduced to three-quarters.

The outstanding difficulty at first was to find a sufficiency of cooks, about 50,000 of whom were required for every million men enlisted. The regimental cook was by tradition a member of what may be described as the 'depressed classes', the office being bestowed, as a rule, upon men who were not considered much use at anything else. The result was dirt, waste and indigestion. Of late, however, a resolute effort had been made to better this state of affairs, and the setting up of the Army School of Cookery at Aldershot had gone far to establish an improved and constant standard. But the school had been closed down with the departure of the B.E.F. overseas, and

until this indispensable institution could be resuscitated and reproduced all over the country, the troops had to suffer the well-inten-
tioned but empirical efforts of a cohort of amateurs proceeding
along the tortuous path of trial and error.

Next came the far more difficult problem of housing. Throughout
the British Isles there existed only enough barrack accommodation
for 175,000 men, and in the very first month of the war more than
that number of men enlisted, without counting the Reservists, who
poured in at the rate of 40,000 a week, and the Territorials, who had
reached their full establishment within four days. Considerable
contingents of Canadian troops, too, began to arrive almost immediately.

By clearing married quarters and other subsidiary buildings, and
introducing a ruthless system of 'doubling up' (from which officers'
messes and bedrooms were not exempt), barrack accommodation
was increased to take another 100,000 men. Thousands more were
put under canvas—fortunately the late summer and early autumn of
1914 were phenomenally warm and sunny—while countless others
'dossed down' in schools or public buildings or were billeted in
private houses.

This last expedient gave rise to endless inequalities. Besides involving special assessments in the matter of rents and damages, it
scattered the men far and wide over the countryside, making it
difficult to collect them for daily drill and training. Billeting 'with
subsistence' presented a special problem, for here standards of
hospitality varied considerably, and comparisons, especially where
food is concerned, are proverbially odious.

But, pending the erection of comfortably warm and electrically
lighted hutments, which presently sprang up all over the country, all these makeshifts were endured by the troops with
surprising cheerfulness and philosophy. The exhilaration of novelty
had not yet worn off, and the spirit of adventure was still strong
within them.

That spirit was not entirely dashed by an equal, if not greater trial,
the shortage of army clothing. No soldier can be expected to feel like
a soldier unless he looks like one, or for that matter to march without
boots, and in these respects the game of cheerful make-believe had
sometimes to be stretched to the limit. It must be confessed that in
some of the less-favoured divisions—those composed of men outside
the first hundred thousand or so who had been the earliest to answer
Lord Kitchener's call—it would be a gross contradiction of terms to
describe the apparel worn as 'uniform', for never was there a more

variegated display of sartorial odds and ends. Some men wore their civilian clothing, others were issued with an old scarlet tunic dyed blue and bereft of its buttons. It was no uncommon experience to meet a soldier attired in the tunic aforesaid, flapping open, a pair of corduroy trousers, and a debilitated bowler hat.

Here is a contemporary reminiscence. It deals with the sumptuary situation at that time.

We are more or less in possession of our proper equipment now. That is to say, our wearing apparel and the appurtenances thereof are no longer held in position with string. The men have belts, pouches, and slings in which to carry their greatcoats. The greatcoats were the last to materialise. Since their arrival we have lost in decorative effect what we have gained in martial appearance. For a month or two each man wore over his uniform during wet weather—in other words, all day—a garment which the Army Ordnance Department described as: 'Greatcoat, Civilian, One'. An Old Testament writer would have termed it 'a coat of many colours'. A tailor would have said that it was a 'superb vicuna raglan sack'. You and I would have called it, quite simply, a reach-me-down. Anyhow, the combined effect was unique. As we plodded patiently along the road in our tarnished finery, with our eye-arresting checks and imitation velvet collars, caked with mud and wrinkled with rain, we looked like nothing so much on earth as a gang of welshers returning from an unsuccessful day at a suburban race-meeting.[1]

It was certainly a hard schooling for all concerned during the pitiless winter of 1914–15, especially since fully ninety per cent of the men had enlisted under the firm conviction that they would be provided forthwith with uniform, rifle and ammunition and dispatched overseas to shoot Germans. Eight months of foot-slogging, floor-scrubbing, trench-digging and make-believe warfare with dummy weapons had not entered into their calculations.

But the winter of their discontent ended at last; the spring came, and lo! they found themselves trained soldiers, hard as nails, fully equipped, and thrilled by the promise of immediate active service.

~⅏(5)⅏~

We turn now further afield, overseas in fact, to study the lessons in army organisation and administration learned by the British Expeditionary Force and those who followed them along the road of practical experience.

[1] *The First Hundred Thousand* (Ian Hay).

The whole question of army training and equipment in general will be discussed in future chapters, but it may be well at this point to inquire how far the planning and prevision of the general staff for this particular campaign satisfied hope and expectation.

And here let us remember that from the point of view of grand strategy it is never possible to plan ahead with an absolute degree of certainty. So swift is the march of modern military science that the most carefully formulated schemes (especially defence schemes, which must depend for their success very largely upon accurate divination of the enemy's intentions) may be rendered totally inapplicable, as we shall immediately discover, by some unforeseen development in tactics or equipment. In this eventuality the primary safeguard against disaster is an army well disciplined and intelligently grounded in the lessons of the past, especially the immediate past. It is this insistence, incidentally, by wise commanders, upon the inculcation in the soldier of the indispensable elements of his trade that so frequently attracts the unfavourable attention of amateur strategists, who are fond of complaining that an army is being compelled to train, 'not for the next war but for the last one'.

By all essential standards the preparedness of the B.E.F. in 1914 was beyond, or almost beyond, criticism. The South African War had taught the troops the value of mobility, marksmanship and the intelligent use of cover. Supply, transport and medical services had been modernised. Musketry in particular had improved out of all knowledge: so devastating was our fire along the line of the Mons Canal in August 1914 that the Germans concluded that we were quite unexpectedly strong in machine-guns.

Here they were wrong, and so had we been, for we had entirely failed to foresee the destructive effect upon closely massed troops of this particular weapon. Our establishment at that time consisted of two semi-obsolete Maxims per infantry battalion (though these were being replaced by the greatly superior Light Vickers), while the Germans, who had not overlooked the possibilities of intensified small-arms fire, had about 50,000 such instruments of destruction.

This lapse in our prescience was doubly unfortunate, because for the next two years at least machine-guns, aided by quick-firing artillery, dictated the whole conduct of the war on the Western Front. In other words, they speedily drove everyone underground, and the Western Front resolved itself into a trench-line extending from the North Sea to the Alps, with the artillery monotonously shelling the back areas, while a symmetrical interlacement of machine-gun bullets rendered no-man's-land a desert. Strategic warfare had come to a standstill, for you cannot outflank an opponent who has no flank, and who, if you do achieve a break-through at any point, merely retires to an even stronger position slightly to the rear.

This unforeseen turn of events took both sides by surprise: ourselves because we were at the outset but scantily provided with machine-guns, and the enemy because an elaborate strategic design for the overrunning of Western Europe by orthodox mass invasion had been brought to a standstill by a concentration of fire-power even more deadly than he had expected.

Naturally, an immediate effort was made to remedy our defences in this respect. Infantry battalions were provided with four Vickers guns in place of the two Maxims, and a thorough and methodical course of machine-gun training was instituted for the gunners themselves. Up till 1916 no separate official manual of such training had existed. But experience soon taught its own lessons, and improvements in tactical handling followed almost automatically. Within a year's time Battalion Machine-gun Sections were in course of conversion into a single Brigade Machine-gun Company, of sixteen guns, under the direct control of the Brigadier; and a little later all were merged into a new corporate body known as the Machine-gun Corps. Their place as battalion weapons was taken by the Light Lewis gun, firing, like the Vickers, at the rate of 500 rounds per minute, and capable of being aimed either from a position of rest or the shoulder. The Lewis was thus our first effective automatic rifle.

Quick-firing field artillery was increased in proportion, and in some of the intensive bombardments which presently became the preliminary feature of a mass attack, the guns stood parked sometimes almost wheel to wheel.

But still the trench-barrier stood firm. The enemy remained for the most part on the defensive, well content to hold the valuable French and Belgian territory which he had already overrun. His defences were sited mostly in commanding positions, notably on the Chemin des Dames (in the French sector), and along Vimy Ridge (which changed hands more than once), on the Somme, and in the dread Salient of Ypres. The only way to carry these defences was by frontal assault, covered by a carefully timed 'creeping' artillery barrage, and various elaborately planned attempts were made to do so. But though by desperate valour and at enormous cost a small gain of ground was made here and there, the Western Front stood unpierced until 1918; for the attacking troops were met not only by aimed artillery fire and never-ceasing diagonal streams of machine-gun bullets, but by a continuous and almost impenetrable hedge of barbed wire.

Except for an occasional gap blown by concentrated artillery fire, barbed wire remained practically indestructible until, as always eventually happens, a weapon had been evolved capable of dealing with the situation—in other words, the tank, destined in future years to dominate all military operations on land.

Tanks were a British invention, and a small number of them, of a somewhat primitive type, were first sent into action on September 15th, 1916, during a critical phase of the battle of the Somme. They achieved a dramatic surprise effect but little else, and a precious and carefully guarded secret was sprung all too soon. Experience was to show that the true value of the tank lies in its employment in very large numbers handled upon a concerted tactical plan, as naval vessels are manœuvred in action at sea. For such an operation unlimited open ground is required, as was exemplified thirty years later in the spectacular tank battles in the African desert.

But in the First World War the tanks undoubtedly served an immediate if minor end: they broke through the barbed wire and enabled an attack to penetrate upon a wider front than ever before.

While upon the subject of static warfare it may be interesting to recall the different methods of trench defence employed by the British, French and Germans respectively. It was said, and with some truth, that for this purpose the British employed men, the French artillery, and the Germans machine-guns.

The British, whose speciality is to stand one's ground at any cost, preferred to line the parapet and maintain continuous rapid rifle-fire, with deadly effect, but at the cost of innumerable casualties from the enemy's artillery barrage. The Germans were accustomed during a bombardment to withdraw most of their front line troops and leave the defence of the whole position to their well-dug-in machine-gunners, each firing along a given line in a pre-arranged and automatic pattern, and so leaving no gap through which our advancing infantry could hope to pass unscathed. The French, whose motto in most things is *reculer pour mieux sauter*, adopted a characteristically elastic system by which, during bombardment, the trenches were abandoned altogether and the men withdrawn to cover and rest—it was even said that they seized this opportunity to cook their dinners—and the subsequent infantry attack dealt with, *en rafale*, by that ramshackle but devastating weapon the Soixante Quinze. After this such enemy elements as had succeeded in occupying the front line system were ejected by a spirited counter-attack.

~⚡(6)⚡~

The tank was the first military novelty of that era. The next, the aeroplane, was no particular novelty in itself, for it had been in established use for some years; but its employment as an adjunct to military operations was still very much in the tentative stage.

Its most obvious function was to supersede the cavalry in the gathering of information as to the enemy's movements and dispositions—to discover, in Wellington's words, 'what was going on on the other side of the hill'. Here it performed invaluable service. It could locate hostile formations and observe transport movements. It could report which trenches were occupied and which empty. It could detect dug-in artillery batteries, especially in winter, when the wheel tracks of ammunition limbers leading to a particular spot and stopping short there could be traced in the snow. It could even take photographs.

All this naturally led to an immediate and enforced improvement in methods of concealment, such as painting a building or a vehicle in a blend of violently contrasting colours, or by the use of overhead netting interwoven with grass or leaves. Thus a new expression, 'camouflage', made its appearance in the lexicon of warfare.

The second service that the aeroplane could perform was that of 'spotting' for artillery. This at first was of no great assistance, for the machines of this period were limited in range and fragile in design. Moreover, until operational wireless came into being intercommunication between ground and air was confined to a few visual signals. In 1915, for example, a German plane passing over a well-manned British trench would drop a long coloured linen streamer which, as it fluttered down, presented the German gunners, far in the rear, with a rough and ready target and aiming mark. Captive observation balloons, too, were extensively employed by both sides: indeed, the spectacle of a double row of these monsters, suspended high in the sky and facing one another all down the endless trench-line, indicated and defined the exact position of the Western Front. Periodically one of these would be shot down in flames, the observer making his escape as best he could by parachute.

Later, when aeroplanes began to be equipped with machine-guns, automatically geared to the propeller and firing between the blades, a good deal of low flying and 'ground-strafing' came into operation. During Allenby's final triumphant advance in Palestine in 1917 the R.A.F. co-operated closely with the ground troops and inflicted heavy losses upon the retreating Turkish Army.

There were air combats, too. Here there were considerable fluctuations of fortune, dependent upon the ability of the combatants to introduce an improved type of machine and so gain a temporary ascendancy. In consequence the sky was frequently in the exclusive possession of one side or the other, and advantage was taken of this circumstance to institute bombing raids. These were at that time more of a nuisance than a danger, for this particular form of aggression was still in the experimental stage.

But compared with the tank, the aeroplane during the First World War had but little effect upon the conduct or outcome of the campaign, which ultimately resolved itself into an affair of massed infantry attacks, under a creeping barrage, against the concentrated resistance of quick-firing artillery and innumerable machine-guns. In the main the defence had the best of it, as the grim record of Verdun and Passchendaele attests.

Lastly, so far as the Western Front was concerned, the First World War and the new tactics which it evolved marked the end, after centuries, of the employment of cavalry as shock troops, or indeed in any other capacity. There were no flanks to encircle, and where a frontal gap was created the ground was too cut up by trenches and shell-craters to permit of their exploitation. Except for a few weeks of open fighting in the autumn of 1914, and during the final victorious advance of the Allied forces (which began on August 8th, 1918, and never ended until the Armistice), with the trench-systems left behind and open country once more available, the cavalryman's occupation was gone—practically for ever.

But cavalry were destined to come to their own again, though in a most unorthodox but, as it happened, far more effective guise.

CHAPTER VI

THE YEARS BETWEEN

~*(1)*~

THE Great War, so called, was over, and it was widely assumed that there would never be another. The idea was unthinkable: this had been a war to end war, and President Wilson's League of Nations would take care of the future. The millennium was just round the corner.

Unfortunately this proved too optimistic an estimate. In the first place, hostilities had not by any means been concluded. True, the war was declared officially at an end on August 31st, 1921, but this merely amounted to crying peace where there was no peace.

That much-enduring public servant the British soldier still had plenty of work on his hands. The aftermath of the Bolshevik Revolution in 1917 necessitated the retention of British troops in north Russia from the summer of 1918 to the autumn of 1919. In 1919 there was serious trouble in Afghanistan, and in 1920 a rebellion in Mesopotamia. There were almost continuous warlike operations in Waziristan on the North West Frontier until 1924. British troops had to be kept in Turkey till 1923, and the Army of Occupation in Germany was not completely withdrawn until December 1929.

At home there was serious and prolonged trouble in Southern Ireland, accompanied by the usual post-war economic and industrial upheavals in Britain itself—trades disputes and stoppages, culminating in the General Strike of 1926, which involved a declaration of emergency and the employment of the Army in considerable numbers for the protection of property and the distribution of food.

All this, however, though it imposed further burdens upon the men responsible for the safety of the Country and Empire, caused them no particular surprise. They were students of military history, and were only too well aware that though the British are the most unmilitary minded of nations, they have seldom been capable, with the best intentions, of avoiding military commitments and entanglements for very long.

Beginning with the Cromwellian era, our periods of *relief* from wars of major importance alone have been roughly as follows:

During the reigns of Charles II and James II, about. . .	10 years
From the Peace of Ryswick to the War of the Spanish Succession	5 years
From the Peace of Utrecht to the War of the Austrian Succession	28 years
From the Peace of Aix-la-Chapelle to the Seven Years' War .	8 years
From the Treaty of Paris to the American Revolution . .	12 years
From the Congress of Vienna to the Crimean War. . .	44 years
From the end of the Mutiny to the Great Boer War . .	40 years
From the Peace of Vereeniging to the Great War (the First World War)	12 years

All these, in 1919, added up to a total of some 157 years of comparative peace. Against that must be set a total period of 118 years occupied by wars which called for the employment of our whole available military strength, and the loss of at least one of which would have marked our extinction as a free people. Moreover, even throughout the so-called intervals of tranquillity we had been engaged in an almost continuous series of 'small' wars all over the globe—some of them not so very small. In short, the longest period for which the British Temple of Janus has remained closed, for nearly three centuries, has been about five years.

So the General Staff and Army Council, leaving the celebration of the latest millennium to those better qualified to enjoy it, set to work to count the cost and study the lessons of the recent world-wide struggle.

And certainly the cost, both in money and human life, had been appalling. In little more than four years we had expended some £8,000,000,000, and income tax in 1919 had reached the unprecedented figure of six shillings. Even now the end was not in sight. In 1919 the Army was still costing the taxpayer £412,000,000. After two years this was reduced to £86,000,000, still about three times the normal figure. By 1925 the sum had been halved, but in 1934, more than fifteen years after the Armistice, the Army Estimates still stood at £39,000,000. Immediately before the war they had been £28,000,000.

Still, staggering though these figures were, they counted for nothing as compared with the toll of human life. To take only the casualties of three of the countries engaged, our Empire had lost 1,000,000 men killed or missing: of these the vast majority came from the United

Kingdom. The Germans had lost 2,000,000 and the French 1,300,000. The massed attacks on the Western Front had resulted in casualties out of all proportion to any ground gained. British dead in the three-weeks' battle of Loos numbered 60,000; during the Somme struggle, which began on July 1st, 1916 and went on until November, 196,000; at Third Ypres, usually known as Passchendaele, in the autumn of 1917, when (with the French Army temporarily crippled by disaster and mutiny) it became necessary for the British to maintain continuous diversive action against the enemy over ground reduced by intensive shelling to a morass into which men sank over their heads, 119,000; and during the last desperate attempt by the enemy to break through in March 1918, 173,000.

Plainly this was sheer murder, though it was not due to callousness or lack of thoughtful planning on the part of our High Command. It was imposed by the conditions of siege warfare which from 1915 to early 1918 had held the Western Front in their grip; for as often happens in these circumstances, the defence had so completely mastered the attack that no other tactics than these could have effected a break-through. In the end the Western Front was only liquidated by a war of attrition. Whether or no it would have been wiser and more economical to create a diversion in another theatre and so divide the enemy's forces is a moot question; but here political considerations intervened. France insisted upon a 'strong' Western Front; so, after the heroic failure of Gallipoli and the half-hearted stalemate of Salonika, no further 'side-shows' were attempted, in Europe at any rate.

But apart from these strategic considerations, it had become quite obvious that in future no country could ever afford such a monstrous and intolerable drain upon its manpower as that which had bled Europe white during those four and a half grim years.

~*(2)*~

Defence, then, having for the time being got the better of attack, two self-evident conclusions followed. First, better protection must be given to the attacker: to launch masses of half-trained and ill-controlled infantry against concentrated artillery and machine-gun fire was to invite promiscuous slaughter. Secondly, some more effective tactical methods of offence must be discovered and put into effect.

For actual protection from small-arms fire some form of body-armour seemed to be indicated; some modern improvement upon that employed in medieval times against flights of arrows and cross-bow bolts, when both man and horse went into action encased in mail or steel armour; or, receding further into history, when a body of Roman legionaries with their shields interlocked horizontally over their heads would advance successfully to the assault in the formation of a *testudo*, or 'tortoise', under a rain of missiles and liquid fire. Indeed, such a device was already available in the tank, which was practically impervious to machine-gun or rifle bullets. But a tank is (or was) a slow and cumbrous vehicle, and could not carry passengers as such. Something much swifter, more capacious, and more dirigible must be provided, and in sufficient numbers to convey a whole infantry battalion into action at high speed, breaking up or out-flanking enemy formations and giving him no time for digging-in or the construction of static defences.

So the armoured car, the platoon truck, and the Bren-gun carrier were born of the inventiveness imposed by necessity, and with their advent the days of serried, slow-moving pedestrian attacks were gone for ever. Mechanisation had arrived. In future armies would fight upon wheels—or at any rate upon fast-moving tractors—reasonably protected from machine-gun fire, and by their mobility enormously increasing the difficulties of hostile artillery direction.

More important still, tractor-fitted vehicles could travel almost anywhere, and were thus independent of roads. In anything like open country they could be manœuvred at will, and employ tactics hitherto confined to the sea.

In addition to the actual bodily protection afforded by armoured vehicles, mechanisation suggested a new, more effective, and far less expensive method of attack—a policy, that is, of dispersion, under which the attacking force could be divided up into a number of highly trained, self-operating units, enjoying a freedom of action denied to more cumbrous formations, and destined in the fullness of time to operate in direct radio communication not merely with one another but with a controlling authority far in rear.

Mention of roads reminds us of another and most important development of this period. It had long been desired, with a view to exploiting the proved value of increased fire-power, to equip as large a proportion of the infantry as possible with an automatic rifle of some kind; but so long as the ammunition supply remained dependent upon horse-drawn, road-bound vehicles, such a project had remained impracticable. A Vickers Brigade Machine-gun Company required for the conveyance of its guns, tripods and belt-boxes some sixteen limbered wagons, each drawn by two or four mules; and since all such traffic was confined to the roads, first-line transport was already too congested to permit of further additions. But with the arrival of mechanisation, armoured carriers could now proceed across country right up into the line, and the ammunition supply be continuously maintained.

Once the principle of universal mechanisation had been established, other developments followed almost automatically. Intercommunication by wireless was approaching perfection, as we shall have cause to discover when we come to examine the conduct of the North African campaigns from 1941 onwards.

On the other hand a new and growing menace had to be faced in the shape of enemy air attack. In former days the chief risks incurred by moving transport or marching troops was at cross-roads or other vulnerable points on the line of route, 'registered' by the enemy artillery and exposed to intermittent shelling. But with the advent of the low-flying bomber this risk became continuous. It was mitigated as far as possible by the employment, first of mobile anti-aircraft weapons, and secondly by the adoption of a policy of systematic dispersal.

Thus, in the post-war schemes of army training it was usual to assume upon route marches that the column was passing through hostile country. Whenever a halt was made each platoon truck was parked, if possible, under cover from the air, while the men themselves fell out among the trees at the side of the road. Or a platoon might at any moment be ordered to extend into open order and advance against an imaginary enemy equipped with low-flying aeroplanes and tanks. Here the new Bren[1] light machine-gun proved particularly useful. It carried an attachment which readily converted it into an anti-aircraft weapon, and was kept constantly in make-believe operation. The new anti-tank rifle too, a weapon capable of piercing more than half an inch of steel, was systematically mounted and discharged.

A motorised column of route was perpetually exercised, for additional security reasons, in rapid alterations in traffic speed and distribution. Roads were all marked off on the map in lettered sectors, and at any moment a dispatch-rider might arrive from the head of the column with some such order as: *For Sector B change to density 15 VTM, in groups of 15 at 20 MPH.* This meant, 'Upon reaching the stretch of road ahead of you marked B, you will spread out your transport to a density of fifteen vehicles to the mile, travelling twenty miles in the hour'. (Twenty miles in the hour, incidentally,

[1] So called from Brno in Czechoslovakia, where it was originally manufactured.

is something very different from a speed of twenty miles per hour as recorded on a speedometer.)

All of which is much more instructive (and exacting) than marching at ease in fours, and means that the soldier of today must keep his wits about him even in affairs of ordinary routine, understand how to read a map, and be prepared to perform some quite complicated manœuvre, without delay or confusion, at a given word.

One of the most beneficial results of the new system of infantry dispersal into small self-contained groups was that it called for considerably fewer men than previously; for it was no longer intended to win battles by mere weight of numbers. (This, of course, is no new idea: it goes back to the days of Gideon and the Book of Judges.) By 1935 a British infantry battalion at full strength consisted not as formerly of a thousand men or so, but of twenty-two officers and 646 other ranks. The number of platoons in a company—a rifle company—had been reduced from four to three, making twelve in all, and each platoon contained three sections.

The headquarters company consisted very largely of specialists. It comprised six platoons. In one the battalion signallers were trained; another was employed in the anti-aircraft and anti-tank defence already mentioned; a third was entrusted with the care and handling of a 3-inch mortar, designed for close support in action and capable of discharging some twenty projectiles per minute. To another were allotted the ten mechanised carriers containing the Bren machine-guns and their ammunition. Then came a pioneer platoon, responsible for the construction or demolition of road obstacles. Last came the administration platoon, which comprised the clerical staff, the transport personnel and the regimental police.

All these dispositions were, of course, largely provisional and experimental, and were destined in the days ahead to undergo considerable development or modification. But they certainly mark a far cry from the days of a battalion composed of 1,000 riflemen and two Maxim guns, with horse-drawn transport. The company commander's charger now was frequently a baby Austin.

~∗(3)∗~

The reader will appreciate that such a complete revolution in tactics, training and equipment as that just described was bound to take time, especially in a country so suspicious of innovation as Great Britain.

We have already examined the difficulties encountered by those two outstanding Army reformers, Cardwell and Haldane. Each had his own: Cardwell's principal battle was over the abolition of Purchase; Haldane was assailed as the man who weakened the Army by liquidating famous battle units, and converted the historic militia into something else.

But the men who were called upon to modernise our Imperial defence scheme—and especially to remodel the Army—in the twenties of this century, were faced with a different and more formidable obstacle: the plain fact that the British electorate as a whole had ceased *pro tem* to think in terms of national security and prestige, and were strongly disinclined to further military effort. The country was not exactly pacifist, but it was ripe for the attentions of the peace-at-any-price propagandist.

This was understandable, for our population had not only been wearied and weakened by a struggle such as the world had never known, but had for the first time in their long history been brought into personal contact with the actual, stark realities of war. German bombers had violated the age-long security and sanctity of their households, while the final establishment of universal military service had imposed upon thousands of those same households, which had hitherto regarded the progress of a war as something to be followed in the morning papers, a new and unfamiliar obligation of personal participation. No wonder that these took a more than passing interest in the possibilities of 'the next war'. If that came the burden would no longer be confined to the willing horse: the Army would be the people, and the people the Army.

On one point public opinion was entirely unanimous: a second Great War would be a disaster of the first magnitude, and might ultimately lead to the disintegration of civilised life in the world. Therefore war as an instrument of policy must be for ever banished from the counsels of men. How? To this question there was only one answer—by mutual and permanent international agreement.

Man proposes. In 1933 Hitler took office in Germany, and from that moment harnessed his whole nation to the intensive mass-production of the newest engines of war. That was the writing on the wall. Hopes of a reasonable, friendly understanding vanished into thin air, and the peace-loving nations, our own included, had to think again.

Opinion in Britain presently resolved itself into two camps: those who held, with Tacitus, that to avoid war you should show yourself ready for it, and those who with equal sincerity believed that to prepare for war is to render it inevitable. The first party (which included those responsible for the safety of the country) were at a disadvantage in this respect, that the measures which they favoured would be enormously expensive, and to impose these upon an impoverished country (suffering from a severe attack of economy-fever) might provoke a dangerous political crisis at a most unseasonable moment. So they hesitated and held back, while the opponents of preparedness did not cease to denounce all militarists and warmongers. The result was a policy of drift, for which both sides were in a measure responsible, and for which ultimately we paid a heavy price.

The effect, so far as the Army was concerned, was a partial paralysis of the plan of the War Office for the increase, re-equipment and thorough training of the troops in the methods of the new mechanised warfare in which Hitler, with all Nazidom behind him, was making such giant strides.

Speed was the crucial need, for mechanisation is a lengthy business, especially when it involves mass-production. Weapons of war are no longer produced by the hand-and-brain work of the highly skilled individual craftsman. His place has been taken by a vast array of power-operated machine-tools of the utmost precision. Merely to prepare the tools required to produce a single large and complicated piece of war equipment may consume eighteen months or two years. (A modern tank is composed of 7,000 different parts.) Much time and labour, too, must be spent in designing, modelling, and the comparison of specifications; for once the final pattern has been selected it can never be altered. Moreover, factories must be built and the essential plant laid down.

Thus, until all the machinery is assembled, and mass-production put into full and effective operation, there must be a time-lag during which nothing can be produced at all, and which may make all the difference between victory and defeat. If at the outbreak of a war the aggressor country has been mass-producing its equipment for two years and the defender country is only just getting to work, that means that for two years at least the aggressor can do with the defender what he will. And that is what happened in September 1939:

> '. . . all along of mess,
> All along of doing things rather more or less.'

~⁕(4)⁕~

Meanwhile, what could be done to mechanise and modernise the Army was done. Not that there was much material to work on, or equipment to work with. As already noted, promiscuous economy was the order of the day.

The Navy, essential for the protection of our Imperial lines of communication and great network of trade-routes, had been dangerously weakened by the reduction in naval armaments mutually agreed upon at the Washington Conference in 1922. The growth of our young Air Force was being stunted by the fact that no agreement had yet been reached as to its future status and usefulness. In the Army, both Regular and Territorial, recruiting had fallen into a steady decline; and since the overseas battalion of each regiment had to be kept up to strength, the home battalions were in most cases about fifty per cent short of their proper complement of men.

The position with regard to equipment was even more lamentable. No serious attempt at mass-production was made until 1937, and then only half-heartedly. Despite the lessons of the early part of the First World War, no Ministry of Supply had been set up,[1] which meant that there was no ordered system of priorities, and that our three defence services were competing against one another for the same goods in a scantily stocked market—a competition in which the Army, the Cinderella of the services in question, usually came off third best.

Equal, even greater, unreadiness prevailed among our principal Allies the French, whose political disunity was heightened by an epidemic of trades disputes and lightning strikes, culminating in the imposition of a forty-hour week at a time when the entire industrial population of Germany were working for sixty. Indeed, strikes in the armament trades were in full swing until within eight days of the issue of mobilisation orders.

The consequences were almost automatic. The Allies had to stand by, helpless and ashamed, while the Italians invaded and annexed Abyssinia, and Mussolini was enabled without rebuke to claim for the Mediterranean, the British highway to the East, the title of *mare nostrum*.

Finally came the humiliating experience of Munich. Into the political issues involved there is no need to enter deeply here, except in so far as they affected the position and prospects of the Army.

[1] This was not done until April 1939.

Much has been said and written regarding Mr. Neville Chamberlain's handling of that situation, most of it unjust and a great deal of it unjustifiable; but whatever Mr. Chamberlain's conduct of the affair, his motives were beyond reproach, for he was a completely honest man and a sincere patriot. He was absolutely convinced of two things. The first was that when Hitler declared that his territorial ambitions were limited to the union of all Germanic communities within a single German State, he was speaking the truth: the second was that the result of another world war, whichever side won it, would be to shatter civilisation and leave Europe in ruins. In the first of these beliefs Mr. Chamberlain was utterly wrong, as the event proved; in the second, who can today deny that he was as utterly right?

Having in due course realised his error, and the full implications of the menace to European freedom now revealed, he had two courses open to him. The first was to declare immediate war. But he knew better than most, better certainly than any of his critics, how desperately unprepared we were for such an Armageddon. True, Hitler was not ready either, or not quite ready; but there is all the difference in the world between being not quite ready and not ready at all—about four years' difference in this case. So, determined as he was to avert the calamity of such a war, avert it at any cost, the Prime Minister chose the only other alternative—abject surrender to an outrageous demand, and with it the inevitable concomitants of loss of face, undermining of British prestige throughout the world, and the Pecksniffian head-shakings of nations more securely placed.

But at least he secured a year's respite, and so gave an apathetic and divided people an opportunity to come to themselves and make up, to some small extent at least, for lost time.

Shame and indignation over Munich had at least one material result, in the shape of an immediate public demand for an all-round increase in the Armed Forces of the Crown. It was still believed that war could be averted, or at least further postponed, and the country had come round to the sensible conclusion that this postponement was much more likely to be rendered permanent if, next time we spoke with our enemy in the gate, we did so in full panoply of war. In any case—here opinion was unanimous—there must never be another Munich. So mass-production of equipment was put in hand at last, and the engines of war began to roll, though all too slowly, off the production line.

So far as the human factor was concerned, it was quite obvious that both Regular and Territorial Army must be brought up to strength at once. There was, as yet, no mention of compulsory service, so an intensive recruiting campaign was inaugurated. A Department of Public Relations had already been set up in the War Office, to publicise the Army and popularise recruiting. Its staff was now increased and its activities extended. Public Relations Officers were stationed at each command headquarters, to establish closer relations between the Army and the Press. Recruiting posters, headed 'The Modern Army' appeared everywhere. An Army Exhibition was opened by the Secretary of State for War at South Kensington, with working models of all the new mechanised army vehicles. The most popular exhibit was an ingenious instrument, the predictor, by means of which the aiming and firing of an anti-aircraft gun could be synchronised with the flight of an approaching hostile aircraft. The public was becoming bomb-shy by anticipation, and not without reason.

A new and enlarged recruiting pamphlet was also issued, less formal and more personal in its appeal than its predecessors. It summarised the history of the British Army, enlarged upon its great traditions, and laid special stress upon the improvement in pay, rations, housing, opportunities for promotion, and recreational facilities offered to the modern recruit.

The results of this concerted effort were immediate and encouraging. Plainly, the country was waking up. But the intake still fell below the needs of that highly critical time.

Something had to be done, too, about the Territorial Army, especially since in his Army Estimates for 1939 Mr. Hore-Belisha, the Secretary of State for War, had foreshadowed an expeditionary force not only of six Regular divisions (two of them armoured) but of twelve Territorial divisions as well.

A further and most onerous duty was also in contemplation for the Territorial Army—the undertaking, no less, of the whole of the anti-aircraft and coastal defences of the country. Mr. Haldane's assumption, sound enough in 1907, that the invasion of Britain was a practical impossibility, had long ceased to carry any weight. In the event of war we would now almost certainly be bombed, and it was more than likely that attempts would be made to invade our shores as well.

But the strength of the Territorial Army had sunk far below establishment. The figure at the moment stood at 130,000 men: it should have been 170,000. So at the end of March it was decided to launch a great campaign for recruits. Not only was the Territorial Army to be brought up to strength, but when that end had been achieved its numbers were to be doubled to a force of 340,000, and all within a space of six months.

The organisation of the campaign was left largely in the hands of the Director General, the Territorial Army, and the County Territorial Associations. So vigorous and wholehearted were the measures employed, and the co-operation everywhere bestowed, that not only were the necessary numbers enlisted, but enlisted in well under the appointed six months. Unfortunately, a good many young men joined the Territorials who might otherwise have enlisted in the Regular Army.[1]

~(5)~

Meantime it had been decided by the Army Council to make one final, eleventh-hour effort to save the voluntary system of recruitment for the Regular Army, by an organised drive for another 50,000 men, to be undertaken and carried out on the most up-to-date lines by one of the leading advertising firms of the country. This was an entirely new departure, for hitherto the idea of employing commercial publicity methods for attracting recruits to the Colours had been strongly repugnant to army sentiment. But the danger was too serious to admit of scrupulous regard for tradition. The situation on the Continent was deteriorating almost from day to day, and it was generally felt, to employ the catch-phrase of the moment, that the 'balloon might go up at any time now'.

A further scheme, of a more orthodox and far more popular character, was set on foot about the same time—to dispatch a complete Mechanised Demonstration Column upon a prolonged tour of the country. Provisional measures to that end had been in hand for some weeks: the column was to halt in public squares and on village greens, where an official welcome would be offered by the local authority, demonstrations staged and recruiting literature distributed. All this called for elaborate organisation and routing: road bridges were even tested to make quite sure that they would bear the weight of the solitary tank which was to be the most prominent feature of the cavalcade.

But the time was too far spent. Upon Good Friday, April 7th, out of a moderately clear sky, the Italian Army suddenly descended upon, overran, and annexed the little kingdom of Albania, a neutral State under Allied protection. This settled all doubts and abolished further hesitation. Three weeks previously Hitler had dissolved the Czechoslovak State, annexing Bohemia and Moravia. Now his henchman

[1] See also pp. 106–7.

Mussolini had joined in, and the conspiracy against the freedom of Europe as a whole stood forth naked and unabashed.

The immediate result, so far as Britain was concerned, was the practical abandonment of the voluntary system of enlistment, though volunteers continued to come in in fair numbers. The idea of an intensive and costly recruiting drive was dropped, and the Mechanised Demonstration Column scrapped on the very eve of its setting out; for the demonstrators were required for sterner duties. Instead, a Bill was introduced into Parliament for the establishment of a 'militia'—a new formation with an old name—under the provisions of which every young man in the country upon reaching the age of twenty would become liable for two years' compulsory service—six months with the Colours and eighteen with the Territorials. This, it was calculated, would bring in about 300,000 recruits during the first twelve months, and fifty per cent more thereafter.

The Bill was officially opposed by the Socialist and Liberal members in the House, but was generally approved by the country, alive to the situation at last. It passed its Third Reading on May 18th, 1939, and upon July 15th the appointed thousands presented themselves for duty. There were no exemptions of any kind. At one particular depot the first three to report were a Duke's son, a market-gardener and an undertaker's assistant.

All registered their names first with the Ministry of Labour, which was in general control of the country's manpower problems. A medical examination followed, from which it emerged that no less than ninety-three per cent of the youth of the country, including every category of health and condition, were fit for general service, while eighty-two per cent were fit for any kind of service, however exacting—a striking tribute to the improved standards of diet and training prevalent throughout the country. Thereafter they were apportioned to their duties in the Navy, Army or Air Force. A few, to their sorrow, were directed to a less spectacular but equally important section of the country's defences, the coal-mining industry.

But the militia scheme, by the force of events, soon had to be implemented. On September 2nd, 1939 a National Service (Armed Forces) Bill was introduced into Parliament, under which all able-bodied men between the ages of eighteen and forty-one were rendered liable for military service for the duration of the war.

By the end of 1939 we had some 1,128,000 in the Army, of whom some 726,000 had joined since the 1st of September, and were thus in various stages of training. That is not to say that all were adequately armed and equipped. Still, we had travelled far since August 1914.

CHAPTER VII

THE PHONEY WAR

～(1)～

UPON August 23rd, 1939, the German and Soviet Governments proclaimed their pact of mutual non-aggression. This left Germany with a free hand for offensive action in other directions, and it became obvious that for the second time in a generation Europe stood upon the brink of total war.

We had not long to wait, for on September 1st the Germans invaded Poland with fifty-four divisions, six of them armoured. The British Government immediately implemented its solemn obligation to the Polish people by issuing an ultimatum to Germany. At 11.15 on Sunday morning, September 3rd, Mr. Neville Chamberlain, the Prime Minister, broadcasting from Downing Street, announced to the world that since no reply had been received from Hitler, a state of war now existed between the British Empire and Germany. Parliament assembled a few minutes later, to the sound of our first air-raid warning. It proved to be a false alarm, but it gave the necessary dramatic touch to the opening of the most tragic period of world history, not by any means ended even today.

London had been largely cleared of children; the War Reserve police, the A.R.P. wardens, and the newly organised fire-services were everywhere in evidence, and the Sunday afternoon civilian strollers in the parks all carried gasmasks in small square containers. There was little or no excitement: people were too busy pondering the future.

A war must always evoke comparison, especially at the beginning, with its immediate predecessor, and thousands upon that Sunday afternoon were comforting themselves with the reflection and hope that matters upon this occasion might turn out no worse than five-and-twenty years ago. Superficially the two situations were not dissimilar. In both cases we had declared war as a gesture of fulfilment to an Ally whose independence we had guaranteed. We had been ill-prepared in 1914, and were in similar plight today. But we had won through once and could do it again. There might be another Mons, but it would be redeemed by another Marne. In any case our Navy was strong and ready, our Air Force growing, and universal military service had been in operation for several months. For a nation of bad starters we were, if anything, a little ahead of our points.

But these reassuring reflections took little or no account of the new and devastating element introduced into warlike operations by the recent perfection of the internal combustion engine—in other words, of the vastly increased menace of the air. The men responsible for the defence of the country were under no delusion upon that score. Indeed, it was considered more than likely that London, in its present undefended condition, would have to be evacuated altogether. In any case the seat of Government and the principal Government departments, especially the Service Ministries, must be dispersed to safer areas. Provisional arrangements to that end had already been concluded, and for many months whole establishments were kept ready for evacuation to the country at twenty-four hours' notice. Hospital accommodation, too, for 300,000 civilian air-raid casualties had been organised throughout the country.

~(2)~

Meanwhile the first task of the War Office was to dispatch the British Expeditionary Force to its battle stations in France, in conformity with an agreement long concluded between ourselves and our French Allies.

But two difficulties, never previously experienced, were outstanding. The first was the possibility—the certainty, it seemed—of an overwhelming attack upon our transports from the air; for it was known that some 950 enemy bombers had been assembled on the aerodromes of west Germany, ready to pounce when the word came that our troops were on the sea. The second was that transport animals had been entirely replaced by mechanical vehicles. This presented, quite literally, a most weighty shipping problem, for space was required for 18,000 motor vehicles of 500 different types, with 100,000 different kinds of spare parts.

In the first case the most pressing need was to conceal our movements from the enemy. Months of painful consideration and preparation had been devoted to that end, the agencies concerned being the War Office, the Admiralty, the Board of Trade, and their French opposite numbers.

Obviously to cross by the shortest route was now out of the question, for Calais and Boulogne were nearer to the German frontier than any other part of the coast, and landing-ports must be found as remote as possible from enemy air-bases. Finally Cherbourg was selected for the troops, and Brest, Nantes and St. Nazaire for their stores and vehicles. Nantes stood some thirty-five miles up the estuary of the River Loire. St. Nazaire, at its mouth in the Bay of Biscay, had been converted during the previous war from a modest coastal port into a considerable base for the use of the American Expeditionary Force, so suited our purpose well.

The actual dispatch of the troops from Britain was conducted with the minimum of advertisement. Gone were the days when a departing troopship was seen off by a cheering crowd, with the regimental band playing 'The Girl I Left Behind Me'. The men were moved only by night, and in small bodies, to escape possible detection by enemy aircraft, and the names of the ports of embarkation were a secret which the local Press were bound in honour not to reveal. To the credit of all, be it said, the pledge was duly observed, and thanks to thorough preparation and co-ordination between the Services concerned, the entire Force arrived at its destination unscathed.

The first to land were the anti-aircraft units (to cover the specially risky process of disembarkation) and the hospital staffs. Advance bodies of civilians were on the spot even earlier, to organise docking arrangements. These had been recruited mainly from the port authorities of Great Britain, and most efficient they proved themselves. The actual troop movement began only a week after the declaration of war.

Upon September 14th, Viscount Gort, v.c., the Commander-in-Chief, followed his men overseas. He sailed in H.M.S. *Skate*, and was accompanied by Lieut.-General Sir John Dill, Commander of the 1st Corps, and his own personal staff. Upon landing at Cherbourg he proceeded to his temporary headquarters at Le Mans, midway between Rennes and Orléans. By September 21st the concentration of G.H.Q. and the essential lines of communication had been completed, and next day the troops began to arrive in the area. In this respect they enjoyed an advantage denied to their predecessors of 1914: they were given ample time to reassemble and reorganise, whereas twenty-five years earlier the B.E.F. had been hurried into action as they set foot upon the soil of France.

So far, so good. But there had been some anxious moments. Naturally the British public was eager for news of the Army, and was inclined to resent security measures and to welcome any rumour. And sometimes it was more than a rumour. Upon September 12th the French Government, doubtless to enhance the morale of their own people, issued an official communiqué to the effect that British troops were now fighting alongside their French comrades in France. In point of fact the only British troops in France at that moment were the anti-aircraft and hospital advance parties already mentioned. But the main body were due to embark at any moment, and the French announcement might result in a swarm of enemy bombers over the Channel, especially since it had been widely quoted, in all sincerity, by the British Press.

The dilemma was obvious. If we repudiated the statement, we would appear to be at loggerheads with our Allies; if we let it pass the public at home would demand details of the fighting and, above all, of the casualties. Nothing could really be done except take steps to prevent the story from circulating further, and hope that the enemy would not act upon it. Fortunately nothing more happened. But it was a tense moment for the General Staff at the War Office.

⇜(3)⇝

The British Expeditionary Force had now been conveyed safely and punctually to France—a proof that the original Cardwell-Haldane conceptions of mobilisation and transport were not only as sound as ever, but were sufficiently elastic to admit of their adaption to the novel conditions imposed by mechanisation and danger from the air.

A word should be said here regarding the actual composition of the Force and of its allotted part in the general Allied scheme.

It had already been agreed that the Allied land forces should be under the supreme direction of the French Commander-in-Chief, General Gamelin. After the success of Marshal Foch in the same capacity in 1918, such an arrangement seemed natural and inevitable, but it depended for its success upon the recognition and employment of the B.E.F. as an acknowledged partner in the Allied scheme, and not as a convenient milch-cow. (It was Pétain's perpetual insistence in early 1918, it will be remembered, that Haig should still further prolong his already undermanned trench-line which led to the almost fatal German break-through in March.)

And to a certain extent, so far as joint action was concerned, history was to repeat itself, for once Lord Gort had taken over his allotted battle-positions he was left very much to himself. Such orders as he received came not from General Gamelin but from (or through) General Georges, Commander of the French Front of the north-east, and in course of time the liaison was destined to grow fainter and Allied co-operation weaker. In the final stages of the battle of Flanders the B.E.F. fought practically alone and unsupported, and such orders as Lord Gort received were manifestly incapable of being carried out.

The Force consisted originally of two corps under the command respectively of Sir John Dill and Sir Alan Brooke, soldiers of great experience and high distinction. It also contained two Divisional Commanders, Major-General Sir H. R. L. G. Alexander (1st Division) and Major-General B. L. Montgomery (3rd Division) of whom much was to be heard in days to come. The 1st Corps comprised the 1st and 2nd Divisions, the 2nd the 3rd and 4th. Towards the end of the year each was augmented by an additional division, the 5th and 48th respectively. In January 1940 the Force stood at 222,000 of all ranks, not including the Air Component,[1] for the maintenance of which the B.E.F. was responsible.

It has been said, with truth, that the Old Contemptibles of 1914 were the best-trained, the best-led and the best-equipped army ever to leave our shores. As regards the first two requisites the same description could most justly be applied to the B.E.F. of 1939—but not the third. Deficiencies in equipment, especially in tanks and heavy artillery, were considerable and serious. This was due to no lack of zeal on the part of the War Office or General Staff, who were compelled to 'make do' with the resources placed at their disposal by the legislature, but to the time-lag, already noted, arising from our tardy decision as a nation to modernise and mechanise our military forces *ab initio*. Again and again in his Flanders Dispatches (not published until 1941) Lord Gort had cause to draw attention to his difficulties in this respect.

'I had been informed', he said, 'that the expansion of the Force was to be continued by the dispatch of the 3rd Corps during the early months of 1940; the Armoured Division was to follow in May, and a fourth Corps, with the 1st Canadian Division, during the late summer. Furthermore it had been decided that the Force should be divided into two Armies as soon

---

[1] This comprised one Fighter Wing and one Bomber Reconnaissance Wing.

as the number of divisions in the field, excluding the Armoured Division, rose above eleven.'

But these expectations were destined, so far as Lord Gort himself was concerned, never to be realised. The 3rd Corps was not fully deployed in France until the end of March, and the 1st Armoured Division, the mechanised equivalent of a sorely needed cavalry arm, arrived too late to participate as a whole in the Flanders operation.

Again Lord Gort reports:

The situation as regards equipment, though there was latterly some improvement in certain directions, caused me serious misgivings even before men and material began to be diverted by the needs of operations elsewhere.[1] I had on several occasions called the attention of the War Office to the shortage of almost every nature of ammunition, of which the stocks of France were not nearly large enough to permit of the rates of expenditure laid down for sustained operations before the War.

Grave words. As matters turned out the ultimate operations lasted for too brief a period for these shortages to be felt. Our disasters arose from other causes. But it is none the less uncomfortable to speculate here as to how our resources would have stood the strain, had the Flanders campaign been prolonged for twenty-five weeks instead of twenty-five days.

The net result, as usual, was that the Army was asked to make the best of what it could get until the machinery of production could provide in full for the needs of all three Services. And to that all-too-familiar appeal, as the event proved, the Army was to make its usual heroic response, and more.

~(4)~

At the end of September 1939, in the largest troop movement ever undertaken with motor transport by the British Army, the 1st Corps left Le Mans for its allotted position along the Franco-Belgian border.

The arrangements were of necessity elaborate, and on lines already rehearsed in peacetime.[2] Tanks, tracked vehicles, and slow-moving artillery were dispatched by train; the remainder of the Force proceeded by three parallel routes. Two 'staging areas' were arranged on each road, south of the Somme and Seine respectively. Anti-aircraft protection was provided at each crossing—another pregnant sign of

[1] e.g. in Norway.   [2] See pp. 61–2.

the times. Five hundred vehicles moved daily over each stage of the route, maintaining a cautious interval of one hundred yards between vehicles, their drivers meanwhile contending with the novel experience of having to keep to the right-hand side of the road. French-speaking British officers maintained liaison with the French road authorities.

Upon the 3rd October the 1st Corps took over the French Sector extending from Maulde to Grison on the Belgian frontier. The 2nd Corps arrived a week later. Work was immediately begun upon an elaborate system of defences in depth, including concrete blockhouses to accommodate anti-tank and machine-guns, with innumerable tank-traps and pillboxes. The Royal Engineers were assisted in their task by other arms, by certain French units, by some thousands of Belgian civilians, and a little later by certain sturdy companies of our newly raised 'Auxiliary Military Pioneer Corps'—a worthier sobriquet than that bestowed upon their predecessors of the First World War, of 'Labour Battalions'.

The line extended for fifty-five miles. It began at Maulde on the right, and ran roughly northward to Hallvin immediately south of Menin, thence south-west along the little River Lys—a name familiar to many of the older soldiers—as far as even more familiar Armentières. Within the salient formed, and protected by it, lay Roubaix, Tourcoing, and the great city of Lille.

This vast defence-work was, as it happened, destined never to be utilised in action; and it seems desirable at this point to offer some comment—from which Lord Gort studiously refrained throughout—upon the whole conception and organisation of the French defence scheme. It depended for its success upon the supposed impregnability of the Maginot Line—and the Maginot Line was already obsolescent. It had been the offspring of experience in the previous war, in which for four years underground defences had proved themselves almost impervious to mass attacks. Hence, it was argued, a permanently manned super-trench system, constructed in peacetime and at leisure along her eastern frontier, would render France practically immune from hostile invasion.

But time marches on, and military science with it. By the thirties of this century no trench system was of any avail against bombers, gliders, troop-carriers or parachutists, and year by year the value of the Maginot defences depreciated. Moreover, to serve its purpose it should have been continued, not along the Franco-Belgian frontier but along the Belgo-German frontier, where it would have carried the line straight on, instead of bending it back almost at right angles, and thus enabling the invader to take northern France, as it were, in flank.

But nothing of the kind was done. The French people had become obsessed by the vision of an impregnable trench system behind which, in the event of war, they could organise an overwhelming offensive and launch it at any point.

It is, of course, possible that if the Maginot Line and the Belgian frontier defences had been given the opportunity, as a completed and occupied whole, to serve the purpose for which they had been designed, the history of 1940 might have been written differently. At least they could have stemmed the first rush. But all such considerations were brought to naught by the excessively cautious attitude of the Belgian Government, who argued that to permit the Maginot Line, or anything like it, to be prolonged along the Belgo-German frontier would be a provocative act, and would certainly cause Belgium to be included in any scheme of aggression which Germany might be meditating against France. Their settled policy was neutrality *à outrance*.

An even greater difficulty with which the Allied authorities had to contend was to discover what the Belgian Government actually proposed to do if, as seemed more than probable, the enemy decided to follow the precedent of 1914 and endeavour to invade France by a sweep through Belgian territory. Upon this question the Belgians were reticent to the point of contumacy. It was obvious that if such a sweep took place, Lord Gort and the B.E.F. could not remain in their frontier trench system and leave Belgium to fight her battle single-handed. They must come to her assistance, and speedily. Yet the Belgian Government steadily refused to allow a British mission, or for that matter a single British staff officer, to cross the frontier and select suitable battle positions for the British Army, or even permit one British reconnaissance plane to fly over. Consequently the whole of Lord Gort's plan for this contingent aid had to be formulated from maps and second-hand information. However, refraining, as usual, from comment (for it was General Gamelin's duty and not his to bring the Belgians to reason in the matter), the British Commander-in-Chief pressed on loyally with the defences of the Franco-Belgian frontier.

One mitigation of the present anxious and embarrassing situation was permitted him. It was agreed between himself and General Georges that in order to give the British force, engaged hitherto on manual labour many miles from the theatre of hostilities, some preliminary experience of actual contact with the enemy, British

units should be transferred to the so-called Saar front beyond the
Maginot Line, and there maintained in rotation, under the command
of a French division.

Here was ample manœuvring and patrolling ground—the enemy
were about fifteen hundred yards away—and full advantage was
taken of the opportunities offered. Raids were frequent on either side.

'Since December 4th,' says Lord Gort in his first Dispatch, 'infantry
brigades[1] of the B.E.F. have successively completed short tours of duty in
this sector, and junior leaders have thus had valuable training in their day
to day duties, when in contact with the enemy.'

~(5)~

Lord Gort and his staff were soon faced with increasing problems
of administration, for the B.E.F. was growing steadily. There was at
this time no threat or prescience of coming disaster: it was assumed
that throughout the course of the war (it might be for years) the soil
of France would be the natural base of the British military forces. To
that end maintenance depots and training-grounds sufficient for a very
large army indeed must be prepared at the earliest possible moment.

Lord Gort's initial difficulty was the extreme length of his lines
of communication. These extended diagonally from the Belgian
frontier to Brest and Nantes—some three hundred miles and more.
A more advanced base was badly needed, and Havre was selected. By
mid-December the staff of the Movement Control was operating
some ninety stations, while fourteen ports were in active use, through
which men, vehicles and stores poured unceasingly. Buildings sprang
up all the way to the forward line: hospitals and reinforcement camps
were put in hand and electric light installed. With the co-operation
of the French Army, artillery practice grounds were established and
other training facilities provided.

Still the numbers grew: by the spring of 1940 the British Army
occupied about a third of France, though its tenure thereof was fated
to be so brief that the actual fact of the occupation has long been
forgotten, if, indeed, it was ever realised.

General Headquarters was established in, or rather about, Arras—
a name pleasantly familiar to thousands of British soldiers of the
previous generation. But conditions now were completely changed.

---

[1] Ultimately a complete British Division (the 51st) was transferred to this area.
It was there on May 10th, and was thus prevented from participating in the
Battle of Flanders.

The Commander-in-Chief and his staff no longer lived in close company in the same street or group of buildings, as at Montreuil during the previous war. Dispersion was the order of the day: G.H.Q., the brain and directing force of the whole Army, must not be exposed to the risk of annihilation by a single bomb. Lord Gort and his principal officers—the Chief of Staff, the Adjutant-General, the Quartermaster-General, the Director of Military Intelligence— were quartered in separate billets some miles apart. That meant that when a conference had to be held, valuable time was taken up in travelling, or in a prolonged struggle with that most exasperating of instruments, the field telephone.[1]

It was the same with the rank and file. Gone was most of the pleasant sociability of crowded streets and brilliantly lighted cafés. Troops resting were dispersed in small contingents all over the countryside, separated from their nearest neighbours by a mile or so of field and plough, and wrapped by night in an impenetrable black- out. What rendered these restrictions particularly galling was the fact that for some months they appeared to be completely unnecessary. The French civilian population took but little notice of them, especially in the matter of lights.

These new conditions of warfare also set a high premium upon secrecy, especially with regard to the strength and location of troops; for to publicise these was to invite the immediate attentions of enemy bombers, and we had not at that time sufficient fighter planes to deal with such visitants. In official dispatches and correspondence place- names were scrupulously avoided. The existence of Arras was never once admitted: it was invariably referred to by its code-name, 'Brassard'; the headquarters of the R.A.F. was 'Panther'. These were thus the forbears of that strange and variegated offspring of a later day—'Pluto', 'Fido' and 'Operation so-and-so'.

The question of security measures in the field in wartime will be dealt with at greater length in a subsequent chapter, but a word may be said here regarding the peculiar difficulties which confronted the D.M.I. and his officers in this particular theatre and at this particu- larly critical period.

In the first place some 8,000 civilian Belgian workers crossed and recrossed the frontier every day, and it was a sheer impossibility to eliminate all opportunities for espionage. Secondly, the modern world is largely populated by persons who demand 'hot news' with their breakfast every morning and over the air at almost every hour

---

[1] We shall have occasion to note an enormous subsequent improvement in this particular respect.

in the twenty-four, and who expect military operations to be reported as promptly and as intimately as League Football matches. This circumstance threw a heavy strain upon the discretion and probity of the host of war correspondents, radio announcers and film representatives gathered at G.H.Q., and an even heavier strain upon the vigilance and tact of the censors.

The D.M.I. and his staff did their best to satisfy legitimate demands, by frequent press conferences and the handing out of regular news bulletins. But journalists are never satisfied with 'hand-outs' or omnibus information. The American correspondents were particularly vocal. They were at that time neutrals, and in the main favourably disposed towards the Allied cause; but they were, first and foremost, journalists. They had travelled, they said, 3,000 miles to report a total war, and there was nothing to report. Their employers were getting restive; in their view this war was not being 'put over at its full publicity value'. In fact, it was a 'Phoney War'.

And, indeed, there was some justification for this statement, for all during that autumn and winter an uneasy peace hung over Western Europe. There was fierce activity at sea—passenger ships were being torpedoed, and the *Graf Spee* had been sent to the bottom off the River Plate—but on land there was nothing to report but a curious hesitancy. Men's minds seemed to be half-numbed by the contemplation of the almost unlimited possibilities of aerial attack, as revealed in the recent destruction of the fine Polish Army within the space of two or three weeks. It was as if the combatants hung back for a moment before proceeding further along a path fraught with such dreadful consequences to the human race.

For several months there was an almost complete absence of bombing upon either side. Possibly Neville Chamberlain's solemn pledge that we would refrain from attacking non-military objectives if the enemy would do likewise had not been entirely without effect: more probably Hitler, supremely confident in his intuition of victory, was merely putting a final polish upon his plan of campaign—or perhaps replacing those of his weapons of war which had grown obsolescent through premature design and construction.

For the Allies the Phoney War was both a help and a hindrance. It helped because it enabled the troops to continue their peacetime training, now conducted under conditions of active service. It was, or should have been, particularly valuable to the vast French conscript army, called up from civil life and hardly trained at all. It also gave the Allied Governments a further period of time in which to overtake their arrears in the output of munitions of war.

On the other hand it initiated a period of monotonous routine, unrelieved by the stimulus of warlike adventure or the hope of speedy victory. Thus the first fine flush of patriotic enthusiasm languished, and in course of time a sense of boredom and frustration took its place. Men, to employ the phrase coined for the occasion, became 'browned-off'.

These sentiments were reflected in their letters home, which were frequent and voluminous : indeed, the B.E.F. had developed a passion for correspondence unprecedented in the annals of the Army Post Office. The reaction of their friends and relations was natural and immediate, and in the absence of any news of operational interest public opinion became concentrated upon those matters now generally summed up under the heading of Army Welfare. Sentimental sympathy rose high : the actual purpose for which the B.E.F. had been sent to France was temporarily obscured, while press and public formulated schemes of aid and refreshment for 'the boys'. These included extension of leave, visits from friends, the provision of such comforts as radio sets and mouth organs, and the organisation of concert parties and theatrical touring companies. One enthusiast wrote to the Press suggesting that a large oil-tanker should be pumped dry and dispatched to France filled with real English beer.

With the setting-in of genuine war conditions this agitation subsided like magic, but it caused a considerable stir while it lasted, and gave significant expression to the fact that the morale of a 'democratic' army must in future be recognised as a psychological problem calling for careful study and sympathetic handling.[1]

The troubles of our Allies, the French, in this matter were more serious than our own. France had been bled white in the First World War, and her people were reluctant to face a repetition of that experience. If the troops could have been sent straight into action, their natural qualities as soldiers would have been called into play at once. Instead, they found themselves cooped up for months in the Maginot Line or back areas, eating their hearts out and longing for home. A French soldier's strength lies in courage and *élan* rather than philosophical endurance of monotony and suspense.

Moreover, one-third of their country, as already noted, was occupied by the British, and the German propaganda machine was busy proffering the well-worn suggestion that while French soldiers toiled and bled in the front line, the British Army was taking its ease in the rear areas and diverting itself with French sweethearts and wives. Pictorial postcards suggesting (and illustrating) such

[1] See p. 321.

possibilities achieved a mysterious circulation among the rank and file.

Above all, the political situation was highly explosive. France was rent by faction; there was little trust in the Government (or series of Governments) and army leaders. Certain army units were frankly Communist: there were disturbing tales of indiscipline and *cafard*.

All of this combined to increase the anxieties of the British Government and High Command. The campaign in Poland had already demonstrated the helplessness of an army in the field, however courageous and well-disciplined, if it is unprovided with the necessary anti-tank weapons and adequate air cover. And in April 1940, to drive the lesson home, came our failure to avert or even arrest the invasion of Norway.

Of this operation[1] there is no need to speak in detail here, except to observe that it was in the nature of a forlorn hope almost from the outset. The little expeditionary force was assembled in haste and shipped without due regard for the necessary priorities in the delivery of equipment. 'Guns', says the official dispatch, 'were landed without their detachments and with little or no ammunition; vehicles arrived without their drivers.' And the enemy were not idle: one ship carrying essential first-line transport was sunk in transit.

The expedition arrived to find the enemy well established. He already held all the aerodromes, and was well provided with heavy artillery and mortars, which kept our troops under bombardment from the moment of landing. It was impossible to disembark artillery or anti-aircraft guns—the tiny harbours of Andalsnes and Namsos offered no facilities for such an undertaking—and the fighters of the Fleet Air Arm were too limited in range to remain for long in the air. Their only landing-ground, the surface of a frozen lake, was speedily disintegrated by a few bombs. However, within the limits imposed they gave a valiant account of themselves. 'The Germans would not face our Fleet Air Arm fighters, which were handled with a boldness that was an inspiration to the troops, who watched their manœuvres from the ground.' No R.A.F. long-range bombers appear to have been available.

The unequal struggle was maintained with great courage and fortitude for a fortnight; but ground was lost rather than gained, and it became plain that nothing could be gained by remaining, and that

---

[1] There were actually two of these. The first, at Narvik in the north, was brilliantly successful, for after the Navy had destroyed a number of enemy war-ships and supply-ships a mixed force of British, French, Polish and Norwegian troops recaptured the town. But subsequent events in Flanders necessitated its almost immediate evacuation.

it would be wise to withdraw before complete disaster overtook the expedition. The withdrawal, thanks to the devoted assistance of the Navy, was effected with great skill and without too serious losses.

The most important feature of this unhappy venture was the lesson which it inculcated—namely that a seaborne invasion of an enemy-occupied coast must be organised upon an overwhelming scale and rehearsed to the last detail; that troops must be prepared and trained to land upon open beaches from specially devised landing craft, and that the invading force must be supreme in the air. And thus out of bitter defeat, in the fullness of time, was evolved the triumphant Combined Operation of D-Day 1944, with its prefabricated artificial harbours, landing craft, airborne troops and overall air supremacy.

The Norway episode was the signal for general action. On May 10th Hitler invaded France and Belgium, and the British Army crossed the frontier, amid the cheers of the Belgian population. Upon the same day Winston Churchill became Prime Minister of England. The Phoney War was over, and the era of 'blood, tears, toil and sweat' had begun.

CHAPTER VIII

DUNKIRK AND AFTER

~(1)~

WE have now to observe how the organisation and administration of the British Expeditionary Force, upon which so much thought and labour had been expended during past months, was to stand up to the strain of the vast operation impending—not forgetting that the success of that operation leaned heavily upon the dispositions and efficiency of the Allied forces as a whole.

There had been much anxious consultation between the French and British commanders as to the action to be taken in the event of a direct German invasion of Belgium. (This seemed to be only too probable, since Hitler had but recently reaffirmed the pacific nature of his intentions towards that country.) Various defence schemes were discussed, each lacking in completeness and finality owing to uncertainty as to Belgian intentions; but finally, at a meeting held at the headquarters of the French First Group of Armies on November 16th, 1939, the following plan was agreed to.

It was known as Plan D, and provided that if the invasion took place the French and British forces should immediately enter Belgium and take up a defence line along the little River Dyle, which ran from south to north, covering Brussels from the east, *and so far as could be gathered from the map*, offered some possibilities as an effective tank obstacle.

The French 7th Army would be on the left of the line, the B.E.F. in the centre (from Louvain to Wavre), and the French 1st Army on the right. The Belgian Army, it was assumed, would occupy prepared positions further forward, along the deep-flowing Meuse and the Albert Canal.[1]

In the event of a failure to hold the line of the Dyle, it was agreed

[1] See Map 1, p. 92.

to fall back to a second position further west, along the line of the Escaut. This was known as Plan E.

On Friday, May 10th, the expected storm burst. Hitler invaded Holland, Belgium and France simultaneously, and Plan D came automatically into operation. The B.E.F., led by the armoured cars of the 12th Royal Lancers, had to cover sixty miles in order to reach its allotted sector on the Dyle, but the position was reached and the defences manned within forty-eight hours.

So far, everything had gone according to schedule; but now came disquieting news from out in front. Belgian cyclist troops were falling back on Huy; important bridges upon the Meuse and Albert Canal had not been demolished, and the so-called anti-tank obstacles designed to cover the dangerous Gembloux gap had proved to be of little or no effect. In other words, the enemy had broken through the frontier defences, and despite the gallant efforts of our small Air Force to impede them, were well into Belgium.

If this had been all, there would have been no particular reason to fear for the immediate safety of the Dyle line, which was solidly held. But to invade France by a sweep through Belgium was no part this time of the German strategic plan, contrived as it was out of deep study of the new and dazzling opportunities presented to an imaginative General Staff by mechanisation, the use of tanks, and command of the air. The intention, in fact, was to strike at a selected point in the Allied line in overwhelming force and cleave a passage right across France to the English Channel.

The essential feature of the operation was that it should be 'non-stop'. There must be no pausing to consolidate ground won, or secure flanks, or bring up reinforcements, or reorganise transport. The thrust must be continuous, and be delivered at the pace, not of marching men, but of armoured vehicles and swift-moving tanks covered from the air.

It was a masterly conception, brilliantly executed. No attempt was made to pierce the Maginot Line; it was merely ignored. Five armoured divisions swept round its northern extremity, traversed the Belgian Ardennes (rendered unusually passable by a dry and early spring) and fell upon the French 9th Army, which was deployed to the south of the 1st. The 9th Army broke and scattered—its reliability had long been suspect—and the invaders crossed the Meuse between Mezières and Sedan. Thence they poured in a wide and irresistible torrent across the old Somme battlefields to Amiens, which was occupied almost within a week. Two days later German motor-cyclists and light tanks were in Abbeville, and the shores of the Channel had been reached.

As a direct consequence, the northern French armies (together with the B.E.F.) found themselves isolated from the rest by a corridor some twenty miles wide, and growing wider. Worse still, Lord Gort's lines of communication, which it will be remembered extended not straight back but diagonally to the south-west, were cut clean across, and the B.E.F. were faced with an immediate shortage of ammunition and supplies. Fortunately, in anticipation of some such emergency as this, a considerable reserve had been accumulated locally, and was for the time being available.

~⊰(2)⊱~

The Allied troops whom we left deployed along the line of the Dyle were now in grave danger of being outflanked and cut off altogether, for south of the French 1st Army on Lord Gort's right there was nothing—nothing but a running river of German divisions advancing westward. The 9th Army, which should have stemmed the tide, had simply disintegrated. On Lord Gort's left now was the Belgian Army, evicted from its frontier defences and in a somewhat shaken condition. The French 7th Army was somewhere further north.

It was high time that a definite scheme of co-ordinated action should be evolved to meet these new dangers, and a meeting of commanders, practically the last of its kind, was held near Mons. It was attended by the King of the Belgians, the French Premier M. Daladier, Lieut.-General Pownall, Chief-of-Staff to Lord Gort (who himself was only too busily occupied elsewhere) and Generals Georges and Billotte, the latter in command of the French 1st Army. The task of co-ordination was deputed by general consent to the last named. The practical effect of this was to remove the British forces from the control of General Georges and, by implication, of General Gamelin.

Obviously it had become impossible to persevere further with Plan D. Fresh measures must be devised at once—possibly a reversion to Plan E and a retirement to the line of the Escaut, a distance of sixty miles. Orders to that effect were issued and the movement effected by the following night, though the troops were much hampered by the crowds of refugees on the roads; also by the fact that, despite Lord Gort's representations, nothing had been done by the Belgian Government to restrict the use of private cars or the sale of petrol.

So much for the position as regards frontal attack. But as rumour clarified into stark fact Lord Gort speedily realised that his real danger was that of encirclement from the south. This danger was intensified by the fact that his rear areas, so called, were not behind him but lay on his right rear, at Arras and in the country surrounding it, in the very path of the advancing enemy. Lord Gort was well aware that in the defence of this area he could look for little help from the French 1st Army, who were in serious difficulties of their own. He must draw from his own slender resources. He had still at his disposal three divisions, the 12th, 23rd and 46th. These, however, had merely been brought out to France to train, and were lacking in much of their equipment, for it had never been expected that they would have to undertake immediate combat duties.

But every man was wanted now, and right valiantly did this improvised defence force rise to the nightmare emergencies of the moment.

'Troops of these Divisions', says Lord Gort, 'fought and marched continuously for a fortnight, and proved, if proof were needed, that they were composed of soldiers who, despite their inexperience and lack of equipment, could hold their own with a better trained and more numerous enemy.'

They were deployed where they could do most good—that is, on a line facing east, to protect Arras and rear G.H.Q., and extending south almost as far as Peronne. Beyond that came the great gap in the French front, now some thirty miles wide.

To formulate a plan for closing this was the business of the French High Command, presumably by means of a strong counter-attack launched both from north and south. Pending such action, Lord Gort had to rely upon his own resources. The defence of Arras itself was entrusted to the O.C. 1st Battalion Welsh Guards, who had under him some engineer units, a battalion of the West Yorkshire Regiment, and an improvised tank squadron. Other emergency units, each called by a name derived from that of their commanding officer, 'Macforce', 'Peterforce', 'Frankforce', 'Patforce', were posted at other key positions, such as the crossings of the River Scarpe.

Various local defence units were extemporised further back, towards the Somme. Few of these or of their commanders had any previous experience of fighting, but their determination made up for much. A Mobile Bath Unit played a stout part in the defence of St. Pol, while General Construction companies of the Royal Engineers and units of the Royal Army Service Corps placed their own areas in a state of defence, and clung to them until they were 'overwhelmed, relieved, or ordered to withdraw'. The spirit of First Ypres still burned bright, after four-and-twenty years.

~⁂(3)⁂~

At home the news of the German attack on May 10th, and of the British entry into Belgium, had been greeted with satisfaction and indeed relief. The Phoney War was over, and we had at long last come to grips with the enemy. The Norwegian episode, it was considered, perhaps with justice, had been a forlorn hope from the start: now, in company with a French Army running into millions, we could meet our opponent on level terms. Mr. Churchill's appointment as Prime Minister inspired additional confidence.

For a week, however, no definite news was forthcoming, beyond an official intimation that the situation was at present 'too fluid for discussion'; but it was reported that the Germans were pressing hard for Brussels—this, if true, meant that the Meuse and the Albert Canal defences had been forced—and that Rotterdam had been heavily bombed. (All Dutch resistance, in point of fact, ceased on the fifth day.) On the other hand there were accounts of successful bombing raids by the R.A.F. upon the German back areas. But of the B.E.F. itself there was, as yet, no word.

Still, the public were in a confident mood. They remembered 1914, and said that we had always been 'sticky starters'. The normal life of London was not disturbed.

But within the War Cabinet and the Service Ministries there was growing anxiety and concern. First had come the news of the break-through from the Ardennes and the liquidation of the French 9th Army, followed less than a week later by the stunning intelligence that the English Channel had been reached. In other words, the coast of England itself was in danger of invasion.

And not merely the coast, for under the new and strange conditions of modern warfare our whole island had become vulnerable, for war was now three-dimensional. Troop-carrying aircraft or parachutists could be dropped anywhere—for choice in some remote and weakly guarded area, where they could quickly coalesce into a united whole and establish a strongpoint or bridge-head. True, new divisions were undergoing training throughout the country, but only one of these was as yet fully equipped. In any case, they could not possibly be everywhere at once.

Obviously, what was needed to meet this new and imminent menace was a vast body of guerrilla troops, composed of men possessed of intimate local knowledge; who knew every backstreet and alley in their own home town, or every lane, by-path and spinney in their own stretch of countryside; who lived right on the spot and would be available at any hour of the day or night to watch the skies and intercept visitants therefrom, before they could disentangle themselves from their parachutes and join forces.

But whatever had to be done in the organisation of such a body must be done quickly. So as early as Sunday, May 12th, only two days after the invasion of France, the matter was put in hand. It was decided that the Secretary of State for War should issue a broadcast appeal for 'Local Defence Volunteers'—a more expressive title, by the way, than that of 'Home Guard', subsequently and somewhat grandiloquently conferred—composed of men not already eligible for military service.

The drafting of the appeal, especially at such short notice, was a difficult and delicate matter, and its wording had to be most carefully considered. It must state clearly the duties of the new force, and say who was eligible for it, and in particular who was not. It must stress the extreme gravity of the situation without causing undue alarm or giving information to the enemy. Above all, it must make no promises which the Government could not fulfil.

This meant that the various departments and officials concerned— the Adjutant-General's department, the Ministry of Labour, the Home Office, the police, and the inevitable Treasury—must be consulted and brought into line within the space of thirty-six hours. But by Tuesday morning, after two nights and a day of continuous drafting and redrafting, the thing was done and the appeal approved.

Its main provisions were clear. Service was to be voluntary, unpaid, and rendered only in spare time, to avoid interfering with the industrial life of the country.

The appeal was broadcast by Mr. Anthony Eden on Tuesday evening, the 14th. Recruits were instructed to report at their local police-station, and Chief Constables of all counties had been previously notified to that effect. But such was the response to the invitation that men were queuing up outside the police-stations before Mr. Eden had finished delivering it—to the embarrassment of those officers of the law to whom the instruction had not yet penetrated.

It had been hoped that 150,000 Local Defence Volunteers might be recruited. In the end they numbered nearly 2,000,000.[1]

To provide these with the usual military equipment was out of the question: there was not for the time being enough of this even for the Regular divisions. So recourse was had, not for the first time in the history of the British Army, to wholesale improvisation. An

[1] See further observations upon the Home Guard in Chap. XX.

appeal was issued for the loan of sporting guns and revolvers, and evoked a generous response; but there were not, of course, nearly enough of these to go round, and various humbler but not entirely despicable weapons were offered and accepted, including more than one ancient blunderbuss and some butchers' knives. Some of the volunteers made shift for a while with pitchforks and home-made pikes. After all, in engaging a newly landed parachutist in single combat, what chiefly matters is to get one's blow in first, whatever the instrument employed.

The reason for the hasty creation of the L.D.V.—the fact that enemy formations had already reached the shores of the Channel— was as yet unknown to the nation at large, for official information as to the actual conditions in Flanders was being withheld in the hope that it might yet be possible to restore the situation, and render it unnecessary to depress national morale prematurely. (As we have seen, a successful Anglo-French counter-attack across the corridor, and the establishment of a strong defensive barrier through Cambrai-Peronne-St. Quentin might well have stemmed the enemy's thrust from the east, while his advanced elements in the west could have been cut off and rounded up.) Consequently there was a good deal of uninformed though natural criticism of the lack of organisation and method evinced in the raising of the new force.

A week later, however, the situation in France had grown so serious that to keep the public in the dark any longer would have been both foolish and reprehensible. So news was 'released' (to employ the popular phrase of the moment) of the break-through at Mézières and Sedan, and of the disaster to the French 9th Army. It was added that in this the German advance had been greatly aided by a new class of unexpectedly heavy tanks. Low-flying bombers, too, had had a most demoralising effect. The situation, in short, was serious, and the B.E.F., though their front was unbroken, had been compelled to fall back in conformity with the French. Louvain was gone, and Brussels would probably go. The Belgian Government had retired to Ostend. On other matters a discreet silence was observed, for to advertise the full extent of the danger threatening the whole of France might have been fatal to French national morale, and to the valiant attempts of M. Reynaud, the new Premier, to maintain it.

But already events had far ̀outrun even this cautious statement. Let us return to Flanders, and resume our study of the actual situation in the theatre of war.

⤳(4)⤶

Here the pattern of the unequal conflict was assuming a more definite and ominous shape.

The line of the Escaut (and Plan E) had already been abandoned, and the Allied Armies on the north side of the enemy-occupied 'corridor' were gathered into a rough triangle of ground with sides about fifty miles in length. The base of the triangle lay along the coast, from Gravelines, through Calais and Dunkirk, to Zeebrugge: the apex was situated south-east, in the neighbourhood of Douai. From Douai to Gravelines ran what was called the Canal Line, a defensive flank facing south-west against the German Panzer divisions in the corridor, and manned by what was left of the various improvised 'Forces' already described. The third side, facing east, consisted roughly of the original Allied front. Brussels and Ghent were now in enemy hands, and so was Arras, after a stout defence by the 5th and 50th Divisions.

The communications of the B.E.F. had thus been finally severed, for the remainder of its forces lay fifty miles away, south of Abbeville and completely removed from Lord Gort's control. They consisted of the 51st Division, withdrawn from the Saar, some battalions of the 12th and 46th Divisions, and the precious Armoured Division.

The R.A.F. had by this time lost their bases in northern France, and were operating from England.

Obviously, the only way to restore the situation was by the double counter-attack across the corridor already indicated, and this called for a clear and co-ordinated plan from the Supreme Command. Here Lord Gort was labouring under a heavy handicap. He had found it almost impossible to maintain liaison with Allied Headquarters: only once in the whole course of the battle had he received written orders therefrom; while from the War Cabinet at home he was constantly receiving instructions to carry out operations which had been rendered impracticable almost before the orders were issued. In fact, our Government seemed to rely for their information more upon General Weygand (who had now succeeded Gamelin) than upon the more candid appreciations of their own Commander-in-Chief.

This was typified by the War Cabinet's insistence upon the execution of a 'Weygand Plan' of counter-attack, based upon their belief, quite erroneous, that the French had recaptured Amiens, Albert and Peronne—the Somme line, in fact. In other words, the plan had no

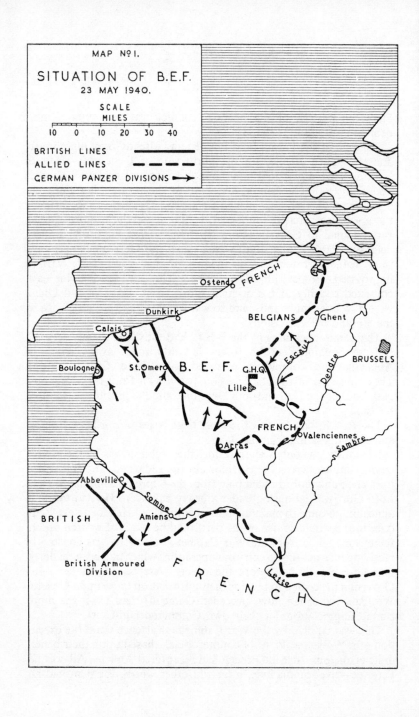

MAP Nº I.

SITUATION OF B.E.F.
23 MAY 1940.

SCALE
MILES
10   0   10   20   30   40

BRITISH LINES ————
ALLIED LINES —————
GERMAN PANZER DIVISIONS ——→

Ostend
Dunkirk
Calais
Boulogne
St.Omer
B. E. F.
G.H.Q.
Lille
FRENCH
BELGIANS
Ghent
BRUSSELS
Escaut
Dendre
FRENCH
Valenciennes
Sambre
Arras
Abbeville
Somme
Amiens
BRITISH
British Armoured
Division
F R E N C H
Lette

substance at all. Nothing had been worked out, verified or co-ordinated. The situation, however, was destined to deteriorate so rapidly that the Weygand Plan was never put into effect.

Upon May 23rd Lord Gort was compelled to place the B.E.F. upon half rations, and upon half rations they fought for the remainder of the campaign.

Upon May 27th Lord Gort was informed, at second hand, that the King of the Belgians had asked for an armistice. This meant that the B.E.F. was now left with an open gap of twenty miles between its left flank and the sea.

The bitter and inevitable end was now at hand. Isolated from all help on either flank, and with supplies dwindling to vanishing point, nothing remained for the B.E.F. but complete evacuation to England, if indeed that evacuation were possible. Lord Gort himself cherished but slight hope in the matter.

'I must not conceal from you', he informed the Secretary of State for War, 'that a great part of the B.E.F. and its equipment will inevitably be lost even in the best circumstances.'

But being the man he was, he saw to it that the circumstances should be the best possible. He had already established a provisional base at Dunkirk, and General Sir Ronald Adam, commander of the 3rd Corps, was busy constructing the famous Perimeter,[1] into which nearly a quarter of a million British soldiers were ultimately withdrawn. They were accompanied by 100,000 French troops, who had decided to share their fortunes. These were embarrassing companions, for, despite the efforts of the British traffic control units, they insisted upon bringing their transport vehicles (mostly horsed) with them, adding to the existing congestion. This transport even found its way to the beaches, where ultimately the horses, lacking food and water, were cut loose by British soldiers and turned inland.

By May 30th the whole of the B.E.F., after days of desperate rearguard action, especially upon the left flank, had been withdrawn within the Perimeter, and the actual evacuation began, just three weeks after the start of the battle. It was an epic operation, but calls for no detailed description in this narrative.

At midnight upon Sunday, June 2nd, Major-General Alexander,[2] accompanied by the Senior Naval Officer, made a final tour of the beaches and harbour, and 'on being satisfied that no British troops were left on shore, they themselves left for England'.

[1] See Map 2, p. 96.
[2] Now Field-Marshal Viscount Alexander of Tunis, Governor-General of Canada.

~✲(5)✲~

The actual deliverance of the B.E.F. and the accompanying Allied troops (to the number of 224,585 and 112,546 respectively) from the beaches of Dunkirk, and their transference to Dover and other south coast ports, was effected by a miracle of courage and teamwork on the part of the Royal Navy, a host of 'little ships' (many of them privately owned and manned by their owners), and the devotion of our home-based Air Force.

But the part played by the Army authorities therein has never been fully realised or justly appreciated, outstanding though the performance was.

The possibility of such a catastrophe as the forced withdrawal of our troops from France had never been overlooked by them, and as early as May 19th contingent plans, long adumbrated, for the evacuation of the B.E.F. from France, and especially for the dispersal and accommodation of the troops upon their arrival in England, were elaborated and put into operation. But for these prompt and far-seeing measures, the state of the homecomers would have been parlous indeed; for it must be remembered that the units of the B.E.F. had no barracks or depot of their own to return to: these had immediately been occupied, on their departure to France in 1939, by new formations.

The plan itself was known as 'Dynamo', and responsibility for its effective working fell chiefly upon the Quartermaster-General's department, especially the Directorate of Quartering, which found itself called upon to make arrangements for the reception, accommodation, clothing, and pay of a mixed multitude of military evacuees running possibly into hundreds of thousands.

At the conference summoned on May 19th to consider Plan 'Dynamo' certain definite conclusions were arrived at. They amounted to the following:

1. All equipment not carried by hand would have to be abandoned.
2. Since the ports of the French coast would probably have been put out of commission by enemy bombing, the great majority of the troops would have to be evacuated from open beaches in small boats. This meant that formations would inevitably be broken up, and the men dispatched haphazard as and when they embarked.
3. Since the ordinary machinery of regimental administration would have ceased to exist, the men would be in immediate need of dry clothing, blankets, and, above all, food.

4. There must be no delays of any kind at the port of arrival: to spend time attempting to sort men out into their original units would cause immediate and perhaps fatal congestion, especially since the port would probably be subjected to heavy bombing. Trains must be dispatched as soon as they were full.

5. Reception areas must be prepared in suitable parts of the south of England, and each train dispatched thither via some nodal point (like Redhill or Ashford) when it would be redirected to its appointed destination.

6. As there would be little time or opportunity for the provision of meals at the port of arrival, arrangements must be made for a series of *halte-repas en route*.

7. The first thing the public would want to be told would be the names of those who had been saved. It would be impracticable, however, to provide universal facilities for the men to do this themselves immediately on arrival, owing to the delay involved.

8. The number of men to be dealt with might run as high as 300,000. Most of these would know to which unit they belonged, but not all to which division they belonged.

These conclusions, it may be added, proved substantially correct, and furnished an excellent basis for Plan 'Dynamo'. This was fortunate, for, as events fell out, the entire plan had to be put into full operation within a few weeks.

The story of the successful evacuation of the B.E.F. from France has been considerably over-simplified by popular tradition. In reality it was a highly complicated operation, and was not confined merely to the conveyance of men from the Dunkirk beaches to Dover, for 'Dynamo' was not the only evacuation plan. Other units had to be evacuated from the south side of the corridor—the 51st Division, the Armoured Division and the Havre base troops. These were dealt with in due course under the so-called 'Cycle' Plan, and were evacuated via Le Havre and St. Valéry.

But even then a very large body of troops remained in France south of the Somme, and, indeed, more were about to be added; for the British Government resolutely declined to accept the evacuation of Dunkirk as the end of the battle of France, and actually dispatched fresh divisions to the aid and encouragement of the French armies south of the Somme. It was a great and most hazardous gesture, but it relieved the British people of all suspicion of wantonly leaving their Allies in the lurch.

Lieut.-General Sir Alan Brooke, who had commanded the 2nd Corps throughout, and had accompanied it upon the withdrawal

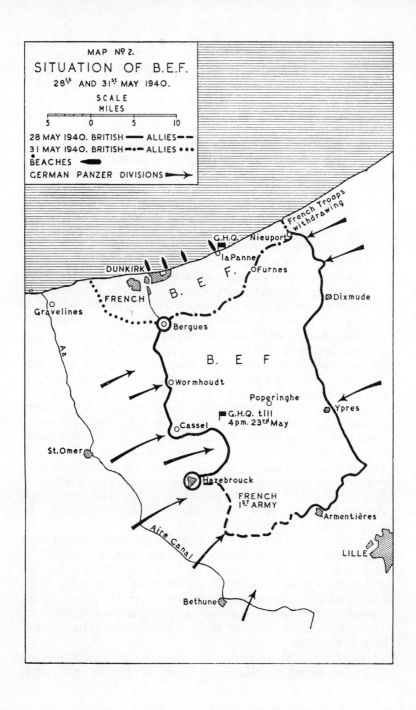

MAP Nº 2.

SITUATION OF B.E.F.
28ᵗʰ AND 31ˢᵗ MAY 1940.

SCALE
MILES

5   0   5   10

28 MAY 1940. BRITISH ▬▬▬ ALLIES ▬ ▬
31 MAY 1940. BRITISH ▬·▬· ALLIES •••
BEACHES ▬▬▬
GERMAN PANZER DIVISIONS ▶▬▬

French Troops
withdrawing

G.H.Q. Nieuport
laPanne
DUNKIRK   Furnes
FRENCH   B. E F.

Gravelines   Dixmude

Bergues

B. E F

Wormhoudt

Poperinghe
                                          Ypres
G.H.Q. till
4pm. 23ʳᵈ May
Cassel

St.Omer
                    Hazebrouck
                    FRENCH
                    1ˢᵀ ARMY

                                    Armentières

Aire Canal   LILLE

Bethune

from Dunkirk, returned to France on June 13th, and established headquarters at Le Mans. Plan 'Cycle' had not been altogether successful, for the 51st Division had encountered disaster. Though a mechanised unit, it had accommodated its pace to that of a slow-moving French infantry corps on its right, with the result that the enemy were able to outflank and encircle the entire force. The 51st Division was pressed back into a cul-de-sac at St. Valéry; and though considerable numbers of men were able to escape down the cliffs to the ships awaiting them, a very large contingent was cut off and captured.

Still, the fight went on; for the 52nd Lowland Division had arrived from England, and the Canadians had landed in Brittany. But the French had reached the limit of their resistance: though another Weygand Plan was mooted, for a last stand in Brittany, it came to nothing. Two days later (on June 15th) the French asked for an armistice. The British Government immediately ordered the British troops home. They were withdrawn to Cherbourg and embarked for England; but the enemy were within three miles of the port when the last troopship left. The battle of France was over at last.

To deal with this final evacuation a third plan had been formulated, Plan 'Aerial'. There was a little more time to prepare this, for it did not begin to operate until June 16th, after French resistance had entirely collapsed and an armistice had been sought. It worked smoothly, and by August 15th nearly 140,000 British and 46,000 Allied troops were safe in England.

We shall have occasion to refer to these Allied troops again. Meanwhile let us return to Dover, and 'Dynamo'.

~*(6)*~

The reception areas of which mention has already been made were provided by the various Commands—Aldershot, Southern, Western and the most southerly district of Northern. These were already occupied by troops in training, some 300,000 men in all, roughly equivalent to the expected numbers of the returning B.E.F.; and the plan was that every man of these should be appointed personal host to a Dunkirk evacuee. He must give him food, find him a knife and fork, provide him with an extra blanket, and 'mother' him generally.

'Dynamo' fell naturally into two parts. The men must first be cleared as rapidly as possible from Dover to their reception area; then, since all units were hopelessly jumbled up, arrangements must be made for sorting them out. For this purpose 'redistribution areas' were established, in which men from the same division could all be reassembled in one place.

The evacuation of certain units, chiefly from the R.A.F. ground force and the Lines of Communication, had begun some time before the formation and occupation of the Perimeter—as early as May 20th, in fact. The full flood did not begin until the end of the month. Then men poured into Dover by night and day, and packed trains left, all round the clock, at intervals of about eight minutes. The Southern Railway employees, from high to low, did memorable work here, and indeed throughout the whole of the Company's system, which served most of the reception areas. The railway authorities acted in close accord with the Directorate of Transportation in the War Office.

The aid and comfort provided by another of His Majesty's Services, the Post Office at Dover, must also be given honourable mention here. More than a quarter of a million men, battered, half-clothed, leaderless, divided between apathetic exhaustion and incredulous joy over their own deliverance, were passed through that port, and the first thought of everyone of them on landing was to communicate with his friends and say he was safe. In normal times the average number of telegrams dealt with by Dover Head Post Office is 800 a day. During the Dunkirk period it ran as high as 4,000. As many as 1,500 were handed in at the little quayside office alone.

The Post Office staff worked all round the clock: they were too deeply moved by the poignancy of their task to worry about meals or time off. The faces of the gaunt, eager men who thrust the hastily scrawled telegrams across the counter or queued up at the telephone-booths established a priority all their own. So the men and girls at the teleprinters and switchboards, aided by many a willing volunteer from outside, worked till they dropped.

Telephoning presented a special problem. Most of the calls were trunk calls, and very often before they could be established the caller had been compelled to entrain and depart. But many a kindly operator contrived to complete the call on her own responsibility, while Authority looked the other way.

Another War Office Directorate, Supply and Transport, was also busily employed, in close conjunction with the Directorate of Ordnance Services, in augmenting the non-stop ferry service between Dunkirk and Dover, and in meeting the bodily needs of the famished B.E.F. (who, it will be remembered, had been on half-rations since May 23rd), not merely on the actual beaches but after arrival at Dover.

To this service the Supply and Transport Directorate was actually able to contribute some sea-going craft of its own, known as 'W.D. Fast Launches'. The normal duty of these vessels was to tow targets out to sea for the benefit of R.A. gunners engaged in off-shore practice. Eight of them were now dedicated to a sterner task, being fitted with machine-guns and supplied with naval ratings as gunners.

Trips by these little vessels began on May 31st, and were continued till the end of the evacuation. They did not go scatheless. The *Haig* was rammed and sunk, but was salved by the R.A.F. and sailed back to Ramsgate; not, however, before she had brought down an enemy aeroplane by Lewis gun fire. The *Kestrel* had her engines disabled, the *Marlborough* lost her propellers and rudder, and the *Pigeon* and *Swallow* were both rendered unseaworthy. But none was actually lost, and between them they evacuated over 2,000 British and Allied troops.

The all-important duty of conveying supplies to the troops on the beaches—and these extended for a full twelve miles—was also undertaken by this Directorate.

'The approximate net tonnage', we are told, 'of supplies dispatched from the Supply Reserve Depots during this period was 6,500 tons. When vessels began crossing to Dunkirk to bring back the B.E.F. they were whenever possible provided with a proportion of food and water. It was not until June 2nd that shipment to Northern France finally ceased, and then'—here follows the characteristic comment of a conscientious Quartermaster—'a considerable amount of stock was returned.'

The Supply and Transport Directorate was also made responsible for the feeding of the evacuees *en route* for their reception areas.

It was decided that, to avoid congestion, no provision of cooked meals would be possible at the ports. Brief halts were therefore arranged upon all the railway-routes to be traversed. At each halt a hot drink and a sandwich was issued, and also cigarettes and matches, supplemented by hard-boiled eggs and fruit as conditions improved. Altogether fourteen halting-points (*halte-repas*) were opened.

It may be added here, to illustrate the thoroughness of this improvised service, that it was found possible to distribute to the French troops arriving in Southampton an issue of their accustomed ration of red wine.

One other Directorate of the Quartermaster-General's department must also be mentioned for valuable first aid administered. This was the Ordnance, which set to work without delay to repair the sartorial ravages of a three-weeks' campaign under more than usually exposed conditions. ('The B.E.F.', says the Report, 'may be said to have arrived practically in rags, at least as regards the "Dynamo" groups.') But:

The returned B.E.F. and Allied troops were re-clothed to the home scale. Within a few months not only had the B.E.F. been brought up to the full home scale, but the Allied troops as well. Allied troops were provided by the War Office (or Allied Forces concerned) with worsted titles, such as 'France', 'Norge', 'Poland', and so on.

And how familiar we were destined to become with these!

~(7)~

It remains only to say a word regarding the troops of our Allies which accompanied the B.E.F. to England.

Incidentally, the one event not foreseen by the Quartermaster-General's department, in its appreciation of the situation on May 20th, had been the arrival of these troops in such overwhelming numbers. It had been expected that not more than 5,000 of them would have to be accommodated, but as we know, more than 100,000 participated in the Dunkirk evacuation alone, of whom the great majority were French.

The French evacuee troops fell into three categories. There were those who had been shipped to England as the quickest and safest method of getting them back to France, where they could be added to Weygand's forces south of the Somme. These were accommodated during their brief sojourn here at Southampton, Bournemouth, Weymouth and Plymouth, where the inhabitants were asked to entertain them as personal guests. In every case the accommodation offered was actually greater than that required.

Then there were those who, inspired by their own patriotic fervour (and also by General de Gaulle's gallant refusal to admit that France was defeated) desired to be quartered and trained in England against the day when they should be able to join in the reoccupation and rescue of their native land.

Finally there were those (chiefly sailors) who, after the final collapse of French resistance, evinced a desire only to return home and enjoy the dubious blessings of life under the Vichy regime. These were ultimately repatriated, but not without difficulty, for no British shipping was at that time available. However, certain French vessels were released from American ports and in due course some 20,000 of these short-sighted mariners were shipped to Marseilles.

For those of our Allies who had decided to stay and share our fortunes at this dark hour much elaborate preparation had to be made. The actual number to be accommodated was uncertain, for scattered military units continued to arrive from all parts of Europe for many months. It was therefore decided to allot a definite area to each nationality. The French were sent to South Lancashire, the Poles to Scotland, the Belgians to Tenby, the Foreign Legion to Trentham, and the Czechs to West Lancashire, all incidentally, except for the Poles, under Western Command.[1]

All of this involved an immense amount of work for the Army departments concerned, especially the Directorate of Quartering. The evacuation from the Dunkirk beaches was the largest and most complicated of these undertakings, and imposed the hardest labour upon those responsible for it. That that labour was not entirely in vain may be gathered from the following letter, written to the Quartermaster-General at the War Office, Sir Walter Venning, on June 14th, 1940, by General Lelong, Chief of the French Mission in London:

Dear Sir Walter,

At the moment when most of the French troops landed in this country from Flanders have already found their way back to France, the time has come to thank the British Army, and in particular your Department, for the help that has been given unhesitatingly, to the full, and sympathetically.

The achievement of this masterpiece of improvised organisation is a success that all Services concerned can look upon with pride.

Please convey to all officers and men who have contributed to it my sincerest thanks, in the name of the French Army.

Yours sincerely,

A. LELONG

---

[1] This applied only to military units: sailors would require to be stationed near their natural element, the sea. Thus there was ultimately a Polish Naval Training Camp at Okehampton, near Plymouth, a Dutch Naval Cadet College at Falmouth, and a colony of Belgian fishermen at Brixham in Devonshire.

CHAPTER IX

UPHILL

~(1)~

ON June 14th, 1940, the Germans had entered Paris. On the 16th the
Reynaud Government made way for a Pétain-Weygand combination,
which issued immediate orders to the French Army to cease fire and
asked Hitler for an armistice. On June 21st, at Compiègne, in the
wagon-lit railway coach in which Foch had dictated terms to the
German delegates in November 1918 (and which had since stood in
the forecourt of the Invalides as a reminder of victory), the Armistice
of 1940 was signed by the French delegates.

On June 24th another armistice was signed, this time with Mussolini, who, deciding that it was high time that he came to the assistance
of the winning side, had declared war upon the Allies on June 10th.

Britain only was left in the path of the conqueror, and it was the
genuine expectation of the world, whether hostile or neutral, that
Britain too would have to ask for terms. But Britain thought otherwise, and, inspired by her Prime Minister, was doggedly determined
not to accept the present disaster as final. On June 18th, in an historic
speech to the House of Commons, Winston Churchill put into words
the sentiment and determination which animated the country as a
whole—to fight on, and on, whatever the cost. The truly desperate
nature of the situation was known to few at the time, but the decision,
it is tolerably certain, would have been the same in any case. So with
that speech and resolution we embarked, though none could have
foreseen it at the time, upon perhaps the most glorious, and certainly
the most heroic, period of our long national existence.

~(2)~

The first thing to do was to appraise the situation, summarise our liabilities, and decide what assets, if any, there were to set against them.

Of these last there were at least two. They were cold comfort, but definitely of value. In the first place we had no longer anyone to consider but ourselves. There was no further need to consider the susceptibilities of an Ally or contribute troops, sorely needed elsewhere, to the defence of other people's territory. Our defence scheme could now be planned solely with a view to the protection of the British Commonwealth and Empire, which meant that we could present a front fortified by a single purpose and undivided counsels. Napoleon had once declared that he would rather fight a campaign against two first-class generals acting in so-called unison than against a single second-class general operating with an absolutely free hand. (Or, as Dogberry once put it to Verges, 'If two men ride on a horse, one must ride behind'.) The same dictum applied with equal force to allied nations. Second-class though British resources might be at this dark moment, we were at least unencumbered by conflicting interests.

Our second asset, unpalatable but wholesome beyond words, was that during the past weeks we had learned some invaluable lessons, by the infallible method of trial and error, in the art of modern warfare, especially in the department of organisation and preparedness.

Still, the debit side of the account was overwhelming, both in fact and implication. The B.E.F. were home again, after one of the greatest rearguard actions in military annals, but they had left all their equipment and their armour behind them. Of the new divisions training at home only one was ready for service. In the whole of England there were only fifty tanks.

Our overworked Navy, suddenly deprived of the assistance of the French Navy, the second strongest in Europe, was fully occupied in fighting the battles both of the Atlantic and the Mediterranean. Our air defences were in a parlous condition. Spitfires and heavy anti-aircraft guns only began coming in numbers off the lines about midsummer, and priority for the latter had to be given to ships. Luckily the Luftwaffe, designed essentially for army co-operation, were extremely short of trained night-bombers: otherwise Hitler might well have attempted the invasion of Britain immediately after Dunkirk instead of wasting his time in Paris.

We were faced with three deadly dangers, two immediate and one prospective—of invasion, of concentrated air attack, and of starvation by submarine blockade.

Immediate invasion seemed the most likely choice, for the simple reason that in June 1940 there was little or nothing to prevent it—except that the shortage of enemy night-bombers was not then fully realised. If Hitler struck, struck at once, with the initiative and choice of landing-place entirely in his hands, a force of 150,000 men, it was calculated, escorted by the German Navy and covered by the Luftwaffe, could be set upon our shores without any serious resistance from our land forces.

Plainly it was high time that something of the true state of affairs should be made known to the country as a whole. The almost miraculous Dunkirk evacuation had relieved public anxiety to such an extent that the operation had been hailed as a victory, and a spirit of quite unjustifiable optimism was in the air. The public in fact was due for a shock. The difficulty was to administer this without administering at the same time a most encouraging tonic to the enemy, who were extremely short of reliable information as to our actual state of preparedness.

It was therefore decided that the Secretary of State for War should call a meeting of the Press at the highest level—newspaper proprietors and editors-in-chief—and present them with a candid picture of the situation, the gist of which they could pass on to their readers in words calculated to rouse them from their present complacency without unduly enlightening the enemy.

The meeting took place on June 18th, directly after the French surrender. It was addressed by Sir John Dill, the new C.I.G.S., who spoke frankly of the high probability of attempted invasion and of our inability to resist it. We had, he said, 1,250,000 men under training, so far as men could be regarded as under training who were restricted to imaginary equipment and dummy weapons. We were particularly short of rifles and small-arms ammunition, though we were importing some from America; but until the time-lag could be overtaken the situation was critical. He spoke also of the fighting south of the Somme, still in progress and already outlined in these pages, but of which little or nothing had been heard in England; and of the hazardous decision reluctantly but resolutely taken by the War Cabinet, to send to France certain promised divisions with the full knowledge that these might become involved in a final French *débâcle* and might never return. However, we had kept our word and sent them. Fortunately, we had got them back again without too serious a loss.

Our defence scheme for the present was to organise mobile brigades ready to be dispatched at short notice to any threatened quarter.

Coastal defences were being constructed at intensive speed, and the L.D.V. were being exercised as fully as possible in their unfamiliar duties. Our hope and determination, the C.I.G.S. concluded, was to fight the enemy to a standstill, and having done that build up a great new expeditionary force of millions and embark upon the reoccupation of France and the invasion of Germany. These brave words were destined to be fulfilled to the last detail, but they could only have been uttered at that time by a man of supreme courage and faith.

⟶(3)⟵

Two immediate and pressing tasks, if we were to survive our present dangers and build for future victory, now confronted the War Cabinet and the War Office. The first was to expand our Army to a size comparable with that of the enemy; the second was to review the whole strategic situation in the light of the Flanders campaign, and especially of the almost illimitable possibilities now presented by the complete mechanisation of warfare.

As a first step to increasing the size of the Army, several age-groups of the Army Class—this was the name given to all those rendered liable to compulsory military service by the National Service (Armed Forces) Act of September 2nd, 1939—were immediately called up for duty, 132,000 in June and 141,000 in July. Indeed, more were called up in the five weeks following the invasion of Belgium than in the first four months of the war.

By the end of June 1940 the strength of the Army in Great Britain was something over 1,500,000, and included the returned B.E.F. These were all embodied, full-time soldiers, and excluded the Home Guard (as the L.D.V. were now called), which stood at 1,400,000. 147,000 of them had been furnished by the Army Class. Over 8,000 cadets were undergoing training for commissions in the O.C.T.U.s.[1] As an evidence of the development of new ideas, a Parachute School had begun training at Ringway, in Cheshire.

For anti-aircraft defence we had about 1,900 guns,[2] ranging from the 4·5-inch and 3·7-inch to the light Bofors 40 mm.

Throughout the country the number of divisions under training was twenty-six, two of them armoured. Few, as already noted, were fully equipped, if equipped at all.

But these were mere instalments of the force required if we were to fight the German Army single-handed. Something upon a far more

[1] See Chap. XII on Army Training. [2] See Chap. XVII.

comprehensive scale was needed. In addition to men for the Armed Forces, enormous provision of manpower had to be made for the construction of the new engines of war, for the building of ships, the output of coal, and the Civil Defence organisations, such as Air-Raid Precautions and National Fire Services. These last two constituted a novel and unfamiliar drain upon our human resources.

In other words, we were faced as a nation with a situation unprecedented in our history—the necessity of numbering the people, and of mobilising every able-bodied man and woman in the prosecution of a total war.

We were handicapped from the start by the fact that despite frequent and additional inducements in the matter of improved pay, accommodation, and freedom to marry offered during Mr. Hore-Belisha's tenure of office as Secretary of State for War, numbers in the Army had fallen far below peace establishment. The range of these inducements, naturally, was limited by the money available to attract recruits, and when it came to a contest for priority in this respect the Army invariably ran third in a field of three. In the spring of 1939 our voluntary Regular Army of 209,700 men (including officers) had fallen nearly 20,000 short of its quota.

It was particularly short of what are known in military language as 'Tradesmen'—that is to say, such skilled craftsmen as artificers, mechanics, and electricians. These were not generally recruited from civilian sources, but from Apprentice Tradesmen's Schools maintained by the War Office.

By 1936 it had already become obvious that future wars, if they came, would be conducted upon a fully mechanised basis. This meant that the demand for army tradesmen would be immeasurably increased. It was not until 1938, however, that financial authority could be obtained for such an increase, modest though it was. On September 1st, 1939, on a peace establishment of 979 armament artificers, the most highly skilled of all army tradesmen, the Army was 410 short.

The doubling of the Territorial Army a few months previously, although it was brought about with gratifying speed, had created certain grievous problems of administration which were never quite overtaken.

It will be remembered that this doubling had been effected by bringing the original Territorial force up to strength and then creating an equal number of new divisions. Unfortunately, though perhaps inevitably, recruits preferred to enlist in the combatant rather than the administrative ranks, with the result that the new divisions were found to be heavily deficient of Royal Army Service Corps and Royal Ordnance Corps units—the very people, in fact, whose duty it was to transport, equip and feed them.

The explanation was simple enough. These young men had joined the Army not to practise their regular occupations but to get away from them. They wanted to fight the Germans, not to repair tank-tracks or wind armatures. Even in the case of those who did enlist as tradesmen, it was more than probable that many would eventually be combed out and sent back to industry, where they were badly needed.

However, these difficulties were gradually overcome by conscription, by the abolition of the Territorial Army as such for the duration, and the merging of the whole British Army into one. This made it possible to direct recruits into any unit for which they might be required, and so achieve a correct 'balance of arms' in each division.

Not much more could be done throughout this period (1938–9), for it must be remembered that the prime necessity of the moment was to fill up gaps with all speed, concentrating on quantity rather than quality or special aptitude for a particular job.

The second period began with the actual outbreak of war in September 1939. The Army now had to direct its energies to two special ends—first the dispatch of the B.E.F. and its reinforcements to Flanders, the conveyance of reinforcements to overseas garrisons such as Malta and Gibraltar, and the mobilising of new units at home; secondly, the solving of the problems of organisation and administration arising from the hasty expansion of the Territorial Army and the equally hasty embodiment of the Army Class. We had the men: now we had to sort them out and assign them to duties consonant with their skill, inclination (where possible), and medical category.

There was considerable need for such action, for already there were complaints in Parliament and Press that throughout the Army innumerable square pegs were serving in round holes; that skilled workmen were scrubbing floors or acting as mess-waiters, or that men of inferior physique were being allotted to arduous front-line duties while their more robust comrades occupied office stools. Making due allowance for the emotional stress of that anxious time, there was no denying that there was considerable ground for some of these assertions, and fresh efforts were made to unravel the situation. A card index system had been instituted, but owing to the impossibility of keeping it up to date its use was discontinued, though not before it had discovered in the Army some 15,000 skilled or partially skilled tradesmen. Commands were now urged to round up all tradesmen within their units and see that they were suitably employed. Those for whom no such employment could be found within their own units were to be reported immediately to the War Office, in order that they might be posted elsewhere.

Army tradesmen themselves had been divided into five groups, according to the relative degree of skill required of them, and this helped further to clarify the needs of the situation. Training centres were established, with the aid of the Ministry of Labour and the Board of Education, in which facilities were provided for the training of 10,000 tradesmen at one time, and a Special Military Training Branch was set up in the War Office to expedite the matter. Finally plans were made for withdrawing a certain number of skilled trades-men and specialist instructors from the B.E.F. to help in training the units at home.

From all of this it will be realised that the implications of mechan-ised warfare had now been fully grasped, and that a real effort was being made to meet the enormously increased need for highly trained mechanics, electricians and other specialists.

Of course, there were the usual priority difficulties. The Royal Navy and Air Force came first, and the Army could expect to find but few skilled technicians in its Army Class intake. Indeed, matters were the other way round, for the Ministry of Labour was pressing to have many army tradesmen returned to industry. Some 8,000 of these were so released early in 1940.

It should be added here that in October 1940, owing to the necessity of evacuating certain branches of the War Office to safer areas, the Directorate of Organisation was moved from London to Cheltenham, at a time when close liaison with the General Staff would have been of the utmost value. It may further be added that these multifarious arrangements had to be organised and carried out amid the daily and nightly visitations of the Luftwaffe, for the blitz was now at its height. About this time we actually had to adventure valuable warships up the Thames, to implement the barrage.

~*(4)*~

Steps were also taken to deal with the admitted fact that some men were being allotted to military duties beyond their strength, while others were retained in comparative sinecures much below their capabilities.

Before the war the Army had been graded under four different medical categories, each of which was supposed to qualify a man for a certain type of duty and no other. The general idea was, first, that every man should find himself in an arm of the service for which he was physically suited, and secondly, that no man should be lost to the Army who could do a useful day's work of *some* kind therein.

But this grading was found to be insufficiently comprehensive, and it was decided to divide men into such categories as would make a clear distinction, not only as to the arm in which a man should serve but the area as well. The following five categories were therefore established, which it may be interesting to study:

A. Men fit for service in any arm or in any theatre of war.

B. Men fit for service in certain arms only, or for employment in Base or Lines of Communication areas.

C. Men fit for home service only.

D. Men temporarily unfit.

E. Men permanently unfit. These last were to be discharged from the Army altogether.

A man at the top or the bottom of this list was in a single definite category: in the one case he 'could endure severe strain' and be employed on any duty; in the other he was fit for no duty at all, and must go. But Category B was a most elastic affair: indeed, it was ultimately divided into eight subdivisions. A man, for instance, might be able to see both to fire a rifle and drive a vehicle; or only to drive; or only to see, without being able to shoot or drive. Or he might suffer from a degree of deafness which precluded him from one type of duty but not from another. Even if he was an individual of low mentality he might still be usefully employed upon some routine duty as an orderly or sanitary man. But whatever the category or sub-category in which he was placed, he knew exactly what duties he could be called upon to perform, and where.

It should be added that all these categories were subject to constant review, and a man could at any time be promoted to a higher category, or downgraded to a lower, or out of the Army altogether.

By careful application of these methods men were gradually allotted to their appropriate duties, square pegs eliminated, and manpower employed with an increasing degree of economy.

In further pursuance of the policy of getting the right man into the right job, a novel and interesting experiment was tried, in the shape of psychological selection tests.

An early and simple form was introduced in October 1939, to assist in the selection of men with special aptitude for certain types of anti-aircraft work. They proved successful, and were adopted for general use in Anti-Aircraft Training Battalions. As an example of the method here employed, a man's quickness in grasping a situation was tested by giving him a limited glimpse (say three seconds) of an approaching aircraft depicted upon a miniature film screen, and then asking him what he had been able to observe, within that brief period, of the make, altitude, direction, and speed of the craft in question.

Further discussions were held (in which the Industrial Health Research Board took part), and during 1940 a series of further simple tests was introduced into various army training units, designed first, to gauge a man's ordinary 'intelligence' and secondly his 'mechanical aptitude'.

In January 1941 proposals were initiated by the Command Psychiatrist, Northern Command, that for the purpose of the more efficient use of manpower, both testing and disposal should be under the control of the Adjutant-General, and that a special department of the War Office should be set up for the purpose.

These proposals were amplified later by the same psychiatrist (Lieut.-Colonel G. R. Hargreaves, R.A.M.C.) and the scheme, after being agreed to by the G.O.C. Northern Command, was considered by an advisory panel of consultants, set up at the instance of the Director-General of Army Medical Services under his chairmanship. The members of this panel toured the commands and held detailed investigations, and as a result of their recommendations the Directorate for the Selection of Personnel came into permanent being in July 1941.

After July 1942 the manpower scheme took a more or less final form. It was decided that the centralisation within the War Office itself of particulars regarding potential tradesmen had become too cumbersome an arrangement; so the collection and maintenance of such particulars was relegated to the various Record Offices. A further step was the establishment of the General Service Corps, whereby all men were posted initially to Primary Training Centres, at which their primary training could be carried on concurrently with the selection procedure. This action was rendered inevitable by the fact that the Ministry of Labour had decided that no more members of the electrical or mechanical trades could be liberated from industry. It was only after a man's capacity or potential had been assessed and compared with the Army's requirements, that he was posted to corps, and began the training special to that corps.

One more source of manpower (if it could be so described) remained to be tapped, by the expansion of the Auxiliary Territorial Service, the Women's Army.

The A.T.S. had originally been formed for the purpose of employing women in certain administration services of the Army, the idea being that every woman enlisting in the A.T.S. would release a soldier for more active duties. There will be more to say about the A.T.S. at a later stage in our story,[1] but by the end of the period just described (1940–1) upwards of 25,000 women were being employed in Signals, and as drivers, cooks, clerks and orderlies. Five thousand more were undergoing training in operational duties. In due course, many of these performed valuable service in the Air Defences of Great Britain as actual members of Anti-Aircraft Batteries.

Such, in brief outline, is the story of those uphill months during which the British people, isolated, disarmed, but indomitable, set themselves to repair the immediate consequences of disaster and build up their resources anew, while never for one moment relinquishing their determination to strike back at the earliest possible moment.

That opportunity, or rather necessity, presented itself all too soon with the entry of Italy into the war. Already the Mediterranean was closed to British merchant shipping, and unless we were prepared to fight a campaign in North Africa, and that immediately, we were in acute danger of losing the Suez Canal and the whole of our life-line to the East.

So the meagre garrison of our Island was cut to the bone, and every available reinforcement sent out to General Wavell in Egypt; with the result that our scene of action is now transferred from Britain to the Middle East. We were by no means ready for such a venture, either with men or equipment, but at least we had the lessons of experience behind us.

⇀≺(5)≻⇀

As we are now approaching a point where it will be necessary to make a closer study of the revolutionary effect upon the conduct of modern warfare brought about by scientific research and discovery, it might be well here to recapitulate the basic principles underlying the organisation and administration of the British Army. These, it will be noted, have changed but little in the last twenty years—a proof both of their soundness and elasticity.

[1] See Chap. XX, Sec. 2.

We are already familiar with the circumstances in which the Imperial General Staff and Army Council were created upon the recommendations of the Esher Committee in 1903.[1] Two world wars have been fought since then, and the scope of their duties has at times been magnified correspondingly. It will suffice here to mention that so far as the Army is concerned, decisions at the highest level regarding its form and use are determined by the Cabinet, assisted by the recommendations of the Defence Committee, which is composed of the Prime Minister (or President), a Chairman, the three Secretaries of State and Chiefs-of-Staff of the Fighting Services, the Chancellor of the Exchequer, the Secretaries of State for Foreign Affairs, Minister of Labour and Minister of Supply, together with the Permanent Under-Secretary for Foreign Affairs. Dominion Ministers may at any time be summoned as members.

The government of the Army is vested in the Crown. The command of the Army is placed in the hands of the Army Council, composed normally as follows:

President: The Secretary of State for War.

Vice-President: The Parliamentary Under-Secretary of State for War (usually in the House of Lords).

First Military Member: The Chief of the Imperial General Staff.

Second Military Member: The Adjutant-General to the Forces.

Third Military Member: The Quartermaster-General to the Forces.

Fourth Military Member: Vice-Chief of the Imperial General Staff.

Fifth Military Member: Deputy Chief of the Imperial General Staff.

Finance Member: The Financial Secretary.

Secretary of the Army Council: The Permanent Under-Secretary of State for War.

(These, needless to say, are the full and formal titles of these officials. In ordinary practice each is usually referred to by the initials of his office: S. of S., C.I.G.S. and so on.)

Coming to the Army itself, the responsibilities of a General Officer Commanding-in-Chief fall under two heads: Command and Training of troops, and Administration. With regard to command and training he exercises his powers through the various divisional and brigade commanders under him. At the head of his administrative staff is the Major-General in charge of Administration, or M.G.A. Speaking generally, administration includes practically everything that concerns the life and purpose of an army except its weapons and actual training for or employment in battle. This comes under the heading of Operations.

[1] See Chap. IV, Sec. 3 (pp. 31-4).

It is interesting and important to follow what is known in the British Army as the Chain of Command, which is designed to fulfil a policy of progressive decentralisation of authority. The first (one might say the golden) rule to be served is that the commander of any unit, from an army downward, although he is responsible for everything in connection with his command, whether it be training, fighting, or administration, should not try to do everything himself, but must apportion the responsibility to his subordinates, and then by personal supervision and inspection satisfy himself that these not only know their duties but carry them out efficiently.

Descending the scale through the various formation levels until we arrive at the infantry battalion or cavalry regiment, we will in every case find an officer or officers representing, in a minor degree, three main sources of authority—the General or 'G' Staff, responsible for operations, intelligence and training; the Adjutant-General's Branch, or 'A' Staff, primarily concerned with Army personnel and its discipline, documentation, medical welfare and educational services; and the Quartermaster-General's Branch, or 'Q' Staff, concerned with the Army's needs in the way of food, quartering, clothing, equipment, stores and movement. Each of these officers is thus connected by an unbroken chain to the supreme head of a particular branch on the Army Council.

Further down the scale, in an infantry brigade for example, the same principle is followed. The Brigadier has under him a Brigade Major, or 'G' Staff Officer, whose duties are concerned with questions of fighting, training and intelligence; and a Staff Captain who combines within himself the 'A' and 'Q' Staff work.

Similarly, in an infantry battalion, although the commander is responsible for the efficient discharge of all regimental functions, he is in practice left as free as possible, while 'G', 'A' and 'Q' duties are performed by the Adjutant, who is assisted by the Quartermaster over 'Q' duties.

The main idea throughout is to keep operational and administrative duties separate and distinct, so that the commander, whatever his status and rank, shall be left free to devote himself to his operational duties without undue distraction.

To that end much thought and ingenuity have been devoted to the simplification, by the employment of certain modern business devices, of what may be called paper-work in army administration.

An army commander must constantly be aware of the numbers, equipment, fighting efficiency, general health and morale of the forces under his control. Formerly this knowledge could be acquired only by close study of reports or statistics, or by perpetual 'briefing'—both of which occupied much time and distracted the commander from his purely operational duties.

Instead, each army headquarters (and for that matter almost any headquarters of importance) is now equipped with a 'graph' room, upon the walls of which the whole internal economy of the formation in question is illustrated in succinct and vivid form by a series of coloured graphs and diagrams, constantly corrected and kept up to date, from which a trained eye can gather almost at a glance any administrative information of which its owner may be in need.

These devices are not, of course, confined to armies in the field. They are in general use in the War Office and throughout the home commands. Let us consider a few examples.

Here is a large diagram in the graph room of the department of the Adjutant-General. It presents to us a row of rectangular figures of equal width, standing side by side, like pillars or columns, upon a horizontal base, at intervals of six inches. Each six inches represents six months of the war: there are thus some ten or twelve columns in all. The height of each column denotes the total fighting strength of army personnel at a given period. A portion of the column is coloured blue, the remainder red. The blue indicates the proportion of men compulsorily enlisted, the red of volunteers.

An examination of the diagram reveals that the column standing upon the section which represents the second half of 1940 is the tallest of the series: this reminds us that the period of the highest intake of personnel during the war was the six months succeeding Dunkirk. Nearly four-fifths of this column is coloured blue, indicating that the ratio of compulsory to voluntary enlistment at this time was roughly 4 : 1. The actual figures are written at the side—809 and 252, denoting thousands—in other words, a total of 1,061,000.

A closer examination reveals that with the advance of the years the columns grow progressively shorter, indicating that our Army strength is dwindling. This, we note, is not so much due to a falling-off in the intake as to the fact that the pillar itself has, so to speak, sunk partly underground—below the level, that is, of its horizontal base. This submerged portion represents wastage due to various causes, each denoted by a different colour—battle casualties, men sick, or men discharged. The most deeply sunken column is that of the second half of 1942, when our battle casualties were 90,000. During and after 1945 the columns sink deeper still. This means that demobilisation has set in.

Summing up, the reader will appreciate that the Adjutant-General, by studying this particular diagram, can quickly estimate:

1. The strength of Army personnel at any given period, and the extent to which it must be reinforced.
2. The intensity of military operations at one period or another, as indicated by the number of casualties. By comparing this diagram with others he may be able to determine to what cause those casualties were due—possibly to inferiority in some particular weapon.
3. The general health of the Army. By comparing this with graphs denoting the various theatres of war, he may be able to decide in which of these theatres an overhaul of the medical services may be called for.

Other graphs are on a smaller and more detailed scale. One may indicate the strength of the various ranks in a single battalion, and so reveal, by the diminution of this or that colour-band, that there is a present shortage of 2nd lieutenants or corporals. Another may divide a formation into its age-groups, and furnish conspicuous evidence, in the form of a too-wide 'brown band', that it is time to weed out some of the 'over forties'.

Perhaps one of the most interesting and illuminating of these diagrams is that which deals with courts-martial. Once again we have a row of columns, the height of each denoting the number of courts-martial held in a given area during a given period. If one of these columns stands noticeably higher than its predecessor, the G.O.C. proceeds to examine its texture. The various colours of which it is comprised denote the nature of the offences committed—desertion, absence without leave, refusal to obey an order, and other and lesser forms of sin, such as 'improperly dressed on parade'—and if the colour which indicates a large number of desertions or a growing tendency to insubordination preponderates, the G.O.C. decides that something is wrong in that area, and orders an inquiry.

Such then are examples of the labour-saving devices by which army administration is simplified today, and the ever-growing demand for conciseness and dispatch satisfied.

CHAPTER X

THE MIDDLE EAST
AND WAVELL

(1)

I⊤ was not until the opening of General Wavell's campaign against the Italians in the Western Desert, in December 1940, that the British Army had a real opportunity to test and demonstrate its efficiency under conditions of modernised warfare; and to these operations we must now devote some attention.

The Middle East Command was created in August 1939. It comprised Egypt, the Sudan, Palestine, and Cyprus. Within this vast area General Wavell exercised control over the land forces, and was responsible for the distribution of such troops and material as were available, as well as for the preparation of war plans, which had to be drawn up in co-operation with the local commanders in British Somaliland, Aden, Iraq, and on the shores of the Persian Gulf.

Under the direction of the Chiefs-of-Staff he was also responsible, in conjunction with the Commander-in-Chief of the British Naval Forces in the Mediterranean and the Naval Commander-in-Chief East Indies Station, for co-ordinating war plans on a wider scale still—namely, with the French in North Africa, Syria and French Somaliland, and with the Turkish and (contingently) Greek Governments.

It will thus be seen that from the point of view of comprehensive planning Allied arrangements in this widespread theatre were well in hand. The troops essential to their execution, however, were sadly lacking, both in numbers and equipment. They consisted at first for the most part of Commonwealth troops—splendid material, but only partially trained and half-equipped. Indeed, General Wavell mentions in his Dispatch that the Egyptian Army was in many respects better supplied than most of the British forces. This, of course, was a mere reflection of the state of affairs at home, where such resources as we possessed were being devoted to the equipment and mobilisation of the B.E.F.

Fortunately, Italy did not enter the war until June 1940, so the situation in the Middle East remained quiescent for some months—during the period of the 'Phoney War', in fact—and the opportunity was taken by General Wavell to train such reinforcements as reached him, consolidate his resources to the best of his ability, and in particular to bring administration under the direct jurisdiction of the Middle East Command.

This last was only achieved after considerable argument and delay. Upon the establishment of Middle East Command in August 1939 General Wavell's staff contained but one administration officer. This meant in effect that in such a widely scattered parish—Egypt, Palestine, and the Sudan—administration had to remain the responsibility of the various individual commands concerned, for it was obviously impossible to gather all the threads into the hands of a single overworked individual in Cairo. In other words, though operational action was vested solely in Middle East Command, control of administration was in the hands of a number of separate commands among which there could be little hope of a settled or unanimous policy.

It was this divorce between operational and administrative control which was to a certain extent responsible, as we shall see, for the loss of British Somaliland. This Protectorate was under the administrative control of the Colonial Office, which meant that General Wavell was debarred from planning for its defence except under the direction of that institution. He was anxious to improve communications and increase his tiny garrison there to an extent commensurate with the French effort at Jibuti, and was confident that if this were done both French and British Somaliland could be held; but he was compelled to apply for sanction and financial approval to the War Office, who referred the matter to the Colonial Office, with consequent and inevitable delays and waste of precious time.

However, at long last, on June 10th, 1940, Middle East Command was permitted to assume complete control of the administration of its own forces. By this time we were on the brink of war with Italy.

The disparity in numbers between the Italian and British forces in North Africa and Palestine by the end of that month was startling. It should be remembered that the defence of the Middle Eastern theatre had originally been an Anglo-French undertaking, with the French troops heavily preponderating. With the collapse of France and the setting-up of the Vichy Government, the French Armies in Syria and North Africa surrendered at once, though General Legentilhomme, in French Somaliland, held out gallantly for a month longer.

Thus General Wavell found himself bereft at a single stroke of almost every one of his Allies, excepting a Polish force some 4,000 strong, previously stationed with the French in Syria, certain French sub-units, and a party of Czechs.

It was reckoned in June 1940 that some 415,000 Italian troops were distributed in Libya and Italian East Africa. Against these General Wavell could only array a force of 42,016 in Egypt, 7,387 in the Sudan, 42,513 in Palestine, 23,098 in East Africa, with inconsiderable garrisons in Aden, British Somaliland and Cyprus; some 118,000 men in all.[1]

Very little equipment had so far arrived in the Middle East, and no single unit or formation was fully furnished. There was a dangerous lack of anti-aircraft and anti-tank guns, as well as other artillery. Tracked vehicles were in a serious state of disrepair. General Wavell mentions that in July, while at Mersa Matruh near the Egyptian western frontier, he was forced to withdraw many of these for overhaul, while of his 300 tanks only 200 were normally available. The enemy were superior, too, in the air, but only in numbers.

The whole-hearted co-operation of the Egyptian Army, moreover, was at this period more than problematical, for naturally the political situation had been profoundly affected by the withdrawal of France from the arena; and the Egyptian Government had not yet made up its mind at what point resistance to the enemy should begin. Yet individual Egyptian units did good service, in the defence of Mersa Matruh against air attack, and also of the naval base at Alexandria.

[1] On a percentage basis, approximately: British Army 47 per cent, Indian Army and Colonial Forces 36 per cent, Australian 11·5 per cent, New Zealand 5·5 per cent.

~·(2)·~

At first, General Wavell was kept fully occupied in maintaining a defensive front in Egypt and guarding certain vital points in the Sudan and Kenya. With the loss of Jibuti, however, and the retention of French Somaliland by Vichy, it became obvious that British Somaliland at any rate could no longer be held by the forces at his disposal. So, in August 1940, after some spirited rear-guard actions on the part of its little garrison of a few battalions against an Italian force of seven brigade groups, the country was evacuated.

The loss of this Protectorate, occurring as it did less than three months after the Dunkirk withdrawal, was an undoubted blow to British pride and prestige, and was criticised both at home and abroad to an extent out of all proportion to its military importance. General Wavell himself had some shrewd comments to make. The temporary loss of Somaliland, he said, was due to four main causes. The first of these was 'our insistence upon running our Colonies on the cheap, especially in matters of defence'. The second was the almost morbid anxiety of the War Cabinet to avoid impairing our relations with Italy by anything in the shape of conspicuous preparation for defence in the Mediterranean: this resulted in long delays in the arrival of reinforcements and refusal to permit an adequate intelligence service to be set up. The third was the inadequacy of Berbera as a port and the lack of any movement to improve it, despite strong recommendations submitted as far back as 1936. The fourth, naturally, was the collapse of French resistance in Jibuti.

During this period all available equipment and troops were being retained in the United Kingdom against the threat of invasion; and it was not until the second half of September that reinforcements in men and material began to reach the Middle East in any quantity.

Towards the close of the year sufficient troops had arrived, both from home and the Empire, to reduce the odds against us to two to one. This, General Wavell decided, was good enough, and since the enemy showed no disposition to advance beyond Sidi Barrani, he determined to take the offensive himself, in the Western Desert.[1]

Hitherto he had maintained his principal defensive line at Mersa Matruh, some hundred miles inside the Egyptian frontier and two hundred west of Alexandria, with a small covering force at Sidi Barrani some seventy miles further west. His planning of the projected offensive is worthy of study, for it included many elements of what

[1] See Map 3, p. 120.

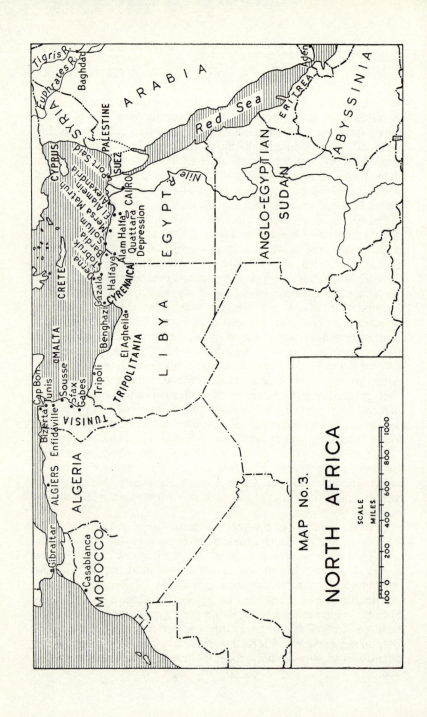

MAP No. 3.

NORTH AFRICA

SCALE

MILES

100 0   200   400   600   800   1000

was to become the recognised pattern for mechanised warfare. The attack was to be delivered without warning, and was to be of the 'non-stop' variety, like the German thrust for the English Channel on May 10th. The operation was not only planned in complete detail by General Wavell's principal lieutenant at the time, General Sir Richard O'Connor, but was carefully rehearsed over ground specially prepared to reproduce the features of the actual arena of battle, including replicas of the entrenched camps in which the enemy had established himself. Paper work was reduced to a minimum, and few orders were written down or issued; the plan of the battle was worked out by verbal consultation between the leaders concerned. The fact that an operation was contemplated at all was concealed not only from the enemy but from the troops themselves. Not more than a dozen senior commanders and officers were aware of the plan until shortly before its execution, and the rehearsals of the battle were represented to the men as a routine training exercise.

The total force engaged consisted of some 31,000 men, with 120 guns and 275 tanks. It included the 7th Armoured Division, destined to achieve world-wide fame as 'The Desert Rats', the equally famous 4th Indian Division (consisting roughly of fifty per cent Indian and fifty per cent British troops), an infantry brigade, a battalion of the Royal Tank Regiment, and a force contributed by the Matruh garrison. The whole force was either mechanised or motorised.

On the administrative side, having regard to the limited amount of transport available, care was taken to establish dumps of ammunition, petrol and water along the 70 miles which separated the British lines at Mersa Matruh from those of the enemy at Sidi Barrani. This was effected without interference from our complacent adversaries.

The battles which followed, and the astonishing success which they achieved, need only be briefly summarised here. The first phase of the operation, which may be called the battle of Sidi Barrani and began the night of December 7th–8th, 1940, resulted in the destruction of the greater part of five enemy divisions, the capture of 38,000 prisoners—a total considerably greater than that of the whole of the attacking force—and 400 guns. British casualties were about 500. From the equipment point of view the infantry tanks, cruiser tanks, and the 25-pounder guns proved themselves to be of excellent quality.[1]

The second phase consisted of the encirclement and capture of Bardia. The forces available now included the 6th Australian

[1] The whole question of equipment will be fully considered in a later chapter.

Division. The final assault was launched on January 3rd, 1941. Complete victory was achieved within three days, and 45,000 prisoners and 462 guns were taken.

Without a moment's delay General Wavell pressed on to his third objective, the considerable seaport of Tobruk. The 7th Battalion the Royal Tank Regiment was now reduced to sixteen tanks. This involved the bold employment of infantry and the increased expenditure of ammunition in their protection; so preparations were made to provide artillery support on a heavy scale. The necessary preparations, which like all General Wavell's undertakings were thorough to the last detail, occupied the next fortnight, and the main assault was delivered upon January 21st. The whole of Tobruk was in our hands next day: nearly 30,000 more prisoners were taken, with 236 guns and eighty-seven tanks. Invaluable aid was rendered upon this occasion by the Royal Navy and Air Force. It was also found possible to establish Tobruk harbour as a base, and this greatly shortened General Wavell's lines of communication.

The final phase threw a considerable strain on administration, for the going was now very rough, and the stocking-up of new advance depots near Mechili had only just begun. Maintenance after the heavy wear and tear of nearly two months of action was an increasing problem. The 7th Armoured Division (now reduced to the tank strength of an armoured brigade) was moving with only two days' supplies, whether of food, petrol or ammunition—a close margin.

The final phase itself may best be described as a rounding-up of what was left of the Italian armies. These were strung out in a confused mass of vehicles, almost twenty miles in length, between our Armoured Brigade in the south and a northern detachment in the Soluch area, some twenty miles south of Benghazi. Fighting all during the 6th February was desperate, but shortly after dawn on the 7th, after a final abortive attempt to break through, the Italian General Bergonzoli was captured, and the victory became final and complete.

In brief, the Army of the Nile (to employ the picturesque title bestowed upon it at that time) had in two months advanced through 500 miles of desert, destroyed an Italian army of nearly ten divisions and captured 130,000 prisoners, 400 tanks and 1,290 guns, with vast quantities of other war material. In these operations General Wavell had never employed a larger force than two divisions, of which one was armoured. The 6th Australian Division had relieved the 4th Indian Division after Sidi Barrani, but the 7th Armoured Division fought throughout. It was reduced, we are told, to a skeleton. Special mention is also made of the only armoured car regiment in the force, the 11th Hussars.

Our casualties were surprisingly light. 500 were killed and 1,373 wounded. Only fifty-five were missing.

The greatness of this military victory, however, was small by comparison with the moral effect which it produced all over the world. To the British people, depressed by a year of mingled stalemate and defeat, and now stolidly enduring the nightly rigours of the blitz, it brought a complete renewal of confidence and hope. To Hitler it revealed the quality of the assistance to be expected from his egregious colleague Mussolini. To the world at large it demonstrated that the British soldier, properly equipped and given a fair chance, is his old doughty, invincible self. Lastly, it introduced upon the stage of history a military strategist and organiser of the first water—the forerunner (and possibly the greatest) of that astonishing array of great captains destined, within the next few years, to lead the British Army to victories undreamed of.

Throughout his triumphant campaign General Wavell was supported at every turn, and was quick to acknowledge the fact, by the Royal Navy along the African coast and the Royal Air Force overhead—a foretaste of that irresistible instrument of conquest later known as Combined Operations.

-*(3)*-

General Wavell's resounding triumph in North Africa had been won, as we have seen, only after he had surmounted the twofold obstacle presented by inadequate forces and divided control thereover. The prospect of speedy and final victory seemed bright.

But his further hopes were doomed to disappointment. In a sense his success had been his own undoing, for the German High Command, impressed by the ignominious failure of their Italian allies not only against the British in Libya but against the Greeks in Albania, had decided to intervene in the Mediterranean theatre on their own account.

They began by enlisting the subservient aid of Rumania and Bulgaria, and equipped those territories with airfields for an offensive against Greece. The Greeks, realising that, however successfully they might hold Italians in check, they were in no position to withstand an all-out German *blitzkrieg*, sought the advice of Great Britain.

The British Government had a hard decision to make. No troops could be spared from Britain itself, where the threat of invasion still loomed large and the training and equipment of the new divisions was in any case far from complete. The only army in being was the Army of the Nile, at present recovering from its tremendous exertions against the Italians, and doing its best to repair and replace the losses in armour and equipment inevitable in a campaign stretched over 500 miles of desert.

Were these troops to be allowed, after due recuperation, to complete their triumphant desert victory, or be diverted, in part at any rate, to the assistance of Greece?

To the lay mind there seemed to be but one course to follow—namely, to make sure of final victory in North Africa before undertaking heavy commitments elsewhere. But the War Cabinet, presumably in view of the strategic situation as a whole, decided otherwise. An expeditionary force, drawn from the Army of the Nile, and consisting of an armoured brigade of the 2nd Armoured Division, the New Zealand Division, the 6th Australian Division, and some corps artillery, was ordered to Greece.

The general purpose of this move seems to have been to interpose a barrier against enemy penetration into Palestine and the East. It might also set up a delaying action which would give the Russians time to prepare for the invasion of their country which Hitler was now plainly contemplating. The gesture was also of value as an indication of Allied solidarity.

Unfortunately the troops available for the purpose could not constitute much more than a token force in the face of German Panzer divisions and overwhelming infantry strength. Worse still, we would be unable to afford adequate fighter protection to these troops against enemy bombing. True, fighter planes were now being produced in mass, but the real problem was to transport them to the scene of action. They could not be flown there, for a fighter's range of flight was then comparatively short: they had to be conveyed by sea round the Cape, a voyage of three months at least, while the Germans could fly their machines direct. (Further west in the Mediterranean the island of Malta was suffering cruelly from a similar disability. The nearest British bases, Alexandria and Gibraltar, were each a thousand miles away, and it was not until April 1942 that it was found possible, even at great cost, to bring Spitfires within flying distance of the Maltese aerodromes.)

The Government decision aroused considerable controversy. The British General Staff were unfavourable to the idea. The Greek military commander supported it, but at a Conference held in Athens in January 1941, attended by General Dill, the British C.I.G.S., and Mr. Anthony Eden, the Greek Prime Minister, General Metaxas, made it plain that in his view—and a most understandable view— British intervention in Greece, unless in overwhelming strength, would merely serve as a justification of the German invasion, and would result in the conversion of the soil of Greece into an Anglo-German battleground.

However, the British War Cabinet adhered to their decision; General Dill and General Wavell loyally acquiesced, and the Expeditionary Force was dispatched.

The troops were transported from North Africa without a hitch, the operation affording to Admiral A. B. Cunningham, Commander-in-Chief of our Naval forces in the Mediterranean, an opportunity, of which he fully availed himself off Cape Matapan, to administer a memorable lesson to the Italian Fleet, which had rashly attempted to interfere. But the almost inevitable withdrawal from Greece which took place a few weeks later, with the complete collapse of Greek resistance, was attended by heavy losses, both in transports and destroyers. Still, thanks to the devoted aid of the Royal Navy, out of a total of some 57,000 men sent to Greece, close on 43,000 were safely re-embarked.

The subsequent struggle to hold Crete was an even more difficult and much more expensive operation. Thanks again to the Navy, no single hostile transport ever succeeded in reaching the island, but parachute and glider-borne troops could not be denied. Seven thousand of them landed in a single day, with their armour and artillery, while low-flying bombers, with little or nothing to resist them, took heavy toll of our exposed forces on the ground.

'Officers', reports General Wavell, 'who had fought through the last war and had been engaged in France during this, have expressed their opinion that the bombardment the troops underwent in Crete was severer and more continuous than anything they had ever experienced. The handicap under which the force laboured in regard to lack of equipment and the difficulties of reinforcing the island with either men or material has been explained, *but it was the enemy air force which was the deciding factor.*'

These last are pregnant words, and should be borne in mind as an early contribution to the debate, still in progress, as to whether the tank or the bomber is to be regarded as the final arbiter of victory in modern warfare.

Our troops in Crete, under the inspiring leadership of General Freyberg, put up a most valiant resistance, and the punishment which they inflicted upon the descending troop-carriers was surprising; but enemy reinforcements arrived unceasingly, some 35,000 in all, and it became clear that evacuation of the island could only be a matter of time. So the order was given, and thanks once more to the self-sacrifice of the Navy more than half the force, which had originally been 27,550 strong, was safely evacuated to Egypt. Of the 13,000 left behind the majority were taken prisoner.

Mention of the Navy should remind us of the peculiar and distressing strain laid upon our seamen, whether naval or mercantile, by politically inspired operations such as these. To risk their lives in conveying essential supplies to vitally important centres like Malta or Archangel was all in the day's work; but to be called upon time and again to evacuate troops from theatres of war to which they should never have been dispatched in the first instance was something entirely different. As Admiral Cunningham truly observes:

It is not easy to convey how heavy was the strain that men and ships sustained. It has to be remembered that in this last instance the ships' companies had none of the inspiration of battle with the enemy to bear them up.

Needless to say, they tackled the job with their accustomed valour, and did all that was required of them. But how much more valuably and cheerfully their labour and lives could have been expended in fighting the U-boats in the Atlantic or seeking out and destroying some enemy capital ship.

So ended our Grecian crusade. The venture had cost us dear, but the account was not entirely on the debit side.

'The attempt to save Crete,' says General Wavell, 'though unsuccessful, undoubtedly frustrated the plan for future enemy operations by destroying so large a portion of his airborne troops. The total enemy losses were at least 12,000–15,000, of whom a very high proportion were killed.

'The defence saved in all probability Cyprus, Syria, Iraq, and perhaps Tobruk.'

That may have been, but the fact remained that the desert campaign had now to be fought all over again, while throughout the world Allied hopes and British prestige had sustained another disheartening setback.

~*(4)*~

Amid the strain and tumult of these distracting events, General Wavell and his staff had succeeded in performing two minor miracles of improvisation, either of which, though little noticed at the time, might have given pause to those critics who had convinced themselves that the British Army had reached the limits of its resources.

In April 1941 a serious Axis-engineered revolt had occurred in the nominally neutral kingdom of Iraq (once Mesopotamia) some 500 miles inland from the Palestinian coast. It was vitally important to guard Allied interests in this country, which afforded an alternative (if circuitous) route from Britain to Haifa and the Mediterranean theatre, should the Red Sea be rendered impassable by enemy action. On May 4th responsibility for the handling of this emergency was passed by the War Cabinet from India to Middle East Command—in other words to General Wavell. Though seriously short of troops everywhere, he contrived to organise a small force which, though obviously inadequate to its task, brought the campaign to a successful conclusion, by the capture of Baghdad and the restoration of the official Government, within three weeks.

'We may consider ourselves extremely fortunate', runs the official report, 'to have liquidated what might have been a very serious commitment with such small forces and little trouble.'

Almost at the same moment, in the very midst of his Cretan preoccupations, General Wavell found himself called upon to cope with a serious threat of German infiltration into Syria, actively supported by French Vichy troops. Once more he had to scrape together a defence force and, more difficult still, provide it with equipment and transport. Indeed, at one time he could only effect his purpose by taking transport, earmarked for service elsewhere, off the ships as they arrived from home and issuing it direct to units.

Some heavy fighting followed, with casualties in proportion, but by the end of July victory had been achieved and Syria had passed into Allied occupation. General Wavell's comment on the matter has a now familiar ring:

We must again be considered fortunate in achieving our objective with forces which were really insufficient for their task. It was only skilful handling and determined fighting, that brought about success.

And, one might add, prompt and vigorous action from higher up.

Meanwhile the possibility, already referred to, that Germany might carry the war into North Africa had grown to actual fact. German troops were in Tripoli by February, and it became obvious that a full-scale German invasion of Cyrenaica, under the redoubtable Rommel, was merely a matter of time.

Before describing the operations which followed, let us pause for a moment to consider General Wavell's position in the spring of

1941, at the moment when he found himself called upon to send an expeditionary force to Greece.

First, as regards the troops at his disposal. In the Western Desert he had the 7th Armoured Division and the 6th Australian Division, which were all he could spare to maintain the ground won during the previous winter. Of these the 7th, the illustrious 'Desert Rats', had been fighting continuously for eight months and was mechanically incapable of further action until after a complete and lengthy overhaul of its equipment. In Egypt itself were the 2nd Armoured Division, the 9th Australian Division, the New Zealand Division, the 6th (British) Division, and the Polish Brigade Group. The remnants of the 2nd Armoured Division had been serving with the 7th, and shared its general exhaustion. The New Zealanders were fully trained and equipped for action, but the 6th Division, which was in process of formation out of various battalions in Egypt, consisted so far of the 22nd (Guards) and 16th Brigades. It was without artillery or supporting arms. The Polish Brigade was available but not fully equipped.

The 4th and the 5th Indian Divisions, together with the Sudan Defence Force, were in Eritrea on the Red Sea, besieging Keren, so were at present unavailable for immediate duty elsewhere. In East Africa, facing a huge Italian army, were the South African Division, furnished by South Africa for operations in East Africa only, together with the King's African Rifles and the Royal West African Frontier Force.

It was from these elements that General Wavell had selected and dispatched the expeditionary force to Greece.

Here is the situation as described by him in May 1941, after the Greek withdrawal:

The situation was full of anxiety. I was threatened with having to undertake operations in no fewer than five theatres, with my resources very seriously depleted by the losses in Greece. There was an obvious possibility, which was soon confirmed, that the enemy would undertake operations against Crete; or he might reinforce his operations in the Western Desert. Responsibility for dealing with the revolt in Iraq[1] was handed over to Middle East from India in the first week of May; the Germans were making use of their air bases in Syria, which might constitute a very serious menace to the defence of the Canal and Egyptian ports, as well as to Palestine. Finally there still remained the remnants of the Italian forces in Abyssinia, to be cleared up if possible before the rainy season set in.

To deal with these many responsibilities my resources were totally inadequate.

[1] See p. 127.

They certainly were. It is little wonder that Rommel had already begun to reoccupy the ground in the Western Desert lost by the Italians in the previous December. By this time his troops were back almost on the frontier of Egypt, though we clung obstinately to Tobruk and were thus able to maintain an active menace to his communications.

In June General Wavell launched a limited counter-attack against Rommel, with the aim of driving him back at any rate as far as Tobruk. He inflicted considerable losses, but failed to gain his objective.

The main reason for the failure was a shortage of armour, coupled with the fact that such as we possessed at this time was not homogeneous. As already stated, the 7th and 2nd Armoured Divisions had by February reached a state of mechanical exhaustion which rendered it imperative that they should be entirely re-equipped. This need now seemed likely of fulfilment, for it was known that 200 fresh tanks were on their way out from home. But the aid and comfort which they brought fell far short of expectation. In the first place fifty-seven of them were lost at sea by mine-action, and the remainder proved to be composed partly of 'Cruisers' and partly of 'I' or infantry tanks, the latter quite incapable of the rapid movement demanded of an armoured division.[1] In the second, the ponderous 'I' tanks proved difficult to unload, and most of them required considerable overhauling and refitting into the bargain. In the third, they were of a type unfamiliar to the crews who took them over, and since it was known that Rommel had also been reinforced and might attack at any time, and since General Wavell was being unduly pressed from home to forestall such action with the least possible delay, there was little space for their crews to become accustomed to their new machines, either from the point of view of driving, gunnery, tactical handling, or maintenance.

So failure resulted. However, the enemy showed no disposition to follow up his advantage, and the opposing forces settled down to their old positions at Matruh.

Several months of comparative stalemate now ensued, by the end of which General Wavell had departed to take command in India, where he was destined within a few months to organise successful resistance, again from inadequate resources, to yet another attempted invasion, this time by the Japanese.

[1] The Cruiser tanks had a speed of fifteen to twenty m.p.h., and the 'I' tanks of not more than five. The whole question of armoured vehicles will be discussed in the next chapter.

~⊰(5)⊱~

General Wavell's achievement in Egypt and the Middle East should be remembered as something unique in the history of the Second World War. In December 1940 his astonishing Libyan campaign first brought victory to British arms and hope to his countrymen. During the following six months he conducted no fewer than six major campaigns—in Greece, in Cyrenaica, in Crete, in Iraq, in Syria, and in Italian East Africa. During May 1941 five of these were being fought simultaneously, and there were never less than three on hand at one time. The theatres of these operations, moreover, were several hundred miles apart, in some instances well over a thousand. He was everywhere and all the time short of troops, equipment and air cover. His lines of communication were some 12,000 miles long. Yet in three of these campaigns—East Africa, Iraq and Syria—he was entirely successful, while in the Western Desert the German effort against Egypt and the Canal was firmly checked and was destined never to penetrate further.

Little of this was known or realised at the time by the people at home, who had their own sufficient preoccupations in the ceaseless bombing of their cities and of the growing U-boat menace to their Island supply-lines. It was certainly no moment to appreciate situations in detail or take comprehensive surveys. Moreover, the African campaign did not end with Wavell; indeed it was only beginning; and the memory of his work was destined inevitably to be somewhat overlaid by the disasters and triumphs of his successors.

But in one respect there can be no ground for comparison between Wavell's achievement and that of the ultimate victors in that long struggle. The resounding successes of Alexander, Montgomery and Eisenhower were founded upon long-term planning and elaborately concerted strategy, backed in ever-increasing strength by great armies and unlimited munitions. Wavell's campaigns, win or lose, were a series, for the most part, of hazardous improvisations imposed by emergency and conducted with totally inadequate resources. Called upon, like many another British Army leader before him, to make bricks without straw, he not only produced the bricks but left behind him a solid foundation upon which those who followed him might build. And build they did, to some purpose; but, as they were the first to admit, it was Archibald Wavell and his sturdy, indomitable following that they had to thank.

CHAPTER XI

A MECHANISED ARMY

~*(1)*~

OUR studies of the battle of Flanders and of General Wavell's diverse operations in the Middle East have made it plain that the art of war has been revolutionised in recent years to an extent unheard of since the introduction of gunpowder into military operations 600 years ago.[1]

The strategy of the Second World War was the direct product of the phenomenal progress achieved during the past half-century in the realm of applied science. To take but two instances, the internal combustion engine gave us the aeroplane and armoured fighting vehicle, while today radio intercommunication can endow a vast, a hitherto invertebrate body of armed men with a nervous system as receptive and almost as swift in reaction as that of a single sentient being.

It seems time then to study all this new and strange equipment in greater detail. But first let us remind ourselves of certain elementary principles of warfare, and consider to what extent these have been modified, or possibly eliminated, by the march of events. Successful warfare, boiled down to its essentials, consists in seeking out your enemy and destroying his power to resist you. This, it might be added, with the utmost possible economy of men and material.

In actual battle there are two ways of achieving this end—by missile-action and by shock-action. The first of these has given us successively bows-and-arrows, giant catapults, artillery, machine-guns, rifles, hand-grenades and bombing aeroplanes; the second, war-chariots, charging cavalry, infantry advancing in mass, and tanks.

[1] A primitive form of cannon is said to have been used at Crécy in 1346.

We should note, however, that though shock-action can gain objectives and occupy enemy ground, missile-action cannot. Indeed, the infantry is the essential and ultimate arm: the other arms are but complements—indispensable complements if you will, but complements for all that. In the old days the archers at Crécy supplied the missile-action, but it was the English men-at-arms who carried the position; just as in older days still it was Hannibal's Balearic slingers who opened the attack at Cannae and Lake Trasimene, but the heavily armed Carthaginian infantry which drove it home. However elaborate or ingenious the weapon or machine, it was the man, when all is said and done, who had the last word. And that truth holds as firmly today as it ever did.

We start naturally with the modern magazine rifle, which is the most potent instrument of its kind ever devised, especially since the invention of the bayonet rendered it capable both of missile- and shock-action.

It began life as a smooth-bore musket, and so remained for a century and a half. Missile-action in the early days of fire-arms was a laborious business. Having discharged his 'matchlock' (by releasing a spring which brought a glowing match into contact with the touch-hole) the musketeer was accustomed to retire to the rear to reload, with the aid of a long wooden ramrod. The matchlock was in due course succeeded by the flintlock, in which the spark required to fire the charge was produced by the trigger-hammer falling sharply on a piece of flint set near the touch-hole. But these weapons were wildly inaccurate and short in range. They were fired from the hip, and no particular effort was made to take aim with them.

The value of rifling had long been realised, but mechanical difficulties were hard to overcome: a rifled barrel fouled easily and was difficult to load from the muzzle. However, by the end of the eighteenth century a battalion of the 60th Rifles was equipped with rifled muskets of a sort.

The first really practical weapon of the kind was invented by a French officer, Captain Minié, and was sighted up to a thousand yards. It was employed by the British Army in the Crimea. The Snider, invented by a Pennsylvania-Dutch wine-merchant, initiated the principle of the breech-loader. The Martini Henry was the first hammerless weapon, and was the last to employ black powder. Then came the magazine rifle, the Lee Metford, the joint offspring of a Canadian watchmaker and a railway engineer. This was supplanted in its turn by the Lee Enfield, with a shorter barrel and longer range— the standard service rifle of the British Army today.

The rifle is a weapon which the British soldier has made peculiarly his own. Upon occasion he can maintain with it a fire of fifteen rounds a minute. At Mons, it will be remembered, so devastating was that fire that the enemy were forced to the conclusion that with our usual national duplicity we had furnished ourselves with far more machine-guns than we had generally admitted.

The development and tactical use of the machine-gun itself, at any rate as far as 1918, we have already studied in some detail.[1] With the coming of universal mechanised transport the difficulty of providing adequate ammunition supplies, which had hitherto stood in the way of all-round employment of machine-guns and automatic rifles in general, ceased to exist. So, in consequence, did the Machine-gun Corps: in future the infantry soldier was to be his own machine-gunner. The Vickers and Lewis were still employed, in special machine-gun units, while the infantry were lavishly equipped with Bren guns and other light automatic weapons, which could be fired from the ground, from the shoulder, or employed as anti-aircraft weapons.

Before abandoning the subject of small-arms fire-power, however, let us not forget that the rifle, or rather the rifle and bayonet in combination, are in their proper environment as indispensable as ever. They may be helpless against tanks, or ineffective compared with automatic weapons; but we have only to recall the jungle fighting in Burma, where roads were non-existent and no transport of any kind could penetrate, to realise that a daring and resourceful rifleman, furnished with a handful of cartridges dropped perhaps from the air, can still render himself master of the situation—as the Japanese discovered to their cost.

❧(2)☙

The tank, as already noted, was a British invention, and was the direct product of the conditions under which, for the greater part of the time, the war of 1914–18 was conducted.

To launch an infantry attack in mass over open ground swept by continuous machine-gun fire was (or should have been) unthinkable: plainly some means must be devised for enabling men to cross no-man's-land with a reasonable prospect of reaching the other side. The obvious solution seemed to be some sort of armoured vehicle, impervious at least to small-arms (which includes machine-gun) fire, capable of negotiating ground pitted by shell-craters and provided

[1] See p. 53.

with sufficient offensive equipment to enable it to deal with enemy machine-gun emplacements. The chief difficulty would be to operate such a vehicle over broken ground and get it across trenches.

A short digression is admissible here, upon the subject of armoured cars in general.

The armoured car, naturally, is older than the tank. It became a military possibility with the advent of the motor-car itself: armoured cars were being constructed by the firm of Charron in France as early as 1902, and by the Daimler Company in Germany a year later.

Armoured cars were extensively employed by the British Army during the First World War. They originated, rather unexpectedly, with the Royal Navy, and many squadrons of them were sent overseas under Admiralty orders. Their usefulness in Flanders ceased perforce with the establishment of continuous trench lines and the elimination of flanks, but elsewhere, especially in the Middle East, their great speed rendered them highly valuable, both for reconnaissance and the transport of machine-guns. In September 1915 they were entirely taken over by the Army, and provided the motor machine-gun battalions of the newly formed Machine-gun Corps.

They were particularly well suited to desert warfare, as was evinced early in 1917, in the highly successful operations conducted by the Duke of Westminster and an Armoured Car Squadron of the R.N.A.S. against the elusive Senussi. It was this occasion, incidentally, which gave rise to the half-opprobrious, half-affectionate sobriquet 'Petrol Hussars', which was subsequently extended to all the mechanised cavalry units of a later day.

Naturally, with the invention and development of the tank, especially the light tank, the armoured car found part of its occupation gone. The tank was not bound to the roads, nor to flat open country, and could stand up to artillery fire, which the armoured car could not. On the other hand the armoured car was a most effective weapon against weakly armed opponents, while its great speed and comparative silence made it highly suitable for reconnaissance work, especially in desert warfare.

The armoured car of today is a most ingeniously designed and highly specialised vehicle. To take a single example, the well-known 'Scout Car' in particular is of great value as an adjunct to armoured units, and, indeed, to the Army as a whole. It has 'independent' springing on each of the four wheels, and a four-wheel drive. It is very speedy, well-armoured, and can travel as fast backwards as forwards. It is practically 'double-ended', for in reverse the steering is transferred to the rear wheels.

The armoured car, then, is unlikely to be displaced by the tank from certain of its duties. Originally produced as a means of transporting a machine-gun, it has become a separate and indispensable weapon in itself.

~*(3)*~

We now return to the tank. Its origin is to a certain extent wrapped in mystery, for from the earliest days of the First World War many keen military minds were being applied to the problem of protecting troops, in their assault upon enemy trenches, from the devastating effect of machine-gun fire. More than one of these made substantial contribution to the ultimate solution; but the man to whom the principal credit should perhaps be ascribed for the evolution of the modern 'Armoured Fighting Vehicle' was Major-General Sir Ernest Swinton, R.E., a well-known and most imaginative writer upon military subjects, who was among the first to conceive the idea of mounting an armoured car of some kind upon a caterpillar tractor, of the type then coming into general use in agriculture for propelling heavy vehicles, even ploughs, across soft and broken ground. That is to say, the new fighting machine was able to lay down its own 'track' as it went along.

General Swinton (or Colonel, as he then was) was also the first to advocate that tanks, if they were to be of real value in battle, must be employed in very large numbers and on a concerted tactical plan, and not sent into action single-handed or haphazard. To that extent he may fairly be regarded as the principal progenitor of tank warfare on its present scale.

The tank, incidentally, was so named because it was the 'top secret' of the First World War: thus its birth and infant nurture were concealed from public curiosity by bestowing upon it a succession of different names—'Landship', 'Mother', and finally 'Tank'. This last, incongruous though it was, stuck, and received the official *imprimatur*. Similarly, the units who operated the tanks were known, as their importance grew, as Armoured Section Motor Machine-gun Corps; Heavy Section Machine-gun Corps; The Tank Corps; the Royal Tank Corps; and finally, when combined with the mechanised cavalry into a single arm in 1939, the Royal Armoured Corps.

The term 'Landship' is of particular interest, because it reminds us that the first tanks were built to the order of the Royal Naval Air Service. Perhaps the fact that Mr. Churchill was First Lord of the

Admiralty at the time had something to do with the matter. At any rate he became keenly interested, and immediately set up an Admiralty Landship Committee, under whose guidance the original plan, which had envisaged a 'ship' 100 feet long, with wheels forty feet in diameter and weighing 1,000 tons, was reduced to more modest and practical proportions.

Meanwhile Colonel Swinton's original proposal and specifications were going the round of the War Office, borne upon the stately current of the 'usual channels'. So far no news of the activities of the Admiralty in the matter had reached the Army Council. Indeed, it was Colonel Swinton himself who was the first to discover that 'The Director of Naval Construction appears to be making land battleships for the Army, which has never asked for them and has done nothing to help.'

But finally a junction of interest and effort was effected between the two Ministries, and early in 1916 a 'tank test' was held in Hatfield Park, at which certain deeply interested and highly important spectators were present, in the persons of Lord Kitchener, Sir William Robertson (C.I.G.S.), Mr. A. J. Balfour and Mr. Lloyd George.[1] So favourably impressed were they that they immediately ordered some machines. A hundred and fifty were put in hand on February 12th, and mechanical warfare was launched.

But the fact remains that the first two tanks in history were constructed to the order of the R.N.A.S. The first, and ancestor of them all, was called 'Little Willie' (no doubt in affectionate reference to the Kaiser's heir), and the second, chiefly because it was larger, was christened 'Mother'. It had the afterwards familiar lozenge profile, and as the tracks passed right over the hull, precluding the employment of a central turret, the guns were mounted in 'bulges' on the sides, known by their naval name of sponsons.

The construction of tanks was now put seriously in hand, and the tanks themselves grew in numbers and efficiency. The first batch, already mentioned, were known as 'Mark I'. No fewer than eight such 'Marks' were produced between 1915 and 1918. Of the Mark I type half were equipped with two 6-pounder guns and four Hotchkiss machine-guns, and the other half with six machine-guns only. Their armour was 10 mm. ($\frac{2}{5}$ inch) thick, and was proof against ordinary small-arms fire but not against the German armour-piercing bullet. The tracks passed right over the body of the hull on either side. To the eye, the tank appeared to be gliding along on a stationary track,

---

[1] Mr. Churchill was by this time in France, commanding a battalion of the Royal Scots Fusiliers.

as indeed it was. Their speed was less than five miles an hour, but they could climb a vertical obstacle $4\frac{1}{2}$ feet high and cross a trench $11\frac{1}{2}$ feet wide.

The chief difficulty was to control them. They carried a crew of eight, no fewer than four of whom were required to assist in the steering. It was not until 1918 that a tank (Mark V) was introduced which could be steered by the driver without assistance from other members of the crew. Finally, the noise inside was deafening, and all orders had to be given by hand signal.[1]

Tanks first appeared in action in September 1916, during the battle of the Somme. For nearly three months the British Army had struggled, on a wide front and with enormous losses, to pierce a practically impenetrable German trench system; and on September 15th, almost as soon as the first tanks were delivered in France, they were launched to the attack. There were forty-nine of them, but not all reached their objective. Some were ditched and others broke down with mechanical trouble; but eighteen made contact with the enemy and acquitted themselves valiantly.

They certainly created a profound sensation, upon friend and foe alike. When the action had been in progress for some time a message was dropped by an airman, which ran: '*A tank is walking up the High Street of Flers, with the British Army cheering behind.*' The news was flashed round the world forthwith, and the great secret was out at last—prematurely, in the view of its original designers.

For another year, against the advice of the newly established Tank Corps Headquarters,[2] the policy of employing tanks in driblets was maintained. The new weapon was at its worst under such conditions, especially in the shell-torn and boggy Salient of Ypres. It was not until November 20th, 1917, that the tank was given a full and fair trial, at Cambrai, against the Hindenburg Line on the 3rd Army front. Firm and open ground was specially selected, and no less than 378 tanks were employed. Each carried a 'fascine' of compressed brushwood, which could be released and lowered to render support in crossing a trench. They were followed into action by ninety-eight 'administrative' tanks (converted from some of the earlier fighting types) conveying petrol, oil and ammunition.

A complete surprise was effected—the noise made by the tanks in assembling had been purposely drowned by low-flying aircraft

[1] But see pp. 184–5.

[2] Tank Corps Headquarters was set up in October 1916, under the command of Brigadier Hugh Elles, who had upon his staff Lieut.-Colonel J. F. C. Fuller and Captain G. le Q. Martel—names all destined to become famous in tank history.

overhead—and the result was a most notable victory—a penetration in less than twelve hours of 10,000 yards upon a front of more than seven miles—a phenomenal advance for those days—with the capture of 100 guns and 8,000 prisoners, many of whom surrendered from sheer panic at the spectacle of the roaring monsters bearing down upon them.

This striking victory was not followed up. The tank was (and still is) a weapon highly susceptible to mechanical trouble, especially as regards tracks—as General Wavell was still to discover in his Middle East campaign[1] more than twenty years later. The remedy is to maintain a very large tank reserve. But there was no reserve at Cambrai, and much of the ground gained was subsequently lost.

Still the tank had proved its worth, and triumphantly vindicated the faith of its creators. In the Third Battle of Ypres a month or two previously, a similar penetration of the enemy's position (without tanks) had taken three months to achieve, at an appalling cost. But Cambrai finally established the tank as a dominant weapon. Much of the technique of its employment then is applicable, as we shall see, to tank warfare of today. Meticulous preliminary reconnaissance, route marking, and intimate co-operation between tanks, infantry and artillery, are among the present commonplaces which were first learnt in 1917.

Most of the actual fighting up to this period had been done by tanks of the Marks I–IV type. They were primitive and clumsy machines, but they improved steadily. By far the best of these was the Mark IV. It had better tracks, a 125-h.p. engine, and special unditching gear for use in heavy going. Lewis guns, too, had been substituted for the Hotchkiss. It weighed twenty-eight tons, carried two 6-pounder guns and four machine-guns, had defensive armour 12 mm. thick, proof now against the German armour-piercing bullet, and travelled at four miles per hour.[2] It was not yet capable of being steered by one man : that was to come with the Mark V. But it was the Mark IV which won the battle of Cambrai : the Mark V, a greatly superior machine, was not to emerge until early 1918.

[1] See p. 129.

[2] Compare the Churchill I in 1941 : 40 tons in weight, one 2-pounder and one 6-pounder gun; armour 102 mm., h.p. 340, speed 18 m.p.h.

~(4)~

The lessons of 1918 were embodied in a great tank programme drawn up for the campaign of 1919. This included provision for more than 10,000 tanks, of which half were to be heavy and half medium. Here we note for the first time that the reversion to open warfare, which began with the battle of Amiens on August 8th, 1918, and continued until the Armistice on November 11th, had indicated the desirability of employing two entirely different types of tank—slow, but powerful machines to attack and penetrate fortified positions, and something lighter and much more speedy to pass through and operate against headquarters, aerodromes and communications; in other words, to do work hitherto performed by cavalry.

Here, so far as cavalry was concerned, came the writing on the wall, writing heavily underlined by the advent of the machine-gun. The traditional role of cavalry is threefold—to obtain information as to the enemy's movements, to interpose a mobile screen between the enemy and the main body, and to break through and employ shock action against a weakening foe. The first of these functions had long been usurped by the aeroplane, the second was destined to be taken over by the cruiser tank. The third, on the other hand, had been brought to naught by the machine-gun battery. From Loos onward (September 1915) cavalry had been held ready behind each of our great offensive 'pushes' to penetrate any gap created, and round up the fly-ing enemy in the ground beyond. But valiantly though they strove, never once did they succeed in getting through a fortified trench sys-tem. Horses were too vulnerable. An infantry soldier advancing to the attack under concentrated fire can usually find some sort of cover or at least lie down, but a man on a horse has no such hope. Together they form too conspicuous a mark, and together they go down.

The evolution of the light 'Whippet' tank was the obvious and inevitable consequence, and it marked the end of cavalry participa-tion in close warfare. Only in Palestine, during General Allenby's brilliant campaign against the Turks in September 1918, were cavalry successfully employed in their traditional role.

Such were the circumstances which led to the division of our tank forces into heavy and cruiser categories respectively. Two new types, Mark VIII and Medium C, were actually ready and available when the end came, quite unexpectedly, in November 1918: there was no 1919 campaign, and neither of the new tanks was ever employed in action. Still, they indicated the line upon which the future design and tactical handling of the dominant weapon must now proceed.

~⊰(5)⊱~

During the early twenties our military activities languished. This was due partly to the natural unwillingness of a people who have just emerged victorious from an exhausting war to envisage the possibility of another, and partly to the strict regime of economy now imposed by the state of the country's finances. The clang of the 'axe' was heard on every side.

In particular the economy campaign retarded both the design and tactical development of that expensive weapon the tank. No heavy tanks were put in hand at all, though an improved medium tank, the Vickers Medium, was produced in 1923. This weapon occupies a unique position in the genealogy of tanks. It probably exerted more influence, we are told, upon the present technique of armoured warfare than any other single type, although it was never employed in action. It was the standard equipment of the Royal Tank Corps for fifteen years, and was the first British tank to have a revolving turret with an all-round traverse.

Considerable progress, nevertheless, was made between the two wars in the study of the organisation and handling of armoured formations. The idea of 'infantry' and 'cruiser' tanks was definitely established, each type performing duties based upon its own weight, speed and armament. A tank can only be heavily armed and armoured at the expense of mobility, and vice versa. Thus the heavy infantry tank, to which speed was a secondary consideration, was for use in close co-operation with infantry advancing against prepared positions: the cruiser, highly mobile at the expense of some security, was to effect deep penetration behind or round the flanks of an enemy's position.

We were also keeping an observant eye upon the progress in tank design made by other countries. Thus in 1939 we contrived to effect a great improvement in the mobility of our cruiser types by the adoption of what was known as the 'Christie high-speed suspension' for tracked vehicles, an American invention which enabled our British Cruiser Mark III to travel at a maximum speed of forty miles per hour. (The Russians adapted the same system to their T34 tank, with results which were to become notable in 1942.)

The principle of employing tanks upon a concerted plan and in large numbers was now universally accepted, though the exact proportions in which the various types were to be commingled was still a matter for prolonged experiment. In 1927 the first 'Armoured Force' was formed. It was composed of a reconnaissance group of armoured cars and tankettes,[1] and a main group with a striking force made up of a battalion of medium tanks, artillery and a machine-gun battalion. The last two were mechanised but unarmoured. This led, in 1931, to a 'Mixed Tank Brigade', and finally, in 1937, to a 'Mobile Division', which became, in 1939, the First Armoured Division, destined to serve as such in Flanders but to come under Lord Gort's command only for a brief period. Its composition is worth noting, for purposes of comparison later. It was made up of two armoured brigades, equipped with the Vickers Mark VI light tank, weighing $5\frac{1}{4}$ tons and capable of a speed of thirty-five miles per hour, and the Cruiser tanks Marks I and III, the latter capable of a speed of forty miles per hour; artillery, engineers, and two infantry battalions. This marked real progress; but one armoured division does not make an army, and Germany, with a start of some years in intensive tank production, was already equipped with a tank strength exceeding that of all the Allies.

By this time, however, we were beginning to produce heavy 'Infantry' tanks again, and in 1939 these actually accompanied the B.E.F. to Flanders, where their service has already been noted. These were the so-called 'Matilda' tanks, Marks I and II. Mark I was a very small tank in which everything was sacrificed to armour. Mark II was greatly superior: it weighed twenty-five tons, carried a powerful 40-mm. gun and a machine-gun, was protected by armour of the unprecedented thickness of 75 mm. (three inches), and could travel at five miles per hour. It was successfully employed in Flanders, the Western Desert, East Africa and the Far East, where the Australians used it against the Japanese up to the end of the war in 1945.

During this same period two cruiser tanks were in production— the Mark III (A.10) and the Mark IV. Of these the first subsequently developed into the Valentine, and the second into the Crusader.

This brings us to the best-known and certainly the most-discussed of all British tanks, the Churchill. In the summer of 1940, as we have seen, there was an alarming shortage of tanks in Britain. (All that could be spared had gone to the Middle East Command.) The Valentine was now coming off the lines, but the Churchill, a much heavier and more powerful tank, was still in the stage of specification and experiment. In view of the urgent need for haste it was decided to put Churchill I into production straight away, without further

---

[1] These were the Morris-Martel and Carden-Lloyd types, lineal descendants, one might say, of the 'Whippet'. In addition to reconnaissance their occupants were trained to alight from their tanks and fight with an automatic machine-gun, just as a cavalryman on occasion could dismount from his horse and fight on foot.

dalliance in the realm of trial and error. Consequently the early
Churchills were handicapped by numerous mechanical faults, and
their performance evoked considerable criticism. Later, however,
these weaknesses were eliminated, and the Churchill became our
standard infantry tank for the rest of the war. It was first employed
in action at Dieppe in early 1942, and subsequently in Tunisia, Italy,
France and Germany.

For the present we need carry our tank history no further. At a
later stage of this narrative we will examine not only the new types
which came into being, but those supplied to us from America under
the terms of the Lend-Lease Act. The design and performance of
Ally and enemy tanks must also be considered; and last but not least,
the inevitable development and growth of tank obstacles and anti-
tank weapons.

~*(6)*~

In April 1939 His Majesty The King formally approved of the
establishment of a new corps, to be designated the Royal Armoured
Corps.

The effect of this proclamation was twofold: it marked the official
recognition of the tank as a permanent arm of the British Army on
the one hand, and the demise of the cavalry, as such, on the other.
Cavalry regiments they would still remain, with their ancient traditions and battle honours faithfully preserved, but their occupation
as horsemen would be gone for ever. Henceforth the petrol-engine
would propel them into action.

The thing was inevitable, but it had been a long time coming. For
twenty years the cavalry and the Royal Tank Corps had existed side
by side, the one maintaining its traditional interest in horse-warfare
and the other experimenting upon a modest scale with the same type
of warfare reduced to mechanical terms.

Throughout the later stages of the First World War, cavalry and
Cruisers had worked together, but never with any degree of success.
On the march the tanks could not keep up with the cavalry, and in
action the cavalry could not always keep up with the tanks. In shock-
action the horse was helpless against the machine-gun. Plainly the
time had arrived when the cavalry must mechanise themselves or
disappear from the Army List.

But sentiment has deep roots, and from 1919 to 1939 the cavalry,
though somewhat reduced in numbers through economic stringency,

stuck to their horses, continued their training, and developed their tactics upon orthodox cavalry lines. The sequel was interesting, for when their horses were finally taken from them those tactical ideas remained. In fact, it was not so much the tanks which swallowed the cavalry as the cavalry which swallowed the tanks. No one had foreseen this, but in retrospect the fact was plain to see.

The process was gradual. As early as 1920 eight yeomanry regiments were converted into Territorial Armoured Car Companies of the Royal Tank Corps, and thus achieved the distinction of being the first cavalry units to be mechanised.

Meanwhile the twenty-eight Regular cavalry regiments had been reduced by amalgamation to twenty. During the period 1928-9 two of these, the 11th Hussars and 12th Lancers, were mechanised, each forming what was known as a Cavalry Armoured Car Regiment. They retained their original cavalry titles.[1] However, cavalry mechanisation did not set in wholesale until ten years later—until the very eve of the Second World War, in fact.

It may be asked, with some reason, why this drastic and fundamental change in the equipment and technique of an outstanding arm of the British Army should have been delayed until the eleventh hour. There were three reasons for this.

The first was the difficulty experienced by the authorities in deciding upon a settled tank policy; the second was the continuous ban imposed upon large-scale army expenditure at this time—after all, tanks are most expensive weapons—and the third (and not the least) was the prolonged rear-guard action put up by the devotees of the horse.

That the cavalry were able, in a comparatively short time, to adapt themselves wholeheartedly to a complete revolution, not only in their equipment and battle practice but in their very point of view and habit of mind, is striking evidence of the resource, loyalty and *esprit de corps* exhibited by all concerned. And they did not go unrewarded; for since 1939 the part played in every theatre of war by our mechanised cavalry has but enhanced the glittering record of their previous incarnation.

Such, in brief outline, is the story of the mechanisation of the British Army. Most stress has been laid upon the development of the tank, destined to become, for the time being, at any rate, the dominant factor in land warfare.

---

[1] The 11th Hussars subsequently served under General Wavell in Libya, and are honourably mentioned in his Dispatch. The 12th Lancers led the B.E.F. into Belgium on May 10th, 1940.

But the conversion to mechanisation was extended to all arms—to the artillery and engineers, for instance, with a resultant enormous increase in mobility and effect. First-line transport was speeded up to an equal intensity, so that supplies—ammunition, petrol, rations and water—could keep pace with the vastly increased demand for them. By 1939 at least twenty per cent of the infantry were conveyed upon wheels or tractors. Moreover, new and ever more ingenious mechanical devices were perpetually in preparation.

War, in other words, had been converted into a species of lightning games of chess—of three-dimensional chess—played over a board a thousand miles square, in the course of which an army might cross a frontier one day and occupy an entire country the next.

Naturally, in order to produce the men capable of handling these mechanical marvels, and of exploiting them at their full value, a new system of training, and a 'hardening' process never before contemplated, had become a vital necessity.

The very thorough steps taken to achieve this end are considered in the following chapter.

CHAPTER XII

MAKING A MODERN SOLDIER

THE complications of military training advance *pari passu* with the development of ever more effective weapons of war. So does the difficulty of handling large bodies of troops in the field; for with the advent of mechanised warfare military operations now have to be conducted at a *tempo* which relegates the historic battles of the past almost to the semblance of a section of the Bayeux tapestry.

Let us consider the formations of the seventeenth or eighteenth century. Cromwell's New Model Army employed pike-men and matchlock-men, or musketeers, in varying proportions. They fought in six open ranks (reduced to three when in close order), with the pikemen in the middle and the musketeers on the flanks. Extended order and individual action were things unknown: men fought in a solid phalanx like the Macedonians of Philip's day, and their orders were given to them in precise detail and without unseemly haste.

The pikemen, who would ultimately have to come to grips with the enemy—a cavalry charge, perhaps—were equipped with a light cuirass and helmet: the musketeers wore long red coats, or cassocks, grey breeches and stockings, and a broad-brimmed hat. They must have offered a picturesque spectacle—and a good mark. But we have to remember that the original purpose of conspicuous uniform was to enable friend to be distinguished from foe: it was only towards the end of the nineteenth century, when artillery and small-arms fire became too accurate to be ignored, that the armies of the world adopted chameleon tactics and clothed themselves in the colours of earth, trees and sky.

Before Cromwell arose a military genius of the first order, in the person of Gustavus Adolphus of Sweden, to revolutionise the whole art of handling troops in the field. He had realised that the key to flexibility of manœuvre and fire-control consists in the establishment of small formations. He reduced infantry battalions to a strength of 500—formerly they had run as high as 3,000—and introduced the use of small 'platoons', firing alternately and to a certain extent independently. It was the first step towards teaching the individual soldier to act, when necessary, for himself—the first step in a very long road; so long, indeed, that for a full century after Marlborough, European battle tactics had altered but little. Troops still went into action with the stately ritual of a full-dress parade, their lines dressed and colours flying.

The performance of men so handled called for perfect fire-discipline and for conduct, on occasion, verging on the heroic. At Fontenoy the Duke of Cumberland, in person, led seventeen battalions of British infantry to the attack. They advanced under murderous fire, with muskets at the shoulder and without firing a shot until within fifty yards of their opponents. Then down came the muskets to the present, and the French firing-line was withered out of existence. Again, to this day upon every 1st of August the men of six of our Line Regiments wear roses in their caps. This is to remind them of the battle of Minden in 1759, at which a spectacle was seen which the French commander declared afterwards he had never thought to be possible—'a single line of infantry break through three lines of cavalry and tumble them to ruin'. Sir John Fortescue describes this particular performance as the most astonishing feat ever accomplished by British infantry.

So far, then, the British soldier had been trained, and very efficiently trained, to fight as an unquestioning, unthinking automaton. But at the beginning of the nineteenth century Sir John Moore, perhaps the most practical of army reformers, introduced an entirely new element into military training. He was the first to recognise that the humblest soldier is a sentient being: he took enormous pains not only to make a man understand what he was doing but to interest him in the reasons for doing it. He achieved his first object by intelligent instruction, and his second by sympathetic understanding and considerate treatment.

Moore himself, as a boy, could load and fire a musket five times in a minute, and he had realised that if men could be trained to do the same thing, not only would collective fire-power be greatly increased, but troops could remain continuously in position without retiring in rotation to the rear to reload. So he taught his men to act individually or in small units, and not to expend vast quantities of ammunition in a series of blind and wasteful volleys.

Moore did not live to see the full fruit of his labours, for he lies buried in the ramparts of Corunna; but it was men so trained and treated who formed the nucleus of the Light Division, destined to win deathless fame for themselves in the Peninsula.

To a certain extent Moore was anticipated by another and even shorter-lived military genius, General James Wolfe, who upon the Heights of Abraham in the battle of Quebec (in the same year as Minden, that *annus mirabilis* 1759) employed a formation of two ranks, thus anticipating Moore and Wellington and, for that matter, the general practice of most armies thereafter.

~❦(2)❦~

Tradition dies hard, especially in the British Army, and in any case long years of peace, such as those which followed Waterloo, do not lend themselves to reforming zeal. The Crimean War, however, administered a rude shock to national complacency, especially in the matter of army administration, and the Cardwell reforms marked the first step towards the creation of a really modern army. The equally painful lessons of the South African War brought further realisation of the need in future of imaginative planning, increased mobility, and the encouragement of individual initiative in action.

In 1914, consequently, the British Expeditionary Force which went to Flanders under Sir John French was not only the most highly trained but the most intelligent army (both in officers and men) that we have ever put into the field. And yet, from force of unforeseen circumstance, it seemed as if much of that training and intelligence must go for nothing; for after a brief period of open and exciting warfare the combatants on either side found themselves committed, as we have seen, to some four years of the corroding monotony of trench warfare, in which strategy stood still and tactics were resolved into a series of primitive, expensive, and mainly ineffective attacks in mass, in which manœuvre was impossible and individual initiative, except in such minor operations as trench-raids, found little opening.

The result was that during 1914–18 military training, so far as hundreds and thousands of men were concerned, resolved itself into teaching a man to march, fire a rifle, throw a hand-grenade, or fight at close quarters with a bayonet or entrenching-tool haft—a return, in other words, to missile- and shock-action in their crudest and most elementary form.

It is to the credit of our military planners, then, that, during what are now usually referred to as the Years Between, they declined to accept the experience of the First World War as a basis for future training or strategy. They were percipient enough to realise that the petrol-engine would be the dominant factor hereafter, and that the intense mobility of the new motorised army formations would relegate static trench warfare to a memory of the past. The next war, if it came, would be a war of strategy on the grand scale, and would be won by the best co-ordinated, best trained, and most mobile side, whether by land, sea or air. And upon that basis, during the next twenty years, in the face of economic stringency, shortage of recruits, lack of equipment, especially tanks, and national apathy, the training of the British Army was formulated and somehow maintained. It was uphill work, but at least the pattern had been outlined.

~⁂(3)⁂~

Let us now consider the full implications of the term 'Military Training' under conditions of total war—of war, that is, which calls for the services not merely of the Regular armed forces of a country, but of every able-bodied inhabitant thereof.

The main point to observe is that when an entire population is mobilised for action, whether in fighting, or in the production of munitions, or in the maintenance of sufficient basic industries to supply the essential needs of the community, the calling up of recruits for purely military duty must be conducted *on a scale proportionate to the ability of the country to supply the necessary sinews of war*; otherwise premature mobilisation will result. That is to say, a right balance must be maintained (and constantly readjusted) between the arms and the men, to obviate a shortage of arms and equipment upon the one hand and of troops to operate them on the other.

The difficulties of such an undertaking were enormous, and were aggravated by the fact that we had never contemplated such a strain upon our manpower resources as that imposed by the emergencies of 1940. It had not been intended, for instance, that in the next war against Germany, if and when it came, British soldiers by the million should be dispatched to the continent of Europe to assist the

French in establishing and maintaining another Western Front.[1] Our costly and wasteful experience during 1914–18 had taught us that lesson. In the event of another war we had merely promised to help the French with a certain number of divisions and no more. For the rest, we would revert to our traditional policy of retaining a free hand and employing our overwhelming seapower to transport troops overseas against the most vulnerable points in the enemy's defences.

But with the surrender of France and the advent of the Vichy Government, anything in the nature of an ordered strategic scheme went by the board overnight, and so far from invading enemy territory, we found ourselves compelled to stay at home, prepared to fight for our very existence.

Consequently, by the summer of 1940, the Commander-in-Chief Home Forces, whose duties in wartime have usually been limited to the efficient training and orderly dispatch of reinforcements for our armies overseas, found himself committed to the unexpected and staggering task of putting our island into a state of defence against the prospect of immediate invasion. However, the critical years were surmounted at last, and with the prospect of invasion reduced to the barest possibility we were able to resume our former hope and intention of invading France—backed in the fullness of time by the overwhelming strength of the United States—and of restoring freedom to the people of Europe.

Throughout the war our methods of training progressed with the lessons of the battlefield. As usual, the enemy had proved an invaluable instructor. We had taken due note of the novel technique of his armoured spearheads thrust forward without flank protection and closely supported from the air. We had also realised that the best way to learn to fight is to engage in battle: failing that, to train troops under conditions as close akin to those of an actual battlefield as possible.

Of course, this idea was not new. During the later stages of the First World War, whenever an important offensive had to be launched, that section of the enemy's trench system earmarked for attack was reproduced upon an identical scale in an area far behind the battle-line, and there the battle was rehearsed in detail. It was upon this principle and upon an appropriately intensified scale that the liberation of Europe, far distant though it might be, was planned and practised from 1940 onwards. These were to be no 'token'

---

[1] In the autumn of 1917, although the British occupied less than one-third of the Western Front, they were opposed by more than fifty per cent of the enemy troops.

exercises: conditions were to be made more realistic than ever before. Moreover, owing to the great increase in various types of weapon, almost every man had to become a specialist of some sort.

To this end the training schemes already in progress in War Office schools and training units were presently augmented by the establishment of so-called Battle Schools. These were originally maintained by the various units involved, which had set up a central depot for the training of instructors at Barnard Castle, in County Durham.

The aim of the new battle drill was first to provide the man under training with a greater sense of realism, and secondly to give the junior leaders—a corporal, say, in charge of a half-section—a grounding in the simple but elastic rules governing minor tactics amid the confusion and distraction of (almost) actual conflict. Its most significant feature was that it came to birth not in the War Office schools or training units but within the companies and battalions of field force divisions. In other words, it was based not only upon imaginative planning but upon hard experience.

By 1942 battle drill was universally accepted and officially adopted by the War Office, which at once set about devising the most effective machinery for the conversion of raw recruits into up-to-date fighters in the shortest possible time.

This was by no means as simple and mechanical an undertaking as might appear, as we shall presently see when we come to examine the question in greater detail. The outstanding problem, which increased rather than decreased with the progress of the war, was that of the most effective and at the same time the most *economical* allocation of manpower; for in this particular allocation the Army, as frequently noted, ran last in the race for priorities.

This last fact was brought home to the House of Commons in no uncertain—indeed, in startling—fashion by the Prime Minister, in a speech delivered in Secret Session on June 25th, 1941.

He began by announcing that in the Battle of the Atlantic no less than 4,500,000 tons of British shipping had been sunk during the past twelve months, and that for the time being the Admiralty was to have an absolute priority on anti-aircraft artillery, Bofors guns, and other defensive weapons. In other words, the Army must go without. An extra 40,000 men, too, would have to be released from the manpower pool for ship-repairing.

'I had to make very severe demands on the War Office', said Mr. Churchill, 'to cut down their manpower requirements.' He added the surprising information that the British Army was not, as the Press and public appeared to imagine, a force of some four or five millions,

A COASTAL DEFENCE POST: ENGLAND 1941

AN ANTI-AIRCRAFT BATTERY: ENGLAND 1941

A ROCKET BATTERY (ANTI-AIRCRAFT) IN ACTION

HOME GUARD INSTRUCTION

A DAIMLER ARMOURED CAR

A.T.S. ON ANTI-AIRCRAFT GUN SITE

THE 5.5-INCH GUN HOWITZER

THE VALENTINE BRIDGE-LAYER

THE 'FLAIL' TANK IN ACTION

THE 'DUKW'

AN EARLY TYPE OF LANDING CRAFT (M)

THE CRUSADER TANK

NORTH AFRICA 1941

NORTH AFRICA 1942

NORTH AFRICA 1943: THE MARETH LINE

ITALY

ITALY

NORTH-WEST EUROPE 1944

NORTH-WEST EUROPE 1944

NORTH-WEST EUROPE 1944: INTO ARNHEM

NORTH BURMA 1944

BURMA: THE ROAD TO KALEWA

BURMA 1945

but of about half that total—excluding the Home Guard, India and the Dominions. Nevertheless, he had felt constrained to ask the Secretary of State for War and the Army Council to accept for the moment a further reduction of 500,000 men. But that was the extreme limit to which he was prepared to go.

'I must warn the House', he concluded, 'that I cannot and will not have the Army drained, mutilated, and knocked about any further. Soldiers must not be taken from their training. *In a few months, or even less, we may be exposed to the most frightful invasion the world has ever seen.* We have a foe who, to wipe us out for ever, would not hesitate to lose a million men; and if he tries to come here we have got to take care that he loses that or better. For this purpose military training must be carried to the highest degree. The men must be active, well-disciplined, competent with their arms, practised in all the latest manœuvres which our hard experience suggests.'

Such was the situation with regard to army training in the summer of 1941. In order to appreciate the extra strain thrown upon the Director of Military Training and his associates at that time, let us briefly consider the normal routine of peacetime.

⤚(4)⤙

There is, or was, a popular impression that in time of peace the British Army does no work worth mentioning. A certain amount of stereotyped, perfunctory marching and counter-marching on the barrack square; a rigid insistence on spit and polish; an occasional route-march or visit to the rifle-range; then the rest of the day spent in loafing about. Such was the general picture of the life of our home forces as conveyed to the public mind by 'anti-militarists' and the less-responsible section of our Press even in the early nineteen-thirties. The officers, it was understood, spent most of their time on leave.

It may, therefore, be of interest to consider what the Army of those days really did.

In the first place it worked practically without a break year by year (except for a brief holiday period round Christmas) from the middle of October until the middle of the following September, and moreover was hard put to it within that period to complete the syllabus laid down for it.

The months from October to February were fully occupied by what may be called individual training—instructing the recruit, first

in the elements of military drill and discipline—including a good deal
of domestic drudgery in the way of floor-scrubbing and coal fatigues
—and in the use and care of his rifle. In addition he had to make
himself familiar with other weapons—the 2-inch mortar, the grenade
and the Bren machine-gun. Then came such not inconsiderable
trifles as visual training and the judging of distance; anti-gas measures
and decontamination; scouting and sniping; packing and loading
vehicles; 'embussing' and 'debussing'; wiring, digging and revet-
ting. To these may be added such exercises as semaphore-training,
instruction in the use of ground both by day and night, and the art
of bridging captured trenches during attack.

After that came six weeks' of musketry training. This carried the
young infantry soldier into April, when the time arrived for sections
and platoons to receive instruction in simple tactical exercises.

Company Training followed: presently companies were welded into
battalions, and the day of elaborate mass operations was at hand. Then
came Brigade Training, under canvas perhaps; and finally a grand
climax in the form of Divisional Training and Autumn Manœuvres.

The officers, in addition to their purely military duties, now devoted
a considerable part of their time to imparting instruction in the
lecture-room: this involved their own attendance at various intensive
'courses' in the subjects they were called upon to teach.

Such was the general routine of army training in peacetime. It
was by no means severe, but it was sufficient to keep officers and men
fully occupied throughout the year; and it was men so trained and
led who ultimately upheld the honour and reputation of the British
soldier from the Dyle to the beaches of Dunkirk.

But with the outbreak of the Second World War everything had to
be intensified. First, troops had to be rendered efficient, not within a
methodically spaced period of training but at the earliest possible
moment, for the demand for reinforcements grew steadily. Secondly,
upon the substructure of the basic exercises enumerated above had
now to be superimposed the strenuous regime of battle-training, with
all its realistic accompaniments and intensified *tempo*. Thirdly, the
process had to be applied, not to a Regular Army of 212,000 men,
but to an army of millions, taken straight from the peaceful pursuits
of civil life.

It will be agreed, then, that the task confronting the Army Council,
the Commander-in-Chief Home Forces, and the Director of Military
Training upon the outbreak of the Second World War was a truly
formidable one. We had, for the moment, as many men as we could
handle, but little or no equipment for them. There was a serious

shortage of training-instructors, and of those available few at that time were possessed of first-hand experience of war; and most of these were either wounded or war-weary men. Even the possession of first-hand knowledge and experience did not invariably mean an efficient instructor. The more highly qualified a man may be to teach, the less successful he frequently proves as a teacher; first because he may not possess the personality necessary to impress himself upon his pupils; secondly because, owing to his own complete mastery of his subject, he fails to appreciate the difficulties of the beginner, and persistently talks over his head.

So the help of the Adjutant-General was invoked, and a special 'Method of Instruction' Wing was opened at the Army School of Education in December 1942. The method adopted was to eliminate straightforward 'lecturing' as far as possible, and to begin at the other end, as it were, by encouraging the pupil to ask questions and so win the knowledge and instruction which he knew himself to be in need of. The primary object was to keep him interested.

The students came from O.C.T.U.s[1] and Primary and Corps Training Units, and the general idea was that when they had graduated they should go back to their original units and spread the gospel. In addition, a travelling team was formed for each arm of the Service, which visited the various training units and conducted small courses at each. Conferences were held periodically at the War Office, and fresh and improved methods discussed. The assistance of army psychiatrists was also invoked and proved of considerable value, as we have seen. The net result was a marked improvement in the efficiency of instructors and the progress of army training.

A third, and even greater problem of this time, was to house and train an army of hundreds of thousands within the confines of a small, densely populated and highly industrialised island, in which unfenced or sparsely inhabited areas were almost non-existent. By contrast the United States, when their time came, were in a position, with 3,250,000 square miles of territory available, to construct great camps and lay out training-grounds, including artillery ranges, almost at will within a single self-contained area. But in Britain troops had frequently to be billeted in hotels or residential blocks sometimes far removed from their training-grounds; and although camps and hutments sprang up subsequently throughout the country, there were never sufficient to meet the perpetual demand. The construction of these, too, was not only an expensive matter, but threw an additional strain upon the administration services.

[1] Officer Cadet Training Units.

A final and outstanding handicap was the character of the British people, as reflected not only in our new conscript armies but in the attitude of Press and public. When as a nation we find ourselves up against reality; when the position is such that nothing but a miracle of effort and endurance and sacrifice can save us from national disaster—or, alternatively, when we suddenly recognise a great moral issue and decide that it is our duty to fight for it—then we are the greatest and most terrible people in the world, because once we start we never give in. But to touch us off we need a detonator, and a powerful one.

In September 1939 and during the following ten months the detonator was not forthcoming. The Phoney War lulled us into a comfortable sense of security and a conviction that everything could come all right, as it always did. It had an especially soporific effect upon the troops in training. The stimulus of realism was entirely lacking: no fighting had taken place in France, and in March 1940 a London stockbroker had won a bet at odds of fifty to one that not a bomb would be dropped on England during the first six months of the war. In such circumstances it was not easy for the troops under training to maintain an attitude of continuous heroism, or for that matter of strained devotion to duty.

On the other hand, the Phoney War afforded the Commander-in-Chief Home Forces and the Directorate of Military Training an invaluable respite in which to overtake some of the arrears both in organisation and equipment.

Then, in May 1940, came Dunkirk—and the requisite detonator. The country sprang to life, conscripts turned into soldiers overnight, and the Second World War began in earnest.

⇜(5)⇝

At the beginning of the war the Directorate of Military Training formed part of the Department of the Chief of the Imperial General Staff. The D.M.T. himself, according to the War Office List for 1939, was responsible to the C.I.G.S. for 'the co-ordination of the military training of the Army, both Regular and Territorial,[1] and of the Supplementary Reserve in Commands, and in all educational and training establishments; also for the organisation of post-mobilisation training'. He was Inspector of Infantry, and was also closely associated with the Directors of Military Operations and Military

---

[1] The Territorials were absorbed into the Regular Army in 1939.

Intelligence, as well as with the Director of Staff Duties, who was responsible for the production of staff officers.

These heavy commitments of the D.M.T. were spread over four branches, each under the control of a General Staff Officer, Grade I. One was mainly concerned with exercises and general co-ordination, two more dealt with arms training, and the fourth with the provision of officers, together with education, the Staff School, and the Senior Officers' School.

Further into the somewhat complicated ramifications of the Directorate we need not penetrate, except to add that with the progress of the war its responsibilities were continuously increased, until by 1943 the number of branches was raised to six, each under a Deputy Director of Military Training. This relieved the Director himself of a great deal of desk-work, and gave him opportunity to travel freely and observe the progress of training among the various formations. There was already in existence a peace establishment of individual inspectors for various arms of the Service. The number of these was now increased to ten, covering every branch of military activity, from artillery training to army education and chemical warfare.

One of the most important and difficult functions of the Directorate throughout the war was that of producing sufficient mechanics and electricians to handle the new and complicated equipment of a mechanised army. The task was rendered the more onerous because the men best qualified for these duties were already being retained in civil life, in 'reserved occupations', to assist in the output of tanks, aircraft, and other engines of war. After 1942 the Ministry of Labour ceased altogether to release such technicians to the Army, and the Army was compelled to manufacture its own, a formidable undertaking when we consider the enormous number required. Still, the thing was done, somehow. Volunteers were attracted by the lure of increased pay, and schools of instruction were set up everywhere, even in garages under civilian instructors.

The history and progress of the Directorate throughout the war fall roughly into five periods. First came the months from September 1939 to August 1940, which can best be described as 'early preparatory'. Next came two years of preparation at the highest pressure, in which, under the perpetual menace of invasion and defeat, active training had to be combined with defence measures. Difficulties during these first two periods were increased by the enforced removal (owing to air-raids) of the greater part of the Directorate to Cheltenham, leaving only the D.M.T. and his Deputy and M.T.1. in London. This involved considerable waste of time in journeys to and from

Cheltenham and in long telephone discussions. But by 1942 the bombing had ceased sufficiently to permit of the return of most of the Directorate to London, and the organisation had assumed its true and almost final shape. Moreover, arms and equipment were now flowing in abundantly.

The third phase lasted until December 1943. We were over the crest now; morale was high and spirits confident, this time with reason. The fourth phase covered the invasion of Europe and the turn of the tide in the Far East. Our training organisation had now reached its maximum size and effect: on the other hand the man-power situation was a perennial source of anxiety. However, Germany was beaten by May 1945, and the fifth and final period set in with the surrender of Japan and the occupation of the British Zone in Germany by the 21st Army Group, subsequently the B.A.O.R.

~(6)~

The reader may be interested to consider the following list of training schools existing in October 1942, all under the control of the D.M.T.

School	*Location*
Staff College	Camberley
Senior Officers' School	Oxford
A.F.V. School	Bovington
School of Artillery	Larkhill
School of A.A. Artillery	Shrivenham
Coast Artillery School	Bude
School of Military Engineering	Ripon
School of Signals	Catterick
School of Infantry	Barnard Castle
Military College of Science	{ Stoke { Bury
Army Gas School	{ Winterborne Gunner { Fort Tregantle
Small-arms School—Hythe Wing	{ Bisley { Netheravon
School of Military Administration	Brockenhurst
R.A. Mech. Traction School	Rhyl
Army School of Physical Training	Aldershot
Intelligence Training Centre	{ Matlock { Cambridge
School of Aircraft Recognition	Deepcut

School	Location
Infantry D. and M. School	Harrogate
Advanced Handling and Fieldcraft School	Llanberis
Allied Special Training Centre	Lochailort
War Dogs Training School	Harringay
Camouflage Div. and Training Centre	Farnham
Mountain and Snow Warfare Training Centre	Glenfeshie
R.A.C. Officers' Tactical School	Tidworth
Canal Defence Light School	Morpeth
Motor Fitters' School	Aldershot
Officers' Training School, R.A.S.C.	Aldershot
Officers' Training School, R.E.M.E.	Kettering
School of Electric Lighting	Gosport
Army Technical School (Boys)	Arborfield

The list is illuminating, first as an indication of the enormous number of specialised services called for by modern warfare, and secondly from its obvious demand for a very large staff of instructors. These at one time numbered no fewer than 90,000, all ranks, including administrative personnel—an establishment calculated to handle a monthly intake of 20,000 men drafted into the Army for training.

To maintain such a large body of instructors was obviously to deprive our armies overseas of some highly experienced and valuable officers and men, and commanding officers in the field struggled hard, and sometimes successfully, to retain possession of these. Yet every one of them was wanted in the home centres, for to reduce their number would be either to lower the standard of training or lengthen the time necessary for the education of the men under their charge. It was the old story—the perpetual tug-of-war between the rate of output and its quality. In due course the number was brought down to 68,000.

The reader may be inclined to be critical of a system which apparently called for such a disproportionate number of instructors, but he may rest assured that for the complications of modern warfare, as evinced in the list of training schools above, and the enormous amount of individual instruction required, especially from the N.C.O. instructors, who were in a large majority, such an establishment is not excessive. This total also included all officers and men employed upon purely administrative duties. In any case we may be tolerably certain that no extravagances would have been permitted by that powerful and independent body, sitting in perpetual judgements on such enterprises, the War Establishments Committee, whose function it was to guard the interests of the taxpayer and, above all, to see that due economy of manpower was observed.

~☆(7)☆~

We pass now from the teachers to the taught, and to the steps by which the recruit proceeded from the status of peaceful civilian to that of seasoned warrior.

By the end of 1942, with abundant equipment at last available, training routine was more or less stabilised. The 'new boy', on arrival, spent his first six weeks in a Primary Training Centre, or Wing. Here he received six weeks' basic infantry training, and was then tested by 'Personnel Selection' boards, who decided upon that arm of the Service for which he seemed best fitted. The decision of the selectors did not always square with the preferences of the selectee, for it depended upon the requirements of a given arm at a given moment; and a would-be gunner, for example, might find himself in the infantry. But these little disappointments were usually accepted philosophically enough. We were fighting for our existence now, and this was no time to insist upon personal predilections. So willing work became the order of the day, and for much longer hours than in peacetime.

It should be noted here that by this time the infantry had come into its own. The authorities had recognised the principle that in every soldier in every arm of the Service the first essential quality must be a sound infantry training, if only to teach a man to use his legs in an enervating world of mechanised transport. Moreover, even in mechanised warfare the man is still more important than the machine. So the infantry now had a proper Arms School at Barnard Castle (formerly the habitat of the Instructors' Training School) and a Director of Infantry Training in the War Office to look after its organisation and maintain its prestige.

It should be added that the strong prejudice against infantry service (based upon certain not altogether unjustifiable misgivings on the subject of 'cannon fodder') which prevailed at the outset of the war, had now been considerably allayed by the sense of reassurance bestowed by mechanised transport and tank support.

After his six week's Primary Training and a week's leave, a man would proceed to a Corps Training Centre of the arm with which he was to serve—an Infantry Training Centre, or an R.A.C. Regiment, or other appropriate establishment. It should be noted that there was little or no battalion training now. There was no time. The urgent need was to put men through an intensive course of Divisional and Corps Training, in order to be able to supply reinforcement drafts, as and when required, in the shortest possible time.

The length of time which a man spent in the centre depended upon the type and standard of training involved. The infantryman received ten weeks' training: this was the shortest of the courses, the longest being that required for Royal Signals, which necessitated instruction in such mysteries as wireless telephoning and radar.

Naturally, each man under training had to attain a definite standard of proficiency before proceeding further. If he displayed unusual application and ability, and his commanding officer, in his capacity of military 'talent-scout', decided that he was likely to make an officer, he was sent before a War Office Selection Board to be considered as a candidate for an Officer Cadet Training Unit, or O.C.T.U. If selected, he was sent to a pre-O.C.T.U., where a final decision was duly taken as to whether or no he had in him the makings of a leader of men.

Since 1938 it had been laid down as a fixed principle that in future no man should be eligible for a commission unless he had served six months in the ranks. It is interesting and significant of the progressive spirit of the War Office of today to note that this sweeping measure of Army reform originated in the Department of the Adjutant-General, and owed nothing to external or political pressure. The rule fulfilled two purposes: first, the road to a commission was now thrown wide open (or even wider, for it had always existed) to every private soldier; secondly, the army officer of the future would carry with him throughout his service a personal and sympathetic knowledge of the point of view and habit of mind of the rank and file. Thus the private would be rendered increasingly aware of the Field-Marshal's baton in his knapsack, while the officer would have become familiar, by actual experience, with the knapsack's humbler and more material contents.

Much careful consideration, backed in time by the lessons of increasing experience, was devoted to deciding upon the essential qualities of a good junior officer. At first there was a tendency, induced perhaps by the fact that there was a desperate shortage of such officers and little time to test a young man's capabilities to the full, to attach more importance to technical aptitude and physical stamina than to character and leadership. Under the searching test of actual warfare, however, it was soon a case of *solvitur ambulando*, and a definite change in official opinion resulted. If it was found impossible to obtain sufficient officers possessed of all four of the qualities just enumerated, then it was decided, inevitably and rightly, that the man of character, the man endowed with confidence in himself and ability to inspire confidence in others, must be preferred to the technical expert, however well-trained or efficient. In its way the decision was a minor triumph for an ancient tradition.

⌁(8)⌁

In his pre-O.C.T.U. the cadet officer was brought up to a certain requisite standard before proceeding to the O.C.T.U. itself. There he might also have to complete his training as a private soldier. His sojourn in the pre-O.C.T.U. might be for anything from one to nine weeks. A certain number of candidates naturally failed to stay the course, and were returned to the ranks. The rest passed on to the O.C.T.U.

The length of the actual O.C.T.U. course varied with the degree of technicality. The Infantry Course lasted seventeen weeks, that of the R.E. about thirty. Then the young officer was posted to a unit in the United Kingdom, where he arrived well charged with theory, but, so far, with no experience in the practical handling of men. Having acquired that, he was ready for his new responsibilities, and was dispatched thereto.

One other form of officers' training must be mentioned here— so-called 'Conversion Training'. This was rendered necessary by the fact that the official calculation of infantry 'wastage' had been underestimated, and it became necessary to convert artillery and engineer officers into infantrymen to make up the deficit—something of a hardship for men who had become proficient in and attached to their present job. But in total war needs must.

Last, but not least, we come to the training of the ordinary private soldier. Upon the completion of his course at the corps centre he was passed on to a unit of one of the so-called Reserve Divisions, or was sent overseas direct to continue his training in surroundings calculated to acclimatise him to actual war conditions. Or he might be attached before departure to a holding unit, which was a sort of waiting-room for men ready to go abroad but for whom there was no present demand. (This last contingency was regulated by the casualty rate.)

These Reserve Divisions were for most of the time three in number : their purpose was to bring the reinforcements for the armies overseas up to a recognised standard of 'elementary collective training' before being dispatched thereto. But it is to be feared that here to a certain extent desire outran performance, and inevitably. In the first place, until the Mediterranean was reopened in 1943 the reinforcements, travelling as they were compelled to do by way of the Cape of Good Hope, took at least three months to reach their destination, and longer still if they were bound for the Far East. After such a time-lag something in the nature of a refresher-course was inevitable upon arrival. True, resolute provision had been made for the continuance of training *en route*; but a crowded (and possibly rolling) ship does not lend itself to military exercises, especially when most of the space not allotted to troops is occupied by stores and equipment. Little of the kind was usually practicable except some routine P.T. exercises. Secondly, newly arrived contingents usually required specialised training in the type of warfare—desert, jungle, or enclosed country—to which they were committed; so the field forces in most theatres gradually adopted the habit of setting up their own local training centres in which to complete the education of the new arrivals.

In other words, collective training was now transferred to the actual theatre of war—the Western Desert, let us say—'a tactician's paradise and a Quartermaster's nightmare'.

⁓(9)⁓

Such, in brief and necessarily condensed outline, is the story of how our citizens' Army of 1939–45 was called to arms and trained in their victorious use.

The method of their instruction was, in a sense, characteristically British, and would have found little favour with the military purists of certain European countries. The reader will probably have noted for himself that throughout the war two forms of military training were going on within the United Kingdom at the same time. One, which concerned the primary or 'individual' training both of officers and men, was under the direct control of the War Office, through the D.M.T.; the other, which could be broadly termed 'collective' training of men much further advanced in their education, came under the Commander-in-Chief Home Forces, and was thus decentralised, to a certain extent, among the commands and the various field-force divisions in training there.

Such a system of divided control may appear an irregular and somewhat clumsy arrangement, leading to such handicaps as the overlapping of interests and the issue of contradictory orders. So it is, and sometimes does. But the only infallible test of a system is the degree of success with which it works. When both sides are determined that it shall work it does work; and this is what happened in the case of our army training scheme. The British people have always been allergic to formal frameworks—witness that curious, haphazard medley of hoary precedents and *ad hoc* legislation the British Constitution itself—and have thriven surprisingly throughout the centuries on rule-of-thumb and common sense. Consequently, the apparently illogical system under which our Army was trained during the Second World War somehow enabled the respective merits of central and decentralised control to be employed to the best advantage of each. When, as sometimes happened, the duties or interests of War Office schools and Command training units touched or overlapped—in the case of weapon training, for instance—close liaison was maintained between the two bodies and the respective claims of 'supervision' and 'assistance' were tactfully balanced. Willingness is all.

Perhaps chief credit for this fortunate consummation should be awarded to the man who so far in this narrative has been referred to merely by his official title—the Commander-in-Chief Home Forces—General Sir Bernard Paget, one of the truly great soldiers of the war. His name is comparatively unfamiliar to the newspaper-reader, yet he was a Commander-in-Chief for a longer period than any other of our war leaders. His outstanding achievement was a twofold one: in 1941, at perhaps our darkest hour, he took command of home forces and contrived, from most inadequate resources, to put our country into a state of defence against invasion; after which he devoted his energies and imagination to the training and equipping of 21st Army Group upon its formation in 1943, against the arrival of D-Day and the invasion of occupied Europe—with what success is now a matter of history.

Previous to this, in 1940, he had contrived, in the face of almost insuperable difficulties and with comparatively small loss, to extricate our Norwegian Expeditionary Force from its unhappy situation at Andalsnes.[1] In 1944 he became Commander-in-Chief Middle East.

It was for his work in forging the weapon which pierced Hitler's Western Wall that General Paget will chiefly be remembered, though

[1] Owing to the starvation of our Intelligence Services during the Years Between, General Paget's information regarding Norwegian terrain was so inadequate that he was forced to fall back on *Baedeker*.

fate denied him the final honour of wielding that weapon himself. As a trainer of troops and an organiser of victory, he performed the same service (on an infinitely greater scale) for Alexander and Montgomery as that rendered by Sir John Moore to Wellington; and his name will be honoured by all soldiers accordingly.

CHAPTER XIII

THE TURN OF THE TIDE

~(1)~

WE return now to North Africa, where we left General Wavell in June 1941 facing Rommel on a line west of Sidi Barrani, with most of his previous gains, except Tobruk, relinquished for the usual reason at that time—lack of means to hold them. On July 5th he had departed to take up even heavier responsibilities in the Far East. He was succeeded by Sir Claude Auchinleck.

An operational stalemate now set in, and persisted for some months. But General Auchinleck was by no means idle: there was much to do, especially in matters of reorganisation and administration.

Before we consider these highly important activities in detail, let us briefly review the general picture and larger events of that most fateful period.

The Battle of the Atlantic was raging as fiercely as ever, and the food supplies of our island were dwindling steadily. Air-raids over Britain had not yet ceased. The Mediterranean was closed, and the loss of Crete, together with the presence of the Luftwaffe in Sicily, had rendered the position of Malta, our principal base for submarine and air attack on enemy supply-lines to Tripoli and North Africa generally, even more precarious than before.

In May came an additional menace to our sea communications, in the shape of the great German commerce-raider *Bismarck*, reputed to be the most powerful battleship afloat. She remained afloat, however, for too short a period to put her reputation to an extended test, for she was rounded up and sunk by units of the Royal Navy within three weeks of her appearance.

This chastening experience may have suggested to Hitler the advisability of intensifying his effort by land. Here he had two obvious choices open to him—either to strike down through Turkey, with the Iraq oilfields and the Persian Gulf as his objective, or to launch an attack on his quasi-ally, Soviet Russia. He chose the latter alternative, and on June 22nd, 1941, that country was invaded upon a thousand-mile front. Mr. Churchill promptly declared the Russians to be our Allies, and with the full backing of Parliament and people, promised them all possible aid.

Incidentally, the invasion of Russia conferred two immediate benefits upon the cause of Britain. It brought considerable relief from bombing to the much-enduring Maltese, at any rate during the summer months; and it aroused the United States to the growing danger to the peace of the New World. The result was the Atlantic Charter, signed by Mr. Churchill and President Roosevelt at sea in the following August.

~*(2)*~

Returning to Middle East Headquarters, we find General Auchinleck busily occupied upon an extensive scheme of reorganisation, rendered necessary by the scattered condition of the troops recently employed by General Wavell in his campaigns in Libya, Eritrea, Abyssinia, Greece, Crete, Iraq and Syria. Brigades had become separated from their divisions, and units from their brigades, while some formations, especially those of the armoured corps, had practically ceased to exist. Here General Auchinleck, in his report, pays just tribute to the skill and resource with which his predecessor had handled and distributed his inadequate forces, and in particular to his overall co-ordination of a command in which British and Allied troops spoke some forty different languages among them.

The actual machinery of organisation and control, then, required but little adjustment. Liaison between the Navy, Army and Air Force was equally satisfactory. The following details may be of interest.

First, and upon the highest level, came the Middle East War Council, with the Minister of State (an office recently created by the Prime Minister himself) in the chair. This body was mainly concerned with political matters affecting the Services in the Middle East. Next came the Middle East Defence Committee, consisting of the Minister of State and the three Commanders-in-Chief, and dealing with major operations and plans. At a slightly lower and wider level the Commanders-in-Chief's Committee (which was also attended by senior staff officers) dealt with operational and administrative questions. Daily liaison was further maintained by Inter-Service Intelligence and Operational Staff Conferences. Another committee was fully employed in the allocation of anti-aircraft sites and units. Finally, General Auchinleck himself was in constant personal touch with the Commander-in-Chief Mediterranean, and Air Force Officer Commanding-in-Chief. And so on down the scale. Thus the Chain of Command[1] within the Army itself was maintained unbroken, while the close co-operation of all three Services was firmly assured.

The ever-present and delicate problem of our relations with our French Allies in the Middle East had now to be approached and adjusted. The Vichy forces in Syria and the Lebanon had by this time capitulated, and in theory the Free French troops under General de Gaulle were in charge of the situation. But this implied a dangerous measure of divided control; so it was agreed between the General and our Minister of State,[2] in the first week of July, that the civil authority in Syria and the Lebanon should be left in the hands of the Free French, provided that British military security was not jeopardised. This, in effect, meant placing the Free French forces throughout the Middle East under the British Commander-in-Chief for operational purposes. To this General de Gaulle also agreed, and the matter appeared to be adjusted.

Unfortunately, the Free French were seriously short of experienced and reliable administrative officers, and there were complaints throughout Syria and the Lebanon that many of the ex-Vichyites who had ostensibly rallied to the cause of Free France, and so retained their official posts, had done so entirely with an eye to their own and Vichy's interests, and were both untrustworthy and corrupt.

Further, there was widespread and frank disappointment that Great Britain had not taken over Syria and Lebanon herself. Such a step, however, though eminently practical, would have been altogether too much for French *amour-propre*. Invaluable work was done at this point by the Spears Mission, who contrived, despite the obvious difficulties of the situation, to come to an amicable arrangement with their Gallic colleagues; while the military security of this vital area was finally guaranteed by an agreement between General Catroux, Délégué Général de France, and the British authorities. It was a somewhat uneasy pact, but it held, and at least Syria and the Lebanon were relieved of the menace of German infiltration.

General Auchinleck had next to apply himself to a problem of an entirely different kind—that presented by the fact that Middle East

[1] See p. 113.   [2] The Rt. Hon. Oliver Lyttelton, M.P.

Command had been growing steadily in extent and unwieldiness, and was now sprawling over a considerable tract of the African continent. A general conference was therefore held, at which it was agreed that an entirely new Command, to be known as East Africa Command, should be set up to embrace Ethiopia, the Somalilands, Kenya, Tanganyika, Nyasaland and Northern Rhodesia; and on September 15th, 1941, this decision took effect, with Lieut.-General Sir William Platt as Commander-in-Chief. This liberated General Auchinleck from the responsibility of the settlement and control of some 1,500,000 square miles of country—a territory larger than Soviet Russia—and left him free to concentrate upon the coming operations in the Western Desert.

⁓(3)⁓

General Auchinleck was determined to renew the offensive at the earliest possible moment. Considerable reinforcements were already available, and more were on the way. The newly arrived units and drafts were being put through their refresher-courses, and vast administrative preparations were in hand.

Rommel was also preparing to attack, but his plans were considerably hampered by the enterprise of the defenders of Tobruk, lying some ninety miles west of the Egyptian border. These, it will be remembered, had been left isolated after General Wavell's withdrawal in the spring of 1941; but so far from behaving like a beleaguered garrison they had maintained a persistently aggressive attitude, and had contained an enemy force twice their strength for several months. They enjoyed the added advantage of being fed from the sea.

In this connection it is appropriate here to make mention of the debt owed and freely acknowledged, now as ever, by the Army to the Royal Navy, especially the so-called Inshore Squadrons. Tobruk is a case in point. For 242 days that beleaguered stronghold was supplied and maintained by the Navy alone in its successful resistance to the enemy. During this period 6,600 men were conveyed thither with 1,400 tons of stores, and 5,000 brought back to Alexandria, at a cost of twenty-seven ships of war and seven merchant vessels. And Tobruk was by no means an isolated instance, but one of a perpetual series.

It was quite obvious then that General Auchinleck's offensive must include in its scope the relief of this garrison. But the general operation was to be upon a much more extensive scale than that, for strength now could be reckoned not in divisions or brigades but in corps. In fact, Auchinleck had under his command by this time two complete armies, the 8th and 9th, the former in Egypt, the latter in Palestine under the command of Sir Henry Maitland Wilson.

The 8th Army, of which we shall hear much, had started life as General Wavell's Army of the Nile, in which capacity we have already encountered it. It now appears, reconditioned and strongly reinforced, under its more familiar and famous designation; and to this force was assigned the task of undertaking the new offensive in the Western Desert.

Naturally, the increase in the strength of Middle East Forces, together with the promise of greater forces to come, involved a considerable extension of administrative routine and planning. These duties had been fulfilled hitherto, under ever-increasing difficulties, by General Auchinleck's Deputy Quartermaster-General and Assistant Adjutant-General. Plainly, it was high time to relieve these two officers of part of their burden. This was done by appointing a Principal Administrative Staff Officer, whose functions should include the co-ordination of the work of the Quartermaster-General's and Adjutant-General's departments and the direction of what may be called the administrative brains-trust. Upon October 18th, Lieut.-General R. S. Riddell-Webster was appointed to the post, and under the supervision of this distinguished officer[1] a comprehensive scheme of engineering and construction work was pressed forward. In this no fewer than sixty-nine pioneer units were employed, including men from Cyprus, India, Malta, Mauritius, Palestine, Sudan and East Africa—an impressive reminder of the resources of the British Empire. It should further be remembered that by contrast with Hitler's army of slave labourers in occupied Europe, these men (and there were women, too) were all volunteers and paid for their services.

Some idea of the work done during this period may be gathered from the fact that seventy-five miles of the extension of the Western Desert Railway were completed and the line between Suez and Ismailia doubled. New roads were built and old ones reconditioned, aerodromes and landing-grounds laid out, and a carefully planned scheme of hospital construction completed in full. A pipe-line was laid down to carry 1,000 tons of oil per day from Suez to Port Said, and—perhaps most essential adjunct of all to desert warfare—a water pipe-line was carried as far west as Mersa Matruh.

[1] General Riddell-Webster was subsequently appointed Quartermaster-General in the War Office.

~×(4)×~

Upon September 26th, 1941, 8th Army Headquarters, under the command of Lieut.-General Sir Alan Cunningham, assumed control of all troops in the Western Desert, with the exception of Tobruk, which for more than six months had exhibited outstanding ability to take care of itself.

The Army comprised two Corps, the 13th and 30th. None of the formations composing these corps was up to strength, even those in actual contact with the enemy: limitations of shipping space were responsible. In consequence, a choice frequently had to be made between the acceptance of fighting and of administration units. At the beginning of July the overall deficiency was sixteen per cent. All that could be done was to distribute personnel to the best advantage, devoting particular attention to the most indispensable formations.

General Auchinleck naturally concentrated upon his armour, with considerable success. At the beginning of July he could put into the field only two armoured-car regiments and the redoubtable 7th Armoured Division: even then the range and mobility of the latter were restricted by the fact that one brigade was equipped with infantry tanks instead of cruisers. By the end of October, however, he had at his disposal the 7th Armoured Division (now completely equipped), the 22nd Armoured Brigade, and the 1st Army Tank Brigade complete except for one battalion. He was also able to equip a third (British) armoured-car regiment, and to complete the equipment of two South African armoured-car regiments.

It is interesting to study the actual composition of these two famous corps, and the widely separated Imperial sources from which they flowed. The 13th, under Lieut.-General Godwin Austen (later under General Gott, at this stage commanding the 'Desert Rats'), consisted mainly of infantry, and included the 2nd New Zealand Division, the 4th Indian Division, and the 1st Army Tank Brigade. The 30th (Lieut.-General Willoughby Norrie), was made up of the 7th Armoured Division, the 1st South African Division, and the 22nd Guards Brigade. Naturally, the composition of the two corps varied with the replacements necessitated by wastage, but such was their original establishment.

We turn now from men to arms—the tanks in particular. The time is late 1941 ; we have been at war for two years, and are at last beginning to overtake our deficiencies in equipment generally. Vehicles of all types are moving in a steady stream from Great Britain, Canada, Australia and the Union of South Africa. These have been augmented since July by tanks and trucks from the United States (still neutral) under the Lend-Lease agreement.

Between the 1st of July and the end of October nearly 34,000 of these American 'trucks' (or motor lorries) and over 2,000 armoured vehicles had arrived. Considerable consignments of artillery and small-arms were also received, including 600 field guns, 200 anti-tank guns, and a quantity of anti-aircraft artillery. Small-arms included nearly 4,000 Bren guns, 1,000 mortars, and 80,000 rifles—substantial reinforcements indeed, but still insufficient for our needs. As in the case of the troops themselves, shortage of shipping space was responsible.

Our tank strength, from the point of view of actual numbers, was much more satisfactory; from that of quality, much less so. The three armoured brigades mustered 487 tanks in all in the 7th Armoured Division, but of these 165 were of the light Stuart (American) type, subsequently rated less as a tank than as an excellent reconnaissance vehicle. The rest were mainly Crusaders. The infantry tanks numbered 120—Matildas and Valentines. The crews, we are told, had great faith in the Matilda, a little out of date now but still a trusted friend. The Valentine, though not quite so effective in action, was almost equally popular for a different reason—the comparatively small maintenance which it required.

There were also some ninety heavy tanks in Tobruk.

It will be instructive at this point to examine the numbers and strength of the forces opposed to us, especially tanks.

Rommel had under his command the 15th and 21st Panzer Divisions—the much-boomed Afrika Korps—and the 90th Light Division, together with an Italian armoured division (Ariete) and seven infantry divisions. Of tanks he could muster 505, and was thus inferior to us in actual numbers; but in the matter of hitting power the situation was very different. More than half the Axis tanks were German Mark IIIs and IVs, both of which were superior to ours in armament, armour and reliability. None of our tanks mounted a gun heavier than the 2-pounder, whereas the German Mark III was equipped with a 50-mm. gun, which not only fired a 4½-pound shell, but far outranged anything of ours. Thus the Mark III tank, by firing from extreme range, could batter ours without fear of reprisal. This long-range superiority was especially valuable in desert fighting, where a target can be observed from over a mile away. The Mark IV had a 75-mm. gun of low velocity, chiefly employed against infantry.

A new tank, the Cromwell, mounting a 6-pounder gun and fully capable of dealing with the Mark III, was in course of production in

England, but was not yet available; so our existing machines had to make what shift they could. It is a tribute to the courage and resource of our tank crews that they were ultimately able, as we shall see, to overcome the tremendous handicap imposed on them and give almost as good as they got.

~❋(5)❋~

General Auchinleck would have welcomed a little more time in which to complete his preparations for the second battle of Libya, particularly from the point of view of training. Many of his troops and their equipment had arrived separately, and some units had had but a brief opportunity of familiarising themselves with their new weapons, especially the tanks. The 30th Corps had only been in existence for six weeks. But it was imperative to attack before Rommel could do so.

The purpose of the battle was to drive the Axis forces right out of Cyrenaica. The opening gambit was to be a turning movement, first west and then north, by the 30th Corps, calculated to threaten the enemy's line of retreat and so compel him to stand and fight. The 13th Corps was to strike northward towards the coast, and contain Bardia and Sollum. The operation was to be backed by a sortie in full force from Tobruk. Thus, if the enemy's main strength could be shattered at the outset, the subsequent drive across Cyrenaica, by way of Tobruk, Derna and Benghazi—names grown familiar by this time—might be achieved with comparative ease.

Matters did not turn out so simply as this—they seldom do—but the subsequent battle was 'one of the most exciting, and perhaps the fastest-moving, ever fought'.

Battle was joined on November 18th, 1941. Seven weeks later, on January 6th, 1942, Rommel, outmanœuvred by superior generalship and bustled westward for some 500 miles by a force inferior to his own both in numbers and equipment, found himself back at El Agheila on the Gulf of Serte, having lost all but fifty of his tanks and some 36,000 men taken prisoner, over 10,000 of whom were Germans.

This second battle of Libya was not a great victory, because it was not conclusive, and the advantage which it brought to British arms was destined to be short-lived. But it was a most notable achievement, though blanketed by the circumstance that it coincided almost exactly with Pearl Harbour and the entry of Japan and the United States into the war: consequently it attracted comparatively little attention in Britain and none at all in America. Nevertheless its course and conduct present certain features of profound interest and considerable educational value.

In the first place the Italians fought far more stoutly than could have been expected from their previous performances. This was largely due to the fact that many Italian units were now working with German troops, who inspired them with the confidence and *élan* which only come with strict discipline. As there were no less than seven divisions of them (in addition to their armoured division) our previous hope of an early and victorious decision in the Tobruk theatre was doomed to disappointment. Secondly, the battle was one of constantly changing movement. The result was considerable confusion at times in either direction. So far as the 8th Army were concerned it was touch and go upon more than one occasion, especially in the second phase of the battle: once only a single division, the 4th Indian, seemed to stand between Rommel's tanks and Cairo. (They proved equal to the occasion.) But hard-pressed and sometimes widely scattered units never failed to rally in the end. In the case of the 30th Corps this was largely due to wireless control, established on a complete scale for the first time. Units thus could not only be directed from rear headquarters but from the air.

Our tanks, too, though hopelessly outranged, developed an ingenious technique of emerging unexpectedly from behind a smokescreen or other cover and engaging the German Mark IIIs at close quarters; or, if attacked at long range, of feigning retreat and so luring the enemy within reach of our field artillery.

Brilliant work was done by a new formation. This consisted of columns of guns and infantry, conveyed in 15-cwt. trucks and extremely mobile. They were trained and led by Brigadier John Campbell, v.c., who organised a system of hit-and-run raids upon the enemy's rear designed to goad him into vain reprisals against an opponent who always had the legs of him. He delighted in leading these in person. The 8th Army paid him the well-deserved tribute of bestowing upon his followers the name 'Jock Columns'.[1]

What really decided the battle, however, was our control of the air. The air-support of the R.A.F., whether in affording overhead protection or in bombing enemy formations and landing-grounds, was superb.

That, perhaps, was why Rommel decided, quite suddenly, to break off the battle; or it may have been that he had decided merely *reculer*

---

[1] An American observer officer remarked of Campbell: 'He is a great guy, but he won't live long.' This prognostication, alas, proved only too true.

pour mieux sauter, especially since he had received news that heavy reinforcements were on the way to him. So he abandoned Derna and Benghazi, and withdrew to El Agheila. The 8th Army were too exhausted to follow him very far; but they had at least the satisfaction of reoccupying the sea coast of Cyrenaica, and thus restoring in some measure British air control over the Mediterranean—a matter of vital consequence to hard-pressed Malta.

The battle, however, was not quite over. A fortnight later Rommel struck back in considerable force. The 8th Army, hampered by long and tenuous communications by land, and having had no time to recondition the port of Benghazi for receiving supplies by sea, fell back; and presently the situation stabilised itself along a line running south from Gazala (midway between Tobruk and Derna) and roughly cutting Cyrenaica into two halves. There it stood fast for more than three months.

⇥(6)⇤

The first six months of 1942 marked the lowest ebb of the Allied fortunes during the war. Japan had come in on December 7th, 1941, and the Pacific battle-fleet of the United States lay sunk or disabled in Pearl Harbour. We ourselves had lost one-third of our battleships or battle-cruisers in seven weeks. The situation to date was revealed by Mr. Churchill in a speech delivered in Secret Session to the House of Commons on April 23rd.

'Before the Japanese entered the War,' he said, 'we were already fully extended in the North Sea, Atlantic, and Mediterranean theatres by sea, land, and air. We have drawn all possible forces to meet our new, fresh, and most formidable antagonist. But in spite of all we could do, and the risks we ran and are running, we are at present outnumbered by the sea, land, and air forces of Japan throughout the Far Eastern Theatre.

'The House must face the position squarely. Not only have we failed to stem the advance of the new enemy, but we have had to weaken seriously the hopeful operations we were carrying on against the old.'

This was ill and ominous news for those responsible for the operation in North Africa, for it meant that sorely needed and long-expected reinforcements would now have to be diverted elsewhere. The Prime Minister's next words confirmed these forebodings.

'The Japanese Army in the A.B.D.A.[1] area threatens simultaneously Australia, India, and, through Burma, China. They have destroyed or

---

[1] i.e. American-British-Dutch-Australian.

captured the following divisions of the Allies, or their equivalent: British and Indian 6; Dutch 3; United States 2; Filipinos 3 or 4. Total 14 or 15.'

The naval situation was even more alarming. The *Nelson* had been put out of action for six months. The new battleship *Prince of Wales* and the battle-cruiser *Repulse* had been destroyed off the coast of Malaya. In the Mediterranean the *Ark Royal* and *Barham* had recently been sunk, while the *Valiant* and *Queen Elizabeth* lay stranded in Alexandria Harbour, disabled by 'limpet' bombs. In other words, we had no battle squadron left in the Mediterranean at all, and the sea-defence of the Nile Valley had to be confined to submarine and destroyer forces and shore-based aircraft.

The Prime Minister referred with tempered satisfaction to the situation in Cyrenaica at that moment.

'I now come to the Middle East. Our strongest and best equipped army overseas stands in close contact with the enemy in Cyrenaica. Twice have we hunted the enemy out of the Benghazi triangle and twice have we been chased back ourselves. The very severe battle which General Auchinleck fought last year just missed being a decisive victory. . . . We inflicted three times the loss on the enemy that we suffered ourselves. Tobruk, after its stubborn defence, was relieved and is now a valuable supply-base. The Gazala position, strongly fortified and strongly held, is 115 miles west of the starting point of our advance.'

Meanwhile at Gazala itself the 8th Army, under its new commander Major-General N. M. Ritchie, was strenuously preparing for the next bout with the enemy. One thing was clear: this time that Army would be fighting to hold what it had gained rather than with the immediate hope of further conquests.

Britain for the moment exercised little or no control over the Central Mediterranean. Malta, under relentless bombing, was almost out of action as an offensive base, and Rommel's reinforcements were crossing in a steady stream from Sicily to Tripoli and Benghazi, while our own still ploughed the endless road round the Cape. Some of them were already being diverted to the Far East, and troops had been dispatched from the Middle East theatre itself (including a complete armoured brigade) to Ceylon, India and Burma; while most of the Australian units under General Auchinleck's command had been sent home to protect their own continent from possible invasion.

The 8th Army was sorely in need of more and better tanks and a really effective anti-tank gun. However, a certain number of American General Grant tanks were now available, and our long-promised 6-pounder guns were beginning to materialise. The R.A.F. were still perilously short of aircraft, especially fighters. Adequate reinforcements of all kinds would doubtless arrive in due course both from Britain and America, but until they did a further offensive was out of the question.

The 8th Army, then, spared no pains or exertion to make its position as strong as possible. The defence scheme was based upon a number of irregularly spaced strong-points (or 'boxes') running from north to south and linked by deep minefields. The focal point was a junction of several desert tracks, known as Knightsbridge, about twenty miles south-west of Tobruk and south-east of Gazala.

Both the 13th and 30th Corps had been to some extent reconstituted. The 13th, as previously, was composed chiefly of infantry, and included the 50th and 1st S. African Divisions, together with the 1st and 32nd Army Tank Brigades. The 30th comprised the 1st and 7th Armoured Divisions, a considerable and highly mobile force of armoured cars, and the Free French garrison of Bir Hacheim, a strong-point on the extreme south of the defensive line. Two brigades of the 2nd South African Division garrisoned Tobruk, which it was expected would be Rommel's primary objective. Most of our armour, therefore, was posted to the north.

Rommel attacked on May 27th, in great force, employing his armour in a wide turning movement round the British left flank, to take us in the rear while his infantry made a frontal attack. He was in a hurry, for he carried only five days' supplies, and his evident intention was to break through at the first rush. He met with a most spirited resistance, and for forty-eight hours the balance hung so evenly that Rommel might well have encountered disaster. He therefore called up all his reserves and launched a furious attack upon the main defensive line. The line held gallantly: a counter-thrust was even attempted, but the odds were too great, and this failed. Still the 8th Army, outnumbered and out-gunned, did not cease to fight all along the line from Gazala down to Bir Hacheim, where the Free French, under General Koenig, made a notable contribution.

At last, on June 13th, that fateful day, it became clear that Rommel was winning, chiefly through overwhelming tank superiority. Knightsbridge, the key to the entire defence system, had to be evacuated (though the 200th Guards Brigade contrived, before withdrawing, to clear everything out except two guns), and a general retirement was ordered. The idea was to withdraw steadily, as Rommel had done in December, keeping only Tobruk as an indispensable port and supply-base from which to harass the enemy.

But here came the final and mortal disaster. Tobruk, which during the previous year had defied the enemy for nine months, fell to a

heavy enemy attack; and although various small formations resolutely fought their way out, our losses both in men and material were
severe.

It was a shattering blow not only to present hope but to British
prestige all over the world—a world which had not yet forgotten or
condoned the surrender of Singapore a few months previously. The
Axis powers were jubilant, and Mussolini hurried to Tripoli in order
to be able to head a triumphant procession into Cairo.

But the 8th Army rose to the occasion. After such losses as they
had now incurred—the entire battle cost them 80,000 men—there
could be no question of establishing a permanent defensive line upon
their present extended front: the rear-guard action must continue,
past Sollum, past Sidi Barrani, past Mersa Matruh, until a position
was reached which could be held by their reduced forces, even if this
meant retreating deeper into Egypt than ever before.

And it was so. Resistance was maintained, furious and desperate,
inflicting continuous loss on the enemy. Units counter-attacked again
and again and even took prisoners: others, encircled and without
ammunition, cut their way out or fought to the last man.

The position selected for the final stand—it had been surveyed as
a precaution more than a year previously—was at El Alamein, sixty
miles west of Alexandria and presenting a thirty-five-mile front. Its
right flank lay on the sea and its left was protected by the great,
almost impassable Qattara Depression. Here the 8th Army, fighting
under the sure shield of the R.A.F. and aided by reinforcements sent
from Cairo, finally arrived, turned at bay, and from this position
was never dislodged.

Mussolini went home again, and in the course of a few months
El Alamein progressed from the status of last ditch to that of starting-
point for one of the most resounding victories in British military
history.

⤙(7)⤚

On August 5th, 1942, the Prime Minister visited Egypt. He was
accompanied by the C.I.G.S. and Field-Marshal Smuts. Evidently
considerable events were pending.

And no wonder, for the time had come at last when it would no
longer be necessary for the 8th Army either to fight on the defensive
or attack without any particular hope of final victory. The output
of munitions of war in Britain was reaching its peak, and two newly
trained and completely equipped divisions, the 44th and 51st, had

already arrived in Egypt. Two fresh armoured divisions, the 8th and 10th, were also available. The 6-pounder anti-tank guns were arriving in quantity at last, and, through the personal initiative of the President of the United States, the 8th Army was now equipped with large numbers of American Sherman tanks, capable of dealing with anything that the Axis could send into action.

One of the earliest fruits of the Prime Minister's arrival was a drastic reconstitution of the Middle East Command, beginning at the top. General Auchinleck, who had been fighting Rommel almost without a break for six months and was badly in need of a rest, was succeeded as Commander-in-Chief by General Sir Harold Alexander, who had been the last man to leave the beaches of Dunkirk, and whose steadily increasing reputation had recently been enhanced by the skill with which he had extricated our small and hard-pressed forces in Burma from almost certain annihilation.[1]

The command of the 8th Army was awarded to General Gott, the distinguished and beloved leader, first of the 7th Armoured Division and later of the XIII Corps. By an unhappy chance the aircraft which was conveying him to Cairo was shot down by two enemy fighters, and he was killed upon the very eve of taking over his new duties. The leadership of the 8th Army thus passed to General Sir Bernard Montgomery, whom we last encountered in command of the 3rd Division in the battle of Flanders,[2] and who was destined, for a variety of reasons, to figure more prominently in the public imagination than any other British soldier of the Second World War. Some of those reasons may briefly be indicated here.

As a strategist, General Montgomery was one of the earliest of the great captains to realise that victory in total warfare is entirely dependent upon integration—the integration of all forces by land, sea and air. To him the term 'Combined Operations' was not enough: all three forces must be absorbed, merged, into a single composite entity. His first act upon taking over the command of the 8th Army was to move his own headquarters to a site adjoining Advanced Air Headquarters, 'where commanders and staff could work together in one team'.

As a commander in the field he was meticulously thorough in his preparation for battle. He invariably declined, like Wellington before him, to move until he was ready, down to the minutest detail of planning, transport and equipment. He was destined more than once to be criticised for over-deliberation, but his reply, in substance, invariably amounted to: 'Where is the harm in taking twice as long

[1] See Chap. XIX.   [2] See p. 74.

over your preparations if you can win the victory in half the time and at half the cost?' His view was subsequently borne out by the comparatively low casualty-rate of his campaigns; also by the fact that the 8th Army gained hundreds of miles 'without ever withdrawing a yard'. The result was the complete trust and affection of his men.

As an individual he was a profound believer in personal fitness, not only for himself but for those about him; and he insisted that his senior officers, even those employed in purely sedentary duties, should indulge in regular and sometimes strenuous exercise. His own life in the field was frugal, almost ascetic; he was averse to formality and (perhaps deliberately) unconventional in his dress. He slept, and conducted his business for the most part, in a travelling caravan. He was sustained by a strong religious faith and was a firm believer in the Sword of the Lord and of Gideon.

As a leader of men he held that the humblest private has the right, in battle, to know where he is, what he is doing, why he is doing it, and how he as an individual fits into the general plan. By the same token he considered that it was the duty of an army commander never to hold himself aloof from his men; that a soldier would fight far better for a leader whom he knew by sight and personal contact than for an unseen entity controlling him from somewhere in the rear.

He was a rigid disciplinarian, but believed that off duty a soldier should be permitted to unbend the bow to an extent which would formerly have been considered almost subversive of discipline. Above all, being no mean psychologist, he had grasped the fact that the soldier of today, especially the somewhat self-conscious, class-conscious product of our modern educational system, is keenly appreciative of a little judicious publicity and an occasional pat on the back. He therefore made it his business to keep the 8th Army well in the public eye, and the 8th Army, conscious that that eye was upon them, played up accordingly, with results memorable in history.

(8)

Rommel had not yet given up hope of a final break-through, and was obviously preparing to strike again. Upon August 28th, therefore, General Montgomery called his officers together and addressed them in words that will never be forgotten by those who heard them. Here is a first-hand description of the impression created upon one of his audience.[1]

[1] From *Operation Victory*, by Major-General Sir Francis de Guingand, Chief of Staff to the 8th Army at this time.

'That address by Montgomery will remain one of my most vivid recollections. It was one of his greatest efforts. We all felt that a cool and refreshing breeze had come to relieve the oppressive and stagnant atmosphere. The effect of the address was electric—it was terrific! And we all went to bed that night with a new hope in our hearts, and a great confidence in the future of our army. . . . He was going (he said) to create a new atmosphere. The question of atmosphere was very important, and he wasn't satisfied with the one he had found. The bad old days were over, and nothing but good was in store for us. A new era had dawned. He then went on to explain the mandate which General Alexander and himself had been given by the Prime Minister. This was to destroy the Axis forces in North Africa. It was written on a half-sheet of notepaper. If anyone didn't think we could do this, then he must go, for there were to be no doubters. "No, I won't have any doubters." Any further retreat or withdrawal was quite out of the question. Forget about it. We must stand and fight where we were. There was to be no question of going back. He had ordered all plans dealing with withdrawal to be burnt. . . .'

'There will be no withdrawals—absolutely none—none whatever—none!' To this characteristically forthright statement the General added as a rider his own estimate of Rommel. 'A very able commander, but he has his weaknesses—he has a tendency to repeat his tactics. A one-track mind.' And it was upon this estimate that Bernard Montgomery based his order of battle, both then and thereafter.

On August 31st Rommel struck, and a heavy action ensued in which he found himself compelled to attack over ground of his opponent's own choosing. The attack was a complete and expensive failure, and by September 7th General Montgomery felt perfectly safe in breaking off the action and resuming his interrupted preparations for his own offensive, which as uJual he was determined not to deliver until he was absolutely ready—and there was still much to do.

But even if it was not followed up, the battle of Alam Halfa, as it came to be called, was an important victory, though it received little or no attention at the time. It was a vital battle, for if we had lost it we should have lost Egypt. Above all, it completely restored the confidence of the 'brave but baffled' 8th Army, as well as establishing their faith in their new leader.

For the coming attack General Montgomery had at his disposal, in addition to a new armoured and two new infantry divisions, the 9th Australian Division, the 5th (later replaced by the 4th) Indian Division, the 2nd New Zealand Division, the 1st South African Division, and the 1st and 7th Armoured Divisions—a truly Imperial aggregation. His recent reinforcements had enabled him to add a third corps, the 10th (General Lumsden) to the 13th (General

Horrocks) and 30th (General Leese). There were also Greek and French contingents. Moreover, he now had over one thousand tanks at his disposal.

Rommel's defences were very strong, and in considerable depth. The position was held by one German and five Italian divisions, the latter stiffened by German elements, together with a German parachute brigade. In reserve northward lay the 15th Panzer and Italian Littorio Armoured Divisions, and further to the rear, on the coast, the 90th Light Division. In reserve in the south were the 21st and Ariete Armoured Divisions. The whole position was guarded by minefields to a depth of 5,000 to 9,000 yards—an average depth of four miles.

A surprise attack was almost out of the question, for the enemy had no flank that could be turned, and the day of massed airborne invasion was not yet. Moreover, troop movements behind the line which were needed to get formations into position could be observed and reported by enemy aircraft. Much, however, was achieved in this respect by skilful employment of 'visual deception'—namely, the preservation of a constant 'density of vehicles' throughout the zone of operations, by the utilisation of a large number of dummy tanks and dummy lorries, which, under cover of night, filled gaps left by genuine formations moving up into the line. Dummy dumps, too, were established towards the south end of the line, and even a dummy pipe-line was laid down, in order to delude the enemy into the belief that the weight of the coming attack would fall there.

In the administrative arrangements bequeathed to him by his predecessor General Montgomery found little to amend, but from an operational point of view he was determined to intensify his policy of closer integration. He therefore abolished the employment of brigade groups and Jock Columns, which had caused divisions, owing to shortage of troops, to be split up into detached and insufficiently controlled units. In future divisions would be concentrated and handled as such.

The great attack was launched on the night of October 23rd, 1942, by bright moonlight.[1] For some days previously General Montgomery, in accordance with his invariable custom, had toured the army, addressing the officers and making clear to all how he proposed to fight, what issues were at stake, and what difficulties were likely to be encountered. Thereafter the officers explained the whole plan of action to their men.

---

[1] The Army Film Unit have immortalised the occasion in a brilliant documentary film, taken not without casualties among themselves—*Desert Victory*.

The glorious victory of El Alamein, which definitely and for the first time marked the turn of the tide in favour of the Allies, calls for no detailed description here. It will suffice to recall that by November 4th Rommel had been utterly defeated and was in full retreat with what was left of his army. Reinforcements were awaiting him at El Agheila, and were soon to be absorbed into his strength; but for all that he had left behind him four crack German divisions and eight Italian, which had ceased to exist as effective formations. Eighty thousand prisoners had been taken, including nine generals.

General Montgomery's aim and hope had been to cut off, round up, and annihilate the entire Axis army in a single operation, and so save his troops a desert pursuit of hundreds of miles; and he would almost certainly have succeeded but for torrential rain which fell during November 6th and 7th, bogging his tanks and transport near Mersa Matruh, while his supplies—especially that vital commodity petrol—were held up for the same reason some miles behind. Rommel made good use of a respite of twenty-four hours to extricate a proportion of his troops and transport; and thus the long pursuit to El Agheila, and ultimately to Tunis, began.

With the consequent and inevitable lengthening of his lines of communication, General Montgomery found himself faced with an administrative problem—that of supply—which increased in seriousness with each day of his triumphant progress. The obvious solution was to take advantage of renewed British naval strength in the Mediterranean to convey those supplies at least part of the way by sea, and dump them at a convenient port adjacent to General Montgomery's line of advance. With the recapture of Tobruk harbour this purpose was effected, and the long overland journey from Cairo to Tobruk eliminated.

The same difficulty recurred in an even more acute form as the pursuit penetrated further west. It had been hoped after the capture and occupation of Benghazi, some 200 miles beyond Tobruk, to extend the sea supply-line to that port; but here, unfortunately, the enemy had had time to carry out demolitions and sabotage on a scale which put the harbour out of action for many weeks. Even after the 8th Army had overleaped that ancient stumbling-block El Agheila, and was advancing upon the Buerat position 1,200 miles west of El Alamein, 800 tons of supplies per day were still being conveyed overland from Tobruk, not only for the 8th Army but for the R.A.F., for whose maintenance, including the construction of ever more advanced airfields, General Montgomery was responsible. It was not until early in January 1943 that Benghazi was rendered available for shipping. After that the situation quickly improved, and the 8th Army swept on, relentlessly.

Tripoli, the greatest and most desirable of our prospective supply-bases, was punctually entered and occupied upon the appointed date, January 23rd. Here again extensive demolitions had been effected: quays and wharves had been destroyed and the entrance to the harbour blocked. However, the combined and furious labours of the naval staffs contrived to restore the *status quo* in less than a fortnight. Upon February 3rd the first transport entered the harbour, and a complete convoy was berthed within three days. General Montgomery's own comment upon this situation is interesting and illuminating.

I have frequently referred to the administrative factor from the time we left El Alamein. The *tempo* of operations was primarily governed by the speed with which petrol, ammunition, air force requirements, and all the necessary stores and materials could be brought forward in sufficient quantities to support the fighting troops. It is important to grasp the distances with which the administrative machine had to contend. From Cairo to Tripoli is 1,600 miles by road: with G.H.Q. at the former and the leading troops at the latter, it was as if G.H.Q. were in London and the leading troops in Moscow, with only one road joining them.

With the capture of Tripoli and the occupation of Tripolitania, the 8th Army were accorded a well-earned 'breather'. They were in great heart. They had been fighting steadily and victoriously for three months, and had covered 1,400 miles. Best of all, the old unhappy routine of 'Benghazi and back' had been relegated now to a memory of the past.

Tunis was the next objective, but first of all a great reserve of stores and munitions must be built up. Two thousand tons were now being unloaded in Tripoli harbour every day. General Montgomery set up his headquarters in a field on the edge of the desert, with his men disposed about him for rest, reinforcement and re-equipment. Not for them were the dubious delights of urban Tripoli: the 8th Army were fighting fit, and fighting fit they must remain. Their task was not yet finished.

During the halt at Tripoli the Prime Minister paid them another visit, and congratulated them, in a characteristically happy phrase, upon having 'nightly pitched their moving tents a day's march nearer home'. Compared with the circumstances of his previous visit it was as if a miracle had been wrought. Moreover, the effects of that miracle were destined to endure, for the tide had begun to turn at last, and henceforth, despite innumerable obstacles and dogged resistance, it was to be progress, progress all the way to the Rhine and beyond.

CHAPTER XIV

COMBINED OPERATIONS

❧(1)❧

GENERAL MONTGOMERY now faced his final goal, Tunis. Thither, for the moment, we need not follow him, for his operations were about to be merged with those of a great Allied force under the supreme command of General Eisenhower. In other words, the Americans had arrived in Africa, while the French Colonial Army had for the most part broken with Vichy and thrown in their lot with the Allies. Gone at last were the days of Britain's splendid isolation and single-handed struggle against overwhelming odds. Henceforth Combined Allied Operations were to be the order of the day.

But before we leave the 8th Army, let us briefly consider the growth and development, under Generals Alexander and Montgomery, of desert warfare. The opportunity may not occur again, for hereafter the battles of Britain will be fought for the most part in enclosed country, built-up areas, or the jungle.

General Montgomery's methods have already been examined, but two are outstanding. The first of these was his theory of 'balance', designed to conserve manpower by never employing more troops in the line than were absolutely necessary, and thus providing an increased reserve to meet emergencies or strike the winning blow. In pursuance of this policy, General Montgomery was accustomed at the height of battle, even when the momentum of his attack was slackening, to withdraw one or more divisions from the line. In this he was supported by the practice of General Alexander, who subsequently employed very similar tactics in the Italian campaign, especially against superior forces. 'The smaller your forces,' said General Alexander, 'the larger percentage you should hold in reserve.'

General Montgomery's second care and preoccupation was the perpetual provision of advanced landing-grounds for the R.A.F., to ensure the destruction of enemy aerodromes and so enable his ground troops to advance into action under an adequate air 'umbrella'. The result in both cases was not only continuous tactical success but a marked economy in the lives of men.

By this time, too, tank warfare had been fully tried out and developed. More and better tanks were available—the Sherman and Churchill, to name only two—and new and more powerful designs were on the way.

Perhaps equally important was the increase in efficiency of devices for improved tank maintenance and the recovery of derelicts. It had long been recognised that a tank is a weapon so precious and so vulnerable that no effort or expense must be spared, first to keep it in condition, and secondly to prevent the enemy from capturing it when stranded or derelict.

To this end two highly useful devices were employed. The first, which had been in use for some time, was the vehicle known as the tank transporter, invaluable in desert warfare, where tanks had to travel long distances before reaching the scene of actual operations. It was an intensely strong vehicle, capable of carrying the largest and heaviest loads. It ran on twenty-four pneumatically tyred wheels—four axles, with six wheels to an axle. The motor-tractor which towed it had ten wheels, making thirty-four in all. (It was little wonder that during the Second World War tyres were unavailable for civilian transport.) The employment of the transporter ensured that the tank arrived in the battle-zone in full working order, with no need to repair or replace tracks; and, perhaps more important still, that tank crews, having had no other driving or maintenance duties to perform through the night, arrived fresh and ready for action.

The second was the Armoured Recovery Vehicle, operated by the R.E.M.E.—a new formation, the Royal Mechanical and Electrical Engineers—and its function was to tow disabled tanks out of action to a place where they could be reconditioned. It had immense tractive power, and in outward appearance resembled a large infantry tank. It even mounted a formidable-looking gun; but this was, in point of fact, a dummy, calculated to keep the enemy at a respectful distance.

Lastly, there had been a steady improvement in tank intercommunication. Tribute here should be paid to the Post Office, which throughout the war performed services for our Armed Forces which were little realised at the time but proved invaluable. Mention has already been made of the difficulty within the earlier tanks of giving or receiving oral orders and information, owing to the noise made by the machinery. The Post Office engineers now set to work, in their great research station at Dollis Hill, in north London (notably in that section devoted to the study of the laws of sound) to discover a remedy for this heavy handicap.

They began by constructing a deep concrete dug-out in the station grounds, in which they set up an apparatus capable, upon the throwing of a switch, of reproducing all the deafening and hideous noises inseparable from the interior economy of a Churchill tank in action. Their aim was to discover some method of damping down these distracting sounds without making spoken orders or messages themselves inaudible. And in due course they succeeded. Upon adjusting to his head the 'fitting' evolved by these experts, the tank commander discovered that the roar of the tank machinery had been miraculously eliminated from his hearing, and that the voice of his neighbour, speaking in his ordinary tones, was clearly audible to him, as was his to his neighbour. This ingenious contrivance improved tank-control, whether from within or without, out of all knowledge.

The increased efficiency and reliability of the later tanks, however, were due less to the excellence of their design and construction than to the skill and resource of their own tank-fitters and repair units. As usual, it was the man and not the machine who counted most in the end.

~(2)~

We turn now to the final phase of the North African campaign. The British and American forces had effected their first landing on November 8th, 1942. This particular operation was known by the code name 'Torch'. Its purpose was to occupy French Morocco and Algeria, to rally the Free French troops to the Allied cause, to invade Tunisia, and ultimately join hands with the 8th Army; thereafter to reopen the Mediterranean, which since June 1940 had been almost sealed to the Allies, and so secure bases for the subsequent assault upon the 'under-belly of the Axis'.

The essential need was speed, for if surprise could be achieved it might be possible to overrun Tunisia and occupy Bizerta and Tunis before the Axis forces could be gathered in sufficient strength to defend them. But an initial and not altogether unexpected hitch intervened, and the opportunity was lost.

Success depended almost entirely upon the degree of opposition or help which might be offered by the French forces in North Africa. These had no particular quarrel with the Americans, for the United States Government, while neutral, had consistently recognised the Vichy regime. The British Government upon the other hand had espoused the cause of General de Gaulle, and British sailors and soldiers had more than once fired upon French ships and troops.

It was therefore obvious that an American Army of Liberation would be likely to receive a more favourable reception in French North Africa than a British. (This was one of the primary reasons for the appointment of General Eisenhower as supreme commander of the Allied Forces, first in the Mediterranean and subsequently in Europe.) It had already been agreed by the Combined Chiefs of Staff that the greater part of the force first landed should be American, and that Lieut-General K. A. N. Anderson, Commander of the British 1st Army, should not take over his duties until after the landing had been effected. He was kept waiting only a day or two, but momentous events occurred during that period.

The landings had extended over a wide front, from Casablanca, on the Atlantic seaboard, to Algiers in the Mediterranean. Opposition at Algiers was slight, and the troops were soon ashore. But there was delay none the less, owing to the fact that the French naval and military authorities here assembled, though now willing to throw in their lot with the Allies, unexpectedly declined to serve under any leader but Admiral Darlan.

Here British and American opinion was somewhat at variance. The British regarded Darlan quite simply as an arch-traitor to the Allied cause, which indeed he had shown himself ever since 1940; but the Americans, as Mr. Churchill pointed out to the House of Commons in a most illuminating speech delivered in Secret Session on December 10th, had no particular animus against him. He had not betrayed *them*, and, moreover, was for some reason incomprehensible to the Anglo-Saxon mind, the only man whom the officers of the French Colonial Army felt that they could obey upon terms compatible with their honour. They were fast bound to 'the chain of command', and by their rigid code Darlan was somehow the lineal representative in North Africa of 'that antique defeatist, who is to them the illustrious and venerable Marshal Pétain, the hero of Verdun'.

So General Eisenhower, whose chief preoccupation was to get his thousands of troops safely and speedily ashore, accepted the responsibility, and acquiesced in this strange proposition. In this he was confirmed by the President of the United States—with a mental reservation, with which Mr. Churchill found himself in cordial agreement, that it was not necessary to employ a discredited quisling for a moment longer than was convenient. However, this uneasy alliance was destined not to be of long duration, for Darlan was assassinated a fortnight later.

Still, he had served his turn, for the result of his appointment had been the immediate cessation of all French resistance to the Allied landings, and the field was now clear for the invasion of Tunisia. But the golden opportunity was gone, and all surprise effect lost. German troops were pouring into Bizerta and Tunis by sea and air, and six months of hard and desperate fighting had to be endured before the elimination of the Axis from Africa could be finally achieved.

~(3)~

The long campaign which now ensued is not easy to follow, especially from the point of view of organisation and administration, for during the early stages both of these were signally lacking. It was a period of much confusion and difficulty.

There were two main reasons for this. The first was the fact that the American landings had taken place at various and somewhat widely separated ports, with the result that, as General Anderson reports:

United States units arrived piecemeal, as fast as the very limited road and rail facilities could carry them, and had perforce to be employed as part and parcel of the British forces under British brigade or divisional commanders, *and not independently, as all of us would have wished.* That the resulting friction was so small speaks volumes for the real desire to pull together which animated all parties. . . . But it was long before our total Allied strength reached a point at which each nation could be made entirely responsible for its own particular sector.

The other reason was political, and arose from the attitude of our French Allies. General Giraud continually refused to place French troops under British command, even though General Eisenhower had placed General Anderson in control of all the Allied forces.

'So', reports General Anderson, 'a series of compromises and makeshifts was adopted, in the course of which I, gradually, and as commander of the only formation equipped and able to undertake the task, became in turn adviser, coordinator, and finally commander of the whole Tunisian front.'

Indeed, the loyalties of all French officers were sharply divided, and some were still maintaining a sort of muddled allegiance to Marshal Pétain. During the first weeks, while the British 1st Army were pressing forward in the hopes of a quick victory, a French General, Barrès, was still negotiating with General Nehring in Tunis—though this, of course, may merely have been a ruse to gain time. Generally speaking, the senior officers were hesitant and afraid to commit themselves, while the junior officers were in favour of the Allies. The rank and file, however, usually obeyed orders unquestioningly. (These were mainly native troops.) Of the civilian population, mayors, railway officials and postmasters were either lukewarm or obstructive.

Altogether, the 1st Army must at times (especially at first) have envied their compatriots of the 8th upon the other side of the Tunisian border—a homogeneous formation, united in spirit and point of view, and with a commander who enjoyed a free hand. Still, trying though the experience was, it proved of considerable value in inculcating the lessons of organisation and integration essential to the unity of a large force composed of troops of different nationalities.

The Allied forces in Algeria at the outset of the Tunisian campaign consisted of the British 1st Army, the American 2nd Corps, and the French 19th Corps, and the campaign itself fell into three main phases. The first was the race for Tunis and Bizerta, undertaken by a force much under strength both in men and equipment. It just failed, after bitter fighting in appalling weather, and its effort faded out soon after Christmas 1942.

The second phase lasted until the end of March 1943, and consisted, so far as the Allies were concerned, in a fluctuating struggle for ground and points of vantage from which to launch a real and substantial offensive. Rains began in December and continued till April.

The 1st Army was much hampered by the length of its lines of communication. From its base at Algiers to Tunis was a distance of 560 miles. Adequate air-support was at first difficult to obtain. All aircraft had to be flown in from Gibraltar or the United Kingdom and airfields were few and far between, the nearest serviceable landing-ground for our advanced formations in Tunisia being at Bône, 114 miles away. Consequently our troops suffered severely at times from dive-bombing.

But there was good will in plenty, and with increasing experience and better means of intercommunication the situation improved steadily. By March liaison was excellent, and all the Allied air forces concerned 'were working as one team'.

The terrain itself was much too extensive for the troops struggling to occupy it, and at one time General Anderson was compelled to employ the infantry battalions of the 6th Armoured Division on ordinary infantry duty away from the armoured brigade. Moreover, the 1st Army was operating in a country which necessitated the employment of much pack-mule transport in place of motorised vehicles. The country was mountainous, and the roads leading into Tunisia ran through a series of narrow parallel passes, which made lateral communication difficult, and the guarding of which called for far more infantry than was available at the time. Positions were taken and retaken, and names such as Longstop Hill and the Kasserine Pass became as familiar to newspaper readers at home as Halfaya Pass and Knightsbridge.

German Tiger tanks made their first appearance about this time. Against these General Anderson found it possible in January 1943 to re-equip the 6th Armoured Division with 241 Sherman tanks. The Valentine tanks thus released were passed on to the French, who received them, we are told, 'with much satisfaction'. The French had started the campaign very poorly equipped indeed, but with the gradual improvement in their armament their efficiency and morale increased steadily, as did the unity and efficiency of the Allied force in general.

The third and final phase began with a great counter-attack by all the Allies on March 28th, and ended, as we shall presently see, with the complete destruction of all the Axis forces in Africa.

⚜(4)⚜

Meanwhile the 8th Army and General Montgomery had not been idle. On March 28th they had turned the immensely strong Mareth Line, and were now pressing up the coast through Gabes and Sousse, with their old opponents the 15th and 21st Panzers and 90th Light Division putting up a dogged rearguard resistance against them, towards Sfax and Enfidaville. General Eisenhower had promised General Montgomery a Flying Fortress 'for his own use' if the 8th Army were in Sfax by the 15th of April. They entered on the 10th, and the Flying Fortress was duly and promptly delivered.

It should be noted that upon the entry of the 8th Army from Tripolitania into Tunisia on February 18th, that Army had passed by preconcerted agreement under the supreme command of General Eisenhower. All the Allied forces thus became united to form the

18th Army Group, under the control of General Alexander as Deputy Commander-in-Chief. This union was made perfect upon April 7th, 1943, when units of General Montgomery's 10th Corps, lunging inland from the coast, made contact and joined hands with elements of the United States 2nd Corps on the Gabes-Gafsa Road.

The ring round the Axis forces was now closed and the stage set for the knockout blow. Upon April 12th, General Montgomery received word from General Alexander that the honour of making the main effort was to be conferred upon the gallant 1st Army, which had survived so much early tribulation and surmounted so many obstacles—an honour in which the Americans and French would thus be able to participate. The role of the 8th Army would be to exert maximum pressure on the southern sector of the enemy's front and pin down as much of his strength as possible.

This arrangement involved a major regrouping between the 1st and 8th Armies, with the object of strengthening the projected thrust of the 1st Army against Tunis and Bizerta. The 1st Army itself was composed mainly of the 5th and 9th Corps. Both these formations had been long in arriving at full strength, particularly the 9th. But to this Corps were now added those famous units of the 8th Army the 7th Armoured and 4th Indian Divisions, together with the 201st Guards Brigade and some medium artillery. Here was strength indeed, and, best of all, by this time the air support rendered to General Anderson was 'intimate, immediate and extremely powerful'.

The great attack was launched on May 6th, over the very ground upon which in 146 B.C. the Roman legions, under Scipio Africanus, had accomplished the final dissolution of the empire of Carthage. It was completely successful : Tunis and Bizerta both fell on the next day. Bizerta was captured by the United States 1st Armoured Division, while the first troops to enter Tunis were our 'Desert Rats', who thus contrived, despite their temporary severance from the parent stem, to be in at the death after all. (They were subsequently restored to the 8th Army, and within three months were participating in the invasion of Sicily.)

A complete collapse of the Axis followed the victory of the 1st Army, and in five days all resistance had ended. The scenes in the Cap Bon Peninsula and to the south-west were fantastic. Prisoners swamped their captors, and drove about in their own transport looking for the cages. On May 12th, Colonel-General von Arnim, Commanding-in-Chief Army Group Afrika, surrendered to the 4th Indian Division. The total of prisoners eventually reached over a quarter of a million : of these over half were Germans. The total British losses of the 1st Army throughout the whole campaign, in killed (4,443), wounded and missing had amounted to 23,610.

On May 13th, General Alexander dispatched the following telegram to 10 Downing Street:

Prime Minister. *Sir, it is my duty to report that the Tunisian campaign is over. All enemy resistance has ceased. We are masters of the North African shores.*

The Tunisian campaign was of intense interest for two reasons. First, it demonstrated the possibility of achieving complete accord between Allies differing in language, process of thought, and military method.

'I say without hesitation', reports General Anderson, 'that the mutual good will, tolerance, understanding, and above all confidence which each of us had in the other was quite remarkable. . . . Even between British and French the initial and very understandable doubts very soon disappeared in mutual open respect and admiration.'

Secondly, this was one of the most perfect examples in history of a battle achieving that at which all commanders aim—the ending of a war by the total elimination of the enemy. At Tannenberg (1914) the Germans claimed to have eclipsed anything since Hannibal's victory over the Romans at Cannae; but neither Tannenberg nor Cannae ended a campaign: the war went on. The Tunisian achievement was final and complete; the merest handful of refugees escaped to Europe.

To General Alexander the triumph must have been particularly gratifying, if only by force of contrast. Just three years previously, to quote the final paragraph of Lord Gort's Flanders Dispatch:

At midnight on Sunday June 2nd, Major-General Alexander and the Senior Naval Officer made a final tour of the [Dunkirk] beaches and harbour; and being satisfied that no British troops were left on shore, they themselves left for England.

It is possible to imagine General Alexander concluding a very different tour of inspection in 1943:

At noon on Wednesday May 12th, General Alexander made a final tour of the beaches and harbour of Tunis; and being satisfied that no Germans remained in North Africa, he himself left for England.

⭐(5)⭐

The immediate result of the expulsion of the Axis forces from Africa was to reopen the Mediterranean to Allied traffic, and so shorten the sea-route to Egypt and the East by thousands of miles. In effect, too, by reducing the length of voyages, it greatly increased the supply of available tonnage.

Even more important, it laid open southern Europe to Allied invasion, with adequate protection from the air. From Bizerta and Tunis Spitfires and Hurricanes, with an operational range of 200 miles, could cover the whole of Sicily, while Beaufighters and Mosquitoes could penetrate almost as far as Venice. Malta, too, and the recently captured island fortress of Pantellaria, were available as bases.

Still, two months had to elapse before any attempt was made to occupy Sicily, and more than three before a landing could be effected in Italy itself. This was unfortunate, and was destined to lead to heavy expenditure both of arms and men in the months to come; but in the circumstances the delay was almost inevitable.

The primary cause was the complete revolution which had taken place in the strategic situation. The Allies were over the crest at last, and were now in a position to take the offensive on a grand scale by the actual invasion of enemy soil. To land a great invading force on a well-defended enemy coast has always been the most difficult and hazardous of military operations, as we had discovered to our cost at Gallipoli in 1915, when men were towed ashore in lighters under concentrated machine-gun fire, with heavy loss.

In 1943, in the face of modern coastal defences, submarine attack and bombing by land-based aircraft, a seaborne invasion of Europe, if it were to be accomplished at all, plainly demanded some entirely new strategic and tactical approach—an approach which would involve the minutest planning and the closest co-operation, not only between the forces of land, sea and air, but between Ally and Ally.

With the advent and development of the armoured fighting vehicle, the obvious solution of the problem lay in the employment of a fleet of shallow-draught, self-propelled, and adequately armoured landing-craft, capable of descending swiftly upon a suitable stretch of beach and of discharging a very large number of men and vehicles in the shortest possible time.

In the spring of 1943 such craft were only just becoming available either in the United Kingdom or in the United States; for their design had to conform with recent experience, and since thousands of them were required, a time lag was inevitable. Fortunately, the intensive methods of production enforced upon the Allied nations by the urgent needs of the moment—notably in the American shipbuilding yards of Henry Kayser—did much to widen the bottle-neck. Even so, the flotilla available by July 1943 was only just sufficient to accommodate the minimum force needed for the invasion of Sicily and Italy.

A further complication arose at this time from the fact that planning for the invasion of occupied France by way of the Normandy coast—for D-Day, 1944, in fact—was already in hand, and even now General Alexander was being pressed to complete the occupation of Italy with all speed in order to liberate his assault-craft for service in the English Channel. Indeed, it required the personal intervention of the Prime Minister himself, at one time, to prevent these invaluable vehicles from being dispatched prematurely to England.

Landing-craft fell into various categories, according to size and employment. There were some ten types in all. The largest and most important was the L.S.T. or Landing-Ship, Tanks. This was of too deep a draught to be available for ordinary beach landings, and was better suited to dockside off-loadings. The most numerous and effective class were L.C.A. (Landing Craft, Assault). Smaller and handier types were the L.C.I., or Landing-Craft, Infantry, and L.C.T., or Landing-Craft, Tanks. There were also specialised craft designed to land artillery, rocket-projectors, and anti-aircraft guns. Finally came an ingenious contrivance known as the D.U.K.W., or Duck, capable either of propelling itself over the surface of the water or of proceeding on its own wheels up the beach.

Parachute troops were now regularly employed, and upon an increasing scale. A complete airborne division had come to birth, and its maroon beret was a familiar sight both at home and overseas. It included parachute and glider troops, and by now both men, artillery and light tanks could be conveyed in glider craft—the two largest types were known as Hengist and Horsa—towed by a powerful plane of the bomber type.

For the landing in Sicily over 2,000 vessels of every kind, from cruisers to D.U.K.W.s, were employed. They came from as near as Malta and Bizerta and from as far away as Britain and the United States, their arrivals being synchronised by the Combined Staffs in a masterly fashion. The landing on Sicily took place at the south-east corner, upon July 10th, 1943. The forces employed were the 8th Army under General Montgomery and the American 7th Army under General Patton, both acting under General Alexander as Deputy Commander-in-Chief.

Considerable airborne forces were included in the operation, taking off from Tunisia. Unfortunately, the weather was not too propitious. A gale blew, and a number of gliders came down into the sea *en route*, while others were blown off their course and came to earth wide of their objective. But the seaborne assault, despite the unheroic but very real handicap of widespread *mal de mer*, was an outstanding success. The enemy was off his guard, and a surprise landing was effected by both invading armies. Opposition from the air, probably owing to the gale, was slight. The port of Syracuse was captured by the 8th Army within twenty-four hours, and this greatly reduced the always difficult and anxious administrative problem of maintenance over open beaches.

In thirty-eight days Sicily was in Allied hands. The immediate result was the overthrow of Mussolini and the Fascist regime. The one aim and desire of the Italian people, now that their own soil had been invaded, was to get out of the war: the Italian troops in Sicily offered but moderate resistance, while the civil population welcomed their conquerors with acclamation. A meeting of the Fascist Grand Council was held—the first for nearly four years—and the King was restored to the throne from which he had practically abdicated and placed in command of all Italian armed forces, thus automatically terminating the dictatorship of Mussolini, who was put under arrest. That supple-minded veteran, Marshal Badoglio, formed a Government, which immediately sued for peace, and on September 3rd an Armistice was signed, by the terms of which the Italians surrendered unconditionally.

But not so the German forces under Kesselring. There were four divisions of these in Sicily, with remnants of three Italian divisions, and these put up a protracted resistance in the north of the island. Their motive here was twofold. In the first place Kesselring was determined that with the Italian surrender Italy should not fall bodily into the hands of the Allies. For this time was needed, to enable German formations to take the place of the defaulting Italians. In the second place Kesselring was anxious for as long as possible to deny to the Allies the use of the airfields in the Catanian plain, from which they could strike with deadly and increasing effect at the heart of Italy. But by August 17th the Sicilian campaign was over, and the Allied armies stood looking out across the narrow waters of the Straits of Messina towards their next objective, the toe of Italy.

The 8th Army, who had been fighting their way up the east coast of Sicily, amid torrid heat in a new and unfamiliar type of country, for nearly six weeks continuously, were badly in need of a rest. Many were suffering from malaria, which despite all precautions assumed serious proportions, especially in the plain of Catania. The casualties incurred in this way by the 8th Army actually exceeded those in battle. But they had the satisfaction of realising that they were not merely a 'desert' army: they had shown that they could acquit themselves equally well under entirely different conditions.

Let us consider how very different those conditions were, not only from the point of view of the operational difficulties of a seaborne invasion, but from that of subsequent maintenance and administrative services. These had to be carried on in enclosed country and over indifferent lines of communication. In the desert there had been no limit to the number of vehicles which could move along the desert tracks: in Sicily the roads were narrow, steep and tortuous, and traffic control presented a complicated problem. Special measures had to be employed to limit the number and type of vehicle on each section of the road, as well as to deal with the ever-present embarrassment of civilian traffic.

In a country, too, where the roads frequently ran along mountain sides, with a cliff-face on the one hand and a sheer drop on the other, twisting round hairpin bends and occasionally running through a tunnel, nothing was easier for the enemy than to blow up a section of road or bring down the whole length of a tunnel. The work done by our sappers and pioneers in dealing quickly with these demolitions and reopening the roads to traffic was quite remarkable. Much bridging was also necessary, whether over rivers or artificially contrived gaps. Fortunately, this contingency had been foreseen and a generous supply of Bailey bridging material was available.

Messina fell on August 17th, and the Germans, aided by a heavy anti-aircraft barrage, withdrew across the Straits, leaving 20,000 dead and 7,000 prisoners behind them.

Still, the victory had been far from conclusive. True, Sicily was in Allied possession; so was the greater part of the Italian Navy. The Germans had evacuated Sardinia, and the French were thrusting them out of Corsica. But the rest had fallen far short of hope and expectation. Crete, the Dodecanese and the Balkans were still in enemy hands. Finally, there were at least fifteen German divisions in Italy, with more on the way. The coming struggle would be hard and bitter.

~*(6)*~

The Italian campaign was perhaps the most disappointing of the Allied offensive operations. Not that it did not ultimately achieve its object; but it was expensive, it was slow, and it was unpunctual.

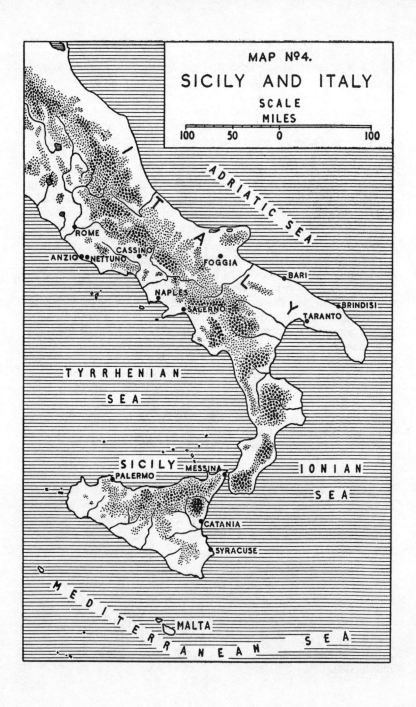

MAP Nº4.

SICILY AND ITALY

SCALE
MILES

100   50   0   100

ITALY

ADRIATIC SEA

ROME
CASSINO
ANZIO NETTUNO   FOGGIA
                              BARI
        NAPLES   BRINDISI
          SALERNO   TARANTO

TYRRHENIAN

SEA

SICILY   IONIAN
PALERMO MESSINA
                              SEA

        CATANIA

        SYRACUSE

MEDITERRANEAN

        MALTA   SEA

This was to some extent due to a circumstance the results of which could hardly have been foreseen. The sudden collapse and surrender of the Italian Government at the height of the Sicilian campaign was a mixed blessing. Instead, automatically, of throwing open the whole of Italy to Allied occupation, it gave the resourceful Kesselring a golden opportunity to thrust his former coadjutors aside and establish the defences of Italy upon a real and formidable basis, all before the Allies were able to set foot upon Italian soil and interfere with his dispositions.

Mussolini, too, had been recaptured in a boldly conceived raid, and his liberation (or rather, the possession of his person) had in a measure restored Fascist pretensions and discouraged the Italian troops from co-operating with their new Allies. Throughout the winter of 1943–4 some two-thirds of the Italian population, including the workers of the industrial north, remained under Nazi domination.

It was to this situation that Combined Headquarters (comprising General Eisenhower's own G.H.Q. and Middle East H.Q., now under the command of General Sir Henry Maitland Wilson) had to address themselves. Their opponent's intention was plain—to compel them to fight a slow and costly battle up the long and narrow leg of Italy, through terrain ideal for defence, against a force whose position could not be turned because its flanks rested on the sea. To achieve such an end only one method seemed feasible, and that was to effect amphibious landings higher up the coast—as far up, in fact, as fighter cover could be extended.

The Allied troops finally assembled for the invasion of Italy consisted of the ubiquitous British 8th Army, under General Montgomery, and the 5th Army, part British and part American, under the American General Mark Clark, both under the command of General Alexander, acting as deputy Commander-in-Chief under General Eisenhower.

Upon September 9th the 5th Army effected a landing at Salerno, some thirty-five miles south of Naples. Fierce resistance was encountered, and for a week the invaders could only hang on precariously to a strip of coast covered by the fire of Allied warships. At the end of that time General Montgomery, who had landed on the heel of Italy with the 8th Army and established a firm base by the capture of Taranto, Brindisi and Bari, moved across to their aid, and the two forces joined hands on September 17th. Two weeks later Naples was in Allied possession. But for the moment the profit was small, for the enemy had not only wrecked the port itself but had destroyed the sewage system and water supply of the city.

Plainly, the conquest of Italy was about to prove a long and expensive operation. Towards the end of November an Allied Conference ('Sextant') was held at Cairo, at which the Prime Minister himself was present and delivered a cogent appreciation of the situation. 'Whoever holds Rome,' he said, 'holds the title-deeds of Italy.' In this opinion he was more than confirmed by Hitler, who in a Special Order issued to his troops about this time (a copy of which was captured a month or two later) stated: '*The Gustav Line must be held at all costs, for the sake of the political consequences which would follow a completely successful defence. The Führer expects the bitterest struggle for every yard.*' In other words, the loss of Rome would strike a mortal blow at Nazi prestige and morale.

The Gustav Line, it should be explained, comprised a series of immensely strong defence works set up by Kesselring across the breadth of Italy. The key to the position, so far as the road to Rome was concerned, was Monte Cassino, which stood crowned by an ancient monastery; and the enemy, not without justification (as we were to learn by hard experience) regarded it as impregnable. Indeed, the Italian Military College had been accustomed to employ this particular 'feature', during manœuvres, as an assault problem.

With the defence of Rome foremost in his mind, Kesselring had massed his principal strength against the 5th Army. This left General Montgomery and the 8th Army, on the eastern side of the Apennine chain, comparatively free, and excellent advantage was taken of the opportunity afforded. The great system of Italian airfields round Foggia was captured, and was employed thereafter as a base both for tactical and strategical bombing, as well as for the rendering of air-cover.

Still, the Gustav Line stood firm, and it became plain that if Rome was to be occupied a large-scale amphibious landing must be effected further north, and effected speedily, for the summer was gone and weather conditions were worsening steadily. Naples having now been cleared, by superhuman exertions, it was decided to employ that port as a base for a landing upon the beaches of Anzio and Nettuno, some sixty miles up the coast and thirty south of Rome.

The landing-party (or assault task-force, as these were beginning to be called) was to be furnished by two divisions of the 5th Army—the 1st British and the 3rd American, with the usual strong support from the Allied fleet. Having captured the beaches the force was to push inland with all speed, cut the enemy's communications between Rome and the Gustav Line, and so trap the enemy between itself and the main body of the 5th Army.

It was a hazardous venture, for both beaches, especially that allotted to the 1st Division, were exposed, shallow and partially masked by sand-bars; while the weather at that time of year—it was now December—could not be relied upon for more than a day or two in advance.

But the outstanding problem was one of administration, or rather of supply and transport—namely, the collection of a sufficient number of landing-craft and the organisation of a system of maintenance which would ensure the landing on the beaches of a daily minimum of 2,500 tons of stores, for so long as the force remained isolated from the rest of the 5th Army. Some two hundred such craft of all types were available, but the largest of these could not be spared for more than a limited time. If the landings were completely successful, and if the break-through could be effected within the allotted period, well and good; but if progress were to be seriously retarded or, worse still, if the enemy succeeded in 'sealing-off' the beaches and so keeping the expedition debarred from aid by land, it must perforce continue to be supplied, for an indefinite period, from the sea—a contingency which might seriously disorganise the vast preparations now in hand elsewhere.

However, it was decided to take the risk, and upon January 22nd, 1944, the landing took place. Weather conditions were perfect and the further forecast favourable. The convoy consisted of 243 warships, transports, landing-craft and various other vessels of the Allied navies, supplemented by Dutch, Greek, Polish and French craft. The assault force itself consisted of some 50,000 troops and more than 5,000 vehicles.

At first all went well. Complete surprise effect was achieved, and the troops were conveyed ashore without loss and in perfect order. Then, when everything depended upon speed and yet greater speed, came an inexplicable delay of three days, while stores were brought ashore, dumps established, and the position consolidated generally. Of any attempt to exploit the advantage of surprise by an immediate advance inland against the enemy's highly vulnerable flank there was none. It was Suvla Bay all over again.[1]

The enemy, once aroused, reacted speedily and in great strength, and in due course the worst happened: the Anzio task force found themselves sealed off and isolated upon an exposed strip of coast nowhere more than eight miles deep.

There, despite all attempts to relieve them, they lay for four months, enduring all the hardships of winter in the open, and scourged by

[1] The second landing on Gallipoli, in 1915.

continuous observed shell-fire from the neighbouring hills. By February 1st the surrounding enemy force numbered five divisions and forty-two batteries of artillery, bent upon driving them into the sea. Every attempt to do so they repulsed with desperate gallantry, but more they could not compass. It was a cruel experience for a most valiant body of men: instead of proving a winning asset in the battle for Rome they found themselves, through no fault of their own, reduced to the status of an expensive liability. But for the fatal delay on the first landing the Anzio Assault Force might have achieved all that was asked of it. But such is the fortune of war.

Meanwhile the battle for the Gustav Line continued, in which General Alexander had at his disposal not only the British and American formations embodied in the 5th and 8th Armies, but a Canadian Corps and New Zealand, South African, Indian, French and Polish formations—a healthy reminder for Hitler of the extent of Allied resources. A body of Italian troops also co-operated. The 5th Army had been reinforced from the 8th in order to enable it to maintain the increasing burden imposed upon it. The role of the 8th Army was to maintain the greatest possible show of force upon the eastern side of the Apennines: later, however, it was moved westward and operated upon the right wing of the 5th.

General Montgomery had been called home in January 1944 to participate in the planning for the invasion of northern France, an undertaking for which he had been earmarked as Commander-in-Chief of all the Allied land forces. Thus ended his long and memorable association with the 8th Army, the command of which now devolved upon Lieut.-General Sir Oliver Leese, a most distinguished Guards officer who, as commander of the 30th Corps, had served as General Montgomery's right hand throughout the African campaign, and was destined later to achieve further distinction in south-eastern Asia.

With increasing command of the air, General Alexander was now able to bring his heavy bombers to bear, and Cassino and the monastery were ultimately reduced to rubble. But this did little to facilitate the actual advance, for the devastation created was such that the assaulting troops were everywhere impeded by wrecked buildings (each of which had been converted into a most effective pocket of resistance) and vast craters filled with water. No wonder that the winter offensive of 1943–4 should have died down to something in the nature of an expensive deadlock.

Still, the effort and sacrifice had not been wholly in vain. More than twenty good German divisions had been contained in Italy throughout many months—a subtraction from Hitler's resources elsewhere which had been of material value to the Russians—while the capture of the Foggia airfield system by the 8th Army had furnished the Strategic Air Force with an invaluable base from which to operate against targets in southern France and central Europe.

In May 1944 General Alexander and his men, assisted by the return of summer conditions, were enabled once more to take the offensive, this time with complete success. Their patience and pertinacity were at last to be rewarded. Within three weeks Cassino had been stormed, the Gustav Line broken, and the Anzio beach head relieved. On June 4th, Rome—the first European capital to be retrieved from Nazi occupation—was entered by Allied troops.

There let us leave them, for the storm-centre is now swinging elsewhere and the Italian campaign is about to become merged in a vastly larger operation, which will presently demand all our attention.

CHAPTER XV

THE WESTERN WALL

⊸(1)⊱

THE reader will recall that throughout 1943, and even earlier, there grew up in this country a persistent demand (even chalked up on walls) for 'The Second Front'.

This was perhaps only natural, for the British people had suffered long and endured all without flinching. Now, they felt, they had grown from weakness to strength, and since the entry of the United States into the war ultimate victory seemed certain. So if Ultimately, why not Now?

What had not been realised by the lay mind was that the initiative had not yet passed into Allied hands. North Africa had been cleared, but elsewhere the situation could only be described as defensive-offensive. Russia was still at death-grips with the German armies; a colossal struggle was in progress between the Americans and Japanese throughout innumerable islands of the Pacific. Burma was the scene of a major campaign in which the British 14th Army was fighting for its life in circumstances of incredible difficulty; while scattered British formations were doggedly withstanding Japanese aggression in the vast theatre of Indonesia. (The Dutch East Indies alone cover an area of about the size of all Europe except Russia.) India itself had to be protected, and we had recently acquired yet another responsibility by our occupation of Madagascar—an island about three times the size of Great Britain.

Finally, and as usual, the amateur strategist had overlooked the fact that Britain's First Front is, and always must be, the Ocean Front; and in 1943 that particular front, since the United States Navy had not yet entirely recovered from the calamity of Pearl Harbour, was more than fully extended. So here were fronts enough, in all conscience.

However, the Second Front, so called—by which, of course, was meant the invasion of Germany via occupied France or the Netherlands—was far from being neglected. Indeed, as we shall presently discover, the most thorough and strenuous preparation for its opening had long been in hand. Thorough it certainly had to be, for when we struck we must strike in overwhelming strength, and before this could happen certain vital conditions must be fulfilled.

In the first place no assault could be contemplated or delivered until German military strength had been bled to reasonable proportions, and German organisation and administration, especially in the matter of supply and transport, had been dislocated by combined and systematic bombing operations, calculated to prevent the rapid transference of reinforcements from east to west.

Secondly, a sufficiency of landing-craft of every type and capacity must be devised, constructed and assembled—and our study of the Italian campaign has shown how woefully short we were in that respect.

Lastly, the American armies on their way across the Atlantic for the invasion—comparatively raw troops, but of the utmost promise—must be given sufficient breathing-space in which to acclimatise themselves to their new and strange surroundings, as well as to undergo a far more strenuous course of training than they had hitherto received. The American Army Commanders were rightly insistent upon this. So during the ensuing months the United Kingdom grew, or rather continued to grow, into one vast training-ground and arsenal for the great host upon whose leadership and exertion depended the whole future of human liberty.

For obvious reasons of security no hint of the extent of these activities could be permitted, even to the British people themselves. The Press, of course, were in fairly full possession of the facts, but for the most part maintained an admirable reticence. Less responsible institutions and individuals, especially those who were inclined to criticise our apparent failure to bring relief to hard-pressed Russia, were more vocal.

But the ultra-Russophiles need have had no misgivings, for the heads of all the Allied nations were in close contact and full accord. In the first place the Anglo-American assault-landing in north-west Africa in November 1942 (described in Chapter XIV), with General Anderson's subsequent campaign in Tunisia, was deliberately undertaken to divert some of Germany's energy from Russia—and succeeded. Secondly, at the conference held at Tehran in November 1943, between Mr. Churchill, President Roosevelt and Marshal Stalin, all the details of a combined plan of action for 1944 were fully worked out, synchronised and agreed.

Let us now turn and contemplate the face of Britain during those hectic, breathless months of preparation for what was already becoming known (though its actual date was a faithfully guarded secret) as D-Day.

~*(2)*~

For all practical purposes the preparation for D-Day began with the return of the British Expeditionary Force from Dunkirk. From that moment the British people dedicated themselves to the purpose not only of recovering what had been lost, but of carrying the war into the enemy's country and pressing it, through untold years if need be, to a victorious conclusion.

Our first care at this time was the supplying of the necessary drafts and new formations for the prosecution of the campaign in the Middle East—a priority in which the Government took a calculated risk in the matter of the defence of Britain against invasion. Thereafter all our energy and resource were devoted to the planning and fulfilment of the supreme effort of the war.

But first a word must be said regarding the steps taken during 1940-2 against the very real possibility of the invasion of our country.[1] This might occur at almost any point, for with Norway in enemy hands Orkney and Shetland lay almost as wide open to assault as southern and eastern England. Indeed, during this period Orkney, especially the area surrounding Scapa Flow, was converted by strenuous exertion into something resembling a second Malta.

The enemy's original intention had been to destroy our airfields and so deprive our ground forces of aerial cover in their resistance to subsequent assault-landings. But with the loss of hundreds of his aircraft in the Battle of Britain during August and September 1940, Hitler found himself bereft of that hope, and thereafter confined himself to the savage and indiscriminate bombing of our cities, especially London, while he assembled a great expeditionary force, to be conveyed in Rhine barges under the escort of the German Navy, for a mass landing upon our shores. Our peril was extreme, for our Navy was already overstretched in the Battle of the Atlantic and our Middle East commitments, and could contribute little to coastal defence.

[1] As late as June 25th, 1941, Mr. Churchill, in Secret Session, had solemnly warned the House of Commons: 'In a few months, or even less, we may be exposed to the most frightful invasion the world has ever seen.' See p. 151.

Meanwhile, our military authorities were not idle. With the gradual building up of our island garrison, a series of defence 'exercises', some of them upon a very large scale, was being inaugurated throughout the country. A single example will suffice—Operation 'Bumper', one of the most considerable of the series, in which it was assumed that the German 6th Army had succeeded in landing a force of six divisions, two of them armoured, with formidable air support, upon the coast of East Anglia.

The invaders found themselves opposed by the British 'Southern Army', under the command of General Alexander (at that time G.O.C.-in-Chief Southern Command) with three British and two Canadian divisions, an armoured division, and two tank brigades.

London having been rendered impassable by heavy bombing, it was presumed that the enemy would advance along a line south of the fen country and the River Ouse and north of the Chilterns. His intention was to make for the Thames Valley, secure crossings at Maidenhead and Oxford, and penetrate to the rolling downs, eminently suited to armoured fighting vehicles, of Berkshire and Wiltshire. He was brought to bay, however, in a great battle in the neighbourhood of Bedford, lasting from September 27th to October 3rd, 1941, in which he was adjudged to have been heavily defeated.

Naturally, some of the tactical features of the operation had to be very much of a 'token' character, especially in such matters as the employment of heavy artillery; but the excitement of fighting under the most realistic possible conditions without cessation for a whole week proved an admirable tonic for the morale of the formations employed, besides applying a searching test to their stamina and fighting spirit. Upon the administrative side, however, there was no need for make-believe, and many valuable and practical lessons were learned in respect of ration supply, the evacuation of casualties, traffic control, and intercommunication between units. Only in the last of these was much fault to be found, and immediate steps were taken to co-ordinate the work of the dispatch riders and wireless operators upon an improved and more reliable basis.

~*(3)*~

The entry of the United States in December 1941 relieved us from our splendid isolation, and at the same time necessitated a complete redrafting of our plan of action. Integration of all arms was still the order of the day, but now it had become necessary to amalgamate the resources and order of battle of the British Commonwealth of Nations with those of the great American Republic. The headquarters of the United Nations was transferred to Washington, well away from the distractions of the war zone—though anti-aircraft batteries now protected the Capitol and White House—and an experienced, representative and highly efficient body known as the Combined Chiefs of Staff Committee was there set up in permanent session to direct the whole course of the war.[1]

With the arrival of the American troops in England in 1942 the outstanding concern of General Sir Bernard Paget (who had succeeded Sir Alan Brooke as Commander-in-Chief Home Forces) was to find room in a small country—smaller than any one of at least half a score of American states—for the housing and training of an army of millions; especially when it is remembered that modern mechanised warfare requires far more freedom of manœuvre than the pedestrian activities of an earlier day.

The discharge of this difficult task (officially described as Operation 'Bolero') was effected for the most part by evacuating all British troops from Southern Command and handing over the entire district to the Americans. These soon filled it to overflowing: indeed, they overflowed into Western Command, where they achieved considerable penetration into Wales and Cheshire. The War Office (and in particular that sorely harassed official the Director of Quartering) were particularly hard put to it whenever one of the two 'Queens' descended unexpectedly on a British port—for these vast and speedy vessels traversed the Atlantic so swiftly and secretly that they occasionally arrived before the news of their departure from New York had been received, decoded, and officially passed from Grosvenor Square to Whitehall—there to discharge some 15,000 troops in immediate need of bed and board.

Accommodation had to be found also for other Allies than American. The Canadians, whose first division arrived in 1939, had grown steadily in strength and now formed an Army. They were the principal occupants of the new South Eastern Command, which covered Kent and that part of our coasts most vulnerable to sudden enemy attack.

Next came the Poles, some 60,000 of them.[2] These were planted in Scotland, where they extended from Forres in Morayshire to the

---

[1] The chief British military representative thereon was General Sir John Dill, who had served as C.I.G.S. throughout the intensely difficult years 1940-1, and now relinquished that office to General Sir Alan Brooke, who discharged it with the utmost distinction to the end of the war. Sir John Dill himself died in Washington in 1943, and was buried in Arlington Cemetery.

[2] To these must be added some 15,000 Poles serving in the R.A.F.

Cheviots, with army headquarters in Edinburgh. To them in due course had to be added some 2,000 convalescents, bearing the honourable scars of Cassino and Breda. There were Belgians in Northern Ireland and the Birmingham district, and a Netherlands brigade at Wolverhampton.

The difficulty of housing this great and ever increasing host was accentuated by the urgent necessity of preserving as much land as possible for agricultural purposes. Formerly Britain had imported something like sixty per cent of her foodstuffs: by intensive cultivation of every available acre of land that proportion had now been reduced to thirty per cent, and it was of vital importance to maintain this level of production and so ease the burden of our hard-driven mercantile marine. The duty of adjudicating between the claims of the warrior and the husbandman was entrusted to a body known as the Training Area Selection Committee, or T.A.S.C., who found their hands more than full, not only owing to the necessity of leaving agricultural land undisturbed, but the difficulty of finding sufficient military *Lebensraum* in an island as densely populated and highly enclosed as England. At one time no fewer than 11,000,000 acres of our soil were in military occupation.

However, the thing was done somehow. Salisbury Plain and the Aldershot district had long been converted to such uses: now such wide-open spaces as Dartmoor were conscripted. Wales and Scotland offered a wider choice, and in due course some of the most remote and lovely districts of the United Kingdom echoed to the thunder of guns and the grinding of tanks. Armoured training naturally called for most space: the two largest Armoured Areas were the Wolds area in East Yorkshire and the Thetford area in Norfolk. Combined training, including the rehearsal of amphibious large-scale assault-landings, was practised, under most realistic conditions, along the shores of Loch Fyne in Argyllshire, once a favourite resort of steamer excursionists from Glasgow.

Larkhill, on Salisbury Plain, was the scene of intensified artillery activity, with live shells whistling over ridges at long range and opposing a barrage to the path of an imaginary advance, while elsewhere 25-pounder batteries laid down smoke-screens or afforded their gunners experience in the art of knocking out processions of mobile dummy tanks.

Modern field artillery, needless to say, is today mechanised like everything else, and is either self-propelled or towed into action by a tractor. Gone is the galloping horse-drawn weapon of old, with the gun-numbers perched rigid upon the limber. The self-propelled gun is carried in a small armoured vehicle resembling a tank: it is fired from the stern and the gunners sit in a species of well, open to the sky but protected by an all-round steel casing which screens them from the view of the enemy, though it is no particular protection against a direct hit.

With regard to modern artillery types in general, the largest weapon employed in 1943 was the intensely powerful 7·2-inch howitzer. Next came the 5·5-inch gun howitzer, then the 4·2-inch mortar, firing a powerful projectile at great range. The 3·7 anti-aircraft gun had been well known to our civil population since the days of the air raids. The standard anti-tank gun was the 6 pounder, whose arrival upon the scene, it will be remembered, was so long and anxiously awaited in the Libyan campaign. The 17 pounder was a most effective and handy weapon, with a traverse of 45 degrees.[1] The famous 25 pounder, or Sexton, when self-propelled, carried its own radio, which meant that it could operate in direct communication with the controlling power behind it. It was capable of a speed of twenty-five miles per hour. Machine-guns and mortars were also conveyed in carriers, though not operated therefrom. Later came a self-propelled vehicle of a purely defensive type—the 'Kangaroo', or 'personnel carrier', which conveyed troops from point to point without exposing them to enemy fire. It carried eight passengers, and was much appreciated by the infantry, who were inclined to regard themselves as the 'unprotected' branch of the Army.

Further north on the Plain, round Imber, tanks of various denominations (most of which have already been described[2]) moving at high speed and mounting various weapons, from the Besa automatic rifle to the 3-inch gun, manœuvred against targets as far as 1,000 yards away.

Another assault vehicle of somewhat different type, destined to perform most valuable service, was now undergoing its tests with a view to a first public appearance on D-Day. This was the A.V.R.E. (or Armoured Vehicle R.E.) designed for work against pill-boxes and concrete emplacements, and operated by the Royal Engineers. It was a Churchill tank, and carried a powerful weapon known as a petard, discharging an explosive projectile capable of disintegrating six feet of concrete.

Elsewhere in the same Command the recently created Airborne Division was making a most impressive first appearance. Here was

---

[1] It was fitted later to the Sherman tank—a truly formidable combination.
[2] See Chap. XI, Sec. 5 (pp. 140–2).

something entirely new in warfare—or rather, here was a great military experiment developed to its full possibilities. By 1942 every member of the Airborne Division (Major-General F. A. S. Browning) travelled habitually by air, descending from the sky by parachute or glider with his own appropriate equipment. The doctor and the padre baled out with the rest. There was a specially trained Regiment of Glider Pilots, skilled first in controlling their frail craft in its rough-riding progress across country until it attained sufficient momentum to take the air, secondly in judging the exact moment at which to detach it from the aircraft towing it, and thirdly in guiding it smoothly to earth at exactly the right spot, whether on landing-wheels or skids.

Besides conveying troops, the gliders were now capable of carrying motor-cycles, Bren-gun carriers, and even artillery, all of which could be brought to earth far behind the enemy's lines: 6-pounder anti-tank guns were actually dropped by parachute at Arnhem.

The famous Dieppe raid took place in August 1942, and the lessons derived from that somewhat expensive venture were immediately applied to the further improvement in the training of troops for assault landings. All during this period, by day and by night, and in all weathers at various coastal training-centres, men fantastically attired and with blackened faces emerged literally from the sea to fight their way up wired and mined beaches, through smoke-screens, to an objective of stoutly defended pill-boxes; or descended from the sky to stage a street battle; or advanced up a valley to storm some fortified position, reminded, by a stream of live bullets directed over-head and on either flank, to keep the correct line and take advantage of every inch of cover.

The Commandos were certainly trained in a hard school, but it is to be doubted if their education was much more severe than the toughening process undergone by some of the Line regiments or airborne troops. Indeed, military opinion on the subject was sharply divided. Many experienced officers held that, magnificent though the work of the Commandos was, it could have been done equally well by properly trained regular units, and that too without 'milking' established formations in order to set up a *corps d'élite*. The most undesirable feature of the system, they added, was that public adula-tion of the Commandos induced a feeling of inferiority in troops employed in less spectacular but equally hazardous ventures; while the degree of licence accorded to such guerrilla formations, whether on or off duty, set an inevitable premium on indiscipline.

These criticisms were justifiable; but it may be argued that Fame is the spur, and that the very publicity which the Commandos enjoyed may have been largely responsible for the brilliance of their achievements. Certainly they cheered the hearts and raised the morale of our civil population at an anxious and difficult time.

~≈(4)≈~

But the training activity just described was confined to no particular arm or district, for training schools had grown up all over the country.[1] General Paget laid especial stress upon the importance of infantry training, a need apt to be overlooked in an era of promiscuous mechanisation. (After all, although infantry were now frequently conveyed to the battlefield on wheels, they still had to do their actual fighting on their feet.)

'The infantry', said General Paget, 'is the cutting-edge of battle'; and like Lord Wavell before him he held that 'it is the platoon and section commanders who do most to win our battles'. So he lost no opportunity of impressing upon his officers the principles inculcated a century and a half earlier by Sir John Moore[2] and consistently neglected in the mass-attacks of the First World War—namely, the training of platoon and section commanders to handle their units, when occasion arose, as self-contained and self-reliant formations, independent of higher direction or synchronised artillery support.

'In France and Belgium during the period 1916–18,' he said in an address to Senior Officers (including Americans) at the School of Artillery in October 1943, 'it was the practice for our infantry to advance in lines close behind an intense and rigidly timed barrage, on which they relied entirely to neutralise the enemy's defences. If, as often happened, the barrage partially failed to achieve its object, the enemy machine-guns which had survived held up the attack. The infantry then went to ground in whatever cover they could find, while the barrage rolled on in accordance with the previously arranged time-table. . . .'

thus leaving the infantry naked to their enemies, with consequent failure of the attack and heavy casualties.

'I do not mean to imply', he continued, 'that we should expect infantry under modern conditions to attack without artillery support. They must always be given the maximum support available. But they must not rely upon it to the extent of ceasing to think and act for themselves: they must be ready at all times to make use of their own weapons, *not only to see them into the assault over the last 200 yards, but to deal with unexpected opposition during any stage of the attack.* . . .

[1] See p. 156 for detailed list. [2] See p. 146.

'This kind of flexible team-work and initiative demands a high standard of junior leadership, such as is taught here. It is the junior leaders who will do most to win the battle, and therefore we must do all in our power to fit them for their task.'

Finally, and at the highest level, the Commander-in-Chief impressed upon all concerned the necessity of the complete integration of staff work as between 'G', and 'A' and 'Q'. He drew certain more than convincing instances from the histories of the Crimea, Gallipoli, and, more recent, Norway, and of what happens when 'G' plans an operation which is administratively impossible.

'Avoid watertight compartments like the plague,' he said; 'let us play as a team, and not as separate branches of the Staff.'

This last injunction was in the nature of a benediction, for General Paget's work as Commander-in-Chief Home Forces was done. The great machine which he had assembled and attuned was now about to pass into other hands, and by these to be launched as part of the mightiest operation in military history.

CHAPTER XVI

'OVERLORD' AND AFTER

⤚(1)⤜

D-DAY was at hand. It had been long in coming, first because of the postponement brought about by the north-west African operations of 1942–3, and subsequently by the Allied decision (after considerable discussion) to open the European campaign by administering the knock-out blow to Italy, thus reopening the short sea route through the Mediterranean and diverting as many German troops as possible from the Russian front to the defence of southern Europe.

Now, at long last, these commitments had been discharged, and all was in readiness for the supreme effort of the war. The Allied forces were approaching maximum strength and munition output was at its peak. May 1st, 1944 was designated as 'target' date, and the coming adventure was christened, not inappropriately, Operation 'Overlord'.

General Montgomery had arrived in England from Italy on January 2nd, 1944, and had been placed by General Eisenhower in operational control of the whole of the Allied land forces about to be engaged. His 'opposite numbers' of the Royal Navy and Royal Air Force were respectively Admiral Sir Bertram Ramsay and Air Chief Marshal Sir Trafford Leigh-Mallory. It should be noted that Montgomery's appointment differed from those of his two colleagues in that he had been placed not in supreme command of the land forces but in 'operational control', pending the moment when General Eisenhower should himself take over the Supreme Command. (This occurred on August 1st, when the United States 12th Army Group had been completed by the arrival in France of the U.S. 3rd Army under General Patton.)

A plan, known as the 'Cossac' plan, for an Allied landing in France had been formulated in 1943 and accepted by the Allied Commanders. The selection of the best possible landing-ground was of chief importance. It must present a stretch of beach suited to the employment of assault landing-craft and capable of accommodating an enormous number at one time. It must lie sufficiently near the south coast of England to allow of a reasonably short passage for the invading flotilla, as well as to ensure the provision of adequate air cover over the beaches themselves. (This ruled out the Biscayan coast.) Conditions of tide and weather must be carefully estimated. The *hinterland* must be suitable for the landing of aircraft and the operation of tanks. Above all, careful consideration must be given to the question of the amount of opposition to be expected at any given spot.

The so-called Western Wall was not by any means of the same strength everywhere. The enemy had assumed that an invader, to have any chance of success, would have to secure one of the French Channel ports as a preliminary to more serious operations, and for that reason had given priority to the work of rendering these bases— Le Havre, Cherbourg and Brest, for instance—virtually impregnable to attack from the sea. Particular attention was also paid to the Pas de Calais, as being the nearest point of approach from the coast of England.

The plans of the Allies were, in point of fact, very different, and of an originality entirely unanticipated by the one-track-minded Rommel, who was in charge of the coastal defences. Instead of incurring heavy casualties in a possibly fruitless attempt to secure a French harbour as a base of operations, the Allies had decided to bring their own harbour, or harbours, with them—in other words, establish a beach-head upon some stretch of open coast and enclose it in an artificial, prefabricated breakwater with blockships and pierheads, conveyed thither for the purpose. Work upon these breakwaters—a top secret which afterwards achieved well-earned fame under the sobriquet 'Mulberry'—had been in progress throughout the United Kingdom for many months. Each section thereof can best be described as a floating caisson or blockship of concrete, capable of being towed to its appropriate berth and there scuttled. No fewer than 146 such vessels were constructed, sufficient to furnish two complete harbours. They were of varying type and draught—six types in all— to accord with the different depths of ocean involved. (The plumbing of those depths must have been a major work of research in itself.)

The location finally selected for the landing was the Baie de la Seine, on the Normandy coast immediately south of the Isle of Wight.

The Baie itself lies wide open to the Channel, and is some seventy miles in breadth: its western side is enclosed by the Cotentin peninsula, on the northern extremity of which stands Cherbourg; on the eastern side are Le Havre and the mouth of the Seine. The strip of coast within the Baie, dotted with former holiday resorts such as Trouville, Deauville, Bayeux and Caen (from which last William the Conqueror had sailed nine centuries before to the invasion of England), was protected by a series of linear defences, arranged as strong points manned by troops mainly of low category. The gun positions, however, were defended by armour and concrete, while the beaches themselves were a maze of mines, wire entanglements, and underwater obstacles only visible at low tide.

It was a formidable commitment, especially since the ground beyond the Caen-Bayeux road in the British sector, consisting of *bocage* (pasture land divided by high banks and hedges), was not particularly favourable to offensive operations; but it seemed to offer the best prospect of success. As General Montgomery reports:

The Normandy beaches were selected because they offered a better shelter for shipping and were less heavily defended than other possible beaches. *They also satisfied the minimum requirements of the air forces, in terms of their distance from home bases, for the provision of air cover.*

General Montgomery had at his disposal the 21st Army Group, comprising the 1st Canadian Army (Lieut.-General Crerar), the 2nd British Army (Lieut.-General Dempsey), the British airborne troops (Lieut.-General Browning), and various Allied contingents; the 1st United States Army (General Omar N. Bradley), and the American 82nd and 101st Airborne Divisions. His plan of battle, as approved by General Eisenhower and agreed by the Combined Chiefs of Staff, can be stated in his own words:

'The intention was to assault, simultaneously, beaches on the Normandy coast immediately north of the Carentan estuary' (i.e. the eastern coast of the Cotentin peninsula) 'and between the Carentan estuary and the River Orne, with the object of securing a lodgement area which was to include airfield sites and the port of Cherbourg. The left or eastern flank of the lodgement area was to include the road centre of Caen.[1]

'Once ashore and firmly established, my plan was to threaten to break out on the eastern flank—that is, the Caen sector; *by this threat to draw main enemy reserves into that sector; to fight them there and keep them there, using the British and Canadian troops for the purpose. Having got the main enemy reserves committed to the eastern flank, my plan was to make the*

[1] See Map 5. This lodgement area was about fifty miles wide, and was designated 'Neptune'.

breakout on the western flank, using for this task the American armies under General Bradley, and pivoting on Caen. This attack was to be delivered down to the Loire and then to proceed eastward in a wide sweep up to the Seine about Paris. This would cut off all the enemy forces south of the Seine, over which river the bridges were to be destroyed by air action.'

That is to say, the plan contemplated a great scythe-like sweep, first south and then east, by the Americans, while the British and Canadians, acting as hinge, kept the main enemy forces pinned down in the neighbourhood of Caen. It was a bold plan in more senses than one, for its outcome was bound to evoke (and did evoke) in both Allied countries certain comparisons between the apparent immobility of the 21st Army Group and the triumphant progress of the American troops out on the wing. But General Montgomery was fully justified by the event, for he had rightly judged that the enemy, determined at all costs to prevent the Allied left wing from advancing on Rouen and Paris, would concentrate his forces against the Caen area, and would thus be compelled to weaken himself elsewhere.

'The operations', he reports, 'developed in June, July and August exactly as planned. I had given D+90 as being target date for being lined up on the Seine: actually the first crossing of the river was made on D+75.'

In other words, Montgomery had forecast that his armies would reach the Seine within three months of D-Day, whereas they actually arrived a fortnight earlier. Which seems to dispose of any suggestion that the advance was unduly delayed by the 21st Army Group having become involved in a 'stalemate'. But this is to anticipate.

D-Day, that long awaited date, emerged from the mists of conjecture into the full light of history upon June 6th, 1944. But D-Day was merely the climax of a long-term scheme, for the invasion operations had really begun some time before. First, an ordered plan of long-range bombing had wrecked the greater part of the German radio-location system, devastated his munition centres and, by destroying roads and railways, severely reduced his mobility. This programme was in full operation by D-Day *minus* 60 (that is, by early April), with a resulting famine in locomotives and stock. By June 6th, seventy-four bridges and tunnels leading to the battle area were rendered impassable; on June 7th all railway bridges over the Seine between Paris and the sea were out of action. Secondly, continuous attack upon aircraft, air factories and landing-grounds had reduced the Luftwaffe to a level which secured for the invaders the mastery of the skies over the Channel and assault coast. (Only two bombing attacks on our assault forces were attempted during the sea passage, or on the beaches, at any time during D-Day.) Thirdly, as D-Day

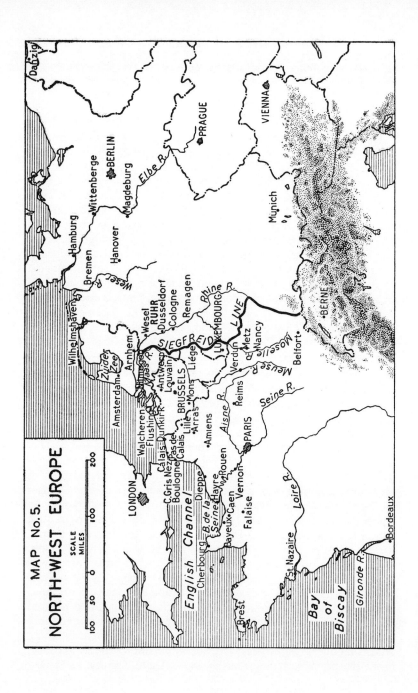

MAP No. 5.
NORTH-WEST EUROPE

SCALE
MILES

100   50   0   100   200

drew near, promiscuous and devastating tactical bombing-raids were delivered against the coastal defences all along the Atlantic Wall, confusing the enemy as to the actual point of the intended invasion and adding to the general demoralisation of the defenders. Particular attention was paid to Cape Gris-Nez, between Calais and Boulogne, with the result that the enemy, convinced that this was to be our point of attack, concentrated there a large force which would have been of the utmost value in the 'Neptune' area.[1]

Thus by deep planning and close integration of all three Arms—for the escorting naval forces played their full part in clearing the Channel of enemy submarines and E-boats—the way was paved for a completely successful large-scale amphibious invasion, and a problem which had baffled successively Philip of Spain, Napoleon Bonaparte and Adolf Hitler was solved for the first time in modern history.

Large-scale it certainly was, for the total of men and machines conveyed across Channel for the initial landing amounted to 130,000 men and 20,000 vehicles, all within three tides. Over 4,000 ships were employed, together with several thousand smaller craft.[2] One British and two American divisions were transported by glider and parachute.

The equipment included various new and ingenious engines of war not previously mentioned in our narrative. Besides the Assault Engineer tanks (the A.V.R.E., already described[3]) there were tank-carried bridges for crossing anti-tank ditches, mat-laying tanks for covering soft clay patches, 'ramp' tanks over which other vehicles could clamber and so surmount sea-walls, and 'flail'-tanks for mine clearance.

The flail-tanks were the outcome of much research and experiment, for in the desert war the enemy's habit of sowing small mines just below the surface of the ground in the path of our advance had become a serious menace. The flail-tank proved a most efficient anti-dote. It carried before it a horizontal axle or drum, to which were attached lengths of steel chain. The drum, revolving at high speed, imparted a flail-like action to the free ends of the chains, which by beating the ground ahead of the advancing tank, like a carpet, detonated all the mines concealed in its path. Since the drum projected some distance ahead of the tank itself the occupants suffered

[1] Supreme Headquarters of the Allied Expeditionary Force 'S.H.A.E.F.' was at Portsmouth, but a duplicate S.H.A.E.F., equally complete, had been established within the cliffs of Dover, from which if need be Operation 'Overlord' could have been launched. Possibly rumours of its existence may have influenced the enemy in his decision to mass troops in the Pas de Calais.

[2] Approximate figures: warships, minesweepers, etc., 1,100; landing craft, 4,200; coasters and liberty ships, 625.

[3] See p. 208.

no harm. The task of eliminating these mines had been performed hitherto by an instrument roughly resembling a Hoover carpet-sweeper, which by means of an electro-magnetic device gave audible warning to its operator of the presence of the mine, which was then dug out and rendered harmless. But this process was naturally slow and risky: the enemy, moreover, began presently to substitute mines made of plastic for those of steel, to the presence of which the electro-magnetic detonator offered no reaction. The flail-tank made short work of both.

Of especial interest, too, was the bridge-carrying tank. This was a Churchill tank with its upper works removed, carrying an arched steel bridge thirty feet long and consisting chiefly of two parallel spans at a distance apart equal to the gauge of a tank or armoured car. To place the bridge in position (say across a trench) it was lifted from its bed on top of the tank by a hinged steel arm, which swung it forward and set it down athwart the obstacle in less than two minutes, without exposing the crew. It could bear a weight of fifty tons.

Such were the preparations, material and moral, for Operation 'Overlord'. What was to happen when the landing had been effected is made plain in the following extract from the official Dispatch.

Once the troops were ashore it was necessary for them to 'crack about'. The need for sustained energy and drive was paramount, as it was necessary to link our beach-heads and penetrate quickly inland before the enemy opposition crystallised.

Plainly General Montgomery was determined that there should be no repetition of the Anzio episode.

⁓(2)⁓

D-Day itself began as early as 1.30 a.m. on June 6th, with the dropping of American airborne troops in the neighbourhood of Ste Mère Église on the right of the selected position. Half an hour later a party of the 6th (British) Airborne Division descended on the left, in the neighbourhood of the Canal de Caen. Thus both right and left flanks were secured. Our bombers had worked up to a furious finale during the night, and by dawn some 6,000 tons of bombs had effected their purpose of 'softening-up' the beach defences.

With full daylight came the Allied Armada, a spectacle almost overwhelming in its extent and majesty, as its naval escort shepherded it through the minefields, while the R.A.F. roared overhead. It comprised two separate Task Forces, Western and Eastern, each with its own allotted beach-objectives. The British were on the left. The weather was atrocious. It had blown, and continued to blow, with a violence unexampled for the time of year, and General Eisenhower took a grave and deliberate risk when at the eleventh hour he gave the word 'Go'. Still, to have postponed the expedition at this moment would have involved a probable delay of three or four weeks. To have delayed further would have left but a scanty margin of time before another winter set in, besides giving the enemy an opportunity to recover from the paralysing effect of our strategic bombing campaign. We should also have lost the advantage of surprise. There was the effect, too, upon the fortunes of Russia to be considered, as well as the reaction of the peoples of occupied Europe to a hope once more deferred.

So General Eisenhower, fully conscious of the appalling risk he was taking—for a disaster on D-Day would have prolonged the war indefinitely, perhaps for years—made his decision and made it unflinchingly. He was more than justified by the event, for the landing was a triumphant success.

Still, the crossing was a severe ordeal for the thousands of men packed close in small unwieldy ships, some of them hardly ships at all—flat-bottomed rectangular contraptions designed for shallow inshore work rather than the rolling Channel. But the men, numbed, soaked and seasick though many of them were, endured everything with their usual blend of grumbling fortitude and sardonic humour— characteristically summarised in the action of one anonymous sufferer, who chalked up along the side of his L.C.A. the Government slogan of the moment: *Is Your Journey Really Necessary?*

Of the great battles which now ensued, and continued almost without a break until the Rhine had been crossed and Germany invaded, there is no need to speak in detail here, except in so far as we are concerned with the personal fortunes of the 21st Army Group.

In one respect only did the subsequent operations fall short of hope and expectation. Owing to the enemy's immense concentration of strength in the Caen area, Caen was not carried at the first assault: indeed, some weeks had to elapse before even a part of the town was occupied. All the other beach-heads, however, were successfully established, and within six days were firmly linked together on a front of about fifty miles, varying in depth from eight to twelve.

Having effected a secure lodgement upon the Normandy coast, General Montgomery was now able to proceed with his considered plan of campaign. His aim was to engage and defeat the forces opposed to him between the Loire and the Seine. To do this he had first to break out of his confined position on the beaches and initiate the great sweeping movement already foreshadowed.

He had three essential objects in view. The first was to draw the bulk of the enemy's armoured strength on to the left (or eastern) Allied flank—in other words, against the 21st Army Group—in order to remove opposition as far as possible to the encircling sweep of the American 12th Army on the right; the second was to maintain and build up his reinforcements and supplies, which until a port could be secured must be brought in over open beaches; and the third was to impose every possible obstacle in the way of a similar build-up by the enemy.

The first of these he achieved by initiating and maintaining a continuous offensive in the Caen area, thus compelling his opponent to divert all his available reserves into that theatre. Casualties in such circumstances were bound to be heavy, but Montgomery had forced his opponents to fight the battle as planned by him and not by them.

In the matter of his 'build-up' he was not so fortunate. Cherbourg was not captured until June 26th, and even then the docks and harbour were found to have been demolished so thoroughly that they could not be rendered serviceable until late in August.

But his worst enemy was the weather. Another and even greater storm rose a fortnight after D-Day, and raged without ceasing for seventy-two hours. Some 800 craft of all kinds were driven ashore and wrecked, and the Mulberry harbours were severely damaged. Indeed, the Mulberry in the Omaha (American) area was put out of action almost entirely, and all resources thereafter were diverted to the completion and strengthening of the Arromanches (British) harbour. The overall loss caused by the storm amounted almost to 20,000 vehicles and 140,000 tons of stores. Shortages of ammunition imposed a special handicap upon the progress of the offensive.

In his third commitment, the prevention of the enemy build-up, General Montgomery was successful to a most encouraging degree. The strategic bombing campaign of the pre-D-Day period was already bearing fruit in the shape of broken bridges, blocked roads, and devastated fuel dumps. Not only had enemy mobility been reduced to a disastrous degree, but low-flying Allied bombers now rendered road movements almost impossible except by night, while rail transport could not be brought nearer to the front than 150 to 100 miles. Routes had to be changed hourly.[1]

---

[1] This information is derived from a report issued by the German Commander-in-Chief, Rundstedt, about this time.

But this by no means marked the end of German tribulations. A fortnight after D-Day the Russians struck back, and struck hard. Vitebsk fell, and five German divisions were wiped out. Mogilev and Minsk, the capital of White Russia, followed. The whole Russian line was in motion, and presently the movement became a landslide from the Baltic States to the south of the Pripet Marshes.

The immediate repercussion within Germany itself was of a truly startling character—namely, an attempt to assassinate Hitler, by means of a bomb concealed in a dispatch-case beside his desk at his headquarters. Hitler was not seriously hurt, but the inevitable 'purge' which followed the failure of the plot resulted in the shooting or hanging of various high officials, including a Field-Marshal and several Generals, and the elevation of Hitler's special *protégé* Himmler, chief of the Gestapo, to the post of the command of the army within Germany. Public alarm and despondency were countered as far as possible by the promise of new and terrible secret weapons. One of these, the V1 bomb, was already in operation and, although it inflicted yet more hardship and death upon the much enduring people of London, proved to be of little or no military value.[1]

Early in August the Russian advance came to a halt, but by this time the Allied armies in the west had taken up the tale. An entirely new American force landed in southern France between Toulon and St. Raphael, and within a week had effected a lodgement of over 200 square miles. In Italy General Alexander had crossed the Arno and driven Kesselring so far to the north that he now stood in danger of invasion from the Riviera.

Meanwhile General Montgomery's Army Groups in Normandy had broken out of their restricted bridge-head, and the great encircling movement had begun—first west, then south along the Biscayan coast, then east, then northward towards Paris. The most reasonable course open to the Germans at this time would have been an orderly withdrawal to the line of the Seine. But Hitler had elected to do what Montgomery had hoped he would do—stay and fight it out between that river and the Loire. As a result the German 7th Army was caught between the British-Canadian 21st Army Group pressing southward from Caen, and the left wing of the American 12th Army Group advancing northward to Falaise. The result was the trapping of that army in the 'Falaise Pocket', the mouth of which was ultimately sealed; and the army itself, enfiladed on either side by artillery fire and smitten from above by ceaseless bombing, practically ceased to exist.

[1] See Chap. XVII, Sec. 8 (pp. 247–9).

Thus ended the Battle of Normandy, which had raged from June 6th to August 19th. The enemy losses in manpower fell not far short of half a million, for 240,000 were killed or wounded and 210,000 taken prisoner. Some 3,500 guns and 1,500 tanks were captured or destroyed.

Our own losses were severe, especially among the 21st Army Group—which was not surprising, considering the preponderance of enemy strength arrayed against it. That preponderance, too, increased steadily. Upon June 25th the German forces in the Caen-Caumont sector included five Panzer divisions and 530 tanks, as compared with 190 tanks and one Panzer division in the Caumont-Cotentin sector. A month later the figures had increased to 645 tanks and six Panzer divisions opposite the one, as compared with 190 tanks and two Panzer divisions opposite the other. In other words, Montgomery's strategic policy of a determined and continuous offensive in the Caen sector had drawn thither all the enemy's available reserves, and so eased the path of the brilliant American scythe-movement on the Allied right.

A word may appropriately be said here regarding the criticism directed at this time against General Montgomery's handling of the Normandy battle. This came chiefly from certain enterprising American journalists, impatient of delays and avid of 'hot news', and was to the effect that the General was dilatory, over-cautious, and disinclined to take legitimate risks. There was a further suggestion that in his handling of operations during the Ardennes counter-attack some four months later the Field-Marshal (as he had by this time become) was inclined to risk American rather than British forces.

Both criticisms are cogently answered by Field-Marshal Montgomery's own Chief-of-Staff:[1]

Some say Montgomery did not take sufficient risks. It is true that he invariably endeavoured to make certain that an operation would succeed.

There were two other factors which influenced him in the risks he was prepared to take.

The first was the fact that he had set himself the task of never again allowing his troops to suffer a major defeat. He had made this vow when he saw the result of such misfortunes on taking over the command of the Eighth Army.

The second was the dwindling British manpower problem. He dared not risk a major reverse now.

In other words, although fresh American units continued to arrive in Europe right up to the end of the war, few British reinforcements

[1] From *Operation Victory*, by Major-General Sir Francis de Guingand, K.B.E., C.B., D.S.O.

appeared on the scene during the final six months. The truth was that after nearly five-and-a-half years of endless battle, largely single-handed, there were none to send. Britain was bled white: she could and did, sustain her effort to the end; increase it further she could not,

~✕(3)✕~

It was now quite clear that the German occupation of France must end. German Administration Headquarters in Paris was the first to recognise the fact, and decamped forthwith in the direction of Metz and Nancy, accompanied by various French quislings. On August 14th the French Resistance Movement, which had been operating so far underground and with great effect, came to the surface once and for all. The French Provisional Government proclaimed a revolt: on August 23rd the Fourth French Republic was born, and France reared her head once more amid the comity of nations. The dawn of freedom was breaking.

Meanwhile American armour was moving swiftly northward, and could possibly have reached Paris ahead of all the Allied forces; but by a happy chance—if chance it was—a French armoured division under General Leclerc was the first to enter Paris and liberate the city.

The chief preoccupation of the enemy now was to extricate his forces from France. Only in the Pas de Calais and the Netherlands were the troops ordered to hold on to the last; partly because the V1 bomb-sites were situated here, and partly to deny to the Allies (who were still compelled to import their supplies via Cherbourg or the Arromanches Mulberry) the use of such invaluable ports as Le Havre, Calais, Dunkirk, and above all Antwerp.[1]

But the rest of the German Army were ordered to make their way eastward, and there to establish a continuous defence wall. They had suffered immense losses, but were still strong and well-equipped; and if they were given time to extend and consolidate the Siegfried Line (once the subject of a ribald marching-chorus, but now a very real obstacle in the path of the Allies) a prolonged and expensive stalemate might ensue.

Plainly the prerequisite of final victory was speed. At the same time the Allied plan of action had to be reviewed and adjusted to the new situation. Ever fresh contingents of young and lusty American troops were arriving in France, and the balance of manpower was

---

[1] A garrison had also been left at the mouth of the Gironde, to prevent Allied access to Bordeaux.

settling down more and more decisively upon the American side. General Eisenhower was due to arrive and take over the Supreme Command in person, and did so upon September 1st. This left Field-Marshal[1] Montgomery in command of the British 2nd and the Canadian 1st Armies, with the remaining units of the 21st Army Group, while General Omar D. Bradley assumed control of the 12th Army Group (1st and 3rd American Armies). A little later General Eisenhower also took over from the Mediterranean Command the American 6th Army Group, operating under General Devers in the Rhône Valley.

The next step was to cross the Rhine, and so consummate the hopes of five long years by the invasion of Germany.

Here two plans of action presented themselves. Each was earnestly considered and debated. The first was a concentrated attack in very great strength upon a narrow front, which if successfully delivered would establish a firm bridge-head beyond the Rhine from which it would be possible to 'fan out' to right and left. The alternative was to deliver a general attack at selected points all along the line. In other words, it was a choice between a torpedo and a broadside.

Field-Marshal Montgomery himself was a strong advocate of the 'torpedo' policy. If the projected thrust, he argued, were to be delivered over the Rhine north of the Ruhr, its immediate objective would become the Ruhr region itself; and with that vast industrial district precluded further from furnishing the essential sinews of war, Germany's resistance must inevitably and speedily collapse.

The Field-Marshal's actual proposal, which was based on the premise that it would be put into effect with the least possible delay and adequately followed up, was a clearance of the Channel coast as far as Antwerp, followed, without waiting to consolidate these gains, by an all-out drive into Germany.

Occupying, as it did, the left and northernmost wing of the Allied line of advance, this task would fall automatically upon the 21st or, as it was now designated, the Northern Group of Armies,[2] backed by such maintenance units as might be furnished by the Supreme Commander from the other formations at his disposal; for though the Northern Group might form a victorious spearhead in the proposed enterprise, it could not continue to operate indefinitely.

[1] He was promoted Field-Marshal upon this date, upon the occasion of his handing over of the Supreme Command.

[2] General Bradley's command was hereafter known as the Central Group of Armies, while a force composed of the 1st French Army (under General de Lattre de Tassigny) and the U.S. 7th Army (under General Patch) were subsequently designated the Southern Group of Armies.

The 'broad front' policy, on the other hand, implied lining up the Allied armies along the River Rhine and there developing operations for the capture both of the Ruhr and Frankfurt areas. Its particular merit lay in the fact that it avoided the risk of initiating a long-range operation upon a narrow front, with attendant danger to exposed flanks in enemy territory.

Field-Marshal Montgomery's objection to this plan was that a 'broad front' would nowhere be strong enough to achieve quick or decisive results, and that in consequence the enemy would have time to recover, with the inevitable corollary of a long winter campaign.

General Eisenhower, with his usual good sense and thoroughness, gave due and impartial consideration to both points of view. Upon the strategic side he had to balance the consequences of a possible failure of the all-out thrust, against the delay inevitable in the organisation of the broad-front movement. As a sagacious commander he must also have been acutely conscious of the effect upon the fighting spirit and *amour-propre* of the Central and Southern Groups of Armies if they found themselves relegated, even for the shortest period, after their recent superhuman exertions, to anything approaching a static role in what might prove the final battle of the war.

In due course he made his decision. In this he was chiefly influenced, not by any question of operational prestige on one side or the other, but by sober consideration of such vital matters as supply and maintenance. The strain upon Allied administrative services, with their over-extended lines of communication, was by this time enormous. Taking fuel alone, 1,000,000 gallons of petrol, delivered by road, pipe-line[1] or aeroplane, were being consumed daily in the headlong advance of the Allied armour; and in all other respects the Allied forces were reaching the limit beyond which a victorious army cannot advance without pausing to reorganise its line of battle and replenish its stores.

This, General Eisenhower decided, was the overriding factor in the situation; so he came down on the side of the 'broad front'. He reports:

As will be indicated in due course, the difficulties of supply eventually forced a halt upon us when we reached Germany, but the very rapidity of our advance across France had made that inevitable. In consequence of the enemy's denial to us of the Brittany ports and the unexpected situation of having to support a dash of such length and speed entirely from our bases on the Normandy shore, only a miracle of hard work and improvisation by the supply services had carried our armoured spearheads so far.

---

[1] Known by its code-name of 'Pluto'. See p. 261.

The difference which this decision made to Field-Marshal Montgomery was that though the Supreme Commander fully concurred in the idea of a direct thrust into Germany, he did not feel justified in withdrawing transport from units on other sections of the 'broad front' in order to back and follow up the Northern Group of Armies.

⟋(4)⟍

We now return to the Northern Group, with whose movements and fortunes we shall chiefly be concerned. But first let us summarise the part—henceforth the major part—played by the American armies in the revised strategic plan.

First, their progress through reoccupied France. On the extreme right the 3rd United States Army had struck eastward of Paris as far as Nancy and Verdun, while another column pressed south-east towards the historic Belfort Gap, there to link up with the 7th United States Army approaching from Marseilles. Meanwhile the 1st United States Army crossed the Aisne, with its right flank directed towards the Duchy of Luxembourg and its left following the line Mons–Liége.

On the extreme left flank moved the British-Canadian Northern Group of Armies, no longer the pivot or hinge, but this time the extreme cutting-edge of the great Allied drive. Its immediate tasks were the destruction of the enemy in north-eastern France, the clearance of the Pas de Calais (with its V1 bomb-sites), the capture of airfields in Belgium, and the occupation of Antwerp.

The first obstacle in the path of General Montgomery was the winding River Seine, which it will be remembered had been stripped of all its bridges between Le Havre and Paris. But on August 29th XII, II Canadian, and I Corps had contrived to establish a bridge-head at Vernon, some thirty miles south-east of Rouen. Thereafter the British armour swept forward in a torrent.

Its progress was phenomenal: inspired perhaps by memories of battles fought both long ago and comparatively recently over this very ground—as long ago as 1918 and as recently as 1940—it had in less than a week liberated Amiens, Arras, Douai, Lille and Tournai. By September 3rd the Guards Division was in Brussels: Antwerp was occupied shortly after. The difficulties of transport and maintenance had been immense, for the Group was now operating 400 miles from its beach-head bases in Normandy; but the pace had never slackened. In these operations our 2nd Army was brilliantly supported on its right by the American 1st Army.

Meanwhile the Canadians on the left were sweeping up the Channel coast, to the liberation of Dieppe, Boulogne and Calais. By their speedy capture of the first of these objectives they put paid to an old account.[1]

So far progress had exceeded every hope. Holland had been reached, and just east of Holland lay the open plain of Hanover, with its promise of Bremen and Hamburg. Below Hanover, too, lay the Ruhr, that great triangle east of the Rhine, which produced most of Germany's mineral wealth.

But to reach this delectable goal it was first necessary to cross the Rhine, which here ran through Dutch territory into the North Sea, in two arms known as the Waal and the Lek, in a flat low-lying countryside intersected everywhere by canals and water barriers. Here was no battleground for the armoured fighting vehicle: the only way to establish a lodgement beyond the Rhine estuary was by glider and parachute troops.

This brings us to the story of what was subsequently known as the Arnhem operation. Its purpose was to outflank the northern extremity of the Western Wall, and so open a direct road for the 2nd Army into the north German plain. To that end no fewer than three airborne divisions, consisting of the 82nd and 101st United States and the 1st British Airborne Divisions, were detailed to be dropped on the further side of the Maas, Waal and Lek, there to establish a bridgehead and subsequently a corridor of invasion for the 30th Corps. The British objective comprised the bridges over the Lek at Arnhem.

The first two landings were successful, and contact was established with the 30th Corps; but the men bound for Arnhem, furthest north, were brought down prematurely by heavy flak, and cut off. They resisted stoutly, and with anything like normal weather would probably have held their ground until the junction with the 30th Corps had been effected. But it was not to be.

'During the eight vital days of battle,' reports Field-Marshal Montgomery, 'there were only two upon which the weather permitted even a reasonable scale of air support and air transportation. . . . Resupply missions were frequently cancelled, and when flown were often upon a greatly reduced scale. Had reasonable weather conditions been obtained I believe that a bridge head would have been established and maintained.'

To the handicap of the weather had to be added the lack of sufficient aircraft to enable the whole force to be carried in one 'lift'

[1] The Canadians had suffered severely in the Dieppe raid in August 1942. About the same time the 51st Highland Division had the gratification, after more than four years, of reoccupying St. Valéry-en-Caux.

instead of piecemeal, and the unexpected strength of the enemy's reaction. The division was kept under perpetual and heavy artillery fire, which rendered almost all attempts at relief abortive. On September 25th a withdrawal was ordered. 2,500 survivors returned.

It was a serious setback, though only local and partial. The Nijmegen bridge-head remained in our hands, and proved of immense value later on, when the 1st Canadian and 2nd British Armies advanced to the liberation of Holland. Where our hope and expectations were disappointed was in our failure to reach sufficiently far north to occupy the area between Arnhem and the Zuider Zee. Still, without such success as was achieved we should not have been able later on to compass our great crossing of the Rhine into Germany.

~(5)~

Meanwhile upon the central sector of the Allied front the 1st and 3rd U.S. Armies were fighting on the Siegfried Line. In the third week of September the 6th U.S. Army Group deployed upon their right, down to the Swiss frontier, and the 'broad front' was in being.

Except upon its extreme left, where the Canadians were kept busy during October clearing the winding Scheldt estuary (including the island of Walcheren) and so opening up the sea-approach to Antwerp, the battle-line along the Western Wall now seemed destined, owing to continued rain and low cloud, to settle down to a winter stalemate, especially in the air. But Rundstedt was not by any means beaten yet; and upon December 16th Field-Marshal Montgomery, busy with the reorganisation of his Northern Army Group and plans for an early invasion of the Rhineland, received the startling news of a great and unexpected enemy offensive further south.

For some time Rundstedt, by withdrawing and refitting a proportion of his best troops, had been contriving to build up a considerable and most powerful reserve, the spearhead of which consisted of eight Panzer divisions. His purpose was to deliver a surprise attack in overwhelming strength—no mere local demonstration, but an all-out attempt to cut the Allied line in two, cross the Meuse, capture the great Allied communication and maintenance centre at Liége, and thence press on to Brussels and Antwerp. He was taking an unwarranted risk, for if he failed his last reserves were gone, and if he succeeded he had little hope of achieving much more than a temporary turn of the tide.

Still, as General Eisenhower observes in his report:

If he could weaken our determination to maintain that flaming, relentless offensive which, regardless of his reaction, had carried us from the beaches to the Siegfried Line, his sacrifices would not be altogether futile.

In either case the responsibility was Hitler's, for the idea had emanated direct from him.

Rundstedt certainly left nothing to chance, and his handling of the earlier stages of the operation was masterly. He had selected for his point of attack a sector in General Bradley's 12th U.S. Army Group, somewhat lightly held owing to heavy American concentrations in the Aachen area further north. (It was by this route, it will be remembered, that the German invasion of France had been effected on May 10th, 1940.)

The assault was launched upon December 16th, with all the panoply of a German major offensive—three armies, mustering some fourteen infantry and ten Panzer and Panzer grenadier divisions, and equipped with 800 tanks of the latest Panther and Tiger types, advancing under an overwhelming artillery barrage; parachute troops descending far ahead and all around; the infiltration of innumerable *saboteurs* in civilian clothing and Allied uniform. The surprise was complete, and the four divisions guarding the position were swept away. The 12th U.S. Army Group was cut completely in two, and before the advance was halted ten days later, a breach had been created some forty-five miles wide and sixty miles deep—a penetration in fact to within four miles of the Meuse and ten from Liége.

By this wide cleavage General Bradley, in his headquarters at Luxembourg south of the break, found himself cut off from all control of the U.S. 9th and most of the U.S. 1st Army, both of which belonged to his group. General Eisenhower, from his own Command Post at Reims, immediately placed these two armies under the operational command of Field-Marshal Montgomery, upon whom now devolved the duty of co-ordinating their movements with those of the Northern Group.

His first care was to secure the line of the Meuse, which lay directly in the path of the enemy advance. To this end he deployed troops along its western bank, keeping the 30th Corps[1] in reserve—a very necessary precaution. Thereafter he organised a series of counter-attacks by the U.S. 1st Army and the rest of the British 2nd against the northern edge, or 'shoulder', of the great salient created by the

[1] The 30th Corps at this time was composed of the Guards Armoured Division and the 43rd, 51st and 53rd Divisions.

enemy advance. Meanwhile the U.S. 3rd Army, under the redoubtable General Patton, was similarly and as strenuously employed against the southern edge.

The struggle continued furiously until the end of the year. The enemy's initial onslaught had been greatly facilitated by dense ground fog and low cloud, which kept the powerful Allied air component almost earthbound. Still, the American troops within the salient, many of them cut off and isolated from outside aid, put up a most gallant and resolute defence, especially round the vital road-centre in the neighbourhood of Bastogne. Meanwhile reinforcements were being rapidly assembled and dispatched from all quarters to the field of battle. Additional American divisions training in England were brought over in advance of scheduled time to form a reserve.

Presently the salient was sealed off, then stabilised, then gradually deflated. The weather cleared, and the Allied Tactical Air Force got to work with shattering effect upon bridges, dumps, and headquarters within the battle area, while the Strategic Force battered marshalling yards and centres of movement far beyond the Rhine.

It was a full month, however, before the salient had been eliminated and its base recovered, by a junction effected on January 16th, 1945, between General Hodges and General Patton, striking respectively south and north with the U.S. 1st and 3rd Armies.

Thereafter the operational control of the U S. 1st Army reverted to the Central Group. The U.S. 9th Army was retained within the Northern Group under Field-Marshal Montgomery.

The assistance rendered to the American armies in these operations is best summarised in Field-Marshal Montgomery's own words:

On the 19th I ordered General Dempsey to move 30th Corps west of the Meuse, to a general line from Liége to Louvain, with patrols forward along the western bank of the river between Liége itself and Dinant. The Corps was thus suitably placed to prevent the enemy crossing the river, and could cover the routes from the south-east leading into Brussels.

It subsequently became necessary, in connection with the regrouping of the American 1st Army, to send some British divisions east of the Meuse. But throughout the battle I was anxious to avoid committing British forces more than was necessary. Had they become involved in large numbers, an acute administrative problem would have resulted, from their lines of communication crossing the axis of the two American armies.

This last is an interesting and instructive point, for it seldom occurs to the lay mind that an army on the move is not a detached and isolated formation, but resembles a great ship towing an unending string of barges behind it; so that another large vessel, similarly impeded, cannot attempt to cross its wake without creating serious complications.

Such was the battle of the Bulge, as it came to be called. It began with a surprise attack which enabled the enemy, aided by fog, to penetrate deeply into the Allied lines. In this respect it bore a close resemblance to Ludendorf's great offensive against the Anglo-French line in March 1918. It failed, as in 1918, very largely through the resolute defence put up week after week by detached and isolated groups of common soldiers and junior leaders.[1] In both cases the enemy was staking his last card: in both cases he lost.

The German casualties in the battle of the Bulge were enormous. Apart from the killed and wounded of eleven picked divisions, 15,000 prisoners were taken, 647 aircraft destroyed, 400 tanks knocked out, and his dwindling stock of petrol drained to the limit. All that Hitler's latest intuition had brought him was a postponement of the Allied invasion of Germany until the spring, delivered against a resistance appreciably weakened by the German losses in the battle of the Bulge.

So ended 1944, that *annus mirabilis* during which, despite severe setbacks here and there, the tide of fortune turned once and for all in favour of the Allies, and continued in full flood thereafter.

We pass now to the home front, where we shall find that activity is as great, and the need for stern endurance as necessary, as further afield.

---

[1] 'The Battle of the Ardennes was won primarily by the staunch fighting qualities of the American soldier.' Field-Marshal Montgomery's Dispatch.

CHAPTER XVII

THE HOME FRONT

⌒(1)⌒

THE Second World War as waged within the United Kingdom presented three outstanding features, all of which had been fore-shadowed in the First World War, but never to any major extent.

The first was the threat of actual invasion, imminent from May 1940 until late 1942; the second was the perpetual and indiscriminate bombing by the enemy of our cities, aerodromes and ordnance factories, which continued, with a comparatively brief respite in 1941–2, until the closing weeks of the German war; the third was the employment upon an ever-increasing scale, owing to man-shortage, of women in the Armed Forces of the country, especially the Army.

The threat of invasion, with some of the measures taken to meet it, has already been described.[1] This brings us to the bombing raids. It cannot be said that these took us by surprise; the only surprise consisted in the fact that they did not come sooner.

It had been obvious for some years that in the event of war such visitations could be expected upon a heavy and continuous scale, and A.D.G.B., or the Air Defence of Great Britain, had been organised accordingly, to the full extent permitted (in the present apathetic mood of People and Parliament) by the meagre funds allotted for the purpose. Steps had also been taken to organise A.R.P. (Air Raid Precautions) for the protection of the civil population. Hospital accommodation had been prepared for 300,000 air-raid casualties, and from the time of the Munich agreement onward preparations were in hand, at a slowly increasing *tempo*, for the construction of underground refuges and so-called Anderson 'back-garden' shelters. Trenches were dug in parks and on village greens,

[1] See p. 205, Operation 'Bumper'.

and gas-masks issued, while the ears of workers in field and factory were periodically assailed by the depressing wailings of various types of experimental siren.

Air-raid rehearsals were regularly held in most of our large cities, at which, in obedience to the tocsin's call, the inmates of Government offices and large commercial establishments left their desks and filed obediently, if a little self-consciously, down innumerable stairs to a presumably safer region.

The air defence of the country was shared by the fighter-planes of the R.A.F. and the anti-aircraft batteries, for the provision and operation of which the War Office was naturally responsible. It is with these latter that we are concerned.

Headquarters both of Anti-Aircraft and Fighter Commands had been established side by side on a site near Stanmore, some ten miles north of London, in two stately country mansions known as Glenthorne and Bentley Priory respectively, each commanding a prospect of the distant spires and chimneys of North London, with a middle distance of raw, red-roofed suburbs intervening To the right lay another hill easily recognisable, by the slender church spire which crowned it, as Harrow. It was from these twin establishments, working in close and cordial liaison throughout, that the Battle of Britain was subsequently directed and won.

In addition to Anti-Aircraft Command Headquarters, seven other Divisional Headquarters were distributed throughout the United Kingdom, with a varying number of brigades in each division and a proportionate number of gun and searchlight units in each brigade. It should be noted that these anti-aircraft divisions were not in any way comparable with the divisions in the field army, being of no fixed size and at times being as much as four times as large, besides being distributed over thousands of square miles of country. At a later date (in 1940) five more such divisions were added, and three anti-aircraft corps created, to cover the southern, midland and northern areas respectively.

Anti-Aircraft Command was placed in the hands of General Sir Frederick A. Pile, and there remained until the closing weeks of the German war. The Air Officer Commanding-in-Chief Fighter Command (Air Chief Marshal Dowding) was, however, in operational control of the whole system.

In 1939 the anti-aircraft defences, like all other arms of the Service, stood sorely in need of further and better equipment The number of heavy guns under General Pile's command was only 695, many of them obsolescent; the approved and recommended total was 2,232.

So far as the lighter guns were concerned, out of an approved total of 1,200 only 253 were available. As regards searchlights, 2,700 were at hand out of a recommended total of 4,700.

However, there is no spur like dire necessity, and by May 1941, under the scourge of a whole winter of continuous bombing, the number of searchlights had grown to 4,532, while 1,691 heavy and 940 light guns were in action. Even so, these numbers still fell short of the recommended quota. Moreover, the shortage of manpower was already making itself felt, and by the end of May some of this equipment had actually to be withdrawn from service through want of gun-crews to operate it.

It should here be mentioned that the original intention of the War Office had been that the anti-aircraft defences of the country should be manned entirely by units of the Territorial Army. No better material could have been employed. The Territorials had won their spurs in the First World War, when whole divisions of the Territorial Army had achieved high distinction both on the Western Front and in the Middle East. They had also furnished the garrison of India. By 1939, therefore, the Territorial Army enjoyed a prestige and *réclame* all its own. It was an army of volunteers, of great keenness, high morale, and an established tradition : and it was a bitter blow to all concerned when, with the coming of Conscription early in 1939 it was decided (probably rightly), in order to avoid undue specialisation of units and invidious comparisons arising therefrom, to abolish the Territorial Army as such and merge it with the Regular Army for the duration. (As a sentimental gesture many an ex-Territorial, upon removing the 'T' badge from the lapel of his tunic, transferred it to the back, and there carried it, out of sight but near to his heart, throughout the period of his service.)

With the submerging of the Territorials the anti-aircraft defences of the country were now entrusted to the new conscript militia. These at first proved a most unsatisfactory substitute, lacking as they did both the experience and *esprit de corps* of an established formation—a circumstance upon which General Pile was moved to justifiable protest.

General Pile's difficulties were further increased by the transfer of many of his A.D.G.B. units overseas.

'The shortage of manpower,' he reports at this time and indeed frequently thereafter, 'and the large demands made on the Command to supply personnel and units for the field army (in all, 170 gun or searchlight regiments went overseas) led first of all to the employment of mixed units, and later to the Home Guard manning anti-aircraft equipment. It led also to drastic reductions in the number of searchlight units.'

~(2)~

At first sight it might appear that the most appropriate source of manpower for the anti-aircraft defences of the country would be found in the Home Guard, now over one million strong. But we have to take into consideration the actual composition of this force, and, above all, its terms of enlistment.

As regards composition, the Home Guard consisted partly of middle-aged or elderly men, few of them suited to the hard and continuous service demanded by anti-aircraft defence, and partly of boys under eighteen, who would be absorbed into the Regular Army just when they had been sufficiently trained in their duties to become useful anti-aircraft gunners.

The terms of enlistment involved still greater complications. Service was voluntary—which meant that strict military discipline was difficult to impose—unpaid,[1] and part-time. This meant that a man was only available for Home Guard duty when not engaged in earning his daily bread; and to earn that bread it was essential in most cases that he should live at home, to be near his work; which meant that it would be impossible to transfer such a man for an indefinite period from some midland village to a remote gun-site on the south coast.

Moreover, the Home Guard under their terms of service were not asked to perform more than forty-eight hours of training and duty every twenty-eight days—an average of less than two hours in twenty-four—and in the event of raids taking place they could only volunteer for extra duty with the permission of their civil employer, whose interests, especially if his factory was engaged in war work of national importance, had obviously to be safeguarded. Plainly it was impracticable for one of the major defences of the country to be maintained upon these lines.

However, with the advent of the Rocket Batteries in late 1941, it was found possible to employ the Home Guard, to a limited extent, in anti-aircraft defence after all. These particular weapons were comparatively simple to handle and called for no prolonged training; so General Pile's proposal for the introduction of the Home Guard into the rocket batteries was immediately approved.

But difficulties still bristled. 178 men were required to keep a rocket battery site in action for one night, but owing to the very limited period for which a member of the Home Guard could be kept on duty—each man was called upon for only one night in eight—no

[1] Compensation for loss of earnings was not awarded until 1943.

fewer than 1,400 men were required to keep such a site continuously manned. It was plainly impossible to furnish Home Guard volunteers on so large a scale as this, so the Ministry of Labour undertook to meet the deficiency. This it did by selecting men not employed in any other form of National Service and 'directing' them to the rocket batteries.

But the scheme was not an outstanding success. Within a year the Ministry of Labour had shown itself unable to meet its obligations, so the expedient was tried of transferring men direct to the rocket batteries from the Home Guard infantry battalions. This was a most unpopular move. The Home Guard had enlisted as infantrymen, and had grown strong in infantry spirit and regimental tradition. Each battalion was a brotherhood, and objected to being cut up into working parties under alien authority. So the men released for service with the batteries were not, as a rule, the battalion's most efficient members.

Arrangements were therefore made under which one or more 'Home Guard General Service Batteries' were affiliated to the local anti-aircraft battery, from which the latter could draw recruits. Those found unsuitable for A-A duty, whether for health reasons or change of civilian employment, were drafted back to the Home Guard battalion concerned. Those actually allotted to A-A duty did much stout work, and it was largely due to their courage and devotion that the rocket batteries became a feature of the anti-aircraft defences which enemy aircraft, at any rate, learned to hold in profound respect.

But enough has been said to emphasise the extreme difficulties attendant upon the employment of this particular force in anti-aircraft defence. As we shall presently see, it was from another source altogether that the necessary help was ultimately obtained.

⤳(3)↩

The air defences of the country had been manned in part since April 1939, for it was realised that if and when war did come it would come practically overnight, accompanied probably by immediate and heavy air-raids, and that there would be no time for the mobilisation and distribution of anti-aircraft units.

The period of the Phoney War, however, gave General Pile and his lieutenants a respite in which to establish training-schools in each of his seven divisions, in which the militia recruits could at least be grounded in their complicated and exacting duties.

This was no easy matter, for anti-aircraft training under what amounted practically to peacetime conditions proved a most unrealistic undertaking. During those uneventful months there were no enemy bombers to aim at, so no live ammunition could be employed; while such dummy targets as could be supplied by the R.A.F. were old and slow, and took no evasive action. Moreover, practice at night was hampered by the fact that all planes were ordered to fly with navigation lights full on, thus rendering the duties of the searchlight units entirely redundant. It was not until the summer of 1940, during the Battle of Britain and under enemy bombs, that the real education of the anti-aircraft gunners began—a course from which in due time they graduated with honours.

Equally urgent at this time was the need for new and more modern equipment, for the art of anti-aircraft gunnery was steadily developing into an exact science, calling for deep and perpetual research and the creation of instruments of the most delicate precision.

The invention of radiolocation emphasised this need; and here General Pile was fortunate in enlisting the services of Professor A. V. Hill, F.R.S., of Trinity College, Cambridge, an outstanding figure in the field of scientific research, who called to his aid a large and most notable band of eminent assistants, recruited from all over the British Empire. (Some were enlisted from the United States, and that, too, before their own country had entered the war.) Ultimately hundreds were in service throughout the Command. Many of them came straight from the Universities: these frequently attached themselves to gun-sites, in order to explain to the officers in charge the complex and uncanny workings of radiolocation, or as it came to be called, 'Radar'.

The word 'Radar', as the reader will have noted, is a palindrome, and indicates in itself the basic principle of radiolocation—namely, that it works both ways, or 'there and back'.

In the Anti-Aircraft Command Radar was employed for the detection of the approach, and, indeed, the exact position from moment to moment in the darkest night, of hostile aircraft. In the simplest and least technical language, its operation was as follows: An invisible radio beam, projected into the ether from a Radar station, would probe the skies until it encountered an approaching aircraft. The metal of which the aircraft was composed intercepted the beam and 'reflected' it back to the operations room, where it took the form of a visual image on a cathode-ray tube, contained in a box-shaped device known as a predictor. By manipulating this remarkable instrument so as to hold the ray constantly in place, it was possible to follow and to plot the direction, elevation and speed of the plane, however evasive the action it might take. From these data the predictor mechanism automatically calculated where the approaching target would be at the moment when the shell burst in the sky, and by means of electric pointers enabled the gun to be aimed at that point.

Unfortunately it was long before Radar and the miracles it performed were made fully available to our air defences. The first sets were only delivered during 1940, and it was not until the long ordeal of the 1940–1 raids had been endured that the system came into complete and efficient operation. Till then Anti-Aircraft Command had to rely for its information as to the approach of hostile aircraft upon the listening device known as the sound-locator. These instruments were effective up to a point, but could only follow one plane at a time and were apt to become hopelessly confused in the event of mass raids.

We revert now to the beginning of the war, and the early preparation of our anti-aircraft defences.

First of all a definite division of labour had to be apportioned between Anti-Aircraft Command and the Royal Air Force, for it was essential, first, that there should be no gap or lacuna in our air defence scheme, and, secondly, that our fighter aircraft should be kept out of range of our own guns.

It was arranged, then, that important cities should be made into gun-defended areas, protected by heavy artillery aided by search-lights. Before reaching these areas the raiders were to be compelled to run the gauntlet of our fighter planes, operating between the cities in question and the coast, in what was known as the Fighter Zone. To assist the fighters, a complete searchlight belt was established from the Solent, round the south and east of London, north to the Humber, and then north-west to the Tyne-Tees area. A further belt was established between the Forth and Clyde. For the protection of important and more isolated points, such as airfields and ordnance factories, light guns were deployed, to guard against what was known as precision bombing at a low level.

Each gun-defence area had its own operations room, a nerve centre which could be employed either to pass information or exercise direct fire-control.

The outstanding weapon of the heavy gun section was the 3·7-inch, mobile or static, probably the finest weapon of its kind ever produced. There were also available by June 1940 (when the Battle of Britain began) 355 4·5-inch guns. Later in the war came a more powerful weapon still, the 5·25-inch. The chief of the lighter weapons was the

40-mm. Bofors, supplemented by 2-pounder guns borrowed from the Royal Navy.

We come now to the actual story of the raids.

~(4)~

The Battle of Britain, so called, during the summer of 1940, which certainly saved our country from invasion and thereby altered the history of the world, was fought and won primarily by the immortal fighter pilots of the Royal Air Force. Those were the epic days when the men and women in the streets of London and the workers in the fields and villages of the Home Counties stood gazing raptly upward into a cloudless summer sky, where our Hurricanes and Spitfires, looking no larger than white moths, fluttered endlessly round among their bewildered opponents and sent them crashing to earth.

But if the airmen played the most spectacular part in the victory, the contribution of the gunners was solid enough. Shortage of equipment and lack of experience were naturally a severe handicap, but no fewer than 296 enemy aircraft were shot down by gunfire—some ten per cent of the Battle total—and seventy-four hit and probably lost. The guns also rendered notable aid to the R.A.F. in breaking up formations and so rendering the enemy planes more vulnerable to the fighters.

The memory of those exultant moments (to which both airmen and gunners had made such worthy contribution) served perhaps to cheer and sustain many a heart during the prolonged and testing experience in store for us with the approach of winter.

Indeed it came sooner than that, for the night raids began on August 8th, with sporadic attacks upon the midlands and west. Over one hundred bombers raided Liverpool upon four successive nights, doing immense damage.

Then, on September 7th, came the first night raid upon London, and these continued night after night for weeks and months. The opening raid was spectacular, for the enemy came up the Thames Estuary and set the vast London dock system in flames. There is no need to describe the events of that winter in further detail, for they are engraved indelibly in the recollection of those who experienced them, and, indeed, of many who merely had read of them, for the story spread horror throughout the civilised world.

The early difficulties of defence were immense. The R.A.F. fighters were exhausted by their previous heroic exertions, and, moreover, both Spitfires and Hurricanes were one-man machines in which the pilot had not only to navigate his craft but act as his own gunner. This made them unsuitable for individual action in the dark: it was not until the Beaufighter was evolved in 1941 that this heavy disability was overcome.

In the defence of London, Anti-Aircraft Command on its part was seriously crippled by local shortage of guns—on the memorable night of September 7th, owing to insistent demands for protection from other parts of the kingdom, only ninety-two heavy guns were available for the defence of the capital[1]—and by the fact that the efficacy of the defence scheme had been seriously overestimated. The instruments employed had been designed only for visual shooting at seen targets by day or targets illuminated by searchlights at night. If the target was invisible, the necessary information as to bearing and angle of sight was obtained by sound-locators, and was passed to the gun positions through the operations room.

The system proved a failure, particularly in London, first because of the vast area to be defended, secondly because enemy aircraft, instead of maintaining a fixed course or 'run', revealed a quite unexpected aptitude for evasive action; and thirdly because the sound-locators proved inadequate to detect the approach of any aircraft flying above a certain height. So the Londoner was compelled for many weeks to 'take it' with what fortitude he could muster, which fortunately proved considerable.

The existing system was therefore abandoned, and for the time being the gunners were given a free hand to deal with the situation according to the apparent needs of time and place. This resulted in what came to be known as The Barrage, and its nightly thunder comforted the civil population mightily. It presented to the lay mind a mental picture of a London hedged about by a continuous, impenetrable curtain of fire which no bomber could pierce. Of course, no such curtain existed: it would. have been impossible to provide sufficient guns or ammunition for such a grandiloquent project. But the continuous roar of the guns undoubtedly inspired confidence, and at least helped to muffle the sound of the exploding bombs. So much so, that when the expedient was tried of having special 'fighter nights', during which the guns lay silent while the R.A.F. took charge overhead, such a storm of protest arose that in the interests of public morale orders were given for the comforting, though comparatively innocuous, din of the barrage to be resumed.

[1] But within forty-eight hours the total of heavy guns defending London had been raised to 203.

But aid and comfort were at hand, for Radar was at last coming into its own. Early developments had been hampered by the difficulty of applying the Radar principle to elevation as well as direction or bearing; but by October 1st, 1940, this disability had been to a certain extent overcome, and Radar-directed guns went into action for the first time, with encouraging results.

Of the lessons learned from practical experience, perhaps the most valuable was that to obtain maximum effect the guns should be sited in groups (usually of eight) and directed from a master-site, which would inform the other sites of the position, height and direction of the target. There was at first some difference of opinion as to whether fire-control could best be directed from the actual gun-sites or from the operations room; but with the gradual improvement in Radar design and working it was ultimately found possible to eliminate operations room control altogether, and make the gun-position officer at each gun-site responsible for obtaining his own gunnery data.

Of course, the enemy did not devote his attention exclusively to London. Upon November 14th, 1940, the main weight of the attack was shifted for the time being to industrial centres and ports, where, owing to the smaller and more concentrated nature of the target, immense damage and suffering were inflicted. Coventry was the first victim, and among others to suffer particularly were Bristol, Liverpool, Cardiff, Portsmouth and Plymouth. This involved Anti-Aircraft Command, with its strictly limited resources in the way of guns and men, in the hasty movement of guns from London to the newly affected areas. Forty-seven were taken from the London area and thirty-six from the Thames Estuary.

Later still, in February 1941, enemy strategic bombing developed upon a definite and more intelligible plan, in the form of heavy attacks for several nights in succession upon our principal Western ports. Those upon the southern and eastern coasts had already been denied to our shipping: if this denial could be extended to the Western Approaches, our Island would stand in acute danger of being isolated altogether. Fifty-eight guns were transferred from the midlands for further protection of the ports in question.

Thus the battle raged, up and down the country, but it centred chiefly upon London. The most devastating raids in the spring of 1941 were those of April 16th–17th and May 10th–11th.

But all the time the air defences improved, both in organisation and performance. Between April 1st and May 12th, seventy-two planes were shot down by anti-aircraft fire, and another eighty-two damaged and probably lost. The R.A.F. fighters, too, were achieving far greater success than before, partly owing to the introduction of the new Beaufighter machine, and partly as a result of the development of air-to-air Radar, which enabled the pilots not only to communicate freely with the authorities on the ground but with one another.

Perhaps all this turned the scale. At any rate, after May 12th the raids ceased as suddenly as they had begun, and for almost a year the United Kingdom enjoyed comparative immunity.[1] The enemy, having realised that his campaign was a military failure, had decided, characteristically, to cut his losses and turn his energies elsewhere—in this case to his erstwhile friend and ally Russia.

So ended the first and most formidable phase of the bombing raids, summarised by General Pile as follows:

'It covers a period in which success in battle was achieved with great difficulty, but in which developments in technique were very considerable. At the beginning of the battle our method of defence was still the same as it had been three years before; at the end I felt we had begun to make real progress; certainly the foundation of later success had been laid. What had especially been achieved was the conversion of a large body of troops from ordinary soldiers into skilled technical operators; and this was an essential prerequisite for successful anti-aircraft gunnery.'

∞(5)∞

As already indicated, Anti-Aircraft Command had been hampered from the outset by shortage both of men and equipment.

Mention has already been made of the heavy drain effected on both by the transference of anti-aircraft units from the defence of Great Britain to the assistance of the field armies overseas. A further reduction in strength was now brought about by the necessity of returning to the Royal Navy certain borrowed Lewis guns. In addition, General Pile was requested, early in 1941, to furnish 300 Bofors guns, with their crews, for the protection of the Merchant Navy from air attack. Thus our light anti-aircraft defences, which already stood at only twenty-two per cent of requirements, were further reduced to fifteen per cent.

But the outstanding problem, as ever, was the increasing shortage of manpower. Indeed, it was only by siting the searchlights in 'clusters' of three instead of singly, and so economising on some of the administration services, that all the guns could be manned.

---

[1] Enemy air activity during this period was confined chiefly to mine-laying off the coast, especially in the Thames Estuary and St. George's Channel.

The time had plainly come when some entirely new source of manpower must be discovered and tapped. The difficulties of tapping the Home Guard have already been set forth. One last expedient remained—to employ the A.T.S. in operational duty with the batteries and searchlights.

To do so, however, would be to challenge all Army tradition, under which women, though they had long been employed on every kind of military duty, had never been asked to participate as combatants.[1] Therefore it was with serious misgivings that on April 25th, 1941, regulations were put in force making members of the A.T.S. eligible for such service.

The experiment proved a triumphant success. In the so-called 'mixed' units, in which women preponderated in a proportion of two to one, it was soon found that the A.T.S. were perfectly capable of discharging every duty except those involving the heavy labour of loading and manning the guns. Even the order to fire was given by a woman.

General Pile's chief difficulties in the matter were administrative. In housing a mixed unit of any kind separate provision has to be made for the comfort, privacy and general welfare of the female section. In the case of the anti-aircraft batteries, where the gunners must live by their guns, this called for a good deal of extra labour in the setting up of suitable quarters.[2] The difficulty was heightened by the fact that the batteries, when mobile, were frequently called upon to move at short notice to fresh sites: moreover, until the end of 1942 care had to be taken that units containing women should not be posted to sites where they might find themselves in the path of an invading army. But the women themselves cheerfully accepted almost any accommodation available, and indeed evinced no particular aversion on occasion to living under canvas, as we shall see. The one thing they were never asked to do, even in the case of light weapons, was to fire a gun.

General Pile's only disappointment in the matter of mixed batteries was in the number of women allotted to his command. He had hoped for 170,000: the largest number ever under his orders at one time was 74,000. But their spirit made up for everything.

'So long as reasonable recreational facilities during periods of inaction,' he reports, 'and satisfactory ablutions at all times, were available for them,

[1] The A.T.S. were classified as 'non-combatant', and possibly to regulate the situation, A.T.S. gun-numbers were also designated as such.

[2] This was supplied ultimately by Construction Batteries composed of men withdrawn from their operational duties.

the morale of the women in an operational rôle was always high, and subsequent events proved their great courage. I cannot praise too highly the valuable work these women performed and the splendid spirit which they brought to it.'

But still the manpower problem persisted. (Indeed, it was never entirely overcome.) In October 1941 another 50,000 men were detached from Anti-Aircraft Command and sent to the field armies overseas. This was the more unfortunate since increased quantities of guns and equipment, including the new rocket batteries, were becoming available. The rocket batteries, with their multiple barrels, were by this time a familiar feature in public parks and other gun-defended areas throughout the country. They were comparatively simple to operate, relying as they did upon mass effect rather than accurate laying. Here, as we have seen, the Home Guard were able to render considerable service.

Equipment was being improved in other respects. The 4·5-inch guns had been lined with 3·7-inch barrels, and heavy 5·25-inch guns were becoming available. Of the lighter weapons the Bofors had been supplemented by the Oerlikon and the twin ·5-inch Browning. The efficacy of the 3·7-inch batteries, too, had been greatly enhanced by the introduction of an automatic fuze-setter, which enabled the gun to be loaded and fired at a much higher speed. This was finally superseded by the 'proximity' fuze (working upon much the same principal as the magnetic mine) which was stimulated to detonate the shell by the actual approach of the hostile plane.

Lastly, to compensate for the shortage of light anti-aircraft guns, successful experiments were made about this time in the creation of protective smoke-screens, especially for reservoirs and dams. These were organised by the Ministry of Home Security and operated by the Pioneer Corps.

～(6)～

It was now clear that if and when the Luftwaffe resumed their nocturnal visits, certain surprises were in store for them.

And it was so, though the surprises were not by any means confined to one side, for in the spring of 1942 enemy air attack was resumed in a new form; and though its military effect was small, it was serious enough from the point of view of civilian safety and morale to call for fresh defence measures.

The raids were of two kinds, and were pithily classified under the headings 'Baedeker' and 'Tip-and-Run' respectively.

The Baedeker raids consisted of sudden and savage night assaults upon hitherto undefended localities—cathedral cities or townships of purely historical or architectural interest. They were probably intended as an act of spectacular retaliation for our ever-increasing bomber campaign over Germany. Exeter, Bath, and, later, Canterbury were among the principal sufferers. Steps were immediately taken to discourage these, from such resources as were available, and within seventy-two hours twenty-eight towns, from Penzance to York, were provided with anti-aircraft batteries drawn from gun-defended areas in the north and west. The R.A.F., needless to say, redoubled their defensive efforts, while the activities of Bomber Command over Germany increased rather than diminished.

The tip-and-run raids were delivered in daylight, usually in the early hours of the morning, against towns upon the south and east coasts, by fast fighter-bombers, arriving as a rule in twos and threes and flying very low—almost at water level, in fact—in order to escape Radar detection. Thus they arrived practically unheralded, and had delivered their attack and were away again before the alert could be sounded or the existing defences come into action.

To deal with these it was obvious that a multiplicity of light and quickly handled guns was needed. These, as we know, were in grievously short supply, for Japan was now in the war, and first call upon all such weapons was for our forces in the Far East. Fifty-seven coastal towns, from St.Ives in Cornwall to Aldeburgh in Suffolk, were subjected to these raids, and though they endured them stoutly, suffered much hardship and suspense during the next three months— until June 1942, in fact, when all guns were no longer being sent overseas, and some became available for home defence. By the end of October 500 Bofors guns had been added, and the situation was at least mitigated, though the nuisance persisted, despite perpetual improvements in defence and warning systems, until April 1943; when (perhaps owing to the fact that our weapon production had at last reached full flood and that our so-called Fringe Defences now mustered over 1,000 Bofors and nearly 700 light machine-guns) they ceased as abruptly as usual.

Then, after a lull of some weeks, they were renewed in very much stronger force, and between May 7th, 1943 and June 6th, fifteen attacks were delivered, a total of almost 300 aircraft participating. But by this time the defence was more than equal to the attack, and the anti-aircraft defences and the R.A.F. between them destroyed about fourteen per cent of the raiders, besides damaging many more. Aircraft losses of over ten per cent are usually regarded as too serious to be ignored, and this, coupled with the fact that the two enemy fighter groups employed in the raids were urgently needed in the Mediterranean theatre, brought about the end of these particular visitations. The tip-and-run raids ceased, never to be renewed. Ninety-four of our coastal towns had been attacked, among which the heaviest sufferers were probably Eastbourne and Hastings, though, as usual, Dover had its share.

⁓(7)⁓

We come now to the last phase of the enemy heavy bombing campaign, so far as piloted aircraft were concerned. This began in the autumn of 1943, and continued throughout the winter.

As usual, it presented certain novel features and imposed fresh problems of defence. The attacks were delivered by fighter-bombers supplemented by a new, fast type of heavy bomber; and despite the fact that our anti-aircraft defences had been improved enormously, both in strength and intercommunication, it was found difficult to hold these raiders in check.

Our difficulty was due to the adoption by the enemy of an ingenious system of interference with Radar communications, which we ourselves had invented, and had practised for some time. This consisted in dropping from the air innumerable strips of metallised paper, which had the effect of producing spurious 'breaks' in the cathode ray tube. These so-called 'breaks' could either be mistaken for actual aircraft, or else produced such a profusion of images that a genuine aircraft 'break' could not be identified and followed. (It was, in effect, the answer to the old question: 'Where would you hide a pebble?' 'On the beach!') Searchlight direction was also seriously affected.

London was their principal objective. The first heavy raid came in January 1944, over the Whitehall area. It was delivered by 200 aircraft, and inflicted serious damage. In another, a month later, in the district of St. James, St. James's Palace had a narrow escape and the London Library was partially destroyed by a direct hit. Still, a heavy toll was taken of the raiders, in which valuable aid was rendered by American anti-aircraft gunners, who had now arrived in our country in force, and were more than anxious to participate in its defence. This particular liaison had been growing closer and more cordial for some time: indeed, in 1943 a specially selected Demonstration Battery from Anti-Aircraft Command had been dispatched to the United States, where it had conducted a most successful tour of six months. The largest number of American anti-aircraft troops deployed in the United Kingdom at any one time was just over 10,000.

From early 1944 onward there had been a steady transfer of anti-aircraft equipment from north to south, until an almost continuous belt of such defences ran round the coast from Great Yarmouth to South Wales. This was to guard against air attacks from Germany against the vast bodies of Allied troops already concentrating for D-Day. These, however, never eventuated.

~(8)~

The raids just described died away during March, and were not renewed except in sporadic form. Hitler had decided that air-raids by piloted aircraft had become too expensive to be profitable. In place of these he was now preparing to launch another, almost the last, of his secret weapons.

As early as December 1943 official information had been received that the enemy's air enterprise was about to take the form of raids by 'pilotless' aircraft discharged from fixed runways along the coast of France. Plans were therefore put in hand to deal with this new development; but it was not until June 12th, 1944, that the first of these 'robots' or flying-bombs arrived; and from their performance it became immediately obvious that a new and terrible danger threatened our civil population, especially in the neighbourhood of London. From the military point of view it was fortunate that these visitants did not arrive a few weeks sooner, when our south-coast harbours were crowded with ships and men mustering for D-Day.

The prepared defence scheme was put into immediate operation, but a brief experience revealed that it stood in considerable need of revision and amendment; for the proportion of bombs intercepted and brought down was disappointingly small, and London was beginning to suffer severely.[1] This, it was realised, was to be no mere affair of periodic mass raids lasting for an hour or two, but a savage and unrelenting process of attrition, continued night and day without intermission, and as destructive to morale as to human life. It was no uncommon occurrence during these months for an alert to last for the best part of twenty-four hours.

[1] One of the earliest and most distres.ing incidents of this period was the destruction of the Guards Chapel in Birdcage Walk, on a Sunday morning with a full congregation assembled.

In appreciating the demands of the new situation two points stood out clearly. The first was that no advantage could be gained by shooting these bombs down over a crowded urban area: they were descending there of their own volition all too successfully already. It would be better, if possible, to allow them to continue their flight to a more sparsely inhabited district. The other was that the only effective way to deal with the V1 bomb (as it came to be called) was to intercept it before it could reach its target, and that to give full effect to this scheme the R.A.F. fighters and the anti-aircraft artillery must each be given separate and distinct fields of action, to avoid overlapping. The guns, in other words, must be sure that in opening fire the 'break' in their Radar was not caused by friendly aircraft, while the fighter-planes in pursuit of V1 bombs must not be compelled to give up the chase for fear of our own anti-aircraft shells.

So, after the usual and inevitable experiments in the field of trial and error, a new and comprehensive plan was worked out and put into execution. The gun batteries were moved right down to the coast, to form a continuous belt, or 'fringe', from Cuckmere Haven near Bexhill to St. Margaret's Bay just east of Dover. Since the low height at which the V1s flew required a higher rate of traverse by the guns than the mobile 3·7-inch gun could compass, as many of these as possible were converted to static form by the employment of a specially contrived stable platform, which proved of the greatest value. Behind the guns came the barrage-balloons, the cables of which proved of considerable value in intercepting and bringing down specially low flying-bombs. The space before and behind the guns, either over the Channel or the country lying between the coast and London, was left free for the R.A.F. fighters—a belt varying from fifty to seventy miles deep.

Thus the bombs could first be attacked far out at sea, then be compelled to run the gauntlet of the gun-belt, like birds driven over a line of butts, to be tackled for the third time by fighter planes patrolling in the rear.

Needless to say, the entire defence scheme called for the closest telecommunication between all units engaged. Fortunately preparations to this end had long been completed.

After this matters improved steadily. New and more effective Radar equipment arrived from America, and combined with the British No. 10 Predictor to produce most encouraging results. The new 'proximity' fuse, already mentioned, also proved of great service. Finally, American anti-aircraft guns and gunners became available to augment the resources of the belt, contributing no fewer than ninety heavy guns to the 1,000 weapons of various types already in operation, 600 of which were of the heavy type. Increasing relief was furnished by the victorious advance of the 21st Army Group through France and the progressive capture of launching sites. By the beginning of September all the south coast of England west of Newhaven had been put out of range of the V1 bomb, and the Cuckmere end of the belt was closed down and employed to extend the belt eastward to Sandwich. There was great improvement, too, in the marksmanship of the anti-aircraft gunners. Firing from their original sites at the V1 bombs, their successes had been under ten per cent of the targets aimed at. After the establishment of the coastal belt these rose in five successive weeks from seventeen to fifty-five per cent. Later (in a different area of deployment) a further improvement to seventy-four per cent was recorded.

In two respects at least, the V1 bomb was a more satisfactory target to deal with than a piloted aircraft. In the first place it flew blindly, so could take no evasive action: in the second, dead men tell no tales, and no V1 bomb launched by the enemy could ever return to describe the various new and secret devices tried out against it. Our research and experimental departments were thus given a free hand, with the result, to quote General Pile, that: 'More was learnt about the potentialities of anti-aircraft work in eighty days than had been learned in the previous thirty years.'

~(9)~

But the battle of the flying-bombs was not yet over.

'It had been established early in July 1944 that the Germans were not only launching their flying-bombs from ground sites on the French coast, but were launching a few from specially adapted aircraft. Some of these flew westward, aimed either at Southampton or Bristol; others came in from the North Sea towards London. The latter threat was the more serious, and a deployment was ordered along the coast from the River Blackwater to Whitstable, known as "Diver Box". The Maunsell Forts in the Thames Estuary proved an invaluable addition to this defence scheme.'[1]

By mid-September these attacks had been renewed upon an increasing scale. The 'pick-a-back' planes were now outflanking Diver Box northward, and a further deployment of anti-aircraft batteries

[1] The Maunsell Forts here mentioned were tall spider-legged towers, set up originally to deal with mine-layers flying up the Estuary itself. They were equipped with four 3·7-inch guns and two Bofors.

was rendered necessary for the defence of the east coast. Diver Strip, as it was designated, was completed in mid-October: it extended as far north as Great Yarmouth, and was composed of thirty-four heavy and thirty-six light batteries.

By January 1945 some 1,012 of these air-launched bombing attacks had been plotted. The bombs themselves rarely came within range of the guns, largely owing to continuous outflanking further north. Some even flew across Yorkshire into Lancashire. Nevertheless, of this total only sixty succeeded in penetrating to London.

It had for some time become obvious that these raids would continue throughout the winter, and would involve a still further deployment of our anti-aircraft defences northward. This aggravated the administrational problem of accommodation for the gunners, especially those of the mobile batteries (which were subject to frequent changes of site), to a formidable degree. Living conditions during the wet autumn of 1944 had been uncomfortable enough, especially for the women employed: indeed, the mixed batteries were offered the opportunity at this time to leave Diver Strip for better quarters. One and all asked to be allowed to remain—a further illustration, if any were needed, of the gallantry and fortitude of the A.T.S.

Still, it was plain that this state of affairs could not be allowed to persist throughout the winter, so a substantial and comprehensive housing scheme was put in hand for the gunners in the Strip. The project, which involved, *inter alia*, the building of 3,500 huts and the laying out of sixty miles of road, at a cost of £2,000,000, was completed within 2½ months. This was just as well, for in December 1944 a further deployment northward had been rendered necessary, as already indicated, by the extension of the pick-a-back raids to the Yorkshire coast. These new defences were known as Diver Fringe.

But the end was almost at hand, for the enemy effort was spent. The V1 bomb offensive dwindled steadily, and by the time the attacks ceased altogether the Royal Air Force had actually withdrawn all but two of its fighter squadrons from the defence of Great Britain for offensive operations overseas. For the rest of the war the defence was vested mainly in the guns.

Still, Hitler had one final weapon in reserve, the Rocket Bomb, or V2, of a size and power of devastation equivalent to that of a 1-ton high capacity bomb. The first of these fell upon London on September 8th, 1944, and their visitations grew in intensity throughout the winter. Their range was about 200 miles, their maximum speed 3,000 miles per hour, and the height from which they descended approximately fifty miles.

Nothing could be done, so long as their launching-sites remained in enemy hands, to prevent their arrival or counteract their effect. They came unheralded and unseen, and the first indication of their arrival was the *fait accompli* of a resounding detonation and a freshly devastated area. It was possible by means of Radar to plot with a certain degree of accuracy the space of ground within which a given rocket would fall; but the satisfaction thus furnished was purely academic. Fortunately, they were too inaccurately aimed to have any decisive effect.

General Pile, indeed, was most anxious to employ his guns in shooting at these projectiles and so detonating them in mid-air; but the argument involved by such an unorthodox suggestion as that of 'firing shells at shells' was still in progress when the problem was solved by the capture of the actual launching sites overseas.

The last V2 bomb fell upon March 27th, 1945. Piloted 'intruder' planes continued their visits until the end of April 1945, when the war in the air ceased.

Thus ends the epic tale of the air defence of Great Britain. Its vast scope and responsibility were never fully realised by the people of this country; for though the memory of this or that nightmare experience is indelibly imprinted upon the hearts of most of us, our knowledge has been in the main local and personal. Only those responsible for the overall defence of our Island knew how widespread and systematic the air-raids were, how perilously near they came to complete success, and what profound planning, close co-operation and devoted service were necessary to achieve the final victory.

Over 60,000 civilians, men, women and children, had lost their lives in the raids.

CHAPTER XVIII

VICTORY AND BEYOND

━━

⇜(1)⇝

1945 dawned with all the world still locked in conflict, and with no visible prospect of immediate victory or peace.

In Europe the Allied armies had reoccupied France and Belgium, and were now lined up along the German frontier; but the barrier of the Rhine had still to be negotiated, while the enemy were fighting with as much resolution and resource as ever. Indeed, as we have seen, the triumphant Allied advance had, with the close of the year, suffered a serious, if temporary, check through Rundstedt's surprise counter-thrust against the U.S. 12th Army Group in the Ardennes. Further north, the 21st Army Group were still contending with the inundations and other almost impassable obstacles in the region of Nijmegen and Arnhem. In Italy the Allies had been in occupation of Rome since June 4th, but further north Kesselring was still holding out against Field-Marshal Alexander, who was seriously starved of reinforcements.

Upon our own home front the V1 flying-bombs had been reduced to a comparative trickle, while raids by piloted aircraft had practically ceased; but their place had been taken by an even more formidable engine of destruction in the shape of the V2 rocket bomb. The submarine battle was not yet decided, and food, clothing and petrol supplies were more closely rationed than ever. The war was costing upwards of thirteen million pounds sterling per day, and even with income tax at ten shillings in the pound our immediate financial resources were almost exhausted and our national credit pledged for a generation to come.

In the Far East the United States Navy had recovered, with characteristic resilience, from the initial disaster of Pearl Harbour, and was beginning to exert a stranglehold upon the Japanese; but the latter still clung tenaciously to the Philippines, the Dutch East Indies, Malaya and Burma.

Still, wonders had been achieved in the past two years. North Africa had been entirely cleared of Axis troops, and the Middle East rendered secure. The Italians were out of the war, and Mussolini was heading for a dishonoured grave. Malta had triumphantly withstood all the assaults of her enemies, and the Mediterranean was open again to Allied traffic. Russia had regained practically the whole of her temporarily lost territories, and had actually invaded Rumania and occupied Bucharest. The British Navy, though overstretched and overworked, still contrived, everywhere and at all times, to do everything asked of it. The Allies were steadily acquiring complete control of the air. And now, with the dawn of 1945 and the promise of spring, the Allied forces by land, sea and air were awakening everywhere to fresh and concerted activity.

Early in January the Russians launched a new and vast offensive which broke the German front on a line of more than 260 miles. They captured Warsaw, Lodz and Cracow, and by occupying Danzig and Königsberg isolated East Prussia from the rest of Germany. About the same time the Americans landed in force on Luzon, the largest of the Philippine Islands, while British troops effected a lodgement upon the Japanese left flank at Akyab, in the Bay of Bengal.

Finally came a great stirring all along the Allied Western Front from the Zuider Zee to Switzerland, as General Eisenhower and Field-Marshal Montgomery matured and put into motion the plan of their combined assault against Germany's last barrier and of the final occupation of her soil.

Such was the general picture at the beginning of 1945. Let us pick out those portions thereof with which the British Army is particularly concerned, and develop them in greater detail.

(2)

The final campaign of the war in Western Europe, which covered the first five months of 1945, fell roughly into two parts—the great battles fought west of the Rhine during January and February, and the crossing of the Rhine, followed by an immediate Allied advance into the heart of Germany.

'The main objective of the Allies on the Western Front', reports Field-Marshal Montgomery, 'remained the Ruhr. . . . Beyond this, the object of our operations was to force mobile war on the enemy by developing operations into the northern plains of Germany. It was necessary first to line up on the Rhine; then to bridge the river and gain a suitable jumping-off position for a mobile campaign in the spring.'

At the beginning of 1945 the line-up was as follows. On the extreme left, and furthest north, came the 1st Canadian Army (General Crerar), then the (British) 2nd Army (General Dempsey), then the 9th U.S. Army (General Simpson), which had been left by General Eisenhower under Field-Marshal Montgomery's operational command. These formations comprised the 21st Army Group, with a front extending as far south as Düsseldorf. South of them came the 1st U.S. Army, then the 3rd, then the 7th. To the south of these the line was continued to the Swiss frontier by the 1st French Army.

As already indicated, the main objective of the Allies was the Ruhr, lying east of the Rhine and north of Cologne. Once that rich industrial district had been by-passed and isolated from the rest of Germany, it was felt that the end of enemy resistance would merely be a matter of time.

To ensure the earliest fulfilment of his hopes, Field-Marshal Montgomery was determined to bring the enemy to battle upon the left or western bank of the Rhine, thereby ensuring that the great river should act as an obstacle to retirement in the hoped-for event of enemy defeat; whereas if the enemy were permitted to cross without fighting, the Rhine would offer a serious impediment to the Allied advance.

The battle of the Rhineland was based on two converging offensives between the Rhine and the Meuse, with the object of destroying the enemy forces masking the Ruhr. It was intended, by interdiction from the air and by employing the maximum available forces on the ground, to prevent the enemy withdrawing to the east bank of the Rhine. In this success was largely achieved.

It certainly was. But before proceeding further, let us pause for a moment to note the enormous improvement recently effected in the administrative and maintenance situation by the clearance, in November 1944, of the Scheldt estuary, and the reopening to the Allies of the great port and base of Antwerp.

A glance at the map[1] will reveal that the estuary winds inland (for the most part between Holland and Belgium) for some seventy miles, and that its entrance is covered by the low-lying island of Walcheren, with its important harbour of Flushing (or Vlissingen)

[1] See Map 5.

at its southernmost extremity—in more peaceful days the principal terminus of the mail steamers from Harwich and Queenborough. Needless to say, the island was fully garrisoned, and powerfully defended by artillery in concrete emplacements. It was too closely intersected by dykes and deep banks to offer any scope for airborne landing, but it lay somewhat below sea-level, fenced in all round by strong sea-dykes. It was therefore decided to break down the dykes and so submerge the island as to put most of its artillery positions out of action, thus rendering feasible an assault by landing-craft.

As a result of some precision bombing by the R.A.F., of the most admirable accuracy, the dykes were breached in four places, and the island so flooded as to 'resemble a saucer filled with water'. Commandos now took over the attack, aided by Force 'T' of the Royal Navy and a heavy bombardment from the veteran H.M.S. *Warspite*, with H.M.S. *Roberts, Erebus*, and many supporting craft. The main assault was begun upon November 1st, and after more than a week of the most desperate fighting, in which the Canadian Army participated, Walcheren, together with 8,000 prisoners, was in Allied hands.

Immediate and intensive mine-sweeping operations followed, 300 craft being required for the task. By November 28th the first convoy from England was safely berthed at Antwerp, and the port lay open for the maintenance of both British and American armies. The long road from the Arromanches beaches was closed at last, and the task of the gallant Mulberry Harbours finally accomplished.

~✳(3)✳~

We return now to the 'two converging offensives' between the Rhine and the Meuse, already mentioned.

The first (known as 'Veritable') was to be launched by the 1st Canadian Army, reinforced to a strength of 500,000, in a south-easterly direction, from the area of the Nijmegen bridge-head towards the Reichswald Forest. The second ('Grenade') was to comprise a north-easterly thrust by the 9th U.S. Army, from the Jülich-Linnich sector, towards the Rhine, between Düsseldorf and Mors. A successful junction of the two forces would complete a most important pincer operation.

It had originally been intended that these attacks should be launched almost simultaneously, and the necessary concentrations for the 1st Canadian Army were completed in the first week of February 1945; but the thrust from the south-east was perforce delayed by the fact that the date upon which the 9th U.S. Army could attack depended upon the rate at which U.S. divisions could be released from other sectors, since its strength was to be increased to no fewer than twelve divisions. The delay was somewhat aggravated by the circumstance that the 12th U.S. Army Group was still involved in the Ardennes, and especial watch had to be kept upon the dams on the River Roer, from which it was known that the enemy might release, as he did, a quantity of flood-water. Heavy fighting was also in progress in the Saar and the so-called Colmar pocket.

'Veritable', however, could be set in motion without delay; so upon February 8th the 30th Corps, under the 1st Canadian Army, launched an attack against the Reichswald Forest and the northern end of the Siegfried Line, upon a front of five divisions. The Corps upon this occasion comprised six infantry divisions, one armoured division, three armoured brigades, eleven regiments of specialised armour, five groups of Royal Artillery, and two anti-aircraft artillery brigades. The main feature of this assault was to be the development of a tremendous weight of artillery from well over a thousand guns, together with a comprehensive 'interdiction programme' by the Allied air forces.

This, of course, was a mere beginning, for it was intended that the full weight not only of the 1st Canadian Army but of the British 2nd Army should ultimately be thrown into the battle. And, indeed, there was need, for the enemy reacted speedily and ferociously, with eleven equivalent divisions, including four parachute and two armoured divisions. The battle which followed was one of the bloodiest and most memorable of the whole war.

The 9th U.S. Army launched their attack 'Grenade' upon February 23rd, a fortnight later. They were fortunate in the fact that owing to the growing intensity of the fighting further north some enemy strength had been absorbed from their own sector. They were quick to seize the proffered advantage, and advanced at remarkable speed. Upon March 3rd the two armies linked up in Geldern, where the 35th Division of the U.S. 16th Corps joined hands with the British 53rd Division.

But the effort had been tremendous, and the strain almost unprecedented, even for those days.

'The keynotes of the battle of the Rhineland', reports Field-Marshal Montgomery, 'were the intense and fanatical opposition of the enemy, who, as we had hoped, accepted battle west of the Rhine; and secondly, the appalling weather conditions. The northern flank of the Reichswald operation was conducted mainly in various types of amphibious vehicles: in general the mud and slush were indescribable and greatly hampered the movement of troops and supplies through the heavily wooded areas, which are so lacking in roads.'

General Eisenhower's tribute to the part played by 21st Army Group in their operations is remarkable.

The weather conditions could hardly have been more unfavourable. January had been exceptionally severe, with snow lying on the ground through the month, and when the thaw set in at the beginning of February the ground became extremely soft and water-logged, while floods spread far and wide in the area over which our advance had been planned to take place. The difficulties thus imposed were immense, and the men had sometimes to fight waist-deep in water. The privations which they underwent were appalling, but their spirit was indomitable, and they overcame their personal hardships with great gallantry, to inflict a major defeat upon the enemy in some of the fiercest fighting of the whole war.

Despite the comparative slowness of our progress, 'Veritable' achieved its strategic objectives. We gained a footing on the west bank of the Rhine in the area where our major crossings were subsequently to be launched; and, equally important, heavy losses were inflicted on the Germans west of the river. Moreover, the offensive steadily drew in the enemy's slender reserves, and thus cleared the way for very rapid progress by the 9th Army when Operation 'Grenade' was initiated on February 23rd.

So ended the battle of the Rhineland, with the gaining of all objectives and a loss to the enemy of 100,000 men in killed, wounded and prisoners. 21st Army Group was now lined up along the Rhine as far south as Düsseldorf, ready to participate in the next and final step towards complete victory.

~(4)~

Thanks to very thorough preliminary planning and the accumulation of 130,000 tons of stores of every kind, 21st Army Group was ready to proceed with the new operations within a fortnight. In order to give the enemy no rest speed was essential, so the fortnight was a busy one. Formations were reorganised and lined up in their correct positions, covered by a screen of troops holding the river bank, and concealed from enemy observations by dense and continuous clouds of smoke.

Already, further south, the American armies were in victorious action. Upon March 7th, with great enterprise and dash, the 1st U.S.

Army had secured a footing beyond the Rhine itself by capturing the railway-bridge at Remagen intact—a gain of the highest importance. Shortly after this the 3rd U.S. Army established a bridge-head across the River Moselle, near its junction with the Rhine at Coblenz; and, with the 7th U.S. Army maintaining a steady pressure against the Siegfried Line, columns of the 3rd Army were enabled to penetrate to the rear of the enemy positions. Resistance east of the Moselle crumbled; the Saar was enveloped, and the Rhine cities of Mainz and Worms captured. By the third week in March the Rhine was closed throughout its entire length. All was now ready for the great assault.

Field-Marshal Montgomery's own target date for the crossing of the Rhine, as a preliminary to the isolation of the Ruhr and a deep penetration into the northern plain of Germany, was March 24th; and, as usual, he was more than punctual, for the operation was launched on the night of the 23rd.

His general plan was to cross the Rhine on a front of some twenty-five miles, and there establish a bridge-head deep enough to enable him to assemble there all the troops necessary for his immediate advance.

The crossing would be upon the minutely planned, closely timed, and overwhelming scale already rendered familiar by the operations of D-Day. There would be a preliminary last-minute scourging of the enemy defences by our heavy bombers; then a great artillery barrage to cover the crossing of innumerable amphibious assault craft (to whose strength the Royal Navy had actually contributed a number dragged by road all the way across Belgium, southern Holland, and the Rhineland). Airborne troops would be employed in thousands—the actual figure was 14,000, conveyed in 1,700 aircraft and 1,300 gliders—protected both by anti-flak devices and air interdiction generally. The only departure from precedent was that the airborne troops would be landed after the assault across the river had taken place and not before. There was a twofold reason for this: daylight was essential for the employment of such troops, and it would be impossible to make full use of our artillery for the ground assault if airborne troops were dropped in the target area before we had crossed the river. In other words, the airborne troops would be dropped within the range of the artillery sited on the west bank of the Rhine, in order to share in the artillery support afforded to the ground troops.

The width of the Rhine at this point was some 400 or 500 yards, and was liable to be increased at times by flood-water. The current averaged some 3½ knots. The river-bed was composed of sand and gravel, and was expected to give a good bearing surface for amphibious tanks and trestle-bridges. The engineering effort involved in organising the transfer of two armies over such a width of water was prodigious: indeed, no fewer than 37,000 Royal Engineers and Pioneers, and 22,000 American engineers, were employed in the battle.

Field-Marshal Montgomery's actual plan of action was to cross the Rhine, on a front of two armies, between Rheinberg and Rees, with the 9th U.S. Army on the right and the 2nd British Army on the left. His principal initial objective was the important communications centre of Wesel, on the River Lippe, almost at the junction of the two armies. From the Lippe the 1st U.S. Army stretched southward to a point twelve miles south of Düsseldorf; our 2nd Army extended northward to the Dutch frontier, whence the Canadians carried on the line to the North Sea.[1]

Field-Marshal Montgomery had at his disposal in the 9th U.S. Army three corps, the 13th, 16th and 19th, with a total of three armoured and nine infantry divisions. Our own 2nd Army comprised for the initial stages of the operation, besides the 8th, 12th and 30th Corps, the Canadian 2nd Corps and 17th U.S. Airborne Corps; the latter consisted of the 6th British and 17th American Airborne Divisions. The total forces in the 2nd Army were four armoured, two airborne, and eight infantry divisions, five independent armoured brigades, one commando brigade and one independent infantry brigade. The 79th Armoured Division was in support, with all its peculiar resources of specialised armour and amphibious devices.

So far as the enemy was concerned, the most significant fact to note was that Kesselring had now superseded Rundstedt as Commander-in-Chief of the German forces in the west. The opposition facing the 21st Army Group was mainly contributed by Army Group 'H', under Blaskowitz.

~*(5)*~

The attack began on the night of March 23rd, and by next morning all four assaulting divisions—the 51st and 15th British, and the 30th and 79th American, together with the 1st Commando Brigade—had accomplished their initial crossings between Rheinberg and Rees.

[1] It may be added here that 21st Army Group had been reinforced about this time (few troops being available from home) by the transfer of a number of Canadian divisions from Italy. On March 15th the 1st Canadian Corps took over a sector on the River Maas.

The key-position, Wesel, at the junction of the two armies, was captured by the 1st Commando Brigade, after an intensive air-attack by Bomber Command. On the morning of the 24th, 18th U.S. Airborne Corps dropped on the east bank of the Rhine within supporting distance of the Allied guns on the opposite bank.

The Allied operations had been expedited by certain new factors which should be noted here. In the first place Allied command of the air was now almost supreme, both tactically along the battle-fronts and strategically in Germany beyond. Secondly, thanks to further developments in Radar, our airmen could hit targets invisible to them, while 'Fido' (a British invention for the dispersal of fog) enabled them to take off and land almost at will. The enemy, rendered desperately short of petrol by the loss of the Rumanian oilfields and the destruction of many of their synthetic plants, were unable to employ their new jet-propelled fighters in any considerable number, and had to rely mainly on flak. Their mechanised transport and armour were crippled to a corresponding degree. Finally, the weather cleared at the end of January, and almost for the first time the Allies were able to operate under reasonable campaigning conditions.

The enemy's resistance was strongest on the northern flank, but his power of manœuvre, as already noted, had been greatly weakened everywhere by our interdiction bombing programme, and the British and American bridge-heads were speedily united. Airborne troops and ground troops joined hands on the east side of the river.

Within four days the crossing of the Rhine had been triumphantly effected, and on March 28th the advance to the Elbe began.

-*(6)*-

It remains to summarise the part played by 21st Army Group in these final operations—the conquest and occupation of the soil of Western Germany. First, a word regarding the administrative situation.

By comparison with the resources at his disposal on D-Day and during the months following, Field-Marshal Montgomery was now in control of a well-tried and almost perfectly running machine.

His communications had been improved out of all knowledge, for most of his supplies now came by the short sea-route through Antwerp, instead of via the exposed and distant Normandy beaches. Petrol was laid on direct from England to his very doorstep, as it were. For this he had to thank the great and ingenious system of pipe-lines known as 'Pluto'. These were first laid down in England, then continued under the sea after D-Day to Cherbourg, and subsequently extended, via Boulogne, across the Rhine itself. More than 1,000,000 tons of petrol were conveyed in this way.

Intercommunication, too, had been brought to a high pitch of perfection. Field-Marshal Montgomery's Tactical Headquarters—a highly peripatetic establishment at any time—was now furnished with an ultra high-frequency wireless of an entirely new type (No. 10 Set), which gave the Commander-in-Chief continuous and secure speech communication with his own armies and main headquarters.

Movement and transport had been further perfected and speeded up. A particular advance in this respect had been effected by the employment of the Armoured Personnel Carrier, known as the Kangaroo. These vehicles enabled infantry to be conveyed at high speed, with enhanced security and economy of casualties, to the very edge of the battle-line. (Compare this with the distant days of an attack on foot across no-man's-land through a cross-fire of machine-gun bullets.)

Finally, mention should be made of the provision at night of 'artificial moonlight'. This was supplied by the searchlight batteries, and was not only of the greatest help to the infantry, but proved a boon to bridge-builders and other night-workers in the rear areas.

A word may appropriately be added here with regard to the medical services in the Normandy campaign.

First, sickness among troops, owing partly to the preventive measures employed and partly to the superb physical condition of the troops themselves, was almost halved, compared with that in the First World War. In sweeping through conquered Germany, liberating such prison camps as Belsen and Sandböstel, where thousands of persons were dying of typhus, only twenty-five British soldiers contracted the disease.

Secondly, we have to note the inestimable aid rendered by air transport in the evacuation of casualties; thirdly, the extensive and highly successful employment of blood-transfusion methods. A co-ordinated service of air-transport and refrigerator-trucks ensured that fresh blood was always available for surgeons working behind the line.

The devotion of the Field Surgical Units, operating as they did right up to the line, was responsible for a remarkable and gratifying reduction in the number of deaths from intestinal wounds. In the First World War two out of every three men wounded in the belly died; in the Normandy campaign two out of every three men so wounded recovered.

The net result of this phenomenal progress in medical and surgical practice, coupled with the increased 'expectation of life' afforded to the soldier by the virtual elimination of unwieldy mass-attack, has been a marked decrease in the size of the casualty lists, as compared with those of the First World War (see pp. 58–9). The losses of the British Army during the Second World War in killed, died of wounds and missing came to 177,850. Of these over 27,000 died in fighting the Japanese. Some 20,000 others also died in captivity as prisoners of war.

We come now to the battle itself.

The 9th U.S. Army, still operating under Field-Marshal Montgomery's command, was directed by him towards the line Magdeburg-Wittenberge, both of which cities, as will be seen from a further examination of the map, lay upon the Elbe some sixty miles apart.

The line of advance of the British 2nd Army was also directed towards the Elbe, northward of Wittenberge and extending thence to Hamburg, a distance of some ninety miles. Upon the left of the 2nd Army the Canadians were to advance directly northward, clear the Germans out of northern Holland, and then turn eastward towards Emden and Wilhelmshaven, thus permitting the 2nd Army to strike for the Elbe with its left flank protected.

The core of the enemy's defence was the Ems-Dortmund canal, which lay opposite the left and centre of the 2nd Army; and here a desperate resistance was offered. Meanwhile the right wing of the 2nd Army and the 9th U.S. Army, more lightly opposed, were able to effect far more rapid progress, in conformity with the advance of the 1st U.S. Army from the Remagen bridge-head. So successful was this advance, together with that of the American troops further south, that presently it opened a wide gate into central and southern Germany. Its chief impediment by this time was the bomb-shattered masonry and rubble of the built-up areas through which it was made.

By April 3rd, 1945, the 9th U.S. Army had reached the river Weser, and the bulk of it pushed on to the Elbe. This brought about a readjustment of the Supreme Commander's plans. On April 4th the 9th U.S. Army was restored to the 12th U.S. Army Group, and in company with the 1st Army proceeded with the isolation of the Ruhr: while 21st Army Group operated separately further north.

The 8th Corps of the 2nd Army crossed the Weser near Minden on April 5th, followed shortly and further north by the 12th Corps, which presently reached the outskirts of Hamburg. This movement disorganised enemy resistance on the left, and by the end of the month, despite a defence assisted by skilful demolitions and widespread inundations, Bremen was in the hands of the 30th Corps; which, after the necessary mopping up, crossed the Weser and pressed on. Of this Corps the Guards Armoured Division drove through Bremervorde to capture Stade, and reached the Elbe estuary below Hamburg, while the 51st Division branched north towards the naval base of Cuxhaven.

Meanwhile, the Canadians were proceeding steadily with their allotted task. By mid-April most of northern Holland had been liberated and a large enemy garrison isolated in west Holland.

The crowning point of the advance, obviously, must be the investment and occupation of the great city of Hamburg, at the mouth of the Elbe, followed by the crossing of the Elbe itself, and the capture of the Kiel Canal; then, onward to the shores of the Baltic; and to this supreme effort, aided by the 18th U.S. Airborne Corps, Field-Marshal Montgomery now directed 21st Army Group.

But the enemy had had enough. Everywhere the German armies were disintegrating. Upon the day before the fall of Bremen American and Russian troops had joined hands on the Elbe. The Americans themselves had captured Hanover, Brunswick, Magdeburg, Halle, Leipzig, Nuremberg, and Stuttgart; while the Russians, having occupied Vienna and Königsberg, were now battering their way into Berlin. By April 16th German prisoners captured on the British-American-French front numbered over two million. The end was near: indeed, it had arrived.

'Our plan', says Field-Marshal Montgomery, 'for outflanking Hamburg by a manœuvre similar to that used at Bremen was actually under way, when, on May 2nd, the Germans came out to negotiate its surrender. Across the Elbe the countryside was packed with a mass of German soldiers and refugees, fleeing from our advance and from that of the Russians, with whom we established contact on May 2nd.'

The negotiations for the surrender of Hamburg led upon May 3rd to a far more momentous event—the dispatch of envoys by Grand Admiral Doenitz (who had proclaimed himself the successor of the now presumably defunct Hitler) to Field-Marshal Montgomery's Tactical Headquarters at Lüneburg Heath, there to seek an armistice for the purpose of discussing peace plans in general.

It was quite obvious to the Field-Marshal that the real purpose of this deputation was to obtain from him (and subsequently General Eisenhower), upon what terms they could, a cessation of hostilities which would enable them to employ the whole of their remaining strength against the Russians—an all too patent device to create trouble between Russia and her Allies. He bluntly informed them that no discussion of any kind could be permitted: it must be unconditional surrender or nothing; and if they wished to continue fighting he was perfectly willing to oblige them.

He concluded by showing to the leader of the party, General-Admiral von Friedeberg, a map of the actual operational situation. This revelation reduced the General-Admiral to tears. He then departed whence he came, in order to report to Doenitz in Schleswig-Holstein. He was not long in returning; and at 6.30 that evening (May 4th, 1945) he signed the Instrument of Unconditional Surrender of all German naval, land and air forces opposed to the 21st Army Group—in other words, all German armed forces in Holland and north-west Germany, including the Frisian Islands, Schleswig-Holstein and Denmark, together with all naval ships in these areas. The surrender was received by Field-Marshal Montgomery under the powers conferred on him for the purpose by General Eisenhower, the Supreme Commander-in-Chief.

Cease Fire was ordered for 8 o'clock next morning.

The Instrument of Surrender signed by Von Friedeberg was in due course superseded by, and absorbed in, a General Instrument of Surrender, signed by Colonel-General Jodl at 2.41 a.m. on May 7th, at General Eisenhower's headquarters at Reims.[1] As for Italy, the Allies under Field-Marshal Alexander had at last emerged triumphant from their arduous and long-drawn campaign. During the closing days of April Bologna and Genoa had fallen, Milan had been liberated by partisans, and Mussolini 'liquidated' by his own countrymen. On the 29th all German forces in Italy and Tirol had surrendered unconditionally to Field-Marshal Alexander, to the number of nearly 1,000,000 men.

Three months later, on August 25th, 1945, the 21st Army Group became the British Army of the Rhine, or B.A.O.R.; and pending the establishment of civilian Control Commissions, was called upon to shoulder the responsibilities of government within the British Zone, an area as large as England and with a population of some 20,000,000.

Upon that date Field-Marshal Montgomery issued to all ranks under his command the following personal message. Though addressed primarily to the 21st Army Group, it summarised the achievement of the British Army as a whole, and also foreshadowed

---

[1] A similar Instrument of Surrender was also signed at Marshal Zhukov's Headquarters in Berlin.

the new and heavy responsibilities awaiting it in various quarters of the post-war world; so may be quoted here in that sense.

BRITISH ARMY OF THE RHINE
PERSONAL MESSAGE
FROM THE C.-IN-C.
(To be read out to all troops)

1. On Saturday, August 25, 1945, the 21st Army Group will cease to exist and the British forces in north-west Europe will be known as 'The British Army of the Rhine'.

2. I cannot let this moment pass without a reference to the past achievements of 21st Army Group. This Group of Armies fought on the left or northern flank of the Allied forces that invaded Normandy in June, 1944; these forces liberated France, Belgium, Holland, Luxemburg and Denmark; they invaded Germany, and fought their way to the centre of that country where they joined hands with our Russian Allies; and thus ended the German war.

   The Army Group completed its active operations by gathering as captives on the northern flank, in the space of a few days, upwards of two million of the once renowned German Army. The fame of the Army Group will long shine in history, and other generations besides our own will honour its deeds.

3. Officers and men of the Army Group are now scattered throughout the world; many are serving in other theatres; many have returned to civil life.

   To all of you, wherever you may be, I send my best wishes and my grateful thanks for your loyal help and co-operation.

4. To those who still serve in Germany I would say that, though our name is changed, we still have the same task.

   As a result of this war much of Europe has been destroyed, and the whole economic framework of the continent lies in ruins. We have a job to do which will call for all our energy and purpose; we have got to help to rebuild a new Europe out of the ruins of the old.

   It is a gigantic task. But we must face up to it with that same spirit of service to the common cause of freedom which has so strengthened us during the stress and strain of war.

   Together we have achieved much in war; let us achieve even more in peace.

B. L. MONTGOMERY.
Field-Marshal,
Commander-in-Chief
British Army of the Rhine.

August 25, 1945.

So Germany was defeated, after a struggle waged without ceasing for five years and nine months. Only Japan remained.

CHAPTER XIX

THE BURMA CAMPAIGNS

~(1)~

WE turn finally to a very different theatre of operations. So far, our survey has included desert warfare, mountain warfare, seaborne invasion, battles amid enclosed country and built-up areas, and purely defensive operations against the aerial invasion of our own Island.

In the South-East Asia Command we revert to warfare at its most primitive—hand-to-hand fighting in an almost roadless country of mountain ranges and jungle, in which concerted action by ordered formations is frequently impracticable, and nearly everything depends upon the courage and initiative of individual groups. The climate is demoralising both to physical and moral stamina; noxious insects are ubiquitous and malaria rife; we are many thousands of miles from home, and inclined at times to feel forgotten; and we are engaged (and for many months hopelessly outnumbered) by a well-equipped, resourceful and fanatical enemy.

The main theatre in our land campaign against Japan was Burma. Burma itself covers an area of some 216,000 square miles: that is to say, it is about the size of Germany in 1939, or more than twice the size of Great Britain and Northern Ireland. On the west and north it lies enclosed by India and Tibet, in the north-east by the Chinese province of Yunnan, and on the south-east by French Indo-China and Siam. Upon its south-western seaboard the province of Arakan abuts upon the Bay of Bengal, extending some 400 miles from Maungdaw; thence southward from the Gulf of Martaban for another 400 miles, reduced now to a mere fringe along the western coast of the long, narrow peninsula (Tenasserim) leading down to Malaya.[1]

[1] See Map No. 6, facing p. 268.

The country as a whole is seamed with parallel mountain ridges, imposing a series of well-nigh impassable barriers between Assam on the western and China on the eastern flank. Three considerable rivers, also running parallel and from north to south, provide the country's principal means of transport. Of these the great Irrawaddy is the most westerly; then come the Sittang River and the Salween. The last two flow into the Gulf of Martaban.

The Irrawaddy itself is navigable by fairly large steamers as far north as Bhamo, 900 miles above Rangoon and only fifty from the Chinese frontier: thence light river craft can proceed another 100 miles or so to Myitkyina. The navigability of all Burmese rivers is largely controlled by the state of the monsoon, which lasts from May till October and is responsible for heavy rainfall and much flooding. (On the exposed Arakan coast the annual rainfall is as high as 200 inches.) During the dry winter and spring season, on the other hand, the rivers are apt to dwindle in volume, and navigation, especially in the upper reaches, becomes difficult.

Three hundred miles north of Rangoon, we may note here, the Irrawaddy is joined by a tributary, flowing almost parallel to and not far from the Indian frontier—the Chindwin River, a name destined to become familiar and famous in the annals of the 14th Army.

Mandalay, the most important inland city of Burma, stands in the centre of the country, in its only level and alluvial district, which occupies about one-fifth of the whole. Mandalay is the starting point of the great Burma Road, the lifeline of China, which winds in a north-easterly direction through Lashio, over lofty passes, into the province of Yunnan and on to Chungking, more than a thousand miles away.

The principal railways and roads, like almost every other physical feature of the country, also run north and south. The main line of railway connects Rangoon and Mandalay, then continues to Myitkyina. There are two trunk roads, both starting from Rangoon and reaching Mandalay by different routes. One of these continues to Lashio, where it joins the Burma Road: the other hardly penetrates beyond Mandalay.

In other words, there was in 1940 no direct east-west road from Burma into India. Between the basin of the Irrawaddy and Assam stretched some 200 miles of practically trackless mountain and jungle.

Such was the terrain which in 1941 General Wavell was called upon, with such resources as he could compass, to defend from invasion—terrain of the highest strategic importance, for through Burma lay the only route by which the armies of our Chinese Allies could be kept supplied, and bases stocked for Allied air attack on Japan itself.

~(2)~

The war in Burma lasted from December 1941 to August 1945. The defence of the country had been gravely hampered by two circumstances. The first was that the possibility of its invasion had seemed most unlikely; for, as already noted, it was buttressed on every side by Allied or neutral territory; and of the neutral countries Tibet seemed *hors concours* as a base for enemy invasion, while Siam and Indo-China had recently professed their intention to withstand any possible Japanese aggression. Consequently, with pressing claims for protection coming in from more immediately vulnerable theatres, the defences of Burma had been left more or less to look after themselves.

Secondly, Authority had exhibited perpetual indecision of mind as to who should be responsible for the actual defence of the country. Burma had been removed from the India Command in November 1940 and included in the Far Eastern Command, which was concerned chiefly with the defence of Hong Kong and Malaya, and had its headquarters at Singapore. Against this arrangement General Auchinleck, the Commander-in-Chief in India, had protested vigorously, but without effect. His successor General Wavell actually paid a visit to the United Kingdom, and in view of the fact that the Japanese had by this time invaded Indo-China (in July 1941) personally urged the Chiefs of Staff to restore responsibility for Burma to India. He met with a similar refusal, although he was supported by Sir Reginald Dorman Smith, the Governor of Burma. General Wavell thus found himself, as Commander-in-Chief of the India Command, left with a highly vulnerable neighbour whom he had no authority to defend.

However, at the eleventh hour, five days after the actual entry of the Japanese into the war, he received a telegram from the Prime Minister placing Burma under his command for defence. As a most necessary concomitant, certain reinforcements were promised.

Less than three weeks later the kaleidoscope was given another twist. General Wavell was now informed that he had been appointed Commander-in-Chief of the newly constituted South-Western Pacific Command, afterwards known as A.B.D.A.,[1] in which Burma was to

[1] See p. 173, footnote.

be included. Against this decision, from his new headquarters in Java, 2,000 miles from Rangoon, General Wavell once more protested, on the ground that since the administration of the forces in Burma must necessarily be conducted from India, it would be utterly wrong to transfer operational control elsewhere. He was once more overruled.

On February 23rd, however, only five weeks later, the loss of Sumatra and Singapore having reduced the responsibilities of the South-Western Pacific Command almost to vanishing point, A.B.D.A. was closed down and Burma once more restored to India Command, this time for good, and General Wavell was at liberty to return to India and direct his defence from there.

Let us consider briefly the resources at his disposal. In Burma itself at the outbreak of war were two British infantry battalions and two Indian infantry brigades. There were also eight battalions of the Burma Rifles,[1] inexperienced troops of untested quality. (The Burma Army only dated from April 1937, when Burma was separated from India.) To these must be added six battalions of Indian troops, recently transferred from the control of the civil power. For artillery there were four mountain batteries, and one 18-pounder battery. Administration and Intelligence Services were practically non-existent. The air strength available was one fighter squadron of Brewster Buffaloes, of an obsolescent type. There were no bombers.

Plainly such forces as these could not hold Burma against highly trained and overwhelming Japanese strength. General Wavell, however, was hopeful of considerable reinforcements. The 18th British Division, which had been primarily intended as a general reinforcement for India, was being sent to Singapore, and the 17th Indian Division (Major-General J. G. Smyth, V.C.), under orders for Iraq, had been made available for Burma instead. Very considerable increases in air and anti-aircraft strength were promised. General Wavell also put in an urgent plea for the dispatch of two brigades of African troops from Italian East Africa.

He also received from Generalissimo Chiang Kai-Shek the offer of the services of the Chinese 5th and 6th Armies. Even though a Chinese army approximates in fire-power to not much more than a British division, this should have been a notable addition to our strength. But the problem of employing Chinese troops under a British Commander-in-Chief in Burma presented serious difficulties, not the least of which were the somewhat leisurely methods of Chinese

[1] They consisted of Chins, Kachins, Kerens and Burmans, speaking four different languages.

troop-movement and the entire absence of Chinese administrative services. (The Chinese had no experience of war except in their own territory, where they lived on the country and requisitioned supplies at will.) It was little wonder that General Wavell should have hesitated about accepting the Generalissimo's offer, especially since, as we know, he was expecting considerable reinforcements of his own. However, he accepted it, but deemed it inopportune to invite two Chinese armies into Burma straight away. He therefore compromised by moving a part of one of these nearer the Burma frontier. His motives were not understood at the time either by the Chinese or the Americans, and both chose to assume that Wavell had declined Chinese aid altogether.

Meanwhile Singapore had fallen, and the Japanese were swarming northward up the Tenasserim Peninsula towards Rangoon, against the dogged but unavailing resistance of the 17th Division, whose difficulties were increased by the speed with which the enemy were able to outflank them and set up road-blocks in their rear. Their movements were further hampered by the fact that they were equipped with wheeled motor transport, which confined them to the roads and prevented them from penetrating into the jungle (through absence of pack equipment) for more than a day's march on either side.

There were also bombing raids upon Rangoon itself: these inflicted little military damage, but had a most demoralising effect upon the civil population, including the dock-labourers and railway servants. India had been drained of her aircraft for employment in other theatres, so could offer little air assistance to Burma; but over Rangoon such air-strength as was available acquitted itself valiantly.

'The air defence of Burma,' reports General Wavell, 'especially the vital port of Rangoon, would have been overwhelmed at once but for the presence in Burma of the American Volunteer Group (A.V.G.), an air force manned by American pilots for the defence of China. One of its two squadrons was alternately made available by the Generalissimo for the defence of Rangoon, and the pilots, together with the Buffalo Fighter Squadrons, saved the situation by their dash and skill.'

Upon returning to India General Wavell visited Rangoon, accompanied by Lieut.-General T. J. Hutton, recently Chief of the General Staff, India, whom he had appointed Commander-in-Chief in Burma. He arrived in time to prevent, or at least postpone, the evacuation of Pegu and of Rangoon itself. The 17th Division were by this time in a most exhausted condition, having lost Moulmein and suffered a major disaster in attempting to withdraw across the

Sittang River.[1] The postponement, though it allowed valuable reinforcements to be landed—notably the 7th Armoured Brigade, which rendered inestimable service, especially in the dry paddy fields of the more open country, throughout the whole of this campaign—availed little, for Rangoon fell a week later. Thus the only gateway for British aid to Burma was irrevocably closed—and opened for the convenient landing of Japanese reinforcements.

~*(3)*~

By this time General Sir Harold Alexander arrived to take over the command of the Burma Army. General Hutton remained with him as Chief of Staff. General Hutton's comment upon the performance of the army in Burma during his own period of command should be noted here.

There is no doubt that although some units and some individuals may have failed, the army in Burma as a whole fought extremely well. For many months they withstood the onslaught of superior numbers, with little reinforcement, no rest, and practically no hope of relief. During most of the time they have suffered heavily from air attack, and have received little or no support from our own air forces. They have had no canteens, few amenities, and practically all lost their complete kit early in the campaign. The climatic conditions have been very trying.

And were to prove more trying still when the monsoon came.

Upon General Alexander now fell the thankless and almost hopeless duty of the further defence of the country. His principal handicap, as ever, was the almost entire absence of air support or reconnaissance. No further reinforcements could be expected, and one bomber squadron, one fighter squadron, and the A.V.G., though individually far superior to any of the Japanese, could avail little against overwhelming numbers. The loss of their remaining airfield, at Magwe in Upper Burma, with the destruction of nineteen bombers and fighters on the ground, completed the disaster. Thereafter, we are told, the Japanese air arm enjoyed almost a free hand.

Besides shortage of troops and lack of air support, General Alexander suffered severely from the inadequacy of his administration services. Upon this subject his predecessor had already offered some pungent comments:

[1] General Hutton remarks: 'If they could have been pulled out for a few weeks to rest and refit, no doubt they would have recovered. . . . This was of course impossible.' See also General Alexander's comment, pp. 275–6.

'Transport, supply, medical, provost, rest camps and mess, ordnance and labour units have all been less than the number required to administer the force. Improvisation has been necessary on a scale which has made confusion inevitable.

'The whole conduct of the military administration has been complicated by army headquarters having to deal with numerous civil departments who do not realise how quickly events move in war, and are thus unable to realise that it is necessary to have unified control well ahead of any likely emergency. The civil railway and inland water transport agencies could not be persuaded until it was too late that it was vital to have unified control and to form some military operating units. The result was a breakdown in railway transportation, which prevented the back-loading of valuable and vital stores from Rangoon to the extent that would otherwise have been possible, and great confusion and waste of effort in the Irrawaddy Flotilla company.'

Amid this overwhelming accumulation of difficulties it must have been obvious to so shrewd and experienced a soldier as General Alexander that, in his present state of isolation, the complete abandonment of Burma could only be a matter of time. But he was determined to fight until the last possible moment, for two outstanding reasons. The first was that a successful defence of Burma meant the immunity of India from land invasion; the second was that the loss of Burma would isolate China from her Allies.

He therefore applied his great powers of organisation to the concentration of the Imperial forces in Burma into a unified whole, by the formation of a Burma Corps (Burforce), composed of the 17th Division, the 1st Burma Division and the 7th Armoured Brigade. The command of the corps he bestowed upon Lieut.-General W. J. Slim—a name destined to become memorable in the subsequent history of the Burma campaign.

It should be added here that the Chinese 5th and 6th Armies were now aiding the Imperial forces in the actual defence of Burma itself. This policy was maintained by General Alexander, who was anxious to formulate an arrangement under which the Chinese forces should protect eastern Burma and the Shan States from invasion from Indo-China while the Imperial troops operated in the Irrawaddy basin and west thereof. To this end he established immediate relations with the Generalissimo, who reciprocated by conferring upon him the command of all the Chinese troops in Burma.

A preliminary difficulty, however, arose from the appearance upon the scene of General Stilwell, of the American Army. This remarkable and forceful soldier had been serving for some time as Chief of Staff to the Generalissimo. He arrived at Maymyo, at General

Alexander's headquarters, on March 14th, and bluntly announced that he had come to take over the command of the Chinese 5th and 6th Armies, independently of General Alexander. A somewhat delicate situation was thus created, which obviously called for a definite ruling from General Chiang Kai-Shek in person.

General Alexander accordingly flew to Chungking, with the following happy result:

'I was warmly received by the Chinese, and had several very satisfactory talks with the Generalissimo, at the last of which he expressed the wish for unity of command of the Imperial and Chinese forces in Burma, and asked me to accept the command of all his troops in that country. On my return to Maymyo I informed General Stilwell of the Generalissimo's wishes, and he readily agreed to serve under me as Supreme Commander in Burma.

'I should like to take this opportunity to add that General Stilwell and his American Staff could not have been more loyal or more co-operative throughout the campaign. General Stilwell had my complete confidence. He was obviously liked and trusted by the Chinese, and he understood them and spoke their language.'

The next six weeks were occupied by Burcorps in a desperate and complicated campaign of extemporised effort, for nowhere had General Slim sufficient troops to establish a continuous front at any time. The Japanese had now established complete air superiority, and only three aerodromes were left in operational use—at Magwe in Upper Burma, Lashio on the Burma Road, and Akyab on the sea coast.

Moreover, Chinese co-operation soon began to involve General Alexander in some of the difficulties foreseen by his predecessor. General Stilwell commanded the Chinese 5th and 6th Armies, under General Alexander, but he had to issue all his orders through a Chinese commander, General Lou. In addition, no orders of a major nature issued by General Stilwell, General Lou or General Alexander himself could be carried out without the sanction of the Generalissimo—a state of affairs wholly incompatible with the high pressure and speed of modern warfare.

The consequences were almost inevitable. For some time the Chinese had been holding Toungoo on the Sittang River in considerable strength. On April 7th, 1942, the Japanese suddenly attacked and drove them out of the town, thus opening the road to the Shan States, and uncovering Burcorps' left flank. The enemy pressed their advantage, and owing to Chinese neglect to carry out certain necessary demolitions, made rapid progress.

About the same time Burcorps had been engaged, along a thinly held front extending from Minhla on the Irrawaddy to

Taungdwindyi forty miles to the east, in a desperate effort to save the vitally important oil-wells at Yenangyaung, some fifty miles further north. Owing to the non-arrival of a Chinese division which had been promised for the defence of Taungdwindyi, General Slim was placed in the dilemma of finding himself incapable both of covering the direct line of approach to the oil-wells and of holding the vital centre of Taungdwindyi, which masked the approaches to Mandalay. General Alexander decided that Taungdwindyi must be held at all costs; so on April 14th the oil-wells were destroyed, to deny them to the enemy.

Unfortunately, destruction of the wells involved the ultimate immobilisation of transport, since it was from here that much of the petrol supply was drawn. General Alexander, however, had already made temporary provision for this contingency, by establishing a great supply centre and petrol dump at Meiktila, on the west side of the Irrawaddy, some sixty miles south of Mandalay. He had also moved his headquarters from Maymyo to Shwebo, on the west bank of the Irrawaddy north of Mandalay. His object was not only to give the Chinese armies every assistance, with a view to keeping China in the war, but to gain time to allow India to build up her defences, and especially to complete the road now under construction between Assam and Burma; for he had realised that, with his troops utterly exhausted and further reinforcement out of the question, Burma could not be held much longer.

'I was of opinion', General Alexander reports, 'that the capture of Lashio by the Japanese was only a question of time,[1] and that there would be nothing to stop them moving on to Bhamo, thus turning my communications with Myitkyina. Subsequent events proved the opinion to be correct, but it was impossible for me to disengage any forces to send to Bhamo. I also thought that the condition of the Chinese armies precluded the possibility of my being able to hold Mandalay and the Irrawaddy for very long.'

In truth, the Chinese were in sore straits. Their administration system worked fairly well so long as operations were not too fluid, but their recent experiences at Toungoo and in the Shan States had been too much for them. They were also running short of their staple food, rice, for the provision of which General Alexander was responsible, and owing to the steady dwindling of the rice-growing area by reason of enemy encroachment, the task was growing almost impossible. In other words, matters were shaping towards the inevitable end—the withdrawal of the Chinese armies into China;

[1] Lashio was actually occupied upon April 30th, 1942.

and after consultation with General Stilwell and General Lin Wei, it was so arranged.

Thus, for the time being, our concern with the Chinese armies ends. They had for the most part fought stoutly, but lack of ordered control and shortage of equipment had been too heavy a handicap.

General Alexander's own objective, as the starting point for the withdrawal of Burcorps through the wide belt of jungle ranges which separated the Imphal area from Assam, was Kalewa, a hundred miles north-west of Mandalay; and thither he now directed his course. He had hoped to establish a line along the Chindwin river and the densely wooded Chin hills. In a hard-fought action at Kyaukse, a little south of Mandalay, he succeeded in withdrawing the 7th Armoured Brigade, which had been operating with the Chinese to the east of the Irrawaddy, across the great Ava bridge, the only bridge across that river. Two spans of the bridge were then blown, and the withdrawal to the Chindwin began. It was a race in two senses —against the enemy, who were following him up at speed, and against time, for the monsoon was almost due. He outstripped the monsoon, but not the enemy, who succeeded, after heavy fighting, in capturing Monywa on the Chindwin, and then getting astride the river itself. Thus ended the hope of establishing a Chindwin defence line.

There is no need here to describe in detail the last heroic struggle: it will suffice to say that the withdrawal to Kalewa was successfully accomplished. The troops were either conveyed up the Chindwin by steamer, or moved up the east bank and ferried across. They were accompanied, and encumbered, by thousands of civilian refugees.

Then began the laborious pilgrimage through Manipur State to the Imphal area and thence into Assam. The new road, however, was not only long and devious but far from complete, and owing to the fact that the last twelve miles of it constituted little more than a footpath, most of the motor-transport and all the tanks had to be abandoned. But 2,000 sick and wounded were safely evacuated.

The troops got through, too, and that was what mattered. They certainly had earned their rest. Here is their Commander's final summary of what they had endured:

'Properly to appreciate the achievements of the Burma army, it is necessary to know something of its experiences before my arrival. At the battle of the Sittang the 17th Division was cut off and had to swim the river. The equivalent of a brigade was lost, and the remainder arrived upon the west bank practically naked, with no equipment and with only some of their personal weapons. It is a high tribute to the commanders in this formation that the division was reformed and re-equipped, and, with the addition of the 63rd Infantry Brigade, fought gallantly for another three months before withdrawing into India.

'The 1st Burma Division suffered constantly from the disintegration of its indigenous units, but it in turn reorganised to include battalions brought in from outside, and remained a fighting formation to the end.

'*Practically every formation in these two divisions had at one time or another been surrounded by the enemy, and had fought its way out. Further, the 17th Division fought for five months without rest and practically without reinforcement, and for only one period of three days did it have another formation between it and the enemy.*'

That tribute, it will be agreed, is both generous and just. But perhaps it is not too much to say that the real inspiration and mainstay of that long-drawn battle was General Alexander himself. He was destined a year later (as we have seen) to achieve prominence and fame as an organiser of a victorious offensive elsewhere; and as such perhaps he is best remembered today. But it may be that, when history comes to be written, and the full story of the Burma war is told, he will be remembered most as the man who, at the darkest hour, held the fort and saved India. It is as such, certainly, that his memory will be cherished, with abiding gratitude and affection, by the men whom he heartened and sustained, isolated and outnumbered as they were, and utterly forgotten as they appeared to be, through those nightmare five months in the Burma jungle.

~⋇(4)⋇~

So ended the first phase of the Burma war, with the occupation by the Japanese for the time being of the whole country. They penetrated to the head-waters of the three rivers, and there established their front, cutting the Burma Road, and with it China's last land-link with her Allies.

The scene, so far as Burcorps was concerned, was now transferred to India, the corps being absorbed into 4th Indian Corps and reverting to the command of General Wavell as Commander-in-Chief in that country. Under that command it remained for more than a year, enjoying the benefits of rest and rehabilitation.

The defences of India itself at this time were inadequate in the extreme, for practically all her available strength had been drained elsewhere: in fact, both India and Ceylon lay under imminent threat of invasion, for the Japanese Navy were in full control of the Bay of Bengal. Still, the British Army could not be everywhere, and it was considered, probably rightly, that in the present strategic situation troops were more urgently needed in Malta and Madagascar than in India; so General Wavell was left to make what shift he could with the forces at his command.[1] He even felt constrained to offer (and send) an anti-tank regiment to Egypt, and the 7th Armoured Brigade (which had done such good service in Burma) to Iraq.

Nevertheless, he never ceased to plan for the resumption of the offensive in Burma. This, he considered, could be effected in two ways—by a seaborne invasion of Arakan and Lower Burma, or by driving a military road through the State of Manipur and launching a great land campaign in Upper Burma.

These hopes, however, for the time being proved impossible of fulfilment.

'The heavy monsoon, the severe incidence of malaria, and the Congress disturbances of August and September delayed the preparations in Assam for the advance into Upper Burma, and interfered with the training of troops; while the continuance of operations in Madagascar deprived India of troops, ships, and landing-craft, which were necessary for the preparation of the seaborne expedition.'

Still, General Wavell (whose motto, as we have already had cause to observe, was *l'audace, l'audace, et toujours l'audace*) was rightly determined to take offensive action, if only upon a strictly limited scale, in order to give his troops the stimulus of forward movement, and at the same time demonstrate to the enemy that he was not to be left in undisputed possession of the field. Therefore in December 1942 he formulated, in consultation with General Stilwell, a plan under which the 14th Indian Division should advance from Chittagong down the coast (sea-transport being unavailable) into Arakan, with the object of capturing the airfields on Akyab Island. To hamper the enemy in any effort he might make to reinforce the position, it was agreed that the Chinese armies in Yunnan should advance simultaneously into Upper Burma, and so create the necessary diversion.

In committing troops only partially trained for offensive action to an arduous campaign in a malarial jungle, General Wavell was taking a calculated but justifiable risk. And the expedition might well have achieved its object, but for the fact that for once General Stilwell was unable to spur the Chinese armies into action. They never stirred from Yunnan, with the result that the Japanese were able to move the necessary reinforcements into Arakan.

[1] In addition to the menace of Japanese aggression, General Wavell had also to contend with internal disorders instigated by Congress after the failure of the Cripps Mission. No fewer than fifty-eight battalions had to be distributed over disaffected areas—a serious setback to much-needed training.

The campaign in consequence was a strategic failure, for Akyab was never reached; and by April 1943 the 14th Division, after much heavy fighting, finished in the same position from which it started, at the cost of some 2,500 battle casualties. Losses at least as heavy were inflicted on the enemy. Our troops and their leaders, moreover, had gained invaluable experience both of the enemy's methods and of the defects in their own training and organisation.

'On balance,' reports General Wavell, 'I shall certainly never regret that I ordered the campaign to take place, in spite of lack of resources.'

~(5)~

We return now to the general situation. The year 1943, as we have seen, brought with it an all-round improvement in Allied prospects and hope. In fact, the tide had turned at last. The improvement extended even to the situation in India and the Assam-Burma border.

The reconstituted 4th Corps, composed of many of the original elements of Burcorps, lay in the Imphal plain among the Manipur hills, preparing for an offensive against the Japanese in Upper Burma. The corps comprised the 17th Indian Division, itself once more, and the 23rd Indian Division. The latter included the 77th 'Independent' Brigade, of which we shall hear more presently. The majority of the troops, naturally, were drawn from the Indian regiments, but also included four British infantry battalions—the 1st West Yorkshires, the 1st Gloucesters, the 1st Seaforths, and the 13th Battalion the King's Regiment.

In the air our resources had improved out of all knowledge. The R.A.F. had not only expanded in numbers but had received some really modern aircraft and equipment, including eighteen fighter squadrons, seventeen squadrons of various types of bomber, six squadrons of flying-boats, and five squadrons of transport aircraft. Spitfires, however, were still in short supply. The strength of the American air force had also been greatly increased.

The function of the R.A.F. was now fivefold: to establish and maintain air supremacy over the enemy in Burma, to supply air-cover to the troops, to disrupt enemy communications (as in the European campaign a year later), to defend India itself from air attack, and to maintain, from the air, land forces which could not be maintained by normal means.

Lastly, to fulfil the all-important end of restoring and maintaining contact with China, American engineers were pressing furiously on with the work of constructing an entirely new road and supply route to that country, starting in the Brahmaputra Valley. This was the so-called Ledo Road, destined ultimately to link up with the Burma Road at a point beyond the area of Japanese occupation.

The Americans had also established a truly remarkable 'non-stop' service of transport planes, carrying supplies over mountain ranges, at a height of 22,000 feet, direct to China. As the result of a conference held in Washington in April 1943, which General Wavell himself attended, this particular organisation, known as the India-China Wing of the U.S.A.A.F. Air Transport Command, had been allotted first priority, with a monthly target of 10,000 tons—striking evidence, if any were needed, of Allied determination to render to China substantial and not merely token aid.

Needless to say, these ever-increasing activities threw a heavy strain, aggravated by the poverty of transportation facilities, upon the administrative services. The 4th Corps in Manipur had to be kept supplied: so had the American and Chinese troops in the Ledo area. Protection and supplies for the American air-route to China were also the responsibility of General Wavell. The civil population of Assam provided an additional burden. Stores and depots had to be built along 350 miles of road; the roads themselves had in many cases to be constructed first. In all, daily maintenance for some 100,000 men had to be provided up to distances over 200 miles from rail-head.

The medical situation called for the constant enlargement of hospitals. Malaria remained the outstanding problem. During the Arakan operations casualties from malaria were extremely heavy; the sick-list in Assam itself was also a long one. In June 1943 admissions to hospital in Eastern army reached 10,000, of which over half were due to malaria. Fortunately the rate of recovery was high.

~≪(6)≫~

We come now to the proposed invasion of Upper Burma by the 4th Corps, an undertaking which presented truly formidable difficulties. As we know, there existed no direct connection by road or rail between India and Burma, and in any case the terrain to be traversed was continuously unfavourable—high hills, dense jungle, and malarial valleys. The rivers and mountain ranges of Burma all ran from north to south, with the result that an invading force would be compelled to advance across the grain of the country, so to speak; whereas the enemy, based on Rangoon and the south, could operate up and down the valleys with comparative freedom. The climate, too, practically restricted offensive operations by land to a period of less than six months in the year.

It was this state of affairs which was primarily responsible for introducing into the Burma campaign a form of warfare both novel and unconventional, and at the same time brought upon the scene one of the most remarkable figures of the Second World War. This was Lieut.-Colonel (later Major-General) Orde Wingate, who had served under General Wavell in Palestine in 1938 and later in Abyssinia, and had so impressed his superiors by his daring, initiative and fertility of resource, that General Wavell now made a special request for his services, as a man perfectly equipped to organise guerrilla warfare in Burma.

And he was justified in his expectation, for Wingate immediately put before him a proposal to train a brigade 'for long-range penetration behind the enemy lines'. This body was to be given a free hand, to be unencumbered by lines of communication, and to be entirely supplied from the air—or, as Wingate put it, 'down the chimney'.

And it was so. General Wavell bestowed upon Wingate the command of a brigade composed of the 13th Battalion the King's Regiment, the 3/2 Gurkha Rifles, the 142nd Commando Company, and the 2nd Battalion the Burma Rifles. The formation was known as the 77th Indian Infantry Brigade, and it is interesting to observe that the units were not hand-picked but merely happened to be available at the time. The British contingent thereof were in no sense trained regulars: for the most part they were young citizens who had been engaged, a few years previously, in the humdrum pursuit of a living in commerce or industry. But they were to prove their worth.

The brigade was organised in seven 'columns', each self-contained, with pack transport only, which meant that it had machine-guns but no artillery. It set out from Imphal upon what may be called its trial trip on February 8th, 1943.

Its initial obstacle was the Chindwin river itself, strongly held by the enemy. A feint attack by troops of the 23rd Division upon Kalewa provided the necessary diversion, and the crossing was successfully effected.

The directive given to the brigade commander was simple. He was to cut the north-and-south railway line between Mandalay and Myitkyina; to harass the enemy in the Shwebo area; and finally, if circumstances permitted, to cross the Irrawaddy itself and cut the railway line Maymyo-Lashio.

Two of the columns failed to penetrate far, and returned; but the remainder reached the railway, where they certainly carried out their instructions. They destroyed four bridges, brought down thousands of tons of rock on the line by judicious blasting, and cut the line in seventy other places.

General Wavell had left it to Wingate to decide whether, after this first exploit, he should bring his men back to Assam or continue across the Irrawaddy. There is no need to say which alternative Wingate chose. His columns crossed the Irrawaddy between March 9th and 18th.

Here the going proved more difficult. The weather grew hotter and water was scarce. The men frequently had to dig for it, and not always successfully. All ranks carried their own personal effects on their backs, a burden of sixty pounds. The air-dropped supplies, which so far had been maintained with an almost hundred per cent regularity, were not so easily come by; for the enemy were more numerous here, and frequently prevented the columns from reaching their supplies, or by sending up false smoke-signals caused them to be dropped where no column was. The health of both men and animals began to suffer, and it became evident that this gallant *tour de force* was approaching the limit of its possibilities. Finally it was decided that the operations against the Maymyo-Lashio railway should be abandoned; and in accordance with a drill already practised in training, the brigade was divided into dispersal groups, with orders to find their way back to India independently. This was successfully done, and by many devious routes: one column actually marched east, to be hospitably received by the Chinese and flown back to India by the Americans. The distances traversed during the four months which the operation lasted varied from 700 to 1,000 miles.

Thus ended the first 'Chindit' experiment. It had no strategic value, and about one-third of the force which entered Burma failed to return. Indeed, there were those who condemned the whole enterprise unreservedly. Yet it had achieved results out of all proportion to its operational importance. The experience gained in supply-dropping from the air, in the intricacies of jungle warfare, and in general knowledge of enemy methods, was invaluable. Its very audacity startled and puzzled the Japanese, who, never quick at any time to adapt themselves to unexpected tactics, were sorely perplexed as to how to deal with such informal methods of warfare.

Above all, the Chindit raids, and the unexpected publicity which they attained throughout the world—a publicity of which the Chindits themselves grew heartily ashamed—administered at the time a most wholesome tonic to British morale, and in particular served to remind both friend and foe alike that the British soldier, given half a chance, is, and always has been, the most resourceful fighter in the world. Wingate himself summed up the matter in a couple of sentences:

'A weapon has been found which may well prove a counter to the obstinate but unimaginative courage of the Japanese soldier, and which will give scope to the military qualities which the British soldier still shares with his ancestors. These qualities, hitherto unsuspected by the world, are intelligence in action—that is, originality in individual fighting—and on the moral side, self-reliance and *the power to give of his best when the audience is smallest.*'

Certainly those qualities were demanded and fulfilled in the Chindit raids. And be it remembered, the men who took part in them were called upon to live, or rather exist, for months on end under conditions of squalor sufficient to sap the manhood of the most insensitive. They could seldom wash, they never shaved, they were fever-ridden and devoured by noxious insects, their clothes were in rags, and their food was uncertain of arrival and primitive in quality. Yet they emerged from their experience stronger and better men, for they had learned the great lesson of 'making do' on a minimum ration of comfort, whether of body or soul. As one of their number has put it, with simple directness:

'One came to realise then how few things in life are really essential, and how very essential those few things are.'[1]

⤚(7)⤙

In June 1943 His Majesty the King appointed General Wavell Viceroy of India, and the long professional career of a great soldier came to an honoured close.

In the last paragraph of his final Dispatch, General Wavell bids farewell to the men whom he had trained and led in almost every quarter of the globe during forty years.

'In this my last dispatch,' he says, 'I should like to pay tribute to the British soldier. He has shown himself in this war, as in all others, the finest all-round fighting man in the world. He has won so many victories that he never doubts of victory; he has suffered so many disasters and defeats on his way to victory that defeat seldom depresses him. He has adapted

[1] From *Beyond the Chindwin*, by Bernard Fergusson. Collins.

himself to desert and to jungle, to open plains and to mountains; to new foes, new conditions, new weapons, with the same courage and humorous endurance of difficulties and dangers which he has always shown. His staying power is a sure guarantee of final success.'

He concludes with this self-evident corollary:

'Whatever the qualities of the soldier, the value of an army depends in the end upon the leadership of the regimental officers; and in the British Army this still remains worthy of the men they lead. Whatever method may be adopted in the future to officer the British Army, it must ensure the same standard of leadership and the same close relations with the soldier.'

General Wavell was succeeded as Commander-in-Chief in India by General Sir Claude Auchinleck, whom we first encountered as Commander-in-Chief Middle East.[1]

The reader will remember that since the evacuation of Burma the troops recently engaged there had reverted to the India Command. With the arrival of General Auchinleck, however, on June 20th, 1943, responsibility for the conduct of operations against the Japanese in this theatre was restored to the Burma Command, and in the following August Lord Louis Mountbatten was appointed Supreme Allied Commander. This relieved General Auchinleck of the planning and execution of future operations against the Japanese. He continued, however, to develop the plans of his predecessor, as amended by the Quebec Conference, until the date of handing over.

Much of the time and energy of his command during this period, incidentally, had been occupied in taking necessary action against the subversive activities of the J.I.F. (Japanese-Inspired Fifth Column) and in organising measures to relieve distress in famine-stricken Bengal.

In Burma, by June 1943, we were in contact with the Japanese upon four fronts—in Arakan, on the Chindwin, in the Chin hills north of Manipur, and in North Burma. Japanese strength in Burma at this time was reckoned at five divisions. Their new railway from Siam to Burma was under construction, and its subsequent completion gave the enemy a new line of entry into the country. The work of construction was performed by prisoners of war, under conditions of bestial cruelty which have become notorious in history, and for which heavy retribution was duly exacted.

With the vesting of the control of the operations in the South-East Asia Command, a complete reorganisation of the control of the land forces was necessitated. An Army Group Headquarters was

[1] See Chap. XIII.

set up (11th Army Group) under the command of General Sir George Giffard, who had recently performed most distinguished service in West Africa. A new army, the 14th, was created to take control of the operations which had previously been directed by G.O.C.-in-Chief the Eastern Army. The command of the 14th Army was bestowed upon Lieut.-General Slim, who had long qualified for such a post both by experience and achievement.

A situation was thus created in the Burma Command roughly analogous to that which came into being in the European theatre in 1944: as Supreme Commander, Lord Louis Mountbatten fulfilled a role comparable to that of General Eisenhower, while General Giffard, as Army Group Commander, assumed duties in Burma corresponding to those of General Montgomery in France. General Stilwell was appointed Deputy Supreme Allied Commander.

Lord Louis Mountbatten brought to his high appointment certain outstanding qualities. He was young, vigorous, and broad in outlook. He was also a man of peculiarly inspiring presence, capable of awakening the faith and enthusiasm of his followers by frank and courageous speech. In addressing the troops he laid special stress upon two points: first, that he now expected them to fight all the year through and not merely in the dry season—a battlefield is not a cricket-pitch, he pointed out—and secondly that they must lose no time in shedding their exaggerated respect for the Japanese soldier as a fighter.

Considerable reinforcements had by this time been made available for 11th Army Group, and it was obvious that the period of offensive-defensive stalemate was nearing its end. Particular advantage was taken of our growing ascendency in the air to expand and intensify the system of feeding and supplying troops 'down the chimney'.

A striking instance of the value of such measures is furnished by the story of the defence of the 'Admin Box', and other isolated areas, by the 7th Division of the 15th Indian Corps (Lieut.-General A. P. F. Christison) during the battle of Arakan in early 1944. The Japanese, under an able and bombastic leader, one Tanahashi, were strongly entrenched astride the Mayu Range. Against this objective General Christison, on December 31st, 1943, launched the 15th Corps, composed of the 5th and 7th Indian and the 81st West African Divisions. Considerable progress had been made when on February 3rd Tanahashi, by a swift flank march, succeeded in delivering a surprise counter-attack not only to the front but from the rear. He almost captured corps headquarters. Part of the 7th Division was completely encircled at Sinzweya (afterwards known as the Admin Box), the 5th was cut off from the coast, and the 81st trapped at Kaladan in the valley, some distance to the east. Tanahashi was exultant: he mounted his artillery on the surrounding heights, and bombarded the isolated areas night and day, while Tokyo proclaimed to the world, in advance, the annihilation of the 15th Corps—a consummation which in truth appeared to be a mere matter of time.

But Tanahashi had overlooked the possibilities of our new technique in the air. The R.A.F. having driven the Japanese Air Force from the skies, a continuous service of transport planes was established and maintained, dropping supplies upon the beleaguered garrisons until, after four weeks of desperate resistance, land reinforcements arrived from Chittagong, and Tanahashi was driven back with heavy loss to his original positions.

'As already mentioned,' reports General Giffard, 'the objects of the Arakan campaign were to improve our general situation and engage and destroy Japanese forces. Our success had led me to hope that we could clear the whole of the Mayu Peninsula, but the need for producing reinforcements (5th and 7th Divisions) for the northern front frustrated this. . . .

'To sum up, the Japanese offensive, from which they confidently expected great results, had been defeated, and we had gained our objectives. Last but not least, we had established a moral ascendency over the enemy which promised well for the future.'

-⚔(8)⚔-

Of the diverse and intricate operations which began in 1944 with the increase of our forces in Burma to adequate strength, to continue with increasing momentum until final victory was achieved, no detailed account will be expected here; but some mention must be made of certain methods adopted at this time for carrying the war into the enemy's country—or rather, into enemy-occupied country—regardless of the obstacles offered by wild nature and military art.

The method employed was the further development, on a vastly increased scale, of the 'Chindit' policy of Long-Range Penetration, or L.R.P. This time the expedition would be no mere raiding force, but an army of invasion. They would not proceed on foot, but would be conveyed over the heads of the enemy in gliders, and upon reaching their objective would embark upon an ordered campaign, continuously supplied and reinforced by air transport from India.

Some idea of the increased scale upon which the new operation was to be conducted may be gathered from the fact that the force to be conveyed comprised not only men but 25-pounder guns and engineering equipment, including bulldozers, for the construction of field defences and air-strips. It totalled 10,000 men, with 1,000 pack-animals.

The man who undoubtedly brought the enterprise to fruition was Orde Wingate. Since his experimental expedition of a year previously he had been thinking hard and maturing his ideas. He had even contrived to visit the United Kingdom and the Quebec Conference for the purpose of pleading his cause, and by sheer pertinacity had succeeded in convincing his superiors—among them Mr. Churchill—of the soundness and feasibility of his plans.

His point was that the enemy would be most vulnerable far behind his own front, where his troops, if he had any, would be of inferior quality. With our new air superiority, he argued, the troops could be conveyed to their objective without the preliminary labour and loss of breaking the enemy's front; we should have no vulnerable lines of land-communication to defend; and, provided that airborne supplies and reinforcements could be regularly delivered, the campaign could be maintained indefinitely, and a shattering blow, at the very least, inflicted upon the enemy's dispositions and morale.

He had his way, and his brigade became a division—the 3rd Indian Division, L.R.P. Groups. This was to a certain extent a camouflage title, designed to deceive the enemy, for most of the troops were British, drawn from the 70th Division: the remainder were Gurkhas and West Africans. There were also some extremely efficient American engineer units.

The necessary transport was provided by a special American air unit known as No. 1 Air Commando, or more familiarly, 'Cochran's Circus', after the name of its intrepid commander.

Of this gallant formation General Giffard reports:

'No. 1 Air Commando had been formed to co-operate both tactically and administratively with 3rd Indian Division. It was a composite force comprising some 250 aircraft. This force carried out the hazardous and difficult glider-borne operations, flying fully laden gliders, some in double tow, over 9,000 feet mountains by night, a distance of 300 miles, to the selected areas.

'Equally important was the action of the fighters and bombers of this force, before, during, and after the actual landings, against targets which it was vital to attack.

'No. 221 Group R.A.F. also did splendid work in these operations.

'I wish to express my appreciation of the work carried out by these forces, without whose assistance 3rd Indian Division could not have operated.'

Previous to actual operations, the Allied Strategic Air Force, by systematic and thorough bombing of Rangoon and the southern areas, had inculcated in the enemy a belief that the invasion of Lower Burma was contemplated. Such of the Japanese air force as remained there were faithfully dealt with by our Spitfires, which were now available to the extent of two complete groups.

'Operation Thursday', as it was called, began on the night of March 5th, 1944, and was led by General Wingate himself. Its object was threefold:

1. To assist the advance of General Stilwell and his Chinese troops from the Ledo Road towards Myitkyina, by drawing off and harassing the Japanese troops opposed to him.

2. To create a situation which could enable Chinese forces to advance westward from Yunnan.

3. To cause confusion, damage, and loss to enemy forces in North Burma.

The aim of the earliest-arriving glider-borne troops was to effect a landing in three clearings, designated 'Piccadilly', 'Broadway' and 'Chowringhi', contained within a circle of forty miles radius from Indaw, on the Rangoon-Myitkyina Railway, there to prepare landing-strips, if possible between dawn and dusk, for the reception of the gliders carrying the main body.

Piccadilly, unfortunately, was found to have been blocked by felled trees, so Piccadilly troops had to be switched to Broadway—a most disconcerting episode in such a meticulously rehearsed operation. There was congestion, confusion, and some crashing, in which valuable equipment for the preparation of the landing-strips was lost. Fortunately there was no serious sacrifice of life, and the strips were prepared in time, mostly with spades and bare hands.

'Our losses during the fly-in,' reports General Giffard, 'amounted to only one per cent of the total personnel transported. The only animal casualty was one mule. The smallness of these losses is remarkable, in view of the fact that, at the peak of the fly-in, double the planned effort was achieved; and aircraft were coming in and taking off at the rate of one landing and one take-off every three minutes.'

'Operation Thursday' demonstrated without doubt the feasibility of conveying a very large force by air over the very heads of the enemy, and landing it safely in his rear. Whether the operations which it undertook upon arrival were of sufficient value to warrant the hazard and cost of the expedition was another matter. In the case of 'Operation Thursday' the enemy neither diverted troops from his forward areas nor was he compelled to alter his main strategical plan—the launching of a heavy offensive against Assam, about which there will be more to say later—neither were his rail communications more than temporarily affected. It is true that he was compelled to detach troops to deal with the invaders of his rear areas, but these did not amount to more than twelve battalions (mostly railway battalions) at any one time. Still the work accomplished, even if it fell short of hope and expectation, was of definite importance, both in the help it gave to General Stilwell and in the temporary havoc it wrought to the enemy's communications.

The 3rd Indian Division continued to operate until May. Then its 16th Brigade, which had proceeded the whole way on foot and not by air, through a trackless jungle in which men had frequently to crawl on hands and knees, in order to furnish a right flank guard for General Stilwell, was evacuated by air, while the remaining three brigades passed under Stilwell's command, to operate in an ordinary infantry role in the Mogaung-Myitkyina sector as part of the army of liberation in northern Burma.

But they had lost their leader and inspiration, Orde Wingate, who had been killed not in action but in an unhappy flying accident late in March. He left an ineffaceable memory in the hearts of the men who had followed him. He was a hard taskmaster, for his standard was perfection; but it was his faith which carried him through, and his followers with him. The following are the closing words of a truly characteristic Order of the Day which he issued to the original Chindits after their first successful crossing of the Chindwin:

'Finally, knowing the vanity of man's effort and the confusion of his purpose, let us pray that God may accept our services and direct our endeavours; so that when we shall have done all, we may see the fruit of our labours and be satisfied.'

⤳(9)⤪

We have now briefly examined two of the three 'fronts' (all isolated from one another) established by the Allied forces during the offensive-defensive period which followed the occupation of Burma by the enemy—the southern Front in Arakan, which we have seen the Japanese make a determined attempt to break through to Chittagong and Calcutta, only frustrated by the gallantry and endurance of General Christison's 15th Corps; and the northern

Front, just described, upon which the Chindits had been so actively employed in rendering aid to General Stilwell in his progress down the Ledo Road.

There remains the central Front, composed mainly of the hilly province of Manipur—the bulwark of Assam and ultimately of India itself—held for the most part by the 4th Corps.

Along this front was fought the most critical and the bloodiest battle of the entire campaign. It began in March 1944 (about the same time as the Chindit landings on the northern Front), when a Japanese army of three divisions strong struck west across the Chindwin, along a front which extended from Tiddim in the south to Kohima in the north, in a last desperate attempt to break out from Burma into India.

The terrain was perfectly adapted to Japanese infiltration tactics, and the defenders, locally outnumbered and in perpetual danger of being outflanked and cut off, were compelled to fall back across the frontier into India, where two villages, Imphal and Kohima, insignificant in themselves but of immense value as supply bases and strategic points, were speedily isolated and closely besieged. It was a great moment for the Japanese and their publicity agencies: a Japanese army stood at last upon the soil of India, and the conquest of the whole country was merely a matter of time! For good measure, the fall both of Imphal and Kohima was officially announced, upon March 30th and April 4th respectively.

But neither had fallen, nor could be allowed to fall. In enemy hands either would have been a perpetual menace not only to India itself but to the air route to China. So the order was issued that Imphal and Kohima were to be held at all costs.

The 4th Corps had been slightly reinforced before the ring closed, and India was being combed for further reinforcements. Above all, we retained command of the air, and in addition to the complete supremacy of our fighters and low-flying bombers, it was found possible, not for the first time in the Burma campaign, to keep the garrisons supplied 'down the chimney'.

Still, it was touch and go, and there were some anxious conferences at Delhi, as well as heavy misgiving in Whitehall and Washington. Kohima in particular was in desperate plight. The only water supply lay within thirty yards of the enemy's lines, and men had to crawl down to it singly, fill their containers, and get back as best they could under snipers' fire, until a new water-supply was discovered.

But Kohima clung on, like a miniature Stalingrad, for more than seven weeks, under perpetual bombardment from surrounding heights, until relieved by a comparatively new formation, Lieut.-General Stopford's 33rd Corps, advancing from the north.

In due course the 33rd Corps swept aside the remnants of the besieging force and reopened the road to Imphal, there to join hands with the 4th Corps under General Scoones. Now it was the turn of the Allies to take the offensive. They had assembled a great force by this time, with immense strength in artillery. With this they inflicted upon the enemy an intensive bombardment, and drove him, beaten and demoralised, across the Chindwin.

With the successful defence of Imphal and Kohima the tide had turned. 'In this year', said General Slim to one of his divisions, 'we have thrashed the Japanese soldier man for man. Next year we shall smash the Japanese Army.'

'In December drums rolled and trumpets sang, and the flags of the 14th Army flew proudly above Imphal plain. In a corner of the battlefield, before Scottish, Gurkha, and Punjab regiments, the Commander of the Army, General Slim, was knighted by the Viceroy, with his three Corps Commanders, Christison, Scoones, and Stopford. Fifty thousand Japanese dead lay upon that field.'[1]

~⟩(10)⟨~

By the end of August 1944 the last Japanese soldier had been driven out of India, and the Japanese Army itself was in full retreat to the Chindwin, whither the 14th Army made haste to pursue them, fighting through the monsoon, as the Supreme Allied Commander had enjoined.

It was heavy going, but for a beaten and demoralised enemy it was heavier still. Harried from the rear and hammered from the air, the Japanese died by thousands, many of them from sheer exhaustion and starvation; for their leaders had not expected to fight *à outrance* during this period, and had made little attempt to establish the necessary supply-dumps. All down the road from Kohima to Tiddim lay Japanese skeletons, eaten clean by white ants, with here and there a group of derelict staff-cars, their occupants sitting dead inside them. Prisoners captured about this time were found to be suffering from acute beriberi, due to malnutrition, for even a Japanese cannot exist exclusively on rice.

The pursuit was continued across the Chindwin and over the plain towards Shwebo and Mandalay, 4th and 33rd Corps competing as

[1] From *The Campaign in Burma*, by Frank Owen. H.M. Stationery Office (1946).

to which should reach the Irrawaddy first. But this was not all: from the northern Front came the British 36th Division (under the American General Dan Sultan) advancing down the Myitkyina-Mandalay corridor.

Down south, in Arakan, General Christison's 15th Corps had now been detached from the 14th Army and placed under the direct command of Headquarters Allied Land Forces, charged with the maintenance and expansion of the Arakan positions. This enabled General Slim to devote his entire attention to the important offensive operations now awaiting the 14th Army in Upper Burma.

In November of this year General Giffard's long, exacting, and ultimately triumphant term of duty as commander of the 11th Army Group came to an end. In his final Dispatch he took the opportunity to pay tribute to the achievements of the 'forgotten' 14th Army.

He began by referring to the difficulties and privations of that army's early days—poverty of equipment, shortage of trained reinforcements, lack of welfare arrangements, long service overseas, sickness, indifferent rations, an apparent lack of interest and appreciation from the people at home, coupled with an exaggerated estimate of the fighting qualities of the Japanese soldier. Then he passed to the resolute and sturdy growth, in all ranks, both of efficiency and morale.

'It has been an immense source of pride to me to watch the growth of confidence and skill which enabled the officers and men of the 14th Army to inflict the first major defeat upon the Japanese. . . . Victory was achieved by fine leading by all commanders, from the highest to the most junior section leader; by the skill of the men in the ranks; by high courage in battle; by steady endurance, under conditions of climate and health worse than almost anywhere in the world; and by that spirit which alone enables an army to exert its maximum strength—co-operation among all ranks and arms.

'Finally, I have no doubt that the defeat of the Japanese forces in Burma is due to the balanced judgement, determination, and skill of Lieut.-General Sir William Slim, upon whom fell the burden of the fighting.'

General Giffard was succeeded as Commander-in-Chief 11th Army Group by Lieut.-General Sir Oliver Leese, a leader of great experience and proved worth. As organiser and trainer of the Guards' Armoured Division in 1942, he had acquired an early familiarity with mechanised warfare, which he was to turn to good account in the desert campaigns of North Africa, where, as commander of the 30th Corps, he became General Montgomery's right-hand man. He had subsequently succeeded General Montgomery as Commander-in-Chief of the 8th Army in Italy.

His responsibilities in Burma were heavy. He controlled some nineteen Allied divisions, and in addition to a command comprising the 14th Army, 15th Corps, and numerous line of communication troops, was also Commander-in-Chief of the Allied land forces in south-east Asia (which included General Dan Sultan's[1] British-American-Chinese Northern Combat Area Command, or N.C.A.C.) with headquarters at Kandy in Ceylon.

His task was threefold—to take Mandalay with the 14th Army and Lashio with the N.C.A.C., both of which operations would contribute to the all-important reopening and security of the Burma Road. At the same time he was under orders to set 15th Corps in motion down the coast of Arakan, so as to secure air bases on Akyab and elsewhere, and so provide the necessary air support to the 14th Army when the time came for the recapture of Rangoon.

To enable the reader to appreciate the immense increase in the Allied forces available for this, the final campaign, it will be well to enumerate them in detail.

In the 14th Army the 4th Corps consisted of the 19th and 23rd Indian Divisions. The 33rd Indian Corps consisted of the 2nd British Division, the 5th and 20th Indian Divisions,[2] the 11th East African Division, the Lushai Brigade, the 268th Indian (Lorry) Brigade, and the 254th Indian Tank Brigade. The 15th Indian Corps consisted of the 25th and 26th Indian Divisions, and 81st and 82nd West African Divisions, the 50th Indian Tank Brigade, and the 3rd Commando Brigade.

The N.C.A.C. comprised the 1st and 6th Chinese Armies, the 36th British Division, which had been flown thither in relief of the Chindits, and the 5332 U.S. 'Mars' Brigade. This last was in point of fact the equivalent of a U.S. light division, and consisted of one U.S. infantry regiment, one cavalry regiment, and one Chinese regiment.

Of the various strengths in the field there were approximately: Indian 340,000, British 100,000, West and East African, 90,000, Chinese 65,000, American 10,000. Forty-seven U.S. air squadrons took part, and fifty-one British, including, besides the R.A.F., Indian, Canadian and Australian formations.

There is no need here to describe the terrain over which the final campaign was fought: it should be familiar enough to the reader by

---

[1] General Sultan had succeeded General Stilwell, who had been recalled to America to supervise the training of all American land forces.

[2] An Indian division consisted normally of two Indian brigades and one British brigade.

this time. The only difference now is that the movements are reversed, as in a film run backwards: it is the Allied forces which advance, while the Japanese retire, almost along the self-same roads by which they came.

Let us first survey the course of events in the Northern Combat Area Command, and in China itself.

During the closing months of 1944 the British 36th Division had been driving steadily southward along the Myitkyina-Mandalay railway, by a route parallel with that of Sultan's two Chinese armies and the American Mars Brigade; struggling through swamps and teak-forests and fed mainly from the air. Their aim was to effect a junction with Slim and the 14th Army. This was achieved on December 16th, when the 36th Division made contact with troops of the 19th Indian Division, which had crossed the Chindwin and proceeded eastward across the Mandalay plain by forced marches, at Naba Junction. Thereafter they pressed southward together on either side of the Irrawaddy, in company with the Mars Brigade and Sultan's Chinese troops.

One more junction had yet to be effected—that with the Chinese Expeditionary Force under Marshal Wei-Li-Huang, which emerged from Yunnan westward bound, to join hands with N.C.A.C. on January 27th, 1945, thereby reopening the road from India, via Burma, into China. The first convoy from Ledo to Chungking crossed the frontier the next day, and Lord Louis Mountbatten was able to cable to the Prime Minister in London:

'*The first part of the orders I received at Quebec has been carried out. The land route to China is open.*'

We now return to the main operation.

It was urgently important to capture both Mandalay and Rangoon before the monsoon began in May 1945. This end was achieved, though not without difficulty and the taking of risks. Rundstedt's counter-offensive in the distant Ardennes had been responsible for a delay in the dispatch of six further divisions, together with an amphibious naval flotilla, to the Far East; and about the same time a sudden Japanese advance in the China theatre threatened Kunming, terminal of the Ledo transport plane service, and necessitated the withdrawal to China of two of Sultan's Chinese divisions.

But Mandalay was captured none the less, and by a brilliant tactical manœuvre on the part of General Slim, who switched the 4th Corps from his left, or northern, flank, and conveyed it, by a direct march southward across the tail of the 33rd Corps, to a point 300 miles down the river. He was thus enabled to attack Mandalay both from north and south. The city was entered by the 19th Indian (Dagger) Division on March 8th, 1945. The enemy withdrew to Fort Dufferin, in the centre. After a fierce resistance of nearly a fortnight Fort Dufferin fell, and Mandalay was wholly occupied.

Outstanding in these brilliant operations were the crossings of the Irrawaddy, and a swift mechanised thrust on Meiktila, which cut in behind the retreating Japanese forces. Even speedier action was needed now, for Rangoon lay nearly 400 miles to the south, and the monsoon was only a few weeks away. General Slim was thus under urgent orders from Sir Oliver Leese to drive on to Rangoon at all costs and at all speed.

The main difficulty, as ever, was one of administration. 11th Army Group lines of communication stretched right back into Manipur, and one section of 100 miles between Kalewa and Shwebo was only capable of sustaining fair-weather traffic. To reach Rangoon in time, therefore, the 14th Army's speed must average ten miles a day. What if it fell short of that? The grave risk involved was obvious.

A quick decision was arrived at—to press forward at any cost. Sir Oliver Leese had at his disposal the 4th and 33rd Corps of Slim's 14th Army, and Christison's 15th Corps. The 33rd Corps he directed to the oilfield area round Yenangyaung, to deal with still formidable enemy resistance: thereafter it could proceed down the Irrawaddy via Prome, to Rangoon. The 4th Corps, as the more mobile, was to start at once and drive with all speed down the Pegu Road (which followed the railway) straight on Rangoon. The 15th Corps would join in the attack, though by a very different route.

The 15th Corps, as we know, held the Arakan Front, and thus lay rather nearer to Rangoon than the other two; but the Arakan terrain south of Maungdaw was practically impassable for troops. It was intersected by innumerable tidal creeks, bordered by mangrove forests which ideally suited Japanese resistance tactics. If Rangoon was to be attacked from Arakan it must be by sea. This was rendered a practicable undertaking by our command both of the sea and the air: indeed, General Christison had already captured the island of Akyab and turned it into an air-base.

The proposed attack on Rangoon thus resolved itself into a closely integrated operation between the three Services—described at the time by Mr. Churchill, in an expressive phrase (though of dubious etymological authenticity) as a 'triphibious' attack.

We will deal first with the advance of the 4th Corps down the road to Pegu—that advance which had to be maintained at not less than ten miles per day. Here General Slim received inestimable aid from the air: indeed, the greater part of his supplies were (and long had been) delivered through this source—in Arakan, Imphal and Kohima, for instance. Under Air Chief Marshal Sir Keith Park (who had succeeded Sir Trafford Leigh-Mallory, killed flying out from home) air supply in Burma reached its zenith. The spirit and determination of the men engaged, whether on the ground or up aloft, soared with the effort demanded of them: the supply pilots doubled their hours and the ground staffs worked all night. As Park wrote: 'The armies advanced on the wings of the air force.'

Note should be made here of the benefit wrought, and the amount of human suffering alleviated, by the R.A.F., in the evacuation of casualties. Aircraft arrived loaded with stores and left carrying sick and wounded men, to the number of thousands every month.

The work of the Allied air forces, however, was not limited to transport services. Ahead of the advancing 4th Corps Allied airmen rained bombs (some 80,000 tons of them) upon the enemy's ports, airfields, railways, and other battle targets. Particular attention was paid to what was now the main Japanese supply-line—the newly completed Siam-Burma Railway, built with the blood and tears of many thousand British, Indian and Chinese prisoners of war.

We turn now to the 15th Corps, and the 'triphibious' operation which had been jointly agreed upon between Admiral Sir Arthur Power, Commander-in-Chief of the East Indies Fleet, Sir Oliver Leese, and Sir Keith Park, under the code-title 'Dracula'. A great fleet of ships-of-war, transports, and landing-craft had been assembled, the troops and air forces were ready, and the operation was timed to begin on May 2nd.

The expedition was to proceed down the coast of Arakan for a distance of some hundreds of miles south of Akyab, round the southern extremity, past the Irrawaddy Delta, and into the Gulf of Martaban, there to effect an assault-landing upon Rangoon itself.

The city lay some twenty miles up the river, a waterway of narrow channels and shifting shoals, guarded by well-placed entrenchments and pill-boxes. The garrison of Rangoon was estimated at 10,000, though not all first-line troops. The sea was shallow for thirty miles out, which meant that the landing-craft would have to approach their objective without the covering fire of the warships.

Landing operations were rendered still more difficult by the fact that the weather broke during the voyage, and when the moment came to lower the troops from the transports into the landing-craft on May 2nd, the storm was at its height. But it was decided not to postpone the operation. 'Guts and good seamanship,' as ordained by the Naval Commander's battle signal, carried the enterprise through, and the assault-troops, seasick but indomitable, set off up the estuary on their twenty-four-mile journey to Rangoon.

On May 1st heavy preliminary air attacks had been delivered upon all known defences upon either bank; and Gurkha parachutists were dropped by the score upon a strong position known as Elephant Point, which they captured.

Then came a real surprise. Air pilots, circling over Rangoon Gaol, which was known to be a prisoner-of-war camp, discerned upon its flat roof a legend inscribed, in staring letters: '*Japs gone !*'

And it was true; the Japanese had evacuated Rangoon without striking a blow in its defence. The landing-parties were put ashore with less than a hundred casualties, and the 15th Corps had the gratification of being the first to reoccupy the city, some fourteen days earlier than the 14th Army, however hard it drove itself along, could have hoped to arrive. Actual contact between the two forces was achieved on May 6th, when the 26th Division of the 15th Corps joined hands with the 14th Army at milestone 29 on the Rangoon-Pegu road.

Thus the Japanese forces were riven in two from south to north, and four-fifths of Burma had been liberated. To complete the task was merely a matter of time.

'With the capture of Rangoon,' reports Sir Oliver Leese, 'a major phase of the war against Japan had been completed—a phase important in itself and decisive so far as Burma was concerned. It will stand to the eternal credit of the armies of the South-East Asia Command that this phase was completed before the 1945 monsoon.'

The road to Malaya now lay open, and upon September 9th Singapore was reoccupied without resistance.

Upon September 12th, 1945, General Itagaki, the Japanese Commander-in-Chief in Malaya, Java and Sumatra, signed the surrender of all Japanese armed forces in south-eastern Asia—and so far as the British Army was concerned the Second World War was over at last.

CHAPTER XX

RETROSPECT

ᵜ(1)ᵜ

In the earlier chapters of this book we devoted considerable attention, for purposes of instructive comparison, to the growth and development of the British Army from the days of the New Model to the outbreak of the Second World War. Therein we noted the changes brought about in each successive century and generation by the steady, sometimes headlong, progress of military science: for instance, the ever-increasing range and intensity of fire-power; the maintenance of larger armies in the field rendered possible by modern methods of food preservation; and the changes in tactics enforced by the invention of smokeless powder.

The outstanding feature of the Second World War, as frequently noted in this narrative, was the revolution brought about, first by the phenomenal development, with all its implications, of the internal combustion engine, and secondly by the perfection achieved in the matter of intercommunication. Today troops are moved and battles fought, not at a foot-pace, but at the speed of an armoured car or tank. Massed infantry attacks, the stand-by of the First World War, have given place to a war of swift, wireless-controlled manœuvre by self-contained units, working upon an integrated plan and closely supported from the air.

But total mechanisation has carried us even further than that. It has been responsible for what is known as total war—and total war has revolutionised our national and even domestic existence.

A generation ago the interest of the average civilian in the soldier in time of war was purely patriotic, or sentimental. After bidding the troops God-speed, with flags flying and bands playing, at dockside or railway-station, he was at liberty to retire to his home and follow the progress of hostilities, anxiously no doubt but in perfect security, in the newspapers. But today the distinction between combatant and non-combatant hardly exists. In total war every one of us is in the war-zone.

Besides being called upon for passive endurance, the majority of our able-bodied population must be summoned to active participation as well. In other words, the events and developments of the recent war necessitated what amounted to conscription, either in name or effect, of our total manpower. (After all, there is little material difference between being called to the Colours and being 'directed' into an essential war industry, sometimes far from home and family.) In truth we needed every man we could get, and speedily. In the first place Great Britain had ceased, from a strategic point of view, to be an island, and now lay as wide open to immediate and sudden invasion as any continental country. Apart from our commitments overseas, a great garrison was required to protect our coasts from seaborne attack, to man anti-aircraft batteries, and to be ready and alert, at almost any interior point, to resist the landing of a glider-borne expeditionary force.

A second and equally important need was to mobilise an industrial army to meet the demand for the intensely elaborate equipment imposed by the total mechanisation of war. In fact, apart from certain industrial and agricultural services essential to the life of the community, our country had to be converted into one vast ordnance factory. The strain thus thrown upon our available manpower was immense, and increasing efforts had to be made to relieve it. The most notable, and certainly the least expected, of these additions to our military potential were the Home Guard and those gallant members of the A.T.S. who participated in anti-aircraft defence. (No woman fired the gun, but a woman usually gave the order.)

The events leading to the formation of the Home Guard have already been described.[1] The essential need at that moment was for speed, for an enemy landing of some kind might occur almost anywhere at any moment. There was little time to think out details or calculate difficulties: the latter, and their name was legion, had to be dealt with as and when they arose.

Having regard to the terms of Home Guard enlistment—that service was to be voluntary and unpaid, and that a man should only be available for duty during such time as he could spare from the pursuit of his trade or profession—the authorities wisely decided that there must be no attempt to 'militarise' the new force beyond what was necessary for purposes of organisation and administration. Training must be carried out piecemeal and at irregular intervals,

[1] See p. 89.

and discipline reduced to its lowest effective terms. So far as any analogy was possible, the Home Guard was intended to resemble an armed special constabulary.

The force was under the operational control of the War Office, but the administration of each unit was entrusted mainly to the County Territorial Association of its own particular district. With the absorption of the Territorial Army into the Regular Army for the duration, the Territorial associations had found their occupation gone, while their administrative machine remained intact and in full working order. By this fortunate chance it was a comparatively simple matter to adapt the machine, which was controlled by men with a wide experience in the personal problems of part-time soldiers, to the needs of the Home Guard.

The Home Guard was divided into the usual battalions, companies, platoons and sections; but the size of these was not constant, and varied with local conditions. A company could be 400 strong. The rank and file were known not as privates but as volunteers; there were no commissioned officers and no particular system of ranks. Commanders of units were simply regarded as holders of appointments. All ranks, however, were subject to military law as private soldiers, even though many of them had at one time or another held the King's Commission in one of the Regular forces. (At one Home Guard post in London three of the volunteers had originally seen service as a Rear-Admiral, a Major-General, and an Ambassador respectively.) A volunteer could not be subjected to summary punishment for breaches of discipline, but he could be discharged, if necessary, from the Home Guard altogether. He could also, if he wished, resign upon giving fourteen days' notice.

Such, roughly, was the original framework of the scheme: it was never expected that adjustments would not have to be made. One of the earliest problems to be faced was that of adequate equipment. The situation was complicated by the fact that the raising of the Home Guard coincided, perforce, with the evacuation of the British Expeditionary Force from Dunkirk and the arrival in England of many thousands of men without weapons or, in many cases, sufficient clothing. Naturally, the re-equipping and rearming of these was allotted first priority; and the Home Guard had to wait, in most cases for months, before the necessary rifles and uniforms were forthcoming.

The question of uniform was much more important than might appear, for Hitler had announced that any British prisoners captured, in his coming invasion of our country, with arms in their hands but without uniforms on their backs, would be treated as *franc-tireurs* and shot. This declaration merely conformed with the recent practice of the Nazis during the invasion of Holland and Norway; and in any case, by the canons of International Law, Hitler was for once within his rights. Fortunately, the threat of immediate invasion was not fulfilled. Meanwhile the emergency was met, to a certain extent, by the issue of denim overalls and field-service caps.

The actual duties of the Home Guard fell roughly into two categories. The first comprised the guarding of factories, railways, and buildings of vital importance. The protection of Government Offices in London was entrusted almost entirely to Home Guard units, composed in this case of civil servants; and everywhere throughout the country the Home Guard relieved regular troops in the defence of industrial key-points.

In course of time it became a regular practice for factories, railway centres and other private commercial institutions to form a Home Guard unit from among their own employees. This particular service achieved considerable popularity, for it appealed to employer and employee alike: on the other hand it absorbed a large number of potentially valuable soldiers into purely static defence, and gave them little opportunity to be trained in really mobile operations. These last consisted, first, in constant patrolling, against the possibility of a sudden descent by enemy paratroops; in manning road-blocks; in preventing sabotage or Fifth Column activities; and in readiness at all times to inform Regular troops of enemy landings.

A familiar spectacle in those days, especially upon a Sunday morning, was that of a Home Guard unit scouring a stretch of countryside in an anti-invasion exercise. The procedure, as many an ex-Home Guard will recollect, was roughly as follows:

At a given and precise moment—say '1024 hours'—a signal was broadcast to all company or platoon headquarters of the local Home Guard unit that a party of enemy parachute troops had descended on a certain field or common, the exact position of which was indicated by a large-scale map reference, and must be rounded up and dealt with immediately. The unit concerned (whose members, possibly, the news had not taken entirely by surprise) arrived with great promptitude on the scene of action, in motor-cars, on bicycles, or at the double on foot.

Meanwhile the 'invaders', each wearing a distinctive brassard to show that he was an enemy, had emerged at the appointed moment from the copse in which they had unobtrusively been assembled—it was seldom that genuine parachutists were available for such exercises—and were now creeping under the lee of hedges or through thick undergrowth for purposes presumably of sabotage, or in search of a given rendezvous with similar bodies. In due course, if all went well, these were rounded up in barns, pigsties or ditches—some even received medical attention as 'token' casualties—and about the hour of noon the exercise terminated in a local house of refreshment, where both victors and vanquished were addressed by their commander (and on state occasions by a regular Staff Officer), who apportioned the necessary praise and blame. A party had perhaps been tardy in arrival, while another had not taken sufficient advantage of available cover; or a third had omitted to 'immobilise' its motor-car—a particularly venal sin. The proceedings, however, usually ended on a note of qualified commendation, and the combatants dispersed to their Sunday dinners well content, and, what was more important, with a growing sense of confidence and comradeship towards one another.

The Home Guard, as we know, was never called upon to discharge the principal duty for which it was created. But it rendered immeasurable service in relieving Regular troops for more active duties; in participation, as we have already noted, with the rocket-battery crews;[1] and in its ever-willing aid to the civil defence services. Above all, its very existence and appearance inspired the British people, especially in remote country districts, with a feeling of comfortable security, coupled with a certain parochial pride in their own particular unit.

And, as already noted, the close association of the members of the Home Guard itself, irrespective of worldly wealth or position, created a brotherhood nearly two million strong, whose traditions and memories still survive, and will never entirely fade.

~(2)~

We come now to the story of the development of our final source of manpower—if so it can be called—the Auxiliary Territorial Service, or A.T.S.

The part played by this body in the mixed A.A. batteries has already been described.[2] It should be added that in the summer of 1944 certain of these batteries were transferred bodily to Belgium and Holland, where their previous experience in dealing with V1 bombs enabled them to render conspicuous service in the protection of

[1] See p. 235. [2] See p. 243.

Antwerp, Brussels and the Scheldt estuary, especially during Rundstedt's Ardennes counter-offensive.

Still, the operational service of the A.T.S., notable and gallant though it was, was but a small part of its general effort and achievement, as we shall presently discover.

But first let us remind ourselves that participation by our women in war activity is no new thing. Before 1914 their service was limited to what may be called welfare work, chiefly the care of the sick and wounded, with the name of Florence Nightingale as an outstanding landmark. In a later connection we should remember with honour the First Aid Nursing Yeomanry, or F.A.N.Y.—more colloquially, 'the Fannys'—a corps of young horsewomen raised in 1909 with the avowed intention of riding on to the field of battle to the succour of the wounded. The scheme was perhaps more romantic than practical, and in a time of profound peace had little opportunity to prove itself; but it undoubtedly fired the imagination of the succeeding generation —young women and girls who at that time were growing rapidly aware of the prospect offered them by modern emancipation. To that extent the F.A.N.Y. may fairly be remembered as the forerunner and inspiration of the A.T.S.

The first-fruits of the movement came in 1914 at the outbreak of the First World War, with the formation of the Women's Voluntary Reserve, recruited to a certain extent from the ranks of the redoubtable Suffragette forces. The members thereof donned khaki and set themselves to drill. They received no official recognition from the military authorities, but their services—as ever in times of national stress—were soon in request for work in canteens and other hard and unspectacular duties, often performed on night-shifts, after a full day's industrial or domestic toil.

The movement grew, and in 1915 a second purely feminine organisation came to birth, in the form of the Women's Legion. Its members specialised chiefly in rendering sorely needed aid in military cookhouses and mess-halls. They were still regarded by the War Department as an unofficial body. By 1916, however, the usual shortage of manpower began to make itself felt, and the military authorities were compelled to look further afield than ever before for reinforcements. It was discovered that no fewer than 12,000 soldiers in France were performing non-combatant duties, at bases and on lines of communication, who could well have been employed further up the line. Why not replace these by able-bodied young women? So the Rubicon was crossed at last. A new force, the Women's Auxiliary Army Corps (the 'Waacs'), with two stalwarts of the original

F.A.N.Y., Mrs. Chalmers Watson as Senior Officer and Mrs. Helen Gwynne Vaughan as Chief Controller Overseas, was set up by the War Office, and for the first time women found themselves enrolled as regular members of the British Army.[1] In the course of the next two years 57,000 women passed through the ranks, 10,000 of them in the western theatre of operations.

The movement was not allowed to languish during the succeeding years of peace—women had the vote now, and were even sitting in Parliament—and in 1934, with the threat of yet another world war already looming, a Women's Legion was established under the leadership of Lady Londonderry and Mrs. Gwynne Vaughan. It received a qualified blessing from the War Department, which changed its name to the Women's Emergency Service.

The anxious days of the Munich crisis in 1938 made ultimate war a tolerable certainty. Preparedness crystallised into action, and upon September 27th the formation of the Auxiliary Territorial Service was officially announced, and its organisation established upon a regular military basis.

In August 1939 came the call, 'Action Stations', and upon September 3rd Britain's declaration of war against Germany was transmitted to the world by an A.T.S. telegraph operator.

During the ensuing months recruits poured in from every quarter, and training camps sprang up throughout the country. Here women of every walk of life—housewives, shop assistants, mannequins, business women and factory hands—lived and worked together under their own officers. The Princess Royal accepted the office of Chief Controller in Yorkshire, and was soon afterwards gazetted Controller Commandant of the entire force. That distinguished and experienced leader among women, now Dame Helen Gwynne Vaughan, was established in the War Office as Director of the A.T.S.

In April 1941 the force achieved final recognition, being granted equal status with men. The Auxiliary Territorial Service came under the Army Act, and assumed the responsibilities and enjoyed the privileges of the rest of the Armed Forces of the Crown. Its officers held the King's Commission.[2]

[1] In 1917, in acknowledgement of its outstanding service, the name of the corps was changed to Queen Mary's Auxiliary Army Corps.

[2] The designations of the various officer ranks of the A.T.S. (with their Regular Army equivalents) were as follows:

Chief Controller (Major-General)	Senior Commander (Major)
Senior Controller (Brigadier)	Junior Commander (Captain)
Controller (Colonel)	Subaltern (Lieutenant)
Chief Commander (Lieut.-Colonel)	2nd Subaltern (2nd Lieutenant)

All other ranks were referred to as 'Auxiliaries'.

In 1942, with the inevitable waning of the voluntary intake, came conscription for all women, who had not been 'directed' to other duties, between the ages of eighteen and forty-three. This naturally resulted in a great upsurge in the numerical strength of the women's services, and the further release of many thousands of men for combatant warfare.

By the end of 1943 the strength of the A.T.S. had grown to 212,000 —roughly the same as that of the Regular Army before the war. Of these nearly one-third were by this time trained technicians, or 'tradeswomen' (to employ the usual army term) fully qualified to take the place of skilled male artificers and craftsmen, such as armourers, draughtsmen, fitters and wireless operators. 7,000 were engaged upon switchboard and teleprinter work. 30,000 were employed in clerical duties, some of them of a highly confidential and secret character, such as the composing or deciphering of code messages for Royal Signals. There were 4,000 cooks—a humbler but equally essential service. Of the non-tradeswomen 30,000 were employed as orderlies.

In many of these duties, it should be noted, women proved themselves more efficient than men. They were intensely eager and quicker to learn—one girl mastered the Morse Code in three hours—and were particularly skilful in the manipulation and maintenance of delicate scientific instruments.

In short, whereas at the outbreak of war only five army employments were open to women, the A.T.S. ultimately became expert in more than one hundred, ranging *inter alia* from baker, shoe-maker, and cycle-repairer to architect's draughtswoman, radiographer, and personnel selection tester.

Special mention should be made of the transport drivers, many of them recruited from the F.A.N.Y., a circumstance of which they were justifiably proud. Every A.T.S. driver was responsible for the care and maintenance of her own vehicle—no male assistance, however unsolicited, was permitted—and must be capable of driving a heavy 3-ton lorry, very often in a long-distance convoy, through the night, in the worst of weathers.

One other department of A.T.S. activity should be mentioned here. Every letter posted to a soldier, wherever stationed, during the war was dealt with mainly by A.T.S. auxiliaries—there were hundreds of them—in the great Army Post Office at Nottingham. Each girl handled on an average 8,000 letters a day.

But the work of the A.T.S. was by no means confined to the home front. The first drafts were dispatched overseas to Egypt and Palestine in December 1941, and in due course the force was represented in theatres as far afield as India, East Africa and Italy. After D-Day, needless to say, A.T.S. contingents followed 21st Army Group to France, Belgium and into Germany. Some of its officers soared high: several achieved the rank of Staff Captain in the Regular Army, and directed the labours of an establishment exclusively male. One of them penetrated into Eritrea, to discharge the duty of Assistant Director of Labour.

Lastly, it should be noted, throughout its service in the Second World War the A.T.S. maintained its efficiency and discipline without the employment of detention barracks or sentences of detention. It maintained its own Military Police Force, or Provost Wing— immaculately turned-out A.T.S. 'Redcaps', patrolling the streets of London or Cairo in stately couples. These were seldom called upon to suppress military 'crime': their task as a rule was to inspect leave-passes, give directions as to route, and generally advise auxiliaries in distress.

As already noted, the first Director of the A.T.S. was Dame Helen Gwynne Vaughan, D.B.E. She was succeeded in July 1941 by Chief Controller J. M. Knox, who in October 1943 was succeeded in her turn as Director by Chief Controller L. V. L. E. Whately, C.B.E., who had served in the A.T.S. since 1938.

The following is a summary of the honours and awards earned by all ranks of the A.T.S. in the course of the war: 1 D.B.E., 11 C.B.E., 31 O.B.E., 123 M.B.E., and 275 British Empire Medals. 87 officers and 151 other ranks have received Mention in Dispatches. Many foreign decorations have also been bestowed.

And the force has not gone unscathed. Its Roll of Honour comprises 3 officers and 64 other ranks killed in action, 9 other ranks died of wounds. Missing, 16 other ranks. 12 officers and 301 other ranks were wounded; 34 officers and 518 other ranks died of disease, and a further 8 officers and 147 other ranks died of injuries incurred in the course of duty—a casualty-list in all of 57 officers and 1,055 other ranks.

Such then, in bare statistical outline, is the record of the Auxiliary Territorial Service. But it is more than a record: it contains the elements of an epic; and it is to be hoped that in the fullness of time the whole story will be forthcoming at first hand, in affectionate detail, from the pen of one or more of its own sturdy 'Auxiliaries'.

Meanwhile it is good to know—and the soldier in particular will welcome the news—that the A.T.S. will continue hereafter as an integral part of the Armed Forces of the Crown, under the style and title of The Women's Royal Army Corps (February 1st, 1949).

⇜(3)⇝

The creation of the Home Guard and Auxiliary Territorial Service went far to economise our military potential, and so apply our active strength where it was most needed. But the strain upon our manpower was not lessened, and with the opening of fresh theatres of war, the resultant tale of casualties increased steadily. Fortunately, except for one critical and heroic period, we did not have to fight alone.

This brings us to the all-important question of mutual co-operation in warfare, and of Allied relations generally.

In the Second World War (as in its predecessor) Germany enjoyed the great advantage of fighting as a single entity, with a fixed policy, under single direction, and with no need to ascertain the views or consider the susceptibilities of any allies. The United Nations on the other hand were compelled at all times to consult one another, defer to one another's opinions, and formulate a joint plan of action acceptable to all. The result was frequently a compromise, in which unison was sacrified for the sake of harmony.

Still, the necessary harmony was somehow achieved and maintained—a triumph of integration at least as noteworthy as the military victory which followed. The machinery creaked at times: the wonder was that it functioned so well.

Let us briefly consider our own relations with our respective Allies, and the mutual and peculiar difficulties which each of us was called upon to overcome during the course of the war.

We will take Russia first. Here, so far as the British Army was concerned, there is little to be said, for British and Russian soldiers never fought side by side or shared any common experience. Perhaps it would have been better if they had; for the Russian soldier laboured under the impression (which his superiors did nothing to correct) that he was bearing the whole brunt of the war. The aid, whether direct or vicarious, rendered to him by the Arctic convoys, or the striking of some calculated blow by the Allied forces in order to create a timely diversion at a given moment, were unrevealed to him.

Our relations with France were of a different and more complicated character. We began by declaring war against Germany simultaneously and taking the field side by side, on an integrated plan long agreed. (Lord Gort's forces, in accordance with the Foch precedent of 1918, were actually placed under the operational control of General Gamelin.) Then came the *débâcle* of May and June 1940. France went down and the Vichy Government was set up, with the result that for the next year or so France and Britain were practically at war with one another, as unhappy memories of Oran and Dakar remind us. Even our subsequent co-operation with the Free French Army in Syria and North Africa was not devoid of constraint and embarrassment, as General Anderson and the 1st Army were to discover in the Tunisian campaign.[1] In the end, however, the breaches were healed, and the French Army, reborn, marched side by side with the British and Americans to the liberation of Paris and the invasion of Germany.

Our relations with our Chinese Allies, though distant in a geographical sense, grew steadily closer, especially in the Burma campaign, when the good understanding established with Generalissimo Chiang Kai-Shek by General Wavell and his successors bore valuable fruit, as we have seen, not only in the maintenance of supplies to China by the Ledo land and air routes, 'over the Hump', but in the ultimate liberation of Burma itself.

The rash intrusion of Japan into the war awoke the American nation, at long last, to the realisation of its world responsibilities. The Pearl Harbour incident, though a most humiliating experience and a naval disaster of the first magnitude, marked, as we can see now in retrospect, the first assured step along the road to Allied victory and the rebirth of human freedom; for it achieved a result for which Franklin Roosevelt had striven in vain: it converted the American nation, overnight, into a united people dedicated to a single purpose.

For months that vast country had been torn by divided counsels. There was the party of Immediate Intervention, bitterly grieved and ashamed that America for so long should have stood neutral upon a moral issue; there was another party, equally friendly disposed but less precipitate, who advocated All Aid to Britain Short of War; and there were the out-and-out Isolationists—the America First party (enthusiastically supported by the powerful Germanic elements of the Middle West)—who declared loudly that Europe was not America's business, and that no American mother must again be called upon to dispatch her son overseas to aid in restoring effete aristocracies or putting kings back on their thrones.

Towards the individual visitor to America at this time feeling was friendly enough, and hospitality more generous than ever; for the

[1] See p. 186.

average American hated Nazi-ism and was, moreover, filled with admiration of the courage and fortitude of the British people in their hopeless struggle. For hopeless in 1941 it was undoubtedly considered to be: Britain had lost the war, and the sun was setting on the great British Empire at last. Such was the conviction of the average American citizen, whether expressed with kindly regret or tempered resignation.

Amid such a welter of conflicting opinion, with the voice of the Isolationist overtopping the rest, it seems doubtful today whether President Roosevelt, with all his courage and skill, could ever have brought the United States to the active aid of the Allied cause; and if he had, those States would not by any means have been United. But Japan solved his problem for him, on that Sabbath dawn in December 1941; and at a single stroke united the two great English-speaking communities, for the first time in history, in firm and formal alliance.[1]

As a significant preliminary, the Combined Chiefs of Staff set up their headquarters in Washington; and from Washington, midway between the German and Japanese theatres, the war was conducted until the end.

So far, so good. But two potential dangers to complete and cordial integration of British and American effort had now to be faced and overcome.

In the first place, the extension of the war to world-wide dimensions necessitated a considerable redrafting of the original strategic scheme. Here there was inevitably some clash of opinion—especially political and Press opinion—between the two principal powers concerned. America, with her Pacific fleet temporarily written off and the Japanese Navy on her western doorstep, had a tough task on hand, and naturally pressed for a good share of the forces available. The British High Command, all too conscious of the critical situation in North Africa and the Mediterranean; of the threat, still imminent, of actual invasion of Britain itself; and, above all, of the possibility of starvation through ever-increasing U-boat activity, were insistent that the defeat and complete subjugation of Germany must have first priority.

The problem was discussed with great thoroughness by the major Allies, and in almost daily telephone conversations between Mr. Churchill and President Roosevelt. In the end the President,

---

[1] There was no formal Alliance in 1917. President Wilson merely declared war on Germany—he did not include Austria, Bulgaria or Turkey—and General Pershing preferred for the most part to keep his troops in the Argonne Forest under his own command.

supported by General Marshall, decided that the European situation must be dealt with first. Even so, Britain was partially disappointed of her hope of the necessary shipping and landing-craft reinforcement, and the invasion of Normandy had to be postponed. This was unfortunate, for D-Day, which had been tentatively fixed for early 1944, had to be deferred until June of that year—a dangerously late season for such an operation, as the event proved.

The second difficulty was of a more delicate and personal character. Who was to be the Supreme Commander of the Allied forces in Europe? The British leaders could claim seniority, experience, and first-hand knowledge of the enemy's methods and mentality. America on the other hand would provide a majority, an increasing majority, of the forces to be employed in the coming operations, and this in the American view clinched the matter.

For a moment an impasse seemed possible; and then the problem was solved by the quite providential discovery of a man whom both sides instinctively recognised as the ideal Supreme Commander—General Dwight Eisenhower, of the United States Army. He was accepted without demur by the British High Command—a gesture greatly appreciated in America—and from the day of his appointment justified every hope and expectation. He was an organiser, a leader of men, and, above all, a diplomat of the first water. He possessed to a rare degree the gift of what may be called stereoscopic vision, which enabled him to reduce the views of other people, however conflicting, to a single steady focus.

He knew his limits, and was invariably willing to listen to advice, though he did not always feel bound to take it. (He overruled Field-Marshal Montgomery, as we have seen, in the matter of the invasion of the Ruhr, and backed Air Chief Marshal Tedder's policy of strategic bombing *à outrance* against the protests of General Koenig, the French Commander-in-Chief.)

His appointment smoothed the way for a satisfactory agreement all round. Field-Marshal Alexander was appointed General Eisenhower's deputy in the Mediterranean theatre, and Air Chief Marshal Tedder became Eisenhower's Deputy Supreme Commander in North-West Europe. Other high posts were filled upon the general plan that wherever, by land, sea or air, a Commander-in-Chief, British or American, was appointed, his deputy should be American or British. The result was a complete integration of command, under which in course of time British and American sailors, soldiers and airmen fought with equal readiness and unity under any commander, whatever his nationality.

~✕(4)✕~

Let us now come nearer home, and summarise the conduct of the Second World War by the British Army, and of the new and strange experiences of those who participated therein.

One of the most striking features of modern warfare is the immense importance attached to secrecy, or security. A century ago little was known about the plans, strength, or dispositions of an enemy beyond what could be observed upon the field of battle. To quote Wellington once more, victory belonged to the general who could guess what was going on on the other side of the hill. But the aeroplane has put an end to what may be called tactical privacy, while the secrets of the home front, unless closely guarded, can be flashed round the world by cable or wireless in a few seconds.

For the sake of security, therefore, certain rigid restrictions have had to be imposed upon modern war reporting. Gone are the days when a war correspondent, upon arriving at the base, bought a horse and 'galloped towards the sound of the guns', while his subsequent dispatch reached home long after its contents had ceased to be of any value to the enemy. There must be no mention nowadays of the names or location of units, nor of troop movements by land or sea. Particular care must be taken not to designate a unit by its number: to reveal the existence, say, of the 9th Battalion of a given regiment might indicate to the enemy not merely that a new battalion had been created but that an entirely new division was in being.

In the case of the British Army the strict enforcement of this rule led to one unfortunate result. During the desert campaigns in the Middle East our official reports, in describing the part played by this or that formation in a major operation, confined themselves, as a rule, to the nationality of the troops concerned—Canadian, or Indian, or, occasionally, Scottish. There was little or no direct reference to the achievements of English soldiers—presumably because it was assumed that their participation in all operations would be expected as a matter of course, and that there was no need to stress the fact. A sporting desire to give due credit to the Empire troops was also partly responsible.

Whatever the motive for such reticence, its consequences became immediately and unhappily apparent, especially in the United States, where an ancient gibe, dating back to a German propaganda campaign of the First World War, to the effect that 'Britain will fight to the last Frenchman', took a new and vigorous lease of life. A British visitor to the United States during 1941–2 was frequently asked: 'Must your Indians and Colonials do all your fighting for you? Haven't you any English troops at all?' This question was posed not merely by carping critics, but by genuinely puzzled friends, whose confidence in the genuineness of the British war effort was being severely shaken. Therefore, after some pressure, security restrictions were sufficiently relaxed to permit of a broadcast speech, most movingly delivered by the newly arrived British Ambassador, Viscount Halifax, which gave to the American people, in percentage figures, the relative strength of the British, Dominion and Indian troops engaged in the Middle East campaign. The proportion of British troops proved to be well over seventy per cent, with casualties to the same scale. This timely revelation went far to adjust a situation which should never have been allowed to arise.

But naturally the party most deeply interested in discovering the nature and extent of our military dispositions was the enemy himself. In addition to the employment of his usual highly organised espionage system, he frequently attempted less direct methods. A single instance will suffice.

One day in 1941 a story was published, and attained immediate world-wide circulation, that there had been serious rioting among some newly arrived Australian troops in Jerusalem. As it happened, there were no Australian troops in Jerusalem, or indeed anywhere in Palestine, at that time, and a simple statement to that effect could have scotched the allegation forthwith. But it was in that hope that the allegation had been launched—to enable the enemy to obtain authentic information as to whether or no the Australian forces had yet arrived in the Middle Eastern theatre. The British Government refused to be drawn, merely stating that there was not a word of truth in the story; and a somewhat naïve ruse failed.

Naturally, the security restrictions bore heavily upon the enterprise of the war correspondents, especially the Americans, the demands of whose editors for a daily ration of 'hot news' were both instant and compelling. But for the most part all concerned accepted the situation with loyalty and good faith. A word may appropriately be said here about the arrangements existing between the military authorities and the Press representatives in regard to this controversial and vitally important matter.

In the first place censorship was conducted upon a voluntary basis. Such an arrangement may appear at first sight to err on the side of over-trustfulness on the part of the authorities; but few correspondents availed themselves of this privilege, and with reason. Once a dispatch had been passed by the censor, the correspondent knew that it would go safely through, and whatever inaccuracies or indiscretions it might contain were the censor's responsibility and not his.

A second and most important factor, especially in the relation between the Army Commanders and the war correspondents, was the steady growth of what may be called the Policy of the Whole Truth. The journalist hates just one thing, and that is to be kept in the dark. He also dislikes mass-produced news, or 'hand-outs'—cautiously worded typed statements issued to all and sundry—from which it is impossible for the individual to formulate a dispatch which will differ by one jot from his neighbour's.

After all, the war correspondent of today is in all but name a soldier himself. He no longer waits for news at the base : he accompanies the troops into action, at the risk and sometimes the sacrifice of his own life, to gather his experience at first hand. His dream, as a good reporter, is to achieve some private 'scoop' of his own ; but he is a reasonable person and does not expect miracles in security warfare. What he does expect, and demand, is to be trusted. If he feels that information is being withheld from him which he, as an accredited correspondent, is entitled to receive, he will be tempted to employ any means in his power to obtain it elsewhere, perhaps in some dangerously garbled form. But tell him the whole story, and then tell him what to leave out, and he will seldom let you down.

Such was the advice habitually tendered by the Directorate of Public Relations in the War Office to high-ranking officers, in the matter of their relations with Press correspondents. 'The more you tell them, the less they will give away.'

How successfully our system of censorship worked out in practice has recently become known to us, for the political and military archives of Germany have fallen, intact, into our hands. These reveal a quite astonishing ignorance as to actual conditions in Great Britain. A single instance will suffice.

In the summer of 1940, after Dunkirk, a detailed plan for the invasion of our country was drawn up and almost put into operation, under the portentous code-name of 'Sea Lion'. We have in our possession Hitler's own 'Directive 17' on the subject. The first phase was to be an assault-landing upon the south coast, between Portsmouth and Dover, by an Army Group of some twenty-six divisions under Rundstedt.

But the project hung fire, largely because the enemy were completely in the dark as to the strength of the resistance to be expected. In an operation order issued by Rundstedt in early September 1940, our strength in Britain was reckoned at some thirty-nine divisions! In point of fact, all we could have mustered at that time was a few fully trained and equipped divisions, and rather less than a hundred tanks.

So the threatened invasion never came. The story to be appreciated must be read in detail,[1] but enough has been told here to demonstrate the success of the British censorship system.

~(5)~

We pass now to a brief consideration of the part played by total mechanisation, and by the novel technique rendered possible by the phenomenal progress of military science between 1939 and 1945.

Of the weapons, the tank excited most public attention and controversy. In Flanders in 1940, and in the early days of the desert campaigns, the British Army suffered severely from the inferiority of its tanks to those of the enemy; thereafter they improved steadily, both in design and performance.[2]

Given suitable terrain, the tank proved itself the predominant factor in the ground fighting of the war; but towards the close signs were not wanting that defence, as usual, was beginning to overhaul offence, and that the tank had lost something of its potency and terror. Its most deadly opponents were now the rocket-firing fighters and the improved anti-tank gun.

Whether the tank has had its day is a matter for debate, but two points seem clear—a modern tank attack, to succeed, must be accompanied by fighter aircraft to protect it from dive-bombers, and by rocket-firing fighters to knock out the anti-tank guns.

One of the horrors of modern warfare from which we had fully expected to suffer, and suffer grievously, and against which most elaborate precautions had been taken—the employment of poison gas—we were mercifully spared. The explanation was probably the enemy's fear, well-founded, of immediate and deadly retaliation in kind. It is perhaps within the bounds of possibility that the same considerations may induce a similar hesitancy in the matter of the atomic bomb.

[1] *Defeat in the West,* by Milton Shulman. Secker & Warburg.

[2] Our crowning achievement in this direction was the Comet tank, which appeared too late in the war to attract much public notice. It was of the cruiser type with armour 102 mm. thick, and weighed 32¾ tons: it carried a 3-inch howitzer and two machine-guns, and attained a speed of thirty miles an hour.

ARMS AND THE MEN

We come next to a new weapon of war which is in no danger of obsolescence, and which has intensified the speed and high pressure of military operations to a degree undreamed of a generation ago. This is the universal employment of radio, whether in the wireless control of large formations, or the directing of artillery fire by target-spotting aircraft, or by oral communication between individuals, by means of such devices as the 'walkie-talkie'.

We have but to look back a short distance into the past to realise the significance of that revolution. In the South African War tele-communication was limited to the employment of semaphore or heliograph signals, or of a telegraph cable unwound from an advancing wagon; while information as to 'what was happening upon the other side of the hill' could only be obtained from 'Joe's eyeglass'—the sobriquet conferred by the British soldier, in affectionate reference to the famous monocle of Mr. Joseph Chamberlain, Secretary for the Colonies, upon a small observation balloon, keeping solitary vigil high above the veldt.

Even during the First World War communication was chiefly maintained by wired field telephone. Wireless was available, but was perpetually subject to tapping and 'interference'. At moments of emergency signal rockets were employed.

But perhaps the most pregnant innovation of the Second World War, and one likely to wax rather than wane, has been the mass employment of airborne troops, whether in self-propelled aircraft or gliders.

Three examples will suffice: first our own desperate preparations, as far back as 1940, against the menace of airborne invasion of our island fortress, though in this case our fear was more of parachutists than of glider-borne troops; secondly the effect produced upon military opinion by Wingate's audacious Long-Range Penetration operations in Burma, in which he proved, by conveying glider-borne troops to the enemy's rear and thereafter supplying them from the air, that it is possible on occasion to dispense with orthodox lines of communication altogether; and lastly by the historic and heroic effort of General F. A. S. Browning's three airborne divisions[1] at Arnhem in September 1944, which only failed by the smallest margin to achieve a penetration into northern Germany which might have shortened the war by many months.

But warfare by airborne troops is still in the experimental stage, and must be judged at present less by its performance than its promise. In any case it seems more than likely that the glider, which is of frail

[1] See p. 227.

construction and difficult to land without crashing, will be superseded entirely in the course of time by self-propelled aircraft manned by parachute troops. But airborne troops of some kind will probably furnish the deciding factor, if ever the world is foolish enough to embark upon another war.

CHAPTER XXI

ALL RANKS

~✦(1)✦~

BUT, when all is said and done, the final issue of battle, today as ever, is decided not by the machinery employed but by the man who operates it. Let us therefore turn, for the last time, from Arms to the Men, and consider the part played by the British soldier, whatever his grade, in winning the Second World War.

We will begin at the top.

The reader will have gathered in the course of this narrative, especially its earlier stages, that in the annals of the British Army organisation and control from above have not invariably been free from blemish or blame. This is not altogether surprising. We are not a military-minded people, and in time of peace have never shown any particular interest in the workings of our military machine, beyond systematically starving it. Not that that has prevented us from criticising and, in a general way, deriding it. To the armchair strategist, the comic cartoonist, and the music-hall comedian, the Army, and in particular the War Office, have always been a legitimate subject for mirth. The other two Services are treated with a certain reserve and respect. The Royal Navy is too deep a mystery for the amateur expert to probe; our young Air Force is still the public's white-headed boy; but everybody knows how to run an Army, and everybody likes to tell the Army so.

No doubt in past days there was much to condemn. There was too much paper-work and not enough head-work; promotion depended less upon merit than on seniority; and the whole Army was shamefully underpaid; with the result that the best type of recruit could not be attracted into the ranks, while the King's

Commission was perforce restricted to young men of means or position.[1]

But the First and Second World Wars have made an end of all such things. We have had to fight for our lives, twice, not merely as an army but as a nation, and the result has been the British Army of today, the most efficient in our history. And that description extends to the War Office as well, despite the enormous difficulties imposed by the sudden and enormous increase in an establishment called upon to control an army not of thousands but of millions. Unlike the Army itself, the War Office possesses no trained and quickly expandable reserve.

And never has the British Army produced so many brilliant leaders in the field. The names of close on thirty of these have already been recorded in these pages, not one of whom has failed to reveal some outstanding quality of military greatness, whether in strategic planning, leadership, administrative ability, or sheer moral ascendancy. At least three of them must be reckoned among the great leaders of all time.

There are two names, however, in a somewhat different category, to whom special reference is necessary; one because not enough has been said about it, and one because it has not so far been mentioned at all. They are those of Field-Marshal Lord Alanbrooke, Chief of the Imperial General Staff from the end of 1941 to the conclusion of the war, and of Sir James Grigg, Secretary of State for War from 1942 onwards.

It will be remembered that we first encountered Lord Alanbrooke in command, as General Sir Alan Brooke, of the 2nd Corps of the British Expeditionary Force in Flanders and at Dunkirk, and later as the organiser of a second evacuation, this time from Cherbourg and Brest. Within a month of this most testing experience he had been appointed Commander-in-Chief Home Forces—in other words, to organise the defence of our Island against what looked like imminent invasion. For eighteen months he laboured, with what resources he could muster, to train our new armies, find equipment for them, and instil into them the morale essential to a campaign of successful resistance.

At the end of 1941 Japan entered the war; so did the United States; and the entire plan of Allied strategy had to be reorientated

---

[1] In October 1899, when it became necessary to increase the size of the Army to meet the needs of the South African War, a number of so-called University Commissions were offered by the War Office to young graduates of Oxford and Cambridge. No previous military experience was required, but candidates for Commissions in the Cavalry and Royal Artillery must be possessed of a private income of not less than £500 a year, and for the Infantry of not less than £150.

to include the Pacific and Far East. Brooke was appointed C.I.G.S., and discharged the duties of that immensely responsible post, in good times or in bad, until the end of the war. In May 1942 he was appointed chairman of the Chiefs of Staff Committee, which meant that he now became Mr. Churchill's principal strategic adviser. He accompanied the Prime Minister to those momentous conferences with President Roosevelt and Marshal Stalin, and was justly regarded as his right-hand man throughout. He was clear-headed, candid and persuasive, gifts which stood him in good stead when it came to discussing with the American High Command the difficult and debatable question as to which country should have the predominant voice in the conduct of Allied operations. Brooke was chiefly responsible for the amicable agreement arrived at.

As C.I.G.S. he made a point of keeping in constant touch with his commanders in the field, however widely dispersed, by full and frank correspondence, whether by private letter or telegram. He contrived thus to keep his subordinates *au fait* with the situation in each theatre of war, and so enable them to time and co-ordinate their efforts the better. As C.I.G.S., too, he was responsible for the smooth working of the army machine as a whole—its organisation, equipment and maintenance—and of the selection and appointment of the army commanders.

Such was the burden borne by Sir Alan Brooke throughout those years. Most of his work was entirely unspectacular; indeed, to the general public, intent on more exciting events elsewhere, it was almost unknown. But it has been said of him by an authority more than usually well qualified to testify:

'He has attracted no limelight, but that does not alter the fact that history may very well in the long run assign to him a place among the Englishmen who have helped to win the war second only to Mr. Churchill himself.'

The second name is that of Sir James Grigg, Secretary of State for War from 1942 to the end of hostilities, here mentioned for the first time. He had enjoyed the advantage, before succeeding to that office, of serving for three years as Permanent Under Secretary for War, in which capacity he presided over the civil side of the War Office and represented the Civil Service upon the Army Council; which meant that he took over the duties of Minister of War with the internal economy of the War Office at his finger's ends—a unique qualification. He had previously served as Finance Member upon the Viceroy's Council in India, being called home in 1938 to succeed Sir Herbert Creedy as P.U.S. in the War Office.

His appointment as Secretary of State for War necessitated, first, his entrance into the field of politics as a candidate for Parliament; secondly, the entire abandonment of his long association with the Civil Service, as well as the renunciation of the pension attached thereto. In other words, the difference between Sir James Grigg and his predecessors was that, whereas the average Secretary of State for War is a politician who has accepted the post regardless of his military knowledge or experience (which may be nil) merely as a further step in his political career, Sir James was an experienced military authority who had to be groomed into a party politician as an essential preliminary to his appointment as Secretary of State.

It was an unconventional appointment, but there was no doubting its success, especially since in Field-Marshal Lord Alanbrooke (as he had now become) the new Secretary of State discovered a colleague of his own metal and after his own heart; with results which became steadily and increasingly apparent.

In certain respects the two were very much alike in character and method. Each was a shrewd judge of character, with a genuine flair for discovering the right man for an appointment. Each was a tremendous worker and a stern taskmaster. Neither suffered fools gladly—Sir James Grigg's sufferings in this respect probably exceeded those of his more phlegmatic colleague by a small margin—yet both could be singularly patient with, and indulgent towards, a man who was honestly trying his best. Both, in consequence, will be remembered with gratitude and affection by those who served under them.

It has been pointed out, with truth, that after Dunkirk those who directed the course of the war never made a single major strategic mistake. The credit for that achievement belongs to three Services and more than one country; but so far as the contribution of the British Army is concerned, it has its roots in the Alanbrooke-Grigg partnership in the War Office.

~*(2)*~

Finally we come to the soldier himself, and his regimental officers.

Of the officers it may be said that they do not differ materially from their predecessors of 1914. They are more highly trained and far better equipped technically; but in their ability to lead and inspire their men, by precept, example, and above all by the human touch, they are merely maintaining a tradition centuries old.

A British subaltern knows, or should know, all his men by name, sight and disposition. On parade he is as stiff a disciplinarian as the regimental sergeant-major himself, but off duty his attitude to his flock undergoes a complete transformation. He organises sports and entertainments for them, and participates in these himself. If a man of his platoon is sick and in hospital, he visits him. If the man gets into trouble with higher authority, he goes and speaks a good word for him. He takes a friendly interest, too, in the man's private life and domestic background. Finally, in action, he never asks a soldier to go anywhere where he himself is not prepared to lead the way. That is the British regimental tradition, and it welds a fighting machine together like nothing else on earth.

To a certain, and at one time to a disturbing extent, during the recent war, these beneficent duties were taken out of the young officer's hands by the sudden burgeoning of public interest in what is known now as Army Welfare, consequent upon the institution of Universal Military Service, which had given every fireside in Britain a direct interest in the soldier. This to a certain extent was all to the good, indicating as it did a long overdue awakening of the public conscience in regard to the soldier's lot; but some of it took an unnecessarily officious form, especially during the Phoney War.[1] More than one well-meaning but over-sentimental publicist informed the troops that they were hardly-used men, unduly oppressed by an outmoded code of discipline, and precluded by 'red tape' from ventilating their grievances. One eminent broadcaster invited them to write and confide their woes to him in detail.

The British soldier, especially when he has no fighting to do, enjoys nothing so much as a good, satisfying 'grouse'—it is his eminently sensible substitute for *cafard*—and the army responded to the invitation with alacrity. They made their self-appointed champion the recipient of a full catalogue of those familiar, and to a certain extent inevitable, hardships of which the soldier has had cause to complain from the beginning of time—grievances connected with such matters as inadequacy of pay, monotony of rations, undue restriction of personal liberty, and the irregular arrival of family allowances—all of which were duly proclaimed to the listening world, with appropriate comment. Ultimately it had to be pointed out to the broadcaster in question that the individual best qualified, and more than willing, to listen to a private soldier's grievances, and if they had any substance at all (which was not by any means invariably the case) to get them redressed, was the soldier's company officer; and that to

[1] See p. 81.

encourage him to appeal elsewhere, over the officer's head, would deprive the soldier of his best friend, besides imbuing the public mind with the belief that the British Army was seething with disaffection. The broadcaster, who besides being a man of genuine human sympathy was also endowed with sound common sense, at once recognised the justice of this view, and undertook henceforth to preface all his future discourses with an appeal to the soldier to take his troubles to his company officer before going further afield. This went far to remove what was becoming a serious threat to an ancient and valuable army tradition.

The incident is mentioned here because it throws an interesting and instructive sidelight upon the character and mentality of the modern private soldier. His predecessors of a generation or century ago were of a very different type: they grumbled from habit, like all men under discipline, but only among themselves or, on occasion, to an understanding subaltern. Otherwise they held that the army, or rather the regiment, should keep its domestic affairs to itself and brook no outside patronage or interference. In other words, they were Regular soldiers of the standard breed—ill-educated, largely inarticulate, and, for all their grumbling, content with a very little.

But today we are dealing with a very different type, or multiplicity of types. They come from every section of the nation: moreover, one and all start life in the ranks, which means that a man of superior education and character cannot attain to the privileges of an officer until he has roughed it with the rest for six months or so. This unites all in at least one point of view—appreciation of the need for better conditions for the private soldier—a need not forgotten by the private after he ascends to commissioned rank.

The modern private soldier, too, is frequently a man of high professional standing, or at least promise, accustomed to a certain standard of living: he has an active and intelligent mind: he rebels instinctively against unimaginative handling by authority; he is irked by monotonous repetition of routine duties, and especially by the emptiness and boredom of his hours of leisure. The traditional recreations of the warrior are not for him. He resents, above all, the entire lack of privacy in the life of the common soldier.

Plainly, if our new National Army is to perform its service with keenness and contentment, these causes of discontent—not unreasonable discontent—must be dealt with and corrected. Let us briefly consider what has been done in recent years—in other words, during the Second World War and after—to improve conditions in this respect.

But first let us remember that this improvement did not begin with the outbreak of war or the coming of conscription. During Mr. Hore-Belisha's tenure of office as Secretary of State for War, most of which occurred under peacetime conditions, many admirable reforms were set on foot, though most of them had to be suspended for the duration by reason of sterner needs.

Prominent among these was a determined effort to improve the conditions of barrack life, whether from the point of view of comfort, or catering, or privacy. Many, indeed most, of our barrack buildings were hopelessly out of date and had long been officially condemned. Men slept, ate, and passed much of their spare time in one long, comfortless barrack-room accommodating thirty or forty, warmed by a single small stove, with a row of beds running down either side and a long trestle table up the middle. Meals were conveyed from a distant cookhouse, and usually arrived in a tepid condition. Wherever else the soldier might wish to go—to the wet canteen, the dry canteen, the reading-room, or in pursuit of other personal comforts—it was ordained that he must go outside to do it, whatever the weather.

The new barracks which began to go up during the thirties aimed, first, at assembling as many as possible of the amenities of barrack life under one roof. Meals were served in a proper dining-hall, where men sat round square 'family' tables accommodating perhaps a dozen, and food was passed hot from the kitchen through a hatch. The old bleak barrack-room itself was abolished in favour of small dormitories, holding half a dozen men, with a sitting-room for every three dormitories. The canteens were amalgamated in a single regimental institute, comprising a cafeteria conducted by N.A.A.F.I., and various recreation rooms. For a wet canteen a single room, furnished with a few tables and chairs, and a service-hatch through which refreshment could be dispensed during statutory hours, was now sufficient for the needs of an army growing steadily more temperate.

Many of the old barracks had been to a certain extent modernised; and in all barracks, old or new, men received four substantial meals a day. Previous to this no food had been obtainable after 4 p.m. The question of a balanced diet was taken in hand scientifically: a weekly bill of fare was made out, to be discussed with appropriate solemnity by a small committee of Other Ranks, assembled under the chairmanship of the P.R.I. (President of Regimental Institutes), usually the Second in Command of the battalion.

Several of the new barracks had been completed, and were in actual use, when the Second World War broke out. Most of these were allotted for the duration to the A.T.S.

But perhaps enough has now been said to dispel the somewhat widely held belief that army reforms cannot be planned or brought about as a matter of ordered routine, but only in times of compelling emergency. Let us return to the consideration of the progress achieved in this respect during and after the war.

Experience has taught us at least three things about the modern soldier. First of all, in the Army of today, as already noted, we have to deal with men far more independent in spirit, and far more responsible in character, than the old one-class rank and file. That means that to render army routine congenial, and, indeed, endurable to the new type, they must be relieved of all petty, outmoded restrictions upon their freedom as individuals. Much has been accomplished in this direction. Today a private soldier is free to marry when he pleases—formerly he had to wait until he was twenty-six—and his pay and dependants' allowance have been adjusted to a scale which should relieve him of financial care. Barrack routine, too, has been lightened of many irksome rules and regulations. A soldier off duty today is more or less his own master. He can wear mufti, he can go in and out when he pleases, visit his friends in neighbouring towns and villages, and need not be perpetually applying for leave or having his pass examined. He is even permitted to keep the light on and read in bed. Church parades are no longer compulsory. Artificial social segregation of the various ranks has been greatly modified. Not all of these concessions are universally approved of by old-fashioned persons, but they have certainly conferred upon the soldier the feeling of being an adult individual and not merely an over-chaperoned schoolboy.

Secondly, we have learned that, whether in war or peace, the curse of soldiering, especially to a man of active mind and varied interests, is its deadly monotony. Fifty years ago a private soldier had nowhere to go during his spare hours except the canteen, or possibly to the reading-room of a so-called Soldier's Home, maintained as a rule by some philanthropic society, where he could sit on a hard chair and peruse out-of-date newspapers and periodicals. Today he has at his disposal all the amenities that are summed up under the head of Army Welfare, from organised games—inter-regimental cup-ties and the like—to dances and theatrical entertainment.

Particular mention must be made of the beneficent activities of N.A.A.F.I. (Navy, Army and Air Force Institutes) the phenomenal development and growth of which during the Second World War, and after, furnish significant evidence of the modern fighting man's need of and demand for organised distraction from the strain of total warfare.

So far as the Army was concerned, the work of N.A.A.F.I. fell into two categories—Home Canteen Service, and R.A.S.C. Expeditionary Force Institutes. The Home Service was furnished by the establishment of N.A.A.F.I. Institutes (of the kind already described) up and down the country wherever soldiers were assembled, from Orkney to Dover. Actual service was provided in the main by a staff of young women, whose overall uniform of butcher-blue will linger pleasantly in the memory of the thousands to whom it ministered. These were all reckoned as civilians, and were paid by N.A.A.F.I. Not that their labours were unattended by military risk : indeed, in the Dover area casualties were so widespread that it was deemed necessary to transfer one canteen to a spot further inland. But the N.A.A.F.I. girls would have none of it : in fact they threatened, if so demeaned, to resign in a body. They were allowed to stay.

The R.A.S.C. Expeditionary Force Institutes were established and conducted upon a more formal and elaborate scale. Personnel consisted entirely of men. These, too, were civilians in N.A.A.F.I. employ and were paid by N.A.A.F.I. ; for overseas service they were put into khaki and placed under military law, though without badges or distinctions of rank ; and wherever an expeditionary force penetrated, a fully equipped N.A.A.F.I. unit went with it, sharing the dangers of each particular enterprise. In the invasion of Normandy, N.A.A.F.I. personnel landed on June 23rd and established a base depot forthwith.

There were N.A.A.F.I. units at Dunkirk, and their activities increased and expanded throughout the war, extending ultimately to stations as far afield and apart as Murmansk, Iceland and Madagascar. A notable and valued feature of the N.A.A.F.I. service was the establishment of mobile canteens, which habitually visited isolated posts and batteries, to supply these with comforts which would otherwise have been beyond their reach.

Later, as an expeditionary force penetrated deeper inland, and the time arrived when the A.T.S. could be dispatched overseas with comparative safety, the A.T.S. Expeditionary Force Institutes came overseas as well, this time with civilian women attendants, likewise in khaki and subject to military law.

It is not generally realised that, besides purveying everywhere the material benefits of a well-run canteen and club, N.A.A.F.I. was also made responsible for all army entertainments. This was effected by the establishment of a group of committees for the organisation and control of the body known as 'Ensa'. More than that, the whole of the cost of E.N.S.A—and it was prodigious—was defrayed by N.A.A.F.I.

Like all army institutions, both N.A.A.F.I. and E.N.S.A. found themselves, as is the way in army service, the subject of sporadic criticism, most of it entirely unjustified, from those for whose benefit they had been brought into existence. It was alleged that N.A.A.F.I. made enormous profits out of the soldier: it seemed almost impossible to convince the soldier in question that N.A.A.F.I. was a strictly non-profit-making institution, and that all surplus balances went back into N.A.A.F.I. itself, for the further extension of its activities. But perhaps E.N.S.A. was the favourite target. Doubtless its offerings were of varying degrees of merit—or acceptability, which is not quite the same thing—but there was no disputing the energy and devotion of its personnel, especially the humbler ranks, and their cheerful acceptance of discomfort and hardship both by land, sea and air in their journeyings over three continents, some of which achieved feats of long-range penetration almost as notable as those of Wingate's Chindits.

In any case, it is to be hoped that in due course the full story both of N.A.A.F.I. and E.N.S.A. will be set forth in the written word by those best qualified for the task. Neither tale should lose anything in the telling, and both will be something of a revelation to the reader.

For a non-combatant organisation N.A.A.F.I. took its full share, and more, in the hazards of active service. It has been calculated that in the Second World War, on a percentage-in-relation-to-numbers basis, the heaviest casualties of all were suffered by the Army Chaplains, but N.A.A.F.I. made its honourable contribution.

Last, and most important, must be our realisation that the greater part of our modern Army is composed not of volunteers, but of young men whose prospects and opportunities of advancement in their chosen trade or profession have been compulsorily interrupted by war service or, more recently, by the continuation of conscription in peacetime. How are these to be delivered from a sense of frustration and time wasted?

The obvious answer is to give to them, while in the Army, every possible opportunity to qualify, by spare-time study and expert coaching, for the trade or profession which they intend to follow upon their return to civil life; or, in the case of University students, to enable them to persevere, between spells of duty, with their interrupted courses.

This has now been done, and in a big way—so big, indeed, that the Royal Army Education Corps has increased in stature and importance to a degree undreamed of ten years ago. The expansion began as far back as 1939, when, in response to appeals from the

Y.M.C.A. and other welfare societies, the Army Education Corps embarked upon a programme which ranged from basic instruction of the illiterate and semi-literate recruit to advanced courses in such diverse subjects as Accountancy, Surveying, Company Law, Engineering, Science, and the Arts. Another most valuable institution came to birth in A.B.C.A. (Army Bureau of Current Affairs), under whose auspices discussion groups, composed both of officers and men, met regularly in informal conclave to consider and debate economic, political and social problems of the day, in which views were freely exchanged and opinions frankly stated, irrespective of differences of rank.

These wise measures went far, not only to chase monotony, but to give those participating an invaluable training in the duties and responsibilities awaiting them upon their return to civil life.

Even so, the educational standards of our Army Other Ranks still present some strange and rather unexpected contrasts. At the top of the scale we find some of the most highly educated and efficient soldiers that our Army has ever seen. Today the proportion of highly skilled craftsmen—mechanics, electricians, and the like—is about twenty-five per cent: in the First World War it was two per cent. At the other end of the scale, however, the situation is very different. In early 1947, Mr. Bellenger, the Secretary of State for War, drew the attention of the House of Commons to the disturbing fact that no less than twenty-six per cent of the present army intake are possessed of a standard of education 'very much below that of the Elementary school-child on leaving school'. This seems to indicate that what the army recruit knew at the age of fourteen he has entirely forgotten at the age of eighteen; with the result that army instructors, instead of concentrating their energies upon their pupils' purely military education, have to waste precious time in reteaching twenty-six per cent of them the three R's.

The explanation probably lies in the hand to mouth, makeshift fashion in which almost every non-military activity had to be carried on during the war years, aggravated by absence of parental authority and supervision; for it is in the home that all education must begin.

On the other hand, no one can say that young people of today are stupid: indeed, most of them are highly precocious and almost unduly worldly-wise. We are therefore forced to the paradoxical conclusion that the rising generation is both less literate and more intelligent than it used to be. It is probable, however, that the extension of the school-leaving age to fifteen (or beyond) will go far to redress the balance.

~✳(3)✳~

Such, in brief review, were the diverse elements which combined to produce the British soldier of the Second World War. The hundreds of thousands of young men who fought and won that war came from every walk of life and represented almost every standard of living and point of view; yet the one thing which distinguished them above everything else in the end was their similarity to one another, whether in their superb physical health, their cheerful acceptance of hardship, or their complete confidence in themselves and their leaders.

Their common denominator was toughness. They were not naturally tough, as General Wavell was the first to discover and remark; they had to be toughened. Once that process was completed they never failed to carry out any task imposed upon them, whether in desert sand-storms, or in the sinister twilight of the Burma jungle, or fighting waist-deep in water during the battle of the Rhineland. The reader has but to turn back the pages of this volume and re-read the tributes paid to them by one high commander after another, from General Eisenhower downwards, to realise how complete was their fulfilment.

Their secret was their ability to suffer setback and even defeat without losing heart. They met triumph and disaster with equal equanimity. General Slim put the whole matter in a nutshell when he said: 'I do not believe that the British soldier is braver than any other; but he is braver for longer, and it is the last ten minutes that count'.

But if the British soldier is ever again called upon to take the field, in defence either of his own soil or of that of a smaller and weaker neighbour, let us pray fervently that he may not again be condemned, through national apathy or political timidity, to start as far behind scratch as upon previous occasions in our history—especially since there will be no respite or breathing-space this time in which to make ready.

LIST OF AUTHORITIES CONSULTED

The History of the British Army (FORTESCUE), *Macmillan.*

The King's Service (IAN HAY), *Methuen.*

The British Expedition to the Crimea (W. H. RUSSELL), *Routledge.*

Mr. Cardwell at the War Office (BIDDULPH), *John Murray.*

The Great Boer War (A. CONAN DOYLE), *Smith Elder.*

The Esher Report, *Wm. Clowes.*

The Life of Lord Haldane, 2 vols. (MAURICE), *Faber.*

History of the Great War, 4 vols. (BUCHAN), *Nelson.*

Raising and Training the New Armies (BASIL WILLIAMS), *Constable.*

The First Hundred Thousand (IAN HAY), *Blackwood.*

The Army of Today (GORMAN), *Blackie.*

This Our Army (KENNEDY), *Hutchinson.*

The R.A.C. (MURLAND), *Methuen.*

The War Office (GORDON), *Putnam.*

Army Organisation and Administration (LINDSELL), *Gale & Polden.*

Annual Reports on the British Army, *H.M.S.O.*

Various Supplements to the *London Gazette* containing the Despatches of GENERALS GORT, WAVELL, ALEXANDER, AUCHINLECK, GIFFARD, LEESE and PILE.

GENERAL EISENHOWER's Official Reports:
  (a) Operations in southern France.
  (b) The Italian Campaign.
  (c) Operations in Europe.

El Alamein to the River Sangro (MONTGOMERY), *Hutchinson.*

The Battle of Flanders (IAN HAY), *H.M.S.O.*

The Campaign in Burma (FRANK OWEN), *H.M.S.O.*

Combined Operations 1940–1942, *H.M.S.O.*

Secret Sessions Speeches (CHURCHILL), *Cassell.*

A Miniature History of the War (R. C. K. ENSOR), *Oxford University Press.*

Beyond the Chindwin (FERGUSSON), *Collins.*

The Home Guard of Britain (GRAVES), *Hutchinson.*

Britain's Home Guard (BROPHY), *Harrap.*

Many War Diaries and Personal Narratives.

INDEX